Feeding
the
Dairy Cow

by

A.T. Chamberlain and J.M. Wilkinson

Chalcombe Publications

Published in Great Britain by

Chalcombe Publications
Mountwood House, Biddenfield Lane
Shedfield, Hampshire SO32 2HP

www.chalcombe.co.uk

First printed 1996
Reprinted with amendments 1998
Reprinted 2000, 2002, 2005, 2009

ISBN 978 0 948617 32 4

CONTENTS

Preface   v
Abbreviations   vi

Chapter 1   Introduction   1

1.1   Why is dairy cow nutrition important?   1
1.2   Outline of the book   2
1.3   How to use this book   2
1.4   Introduction to ruminant nutrition   3
1.5   Nutrients required by animals   5
1.6   Anatomy and physiology of the digestive tract   8

PART 1 FEEDS

Chapter 2   Grass   11

2.1   Introduction   11
2.2   Grass production   11
2.3   Grazing strategies   14
2.4   Assessing grassland productivity   16
2.5   Silage   17
2.6   Specialist silage crops   24
2.7   Assessing the composition of grass and silage   26
2.8   The ideal silage   30
2.9   Silage and health   30

Chapter 3   Supplementary feeds   31

3.1   The need for supplements   31
3.2   Forages and concentrates   31
3.3   Chemical assessment of supplements   32
3.4   Classification of feeds   34
3.5   Compounds and blends   36
3.6   Selecting supplements   39

PART 2 ANIMAL REQUIREMENTS

Chapter 4   Voluntary feed intake   41

4.1   Why is intake important?   41
4.2   Definition   41
4.3   Factors controlling voluntary feed intake   42
4.4   Practical assessment of diet quality   43
4.5   The role of saliva   44
4.6   Diet presentation   45
4.7   Silage   46
4.8   Other factors affecting voluntary feed intake   47
4.9   Conclusions   47

Chapter 5   Energy   49

5.1   Introduction   49
5.2   Units of measurement   49
5.3   Sources of energy   49

5.4	Sites of energy digestion	50
5.5	Optimising microbial growth in the rumen	50
5.6	Energy digestion	51
5.7	Products of energy digestion	52
5.8	Estimating energy requirements	53
5.9	Practical aspects of energy nutrition	54
5.10	Beyond metabolisable energy	59
5.11	Fat	60

Chapter 6   Protein   63

6.1	Introduction	63
6.2	Units of measurement	63
6.3	Protein digestion	64
6.4	The Metabolisable Protein system	65
6.5	The industry's position regarding the MP system	71
6.6	Limitations of the MP system	71
6.7	Beyond the MP system	73
6.8	Amino acids	73
6.9	Response to feeding high protein rations	75
6.10	Practical aspects of protein digestion	75

Chapter 7   Minerals and vitamins   79

7.1	Introduction	79
7.2	Calcium	79
7.3	Magnesium	84
7.4	Phosphorus	86
7.5	Sodium	87
7.6	Sulphur	87
7.7	Trace elements	88
7.8	Vitamins	92

PART 3   DIET FORMULATION

Chapter 8   Predicting feed intake   95

8.1	Introduction	95
8.2	Factors affecting intake	96
8.3	Predicting feed intake	97
8.4	Modifying intake	99
8.5	Examples	99
8.6	Manual exercises	100
8.7	Computer exercises	100

Chapter 9   Calculating metabolisable energy supply and requirements   101

9.1	Introduction	101
9.2	Calculating ME supply	101
9.3	Calculating ME required by the animal	101
9.4	Examples	104
9.5	Manual exercises	105
9.6	Computer exercises	106

Chapter 10   Calculating metabolisable protein supply and requirements   107

10.1	Introduction	107
10.2	Calculating MP supplied	107
10.3	MP required by the animal	109

10.4 Examples   111
10.5 Manual exercises   113
10.6 Computer exercises   113
Appendix: Calculation of ERDP and DUP supplied by a feed from the protein degradation characteristics   114

Chapter 11   Calculating mineral requirements   115

11.1 Introduction   115
11.2 Maintenance   115
11.3 Lactation   117
11.4 Pregnancy   117
11.5 Weight change   117
11.6 Calculating supply of minerals   117
11.7 Examples   118
11.8 Manual exercises   119
11.9 Computer exercises   119

PART 4   PRACTICAL DAIRY COW FEEDING

Chapter 12   Designing Diets and Feeding Systems   121

12.1 Introduction   121
12.2 Designing diets   121
12.3 Assessing feed intake on the farm   123
12.4 Manipulating feed intake on the farm   124
12.5 Supplementary concentrates   125
12.6 Achieving sufficient energy intake   126
12.7 The ideal diet   128

Chapter 13   Manipulating the composition of milk   129

13.1 The importance of manipulating milk composition   129
13.2 Milk protein   130
13.3 Milk fat   133
13.4 Producing milk with minimal milk solids   135
13.5 Conclusions   135

Chapter 14   Feeding the high-yielding cow   137

14.1 Why aim for high yields?   137
14.2 Possible disadvantages of high yields   137
14.3 How to achieve high yields   138
14.4 How to formulate diets for high-yielding cows   139
14.5 How to manage high-yielding cows   142
14.6 Bovine somatotrophin (BST)   143

Chapter 15   Feeding the cow before and after calving   145

15.1 Introduction   145
15.2 Target condition score for dry cows   145
15.3 Preventing milk fever   148
15.4 Preparing the rumen   149
15.5 Feeding the dry cow   149
15.6 Blueprint for managing dry cows   151

Chapter 16   Nutrition, fertility and lameness   153

16.1 Introduction   153
16.2 Nutrition and fertility   153
16.3 Nutrition and lameness   156

Chapter 17   Assessing nutritional status   159

17.1 Introduction   159
17.2 Condition score   159
17.3 Milk yield   161
17.4 Milk composition   152
17.5 Blood metabolic profiles   163
17.6 Milk metabolic profiles   165
17.7 Fertility records   166
17.8 Faeces   166

Chapter 18   Practical diet formulation   167

18.1 Introduction   167
18.2 What are the animals' nutritional requirements?   167
18.3 Determining the diet to be offered   169
18.4 Dry matter intake   169
18.5 Metabolisable energy supply and requirements   170
18.6 Protein supply and requirements   170
18.7 Mineral supply and requirements   171
18.8 Additional nutritional considerations   171
18.9 Comparison with computer-formulated nutrient supply and requirements 172
18.10 On-farm calculation of animal requirements   173
18.11 Case studies   174
18.12 Manual exercises   176
18.13 Computer exercises   176

PART 5 EXERCISES

Chapter 19   Exercises   177

19.1 Computer program   177
19.2 Predicting feed intake - Chapter 8   179
19.3 Energy - Chapter 9   182
19.4 Protein - Chapter 10   186
19.5 Minerals - Chapter 11   191
19.6 Diet formulation - Chapter 18   193
19.7 Case studies   199

PART 6 TABLES

Chapter 20   Tables of requirements and feed analyses   204

References   225

Index   229

Preface

Feeding the dairy cow successfully requires a blending of theoretical knowledge of nutritional principles with practical stockmanship and an ability to work with numbers. The successful dairy farmer achieves the blend of skills by combining astute observation with timely decision-making, and by constantly seeking advice from others in a desire to improve the business. Thus new information is refined, tested, adapted and put into daily practice.

What we aim to achieve in this book is a distillation of nutrition, physiology and clinical diagnosis into an integrated guide to the feeding of the dairy cow for the farmer. If you disagree with the value of this approach, visit the leading dairy farmers of Europe and discover the large amount of detailed biological knowledge which they apply to support their business management.

This book has arisen from a short course taught annually since 1986 by the authors. The course brings together practising veterinary surgeons and animal nutritionists to update participants in recent developments in ruminant nutrition and health. The emphasis is on practical diet formulation and on nutritional diagnosis to solve problems on farms.

A special version of a computer program developed for the course is included with this book. The program has been designed to allow the user to test options rapidly. This facility is important because nutrition is not an exact science - there is usually more than one acceptable solution to a problem. We have deliberately avoided an attempt to advance academic knowledge of dairy cow nutrition, but have chosen to work with current feeding systems, whilst accepting their faults and limitations. Better approaches will be devised in the future, but there is a need to do a better job of feeding today's dairy cows.

We thank the many students who helped us; without their enthusiastic participation we could not have produced this guide. Franziska Wadephul's typesetting and Dr Julian Hill's editing is gratefully acknowledged. Finally, without the constant support and encouragement of our wives, this book would not have been possible.

AT Chamberlain
JM Wilkinson

April 1996

Abbreviations

ADAS	Agricultural Development and Advisory Service
ADF	Acid detergent fibre
ADIN	Acid detergent insoluble nitrogen
"ADIP"	"Acid detergent insoluble protein"
ATP	Adenosine triphosphate
AFRC	Agricultural and Food Research Council
APL	Animal production level
ARC	Agricultural Research Council
βHB	Beta-hydroxy-butyrate
BF	Butterfat
BSE	Bovine spongiform encephalopathy
BST	Bovine somatotrophin
CCN	Cerebro-cortical necrosis
CDM	Corrected dry matter
CFU	Colony-forming units
CP	Crude protein
CS	Condition score
DCAB	Dietary cation-anion balance
DCP	Digestible crude protein
DE	Digestible energy
DLWG	Daily live weight gain
DLWL	Daily live weight loss
DM	Dry matter
DMI	Dry matter intake
DNA	Deoxyribonucleic acid
DOMD	Digestible organic matter in the dry matter
DOMD$_c$	Digestible organic matter in the corrected dry matter
DOMD$_o$	Digestible organic matter in the oven dry matter
DUP	Digestible undegraded protein
ECF	Extra-cellular fluids
EDTA	Ethylenediamine tetra-acetate
ERDP	Effective rumen degradable protein
FCM	Fat corrected milk
FFA	Free fatty acids
FME	Fermentable metabolisable energy
GE	Gross energy
GSPx	Glutathione-peroxidase
LCFA	Long-chain fatty acids
MADF	Modified acid detergent fibre
MAFF	Ministry of Agriculture, Fisheries and Food
MCP	Microbial crude protein
M/D	Metabolisable energy in the total diet dry matter
ME	Metabolisable energy
MMA	Methylmalonic acid
MP	Metabolisable protein
NCGD	Neutral cellulase gammanase digestibility
NDF	Neutral detergent fibre
NE	Net energy
NEFA	Non-esterified fatty acids
NIRs	Near infra-red spectroscopy
NMJ	Neuro-muscular function
NP	Net protein
NPN	Non-protein nitrogen
OAA	Oxalo-acetic acid
ODM	Oven dry matter
OMD	Organic matter digestibility
PTH	Parathyroid hormone
QDP	Quickly degraded protein
RDP	Rumen degradable protein
RRS	Rumen-resistant starch
SBF	Sugar beet feed
SCC	Somatic cell count
SDP	Slowly degraded protein
SOD	Super-oxide dismutase
TMR	Total mixed rations
TP	Tissue protein
UDP	Undegraded dietary protein
UME	Utilised metabolisable energy
VFA	Volatile fatty acids
WCS	Water soluble carbohydrates
Y	Yield

CHAPTER 1

INTRODUCTION

1.1   Why is dairy cow nutrition important?

1.2   Outline of the book
  1.2.1   Part 1 - Feeds
  1.2.2   Part 2 - Animal requirements
  1.2.3   Part 3 - Diet formulation
  1.2.4   Part 4 - Practical dairy cow feeding
  1.2.5   Part 5 - Exercises
  1.2.6   Part 6 - Tables

1.3   How to use this book

1.4   Introduction to ruminant nutrition
  1.4.1   Diet formulation
  1.4.2   Computers for diet formulation

1.5   Nutrients required by animals
  1.5.1   Water
  1.5.2   Carbohydrates
  1.5.3   Proteins
  1.5.4   Fats
  1.5.5   Macro elements
  1.5.6   Trace elements
  1.5.7   Vitamins

1.6   Anatomy and physiology of the digestive tract
  1.6.1   Anatomy
  1.6.2   Sources of digestive enzymes
  1.60.3   Physiology

1.1   Why is dairy cow nutrition important?

Milk production is determined by the genetic potential of the cow, her nutrition and her state of health. Of these three factors, nutrition is the most important: it is within the direct control of the farmer, it has a profound influence on production in the healthy animal, it is easy to change and it represents the largest single variable cost (Table 1.1).

With milk production in Europe limited by quotas and milk price increasingly under the control of the purchaser, increased income to the producer can only be achieved by improving the quality of the product or by reducing its cost of production. In the future there is likely to be greater emphasis placed on reducing the cost of producing each litre of milk that leaves the farm. To reduce the cost of production it is useful to know how it is made up. The variable and fixed costs for commercial dairy farms costed by Genus in the UK in 1993 are shown in Table 1.1. The single largest variable cost is that of concentrate feed. Total feed costs account for

approximately one third (33%) of the total variable and fixed costs of milk production. American workers (Galligan, 1991) estimated that by using better nutritional practices a reduction in feeding costs of 14% could be achieved (Table 1.2). Such a reduction would increase profit margin from 3.19 p to 4.03 p per litre for the farms shown in Table 1.1.

Table 1.1   Costs of producing milk in 1993 for recorded herds; average annual milk yield = 5776 l/cow; average herd size = 127 cows (Tomlinson and Perry, 1993)

	Cost per cow (£)	Cost per litre (p)	% of total income
Income			
Milk	1202	20.81	99
+ Calf sales	106		
- Herd replacement cost	-98		
TOTAL	1210	20.95	100
Variable costs			
Concentrate	222	3.84	18
Other purchased feeds	18	0.31	2
Forage costs	98	1.7	8
Vet & med.	33	0.57	3
Office	17	0.29	1
Sundries	81	1.4	7
TOTAL	469	8.11	39
Fixed costs - for dairy unit			
Labour	121	2.09	10
Power and machinery	135	2.34	11
Property charges	66	1.14	5
Interest charges	91	1.58	8
Depreciation	72	1.25	6
Sundries	72	1.25	6
TOTAL	557	9.65	46
Overall total	1026	17.76	85
Profit	184	3.19	15

Table 1.2   Possible savings that might accrue from use of nutrition advice (Galligan, 1991)

Projected savings (%)	Number of farms	Per cent of current cost
0 to 5	0	0
6 to 10	6	40
11 to 15	3	20
16 to 20	4	27
21 to 25	2	13
Mean		14.4

The aim of this book is to provide a better understanding of both the principles and practice of feeding the dairy cow, and so help to realise the profit potential of the herd through better rationing, improved efficiency of production and a higher quality product.

1.2   Outline of the book

1.2.1   Part 1   Feeds
The feeds available for feeding the dairy cow are discussed in the first section. Grass and other forage crops are, and will remain, the foundation of any dairy cow diet. The production and conservation of forages and the assessment of their nutritional value are therefore considered in the first chapter of this section (Chapter 2). Forages alone are insufficient for high-yielding milking cows and usually require supplementing with feeds rich in energy, protein or other nutrients. Many of the supplements used are by-products from human food production and an understanding of their properties and limitations is required before suitable rations can be devised (Chapter 3).

1.2.2   Part 2   Animal requirements
The nutrient requirements of the animal can be expressed in terms of how much the animal will eat (intake) and requirements of energy, protein and minerals. An understanding of the principles of nutrient requirements is necessary in order to understand current and possible future feeding standards or systems of rationing. Without such an understanding the "art" of nutrition cannot be appreciated and mistakes are more likely to be made.

In Chapter 4 the most important requirement, that for feed intake, is discussed together with the factors that control and influence voluntary intake. In the subsequent chapters energy (Chapter 5), protein (Chapter 6) and mineral (Chapter 7) digestion and metabolism are considered.

1.2.3   Part 3   Diet formulation
The digestion and metabolism of nutrients was discussed in Part 2; in Part 3 the prediction of nutrient requirements is considered. The predictions are based on the feeding standards published by the UK Agricultural and Food Research Council (AFRC) in the early 1990s and consider dry matter intake (Chapter 8), metabolisable energy (Chapter 9), metabolisable protein (Chapter 10) and the major minerals (Chapter 11). Each chapter consists of a series of tables and graphs to show how requirements change with changing animal performance. In conjunction with the tables in Chapter 20 this will allow the reader to determine requirements for any given level of animal production. Each chapter concludes with a series of manual and computer exercises to enable the reader to become familiar with the estimation of requirements and to demonstrate some of the more important animal and dietary factors. In order to enable readers to gain the most benefit from these exercises the answers are given in Part 5.

1.2.4   Part 4   Practical dairy cow feeding
Some of the practicalities of feeding dairy cows are considered in this section. The development of diets for milking dairy cows is outlined in Chapter 12. The increasingly important topic of the manipulation of milk quality is considered in Chapter 13. Chapter 14 consider the details of feeding the high-yielding cow. This is followed by a chapter (Chapter 15) on feeding the cow in the weeks immediately before and after calving. The interactions between nutrition and different aspects of health are dealt with in Chapter 16. The on-farm assessment of animal performance and diet adequacy is discussed in Chapter 17. In Chapter 18 the steps involved in the manual calculation of dairy rations are described.

1.2.5   Part 5   Exercises
In Part 5 the various diet formulation exercises in earlier chapters are presented together with solutions. Whilst manual exercises are useful in developing an understanding of the principles of ration formulation, computers have become invaluable in the formulation of diets and in the investigation of dietary and animal effects. A sample of a commercial computer program (RUMNUT) for diet formulation that can be used to tackle many of the exercises outlined in the different chapters is distributed with this book. Therefore instructions on how to install and run the programs are included in this part.

1.2.6   Part 6   Tables
A series of tables of nutrient requirements and feed analyses comprise Part 6. They allow the formulation of diets without the use of a computer. Many of the tables are fuller versions (using smaller steps in animal weight etc.) of those in Part 3.

1.3   How to use this book

We have in mind three groups of readers. The first group comprises those totally new to ruminant nutrition, such as students of agriculture, animal science or veterinary science who, we hope, will find this a useful guide. These readers are recommended to work through the book from start to finish. Hopefully the exercises in Chapters 8 to 11 and 19 will aid their understanding.

The second group are readers wanting to use the new feeding standards to formulate rations on-farm. These readers are recommended to consult Part 2 before tackling the chapters in Part 3 and the associated exercises. Part 4 should also be read to balance the numerical approach of the earlier chapters.

The final group consists of those who want an update on the new feeding standards but who do not need to formulate rations themselves. They should read Part 2, which covers the principles behind the current feeding standards, and Part 4, which applies them to specific topics of dairy cow nutrition.

As some readers may not read all of the chapters consecutively we have tried to make each chapter understandable in its own right. Therefore whilst references are made to sections in other chapters, we have taken the liberty to repeat some of the more important graphs and tables where they are needed.

Equations are only included to allow users to see the interactions between different components, rather than to allow them to make their own calculations. Readers who require the full set of equations behind the current feeding standards are referred to the original AFRC publications (Agricultural and Food Research Council, 1990, Agricultural and Food Research Council, 1992) and the subsequent advisory booklet (Agricultural and Food Research Council, 1993), but they should be warned that all contain a lot of equations (the advisory book contains 184 different equations) and they are a daunting read. Similarly we have endeavoured to remove complex anatomical and physiological terms where this can be done without loss of precision.

1.4 Introduction to ruminant nutrition

When considering ruminant nutrition it must always be remembered that we are dealing with a system within a system. The ruminant animal has its own requirements for energy, protein and minerals, but there is also a second set of requirements: that of the rumen microbes which are responsible for the breakdown of the structural components of plant material, and which produce the majority of the protein absorbed in the small intestine. It is only when microbial requirements are met that the rumen can function optimally and make best use of the feeds offered, especially the cell wall fraction of forages.

Rumen function will be most efficient and stable when diets are formulated to satisfy both the requirements of the rumen microbes and those of the

animal itself. This should result in optimal performance and will minimise disease problems of a nutritional nature. Optimising both sets of requirements is important because in low-yielding animals and dry cows the microbial requirements for protein or nitrogen can exceed those of the animal. For high-yielding dairy cows, on the other hand, the animal's protein requirements are in excess of the synthetic capacity of the rumen microbial population, hence "by-pass" protein must be supplied. Such high-yielding animals must eat as much as possible, which will only occur when rumen function is optimal and the microbial breakdown of plant material maximised.

1.4.1 Diet formulation

As will be seen in later chapters, the nutrient requirements of the animal are highly interlinked with the characteristics of the feeds available: they influence the amount of energy required which then in turn affects the amounts and types of protein required. Before the widespread availability of computers it was common to consider these different requirements in isolation. Although modern feeding standards are beginning to capture some of the interactions between the different requirements but it is still easier to consider them separately in the first instance and then to identify the interactions later. For the formulation of diets the various requirements should be considered in order of importance. Voluntary dry matter intake (DMI) is the factor that limits production most often. After intake, energy is the next most important, followed by protein. Unless the animal is very high-yielding or the ration is composed of some unusual feeds, then once these three requirements are met, the minerals, vitamins and trace elements will usually be found to balance and it is merely a question of checking them. Requirements should therefore be calculated in the following order:

1. Dry matter intake (Chapter 4)
2. Energy (Chapter 5)
3. Protein (Chapter 6)
4. Major minerals: calcium, phosphorus and magnesium (Chapter 7)
5. Sulphur (Chapter 7)
6. Minor minerals such as cobalt, copper, selenium and iodine (Chapter 7)
7. Vitamins (Chapter 7)

For each set of requirements (except voluntary intake) it is usual to subdivide daily requirements into the different "activities" in which the animal may be involved.

These are:

Maintenance The nutrients required to keep the body functioning with no productive output.

Activity   Movement such as standing up and walking requires energy. In practice the energy required for activity is a small proportion of total requirements, and does not vary considerably between different animals. As a result, energy required for activity is usually added into the maintenance energy requirement.

Lactation   The nutrients required to achieve a given level of milk production of a given composition.

Growth   These requirements are important in meat-producing animals but can usually be simplified for dairy cows.

Pregnancy   Nutrient requirements are related to the stage of pregnancy and only become significant in the last third of pregnancy.

The advantage of the above subdivisions are two-fold. Firstly it is possible to express the total requirements for the "activities" of any animal as a combination of the above requirements. Simple tables can then be devised that relate the particular component to the animal's requirements and these can be used to determine the specific requirement for a given animal. Consulting a small number of simple tables therefore allows the total nutrient requirements of any animal to be calculated.

The second advantage of this approach follows on from the first in that the equations used to predict the requirements are also relatively simple. But as long ago as the 1960s it was appreciated that such a factorial approach was incorrect as an animal doing everything at once was going to have a very different voluntary feed intake and metabolism than a cow only doing one productive process. For example, a cow giving 20 litres of milk a day, gaining one kilogram of weight a day in the 30th week of pregnancy and walking 6 miles a day will have far higher total nutrient requirements, feed intake and rate of metabolism than a cow only giving 20 litres of milk a day. Research workers (e.g. Blaxter, 1962) proposed methods for assessing the interactions between different productive processes, but these were not incorporated into practical feeding standards in order to keep equations and tables of requirements simple.

Recent developments in computer power and availability have reduced the benefits of using the factorial approach and modern feeding standards now include the interactions. This has made the prediction equations more complex, but it is still possible to draw up tables of nutrient requirements that can be used to assess total nutrient require-

ments. Such tables are presented in the final section of this book and, whilst certain simplifications have had to be made, they are still accurate enough for most on-farm purposes.

1.4.2   Computers for diet formulation
As our understanding of ruminant nutrition increases, the predictive equations available for formulating diets become more complex. Many requirements are interrelated. For instance protein requirements are related to energy intake which is related to the type of ration. With many dairy cows having *ad libitum* access to one component of their diet, these inter-relationships become very complex.

Advantages of computers
- Computers increase the speed of processing relevant mathematical equations, so the user can proceed with a "what if" approach for much longer than would be possible by hand.
- Computers always get the calculations correct - **if** set up correctly in the first place.
- The more sophisticated formulae are interrelated and iteration (repetition) is needed to reach a solution. Computers can iterate rapidly to a high degree of accuracy. The assumption that everyone uses computers in diet formulation has gone so far that the current feeding standards (AFRC, 1990) actually state that they no longer consider the ease of calculation when deriving the formulae.
- Computers can consider several options at the same time. For example, the program supplied with this book considers four or five different equations to predict dry matter intake and selects that which is limiting.
- Computers allow complex mathematical techniques such as linear and multiple goal criteria programming to be used.

Disadvantages of computers
- The expense and training needed to use computers efficiently can be considerable. Hopefully the former is reducing and the latter can be eased by the design of the program.
- The extensive use of computer programs encourages the user to think that ruminant nutrition and feeding animals on farms is an exact science. However, the predictive equations should merely be considered as giving a "best guess" at what should happen. Whether the animals are actually offered the intended diet, whether they eat it all and whether they respond as predicted is uncertain. Computers should only be used to reduce the time and tedium involved in the complex calculations needed to use the current formulae. In all instances it is vital that formulated rations are validated by checking how the animals perform.
- Dairy cow nutrition is as much an art as it is a science. Much can be done using observation

based on sound experience in the field. There is a growing temptation to hide behind computer programs and not to consider any rationing without their use and to believe totally what the computer produces. No-one should ever attempt to ration dairy cows according to a set of computer "blueprints" without visiting the farm and the cows.

- Some methods such as linear programming can seem like a "black box" in that although the answer is correct you are not sure why! Ideally the machine should only remove the tedious parts of a process, leaving you to apply your mind to the more difficult, skilled areas. In addition they can give the impression that ruminant nutrition is a very precise science; it is not and the art of nutrition will always be as important as the science. Nobody uses linear programming in its true form to formulate rations; arbitrary limits are set on the use of various nutrients and on feed inclusion rates to ensure that sensible results are obtained.

1.5 Nutrients required by animals

This section is intended as a brief revision of the more basic aspects of nutrition. If you are confident about your knowledge of basic nutrition it can be missed by proceeding to Chapter 2. If, however, you find too much is being taken for granted in the later chapters then these sections may warrant closer attention.

1.5.1 Water

Although often forgotten, water is the major and most essential nutrient for all animals. If pigs are deprived of water for more than 12 hours they develop salt poisoning. Cattle, on the other hand, can last at least two to three days without water as they can store considerable amounts in the rumen. While the dairy cow can survive for such periods without water, milk yield is very closely linked to water quality, availability and intake.

Normally a dairy cow will drink about 60 litres of water a day. The provision of a constant supply of **clean** water is therefore crucial to achieving consistent milk production and maintaining healthy animals.

1.5.2 Carbohydrates

The carbohydrates form the main source of energy for ruminants. They are a large family of compounds with the generalised formula $C_n(H_2O)_n$. The five- and six-carbon chain types are probably most important. Carbohydrates are usually drawn in a ring structure as shown in Figure 1.1.

Figure 1.1 Diagrammatic representation of glucose molecule

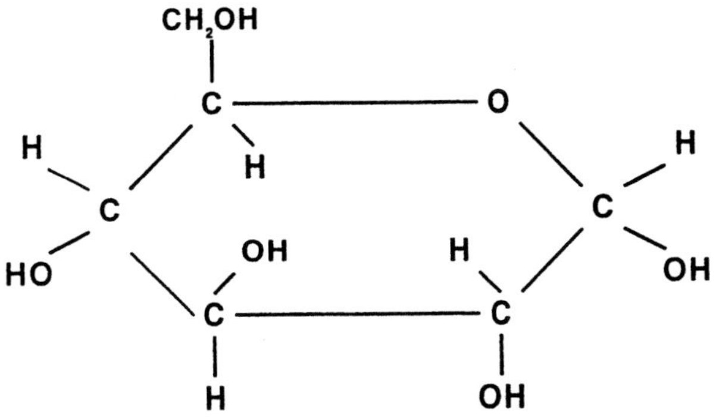

The carbohydrates can be divided into four groups:

- Glucose and the simple sugars, which are all soluble in water and produce a considerable osmotic pressure. The simple sugars are formed of one (monomers) or two (dimers) of the ring structures shown in Figure 1.1.

- Starch, which is a polymeric chain of many six-carbon monomers arranged in a coiled manner. Starch is one of the major forms in which energy is stored in plants, but possesses very little structural strength (cf. cellulose below).

- Pectins are found in large amounts in a few feeds such as sugar beet pulp and citrus pulp, where they are a major source of carbohydrate. For example, pectins represent about 20% of the energy in sugar beet pulp. They are made up of linear chains of the monomer galacturonic acid. Pectins possess considerable gelling properties and this makes them very difficult to measure in the laboratory.

- Cellulose, hemicellulose and lignin. Cellulose and hemicellulose are, like starch, based on polymeric chains of sugar monomers. The monomers are, however, arranged in a linear as opposed to a coiled fashion. The carbohydrates in this group form the major structural components of plant cells and are insoluble in water. They vary in the extent to which they are digestible by the microbes in the rumen. Lignin, which is closely associated with the cell walls and lends strength and rigidity to the plant, is not strictly a carbohydrate but a polymer of phenylpropanoid compounds.

1.5.3 Proteins

The proteins are formed of varying combinations and quantities of the 20 amino acids. All the amino acids contain carbon, hydrogen, oxygen and nitrogen; two, cysteine and methionine, also contain sulphur. The generalised formula of the amino acids is shown in Figure 1.2.

Figure 1.2   Diagrammatic representation of the amino acid family of molecules

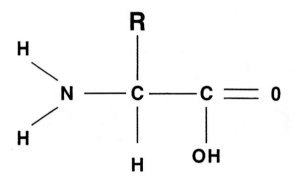

The R group varies between the different amino acids, ranging from a simple hydrogen (glycine) to a complex aromatic group containing a carbon ring (tyrosine and phenylalanine). Proteins are the most complex molecules in animals and plants and have mechanical (collagen), transportation (haemoglobin), enzymatic (trypsin etc.), mobility (muscle) and protective (keratin and the immunoglobulins) functions. One amino acid (tyrosine) forms the basis of the two growth-regulating hormones called tri-iodo-thyronine and tetra-iodo-thyronine.

Monogastric mammals are capable of synthesising about half of the amino acids but some must be present in the diet and are known as "essential amino acids". Ruminants can synthesise all the amino acids via the micro-organisms in the rumen, but the ruminant must have a source of sulphur to synthesise methionine and cysteine. In most instances such a large proportion of the absorbed amino acids comes from microbial sources that the animal does not have any requirement for essential amino acids. However, high-yielding animals on low-protein diets may respond to supplements of specific amino acids, usually methionine and lysine (see Chapter 6, page 74).

1.5.4   Fats

The fats contain carbon, hydrogen and oxygen. Chemically, they are triglyceride molecules: three fatty acids made up of long carbon chains are attached to a molecule of glycerol (Figure 1.3). Each of the fatty acid chains usually contains an even number of carbon molecules but the three differ in length. The fatty acids are subdivided into poly-unsaturated fatty acids and saturated fatty acids. The unsaturated fatty acids contain one or more carbon double bonds. All the animal fats are saturated whereas some of the vegetable fats are unsaturated. Fats are important in the body for long-term energy storage, in a structural role in the cell membranes and as the precursors of the steroid group of hormones. Although the body can synthesise fatty

acids there are a few that are essential in that they cannot be synthesised, for example linoleic acid.

Figure 1.3   Generalised structure of a fat molecule

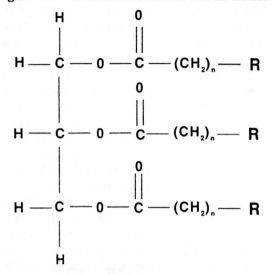

1.5.5   Macro elements

Animals require a range of simple mineral elements in their diets. Some, the macro minerals, are required in large quantities (g per day) and are considered in this section. Others, trace elements, are only required in much smaller quantities and are considered in the next section.

The important elements with respect to ration formulation and disease in dairy cows are considered in detail in Chapter 7.

Sodium. Sodium is one of the major elements in the extra-cellular fluids (ECF) and is present in all body secretions and in urine. The body has extremely good homeostatic control over the concentration of sodium in the ECF with any excesses being cleared via the kidneys. Sodium is involved in maintaining and generating electrical potentials across cell membranes and is involved in numerous active transport mechanisms, e.g. sugar uptake in the small intestine. Some plants, especially those receiving large amounts of potassium fertiliser, are low in sodium; this may lead to deficiencies of sodium in the animal's diet. Deficient animals show a specific craving for sodium and will wander widely in search for it. As the signs of sodium deficiency are so major (reduced appetite, reduced weight gain and reduced milk production) and as the cost of sodium chloride (common salt) is low, modern compound feeds are generally formulated to avoid sodium deficiency. However, there is uncertainty as to precise requirements and responses to supplementary sodium have been seen.

Potassium. In contrast to sodium, this element is found mainly in the intra-cellular fluid. Many of the functions of potassium are in conjunction with sodium in active transport mechanisms and cellular electrical potentials. Potassium deficiency is rare in animals. But high levels of dietary potassium can impair the uptake of magnesium and possibly sodium.

Calcium. Calcium is a major component of bones and, more importantly, is required at the neuro-muscular junction (NMJ), where it regulates the transmission of nerve impulses from nerve to muscle. Most diets are adequate in calcium. Deficiencies in young animals are more often due to deficiencies in vitamin D_3. Vitamin D_3 is involved in the regulation of calcium absorption and metabolism. Deficiency in young animals causes rickets due to poor bone formation. In adult cattle the main form of calcium deficiency is milk fever. Although there are large amounts of calcium stored in the bones, little is mobilisable and the amount decreases with age. Milk has a relatively high content of calcium, and the rapid increase in milk yield after calving can cause a temporary deficiency leading to milk fever.

Magnesium. Magnesium, together with calcium, is involved at the neuro-muscular junction (NMJ). A deficiency of magnesium causes an increased level of excitability. Magnesium deficiency (hypomagnesaemia) is common (grass staggers or grass tetany) as many pastures are low in magnesium. Ruminants have a high turnover of their magnesium stores (40 to 50% a day), so any period of inappetence can cause hypomagnesaemia.

Phosphorus. Like calcium, phosphorus is a major component of bones. In addition, it is involved in numerous metabolic pathways. As it has such a wide range of functions, deficiencies in phosphorus tend to cause a general disability and failure to perform. Much of the phosphorus in plants is bound up in phytates which are only digestible by ruminants. In contrast to sodium and calcium, phosphorus is very expensive to include in rations.

1.5.6 Trace elements
There is a seemingly endless list of trace elements required in small amounts by the body. Many never cause problems and the following section and Chapter 7 are restricted to those which may be involved in problems of nutritional imbalance.

Copper. Deficiencies in copper occur in much of the United Kingdom. Copper absorption is reduced by high concentrations of molybdenum, sulphur and iron in the gut and much of the copper "deficiency" is secondary to an excess intake of these other elements. Clinical signs of copper deficiency in cattle are "spectacles" of poorly pigmented hair around the eyes and general ill-thrift. More commonly, deficiencies are sub-clinical with poor fertility and performance as the only symptoms.

Cobalt. This element is required for the synthesis of vitamin B_{12} in the dairy cow. Vitamin B_{12} is involved in the synthesis of glucose in ruminants, therefore deficiencies result in general ill-thrift.

Selenium. Selenium and vitamin E have a role in the detoxification of oxygen-free radicals and peroxide compounds formed during cellular energy metabolism. If these compounds accumulate in cells they may cause cell death. Deficiencies of selenium cause muscle disorders and weakness such as white muscle disease and heart failure. Selenium supplementation has a very narrow safety range.

Iodine. Iodine is required in the synthesis of thyroxine in the thyroid gland. Deficiencies are uncommon, but may occur where animals do not get sea-derived feeds such as fish meal or sea-salt. The main symptoms are increased still-births and weak calves.

Iron. About 90% of iron in the body is used in haemoglobin in red blood cells. Most animals acquire sufficient iron from soil that is eaten during grazing. However, calves reared indoors away from contact with soil may develop anaemia, and dairy cows housed all year round may require supplementary iron in the diet.

1.5.7 Vitamins
The vitamins are classified as compounds which are essential in small amounts for normal physiological functions. They cannot be synthesised in the body and must therefore be included in the diet. As the original work was based on humans, this definition does not always hold true for ruminants which can synthesise some vitamins in the rumen and liver.

Vitamin A. This vitamin is fat-soluble and also called retinol. It is involved in the synthesis of the light pigments and in the maintenance of normal epithelial structure of the skin and linings of the lungs and intestines. Deficiencies cause night-blindness and ill-thrift.

Vitamin B group. This is a large group of vitamins involved in various biochemical pathways. Deficiencies cause a generalised dehability. Dairy cows are capable of synthesising their own B vitamins via rumen micro-organisms and their requirement usually translates into one for cobalt which is a component of vitamin B_{12}.

Vitamin C. Whilst vitamin C, ascorbic acid, is required by humans in diets, dairy cows can synthesise their own and so supplementation is never required.

Vitamin D_3. Vitamin D_3 is a fat-soluble vitamin which is required in the control of calcium metabolism. Ingested vitamin D_3 is inactive and must be activated in both the liver and the kidneys.

Figure 1.4   **Diagram of the rumen of the cow, seen from the left hand side**

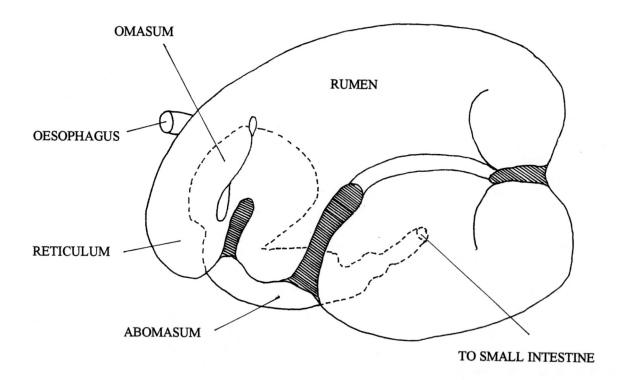

Vitamin E. This is the third fat-soluble vitamin; it is required in conjunction with selenium to prevent the products of metabolic oxidation from destroying cells.

1.6   Anatomy and physiology of the digestive tract

1.6.1   Anatomy

Ruminants have a highly adapted digestive system to enable them to break down cellulose and other cell wall components. Ruminants themselves do not have the ability to break down cellulose but their digestive system is adapted to supply the ideal environment to a range of micro-organisms that break down cellulose and produce volatile fatty acids and synthesise protein.

Although the upper parts of the gastro-intestinal tract are highly modified in the ruminant (Figure 1.4), the digestive mechanisms from the abomasum onwards are much the same as monogastric animals. The teeth of ruminants are highly adapted for eating herbage. The upper incisors are missing and are replaced by a "dental pad" against which the lower incisors bite. Ruminants eat herbage either by cutting it off with their teeth (sheep and goats) or tearing it with their tongue (cattle). The food is briefly ground between the molars by means of a sideways sliding of the upper teeth over the lower teeth before being swallowed.

Table 1.3   **Relative volume of different parts of the digestive tract of an adult dairy cow (Naylor and Ralston, 1991)**

Rumen + reticulum + omasum	52%
Abomasum	6%
Small intestine	28%
Large intestine	14%

The stomach of ruminants is a highly modified development of the monogastric stomach. It consists of four chambers: the rumen, reticulum, omasum and abomasum (see Figure 1.4). The rumen and reticulum are closely connected and together form the largest of the chambers (see Table 1.3). The volume of the rumen and reticulum may be as much as 180 to 225 litres in an adult cow, and they occupy most of the left-hand side of the abdomen. The rumen acts as a large anaerobic (without oxygen) fermentation vat; its main functions are to maximise microbial fermentation by storing feed for a considerable period of time (up to 10 days) and to break down particles of feed to increase surface area and aid microbial penetration.

After initial chewing, food is swallowed and enters the rumen. Here it disperses. Every minute or so a mass of large particles of ingesta is regurgitated and re-chewed ("chewing the cud" or rumination). This further reduces particle size and the ingesta are re-swallowed. In addition, the rumen undergoes a cyclical contraction about every minute which helps to mix the rumen contents.

The volatile fatty acids produced as the result of microbial fermentation of carbohydrates are absorbed into the bloodstream from the rumen and can account for up to 75% of the cow's total energy supply. These acids are continually buffered by salivary bicarbonate and phosphate so that the pH of the rumen rarely falls below pH 6 in dairy cows given a balanced diet. When particle size has been reduced sufficiently by microbial digestion and rumination, the ingesta pass on through the omasum and into the abomasum.

The omasum is a circular organ (about the size of a football in the cow) and of uncertain function and therefore not discussed much by nutritionists! The omasum lies between the neutral rumen (pH = 6.5) and the abomasum which is highly acidic (pH = 1 to 2) and may be involved in ensuring the abomasal contents do not enter the rumen. In cattle the omasum is also an absorptive organ. Between a third and two thirds of the water consumed as well as about half the VFA and considerable amounts of sodium, potassium and other ions are absorbed here.

The final stomach chamber is the abomasum. It is equivalent to the stomach in monogastric animals. The abomasum is maintained at a low pH (1 to 2) by the secretion of hydrochloric acid from specialised glands in the walls. The acid activates the protein digesting enzyme pepsin and partially sterilises the food by killing the microbes.

The abomasum leads into the small intestine which accounts for more than a quarter of the volume of the intestines (Table 1.3). It is a major site of digestion and absorption. Enzymes are secreted into the intestine from the pancreas, gall bladder and the walls of the intestine (see below) to carry out the final breakdown of carbohydrates, protein and fat, which are then absorbed through the intestinal wall and into the blood. The small intestine continues on into the large intestine. By this stage most of the readily digestible feed components have been digested and absorbed. The main functions of the large intestine are to absorb the water and bicarbonate that has been secreted into the intestines during digestion and to store the indigestible fractions of the diet for periodic voiding as faeces. In most ruminants there is a sizable microbial population in the large intestine which breaks down fibrous carbohydrates and produces volatile fatty acids and microbial protein. As in the rumen, these fatty acids are absorbed and may account for as much as 15% of total energy absorbed in certain situations; the microbial protein, however, is lost.

1.6.2   Sources of digestive enzymes

In ruminants, saliva has little or no enzymatic activity but is important as a lubricant for chewing food and cud and as source of buffers to counteract the acidifying effects of the volatile fatty acids. A 600 kg dairy cow on a forage diet can produce up to 170 litres of saliva per day, rich in bicarbonate and phosphate buffers.

The rumen wall absorbs large amounts of VFA but does not secrete any enzymes. Secretory glands in the wall of the abomasum produce hydrochloric acid and pepsinogen, which is converted into the active form, pepsin, by the hydrochloric acid. Bile is produced in the liver and secreted into the small intestine via the bile duct; it is composed of waste products from the detoxifying activities of the liver and emulsifies the fat and helps activate the pancreatic lipases. The pancreas produces lipases (fat digesting), proteases (protein digesting) and carbohydrate digesting enzymes which are also secreted into the small intestine. The protein requirement of the pancreas is large and accounts for half of the protein requirements at maintenance. The wall of the small intestine produces enzymes that complete the final digestive break down of fat, protein and carbohydrates.

1.6.3   Physiology

The gastro-intestinal tract can be considered as a series of storage vessels where digesta are stored. The storage vessels are inter-connected by a series of narrow-bored tubes through which the digesta flow rapidly. The epithelial cells lining the intestines are very specialised as they have to cope with a wide range of compounds, some of which are toxic to normal cells. These compounds must be converted into a form which can be absorbed into the bloodstream and to do this, the cells have a large surface area and a rapid rate of cell turnover.

In the rumen the carbohydrates are broken down by microbial action into the volatile fatty acids (acetic, propionic and butyric acid) and absorbed through the rumen wall (see Chapter 5, page 49). Some starch is formed by the microbes and this, together with any starch that resists microbial breakdown, passes into the small intestine where secretions from the pancreas and lining of the intestine break it down into simple monomeric five- and six-carbon molecules. These simple sugars are then absorbed by active uptake mechanisms involving the sodium pump.

A proportion (0.6 to 0.9) of the dietary protein is degraded by the microbes in the rumen and used to synthesise microbial protein and nucleic acids such as DNA. A mixture of microbial and dietary protein passes into the abomasum where the activated pepsin splits the protein molecules at specific sites. Digestion is continued by the pancreatic enzymes and secretions from the intestinal lining which break the proteins down into separate amino acids. These are absorbed in the small intestine.

Digestion of fat is initially slow as the gut contents are water-based and the fat tends to form into large globules with a small ratio of surface area to mass. Bile has considerable emulsifying activity and this breaks down the fat into small globules and once the particle size is reduced, enzymatic digestion breaks the fat down to its constituent fatty acids.

There is a considerable flux of water into and out of the gut with water being added as saliva, gastric secretions and small intestinal secretions. This water is re-absorbed in the large intestine.

PART 1

FEEDS

CHAPTER 2

GRASS

2.1 Introduction

2.2 Grass production
    2.2.1 Reproductive and vegetative growth
    2.2.2 Factors affecting grass growth
    2.2.3 Species of grass
    2.2.4 Nitrogen
    2.2.5 Phosphorus and potassium
    2.2.6 Density of swards
    2.2.7 White clover
    2.2.8 When to cut for silage

2.3 Grazing strategies
    2.3.1 Sward height
    2.3.2 Buffer grazing
    2.3.3 Buffer feeding

2.4 Assessing grassland productivity

2.5 Silage
    2.5.1 Fermentation in the silo
    2.5.2 Preservability of different crops
    2.5.3 Crop scoring for preservability
    2.5.4 Mowing
    2.5.5 Field wilting
    2.5.6 Harvesting
    2.5.7 Big bale silage
    2.5.8 Silage additives
    2.5.9 Filling and sealing the silo
    2.5.10 Silage making technique

2.6 Specialist silage crops
    2.6.1 Characteristics
    2.6.2 Maize silage
    2.6.3 Whole-crop cereals

2.7 Assessing the composition of grass and silage
    2.7.1 Analytical report for silage

2.8 The ideal silage

2.9 Silage and health

2.1 Introduction

Grass is the most important component of the diet of the dairy cow. At pasture, grazed grass is often the sole feed. In winter and during periods of drought conserved forages, usually silages, are the major feeds in the diet. Ensiled grass is the predominant conserved forage in northern Europe, but in central and southern Europe, and in many other areas of the world, maize (corn) silage is the most important conserved forage for dairy cows, along with lucerne (alfalfa).

In this chapter the growth of the grass crop is described, grazing strategies are discussed and the principles of silage fermentation are outlined in detail. Specialist silage crops like maize silage are also considered. Finally the assessment of the chemical and nutritive composition of grass and silage is reviewed.

2.2 Grass production

The key factors affecting the growth of grass are described in this section together with the effects of defoliation on herbage yield and quality.

2.2.1 Reproductive and vegetative growth

Two types of growth occur in grasses - vegetative growth and reproductive growth. Vegetative growth, otherwise known as tillering, consists of new shoots developing at ground level which ultimately become new plants. Tillering occurs mainly in autumn and winter, when rate of growth is relatively slow, and is stimulated by defoliation at that time of year.

Reproductive growth involves stem elongation and the development of the flowering head; it occurs in spring and summer and is associated with little or no tillering of the plant. It follows that allowing the plant to enter reproductive growth repeatedly is likely to result in an open sward with fewer tillers than in a sward where stem development is interrupted or prevented by frequent cutting or grazing. Paradoxically it also follows that maximum production is achieved with crops which are cut or grazed infrequently, and where reproductive growth is not interrupted by defoliation. This, however, is only true for young grass crops. Eventually, an open sward is likely to suffer from ingress of "weed" grasses and broad-leaved weeds, with consequent deterioration in both sward quality and yield.

The most productive and most persistent grass swards are therefore those which are grazed hard in autumn to stimulate tillering, those which are grazed hard in spring to delay or prevent reproductive growth, and those which are both grazed and cut. The detrimental effects of reproductive growth on tiller numbers and on sward density, usually caused by allowing a crop to bulk up for cutting, can be rectified by subsequent hard grazing later in the growing season.

2.2.2 Factors affecting grass growth

The key factors influencing the annual yield of grass are:

- Grass species
- Site class
- Soil nitrogen (N) status and fertiliser N
- Phosphorus and potassium
- Density of grass plants
- Cutting and grazing strategies

These factors are discussed in the following sections. The **land** best suited to grass production is that which enjoys a long growing season, with significant rainfall during the growing season, and which has moisture-retentive soil of high fertiliser status. The most productive **swards** are those on the most suitable soil, are heavily fertilised, have a high grass plant density, have a high proportion of ryegrass and are cut or grazed infrequently.

2.2.3 Species of grass

The highest yielding grasses are those which are cut at a mature stage of growth, such as whole-crop wheat, forage maize and Italian ryegrass cut for hay or silage. Perennial ryegrass and other sown perennial species such as brome grass, timothy, meadow fescue and cocksfoot (orchard grass) can also be high-yielding, especially if they are cut infrequently.

The lowest yielding grasses are the meadow grasses, bent grass, Yorkshire Fog and other "weed" grasses. Yield differences between different species of perennial grass are greater at high levels of fertiliser N than at lower levels of fertiliser. Ryegrass is the most responsive species to fertiliser N, but well-managed permanent swards with a low proportion of ryegrass can yield as well as leys at medium levels of N.

Italian ryegrass, although higher yielding than perennial ryegrass, requires a high standard of crop management. In wet spring weather Italian ryegrass runs to seed quickly and as a result it can be stemmy and have a low protein content when harvested for silage. The need to reseed after two years makes Italian ryegrass best suited to arable/mixed farms as an entry to wheat.

2.2.4 Nitrogen

The recommended levels of fertiliser nitrogen (N) for grass depend on site class and soil nitrogen status. The more favourable the site class, the more the applied fertiliser N will be utilised, and *vice versa*.

Site class. Land has been classified into site class on a scale of 1 (very good) to 5 (poor) according to soil texture (moisture-holding capacity) and rainfall between April and September (Table 2.1).

Table 2.1 Site classes for assessing potential grass production (Add 1 for northern areas and for sites above 300 m elevation.)

Soil texture	Rainfall, April to September (mm)			
	>500	425-500	350-425	<350
	Site class			
All soils except shallow soils over chalk rock or gravelly and coarse sandy soils	1	2	2	3
Shallow soils over chalk or rock and gravelly and coarse sandy soils	2	3	4	5

Table 2.2 Influence of previous management on soil status

Soil N status	Previous management
Low	Cereals, short term ley given less than 250kg N/ha. Poor quality permanent pasture given less than 100kg N/ha.
Medium	Permanent grass or long ley given 100-250kg N/ha. Grass or arable land given more than 250kg N/ha.
High	Permanent grass or long ley given more than 250 kg N/ha. Permanent grass given large amounts of slurry. Permanent grass containing large amounts of clover.

Soil nitrogen status. Soil nitrogen status depends mainly on previous crop management (Table 2.2).

The higher the soil N status, the lower the response to additional fertiliser N and *vice versa*. The recommended levels of fertiliser N for soils of different N status are shown in Table 2.3.

Table 2.3 Recommended levels of fertiliser N at different soil N status

Site Class	Optimum fertiliser N (kg/hectare/annum)		
	Soil N status		
	Low	Medium	High
1	500	430	380
2	450	380	330
3	390	320	270
4	370	300	250
5	325	255	205

Grass is one of the few crops where the recommended level of fertiliser N is about twice as great as the N offtake by the crop. With other crops, e.g. maize or cereals, the offtake of N is about equal to the fertiliser N applied. The implications for environmental pollution are self-evident.

Grass/clover. Swards should receive a maximum of 50 kg N/ha in spring and thereafter no fertiliser N at all, otherwise clover growth will be suppressed by grass growth and the clover will not rely on nitrogen-fixing bacteria (*rhizobia*) in its root nodules to fix nitrogen from the atmosphere.

Grazing. It is important not to apply compound fertiliser or slurry in spring to grass destined to be grazed because high doses of potassium reduce the availability of magnesium to the plant, leading to increased risk of hypomagnesaemia (grass staggers or grass tetany) in the animal (see Chapter 7, page 85). Pastures which contain ryegrass alone predispose to low levels of magnesium and hence to hypomagnesaemia. Slurry should therefore be applied in the spring to land destined for maize, or on set-aside land. Cereal stubbles are ideal for slurry in summer and autumn. If the farm is all grass, slurry should be stored if possible until it can be applied to grass which has just been cut for silage.

Unless there is a shortage of grass production as the result of a summer drought, there is little merit in applying fertiliser N after July, since soil N status is usually high in the second half of the growing season, especially if the land has been grazed rather than cut. Grass grazed in spring and early summer should be rested from grazing early in June and cut for silage from July onwards to make the best use of N recycled to the sward via faeces and urine earlier in the season by the grazing animal.

2.2.5   Phosphorus and potassium
Phosphorus (P) and potassium (K) are more resistant to leaching from the soil than nitrogen. It is usually adequate to check the P and K status of the soil in late May or early autumn and adjust as necessary.

The normal requirements of grass for P and K are expressed in terms of the oxides phosphorus pentoxide (P_2O_5) and potassium oxide (K_2O) present in fertilisers and are shown in Table 2.4 for soil index 1.

Table 2.4   Requirements (kg/ha/annum) for phosphorus and potassium (MAFF, 1979)

	Phosphorus (P_2O_5)	Potassium (K_2O)
Grazed pasture	30	30
Grass cut twice	90	150
Clover and other legumes (per cut)	80	100

2.2.6   Density of swards
To achieve longevity in a grass sward and reduce the cost of reseeding and the associated risk of failure to establish a new crop, plant density should be maintained at as high a level as possible. Open swards caused by low stocking rate, infrequent cutting or grazing, poaching (treading by grazing in wet weather), severe drought or frost kill in winter are prone to weed ingress.

Grass should occupy at least 90% of total ground cover in spring. If areas of a field show bare ground or significant weed ingress, then it may be necessary to patch up these areas with a partial reseed. In severe cases of grass death or destruction by animals or machinery, reseeding may be inevitable. The reseeding of a perennial grass sward should be regarded as an admission of failed management rather than a planned strategy. There is no reason why a well-managed sward of perennial grass should not remain productive for many years.

The key to increasing plant density is hard grazing in autumn or in spring to stimulate tillering (Section 2.2.1). Removal of surplus herbage at the end of the grazing season is the best way to maintain a high plant population. This is achieved most effectively by intensive sheep grazing. By grazing the grass down to ground level, tillering is stimulated, and the subsequent year's production can be improved significantly as a result. Occasionally a sward can be saved completely from having to be ploughed out by a good hard grazing in late autumn and early winter with sheep.

During the grazing season continuous grazing is to be preferred to rotational grazing. By continuous grazing the same effect of stimulating tillering can be achieved with cattle as with sheep, and the increased sward density makes the crop more resistant to treading by the animal. Herbage intake is also likely to be higher than with less frequent grazing of a more open sward (see Section 2.3.1 below).

2.2.7   White clover
Under good grass growing conditions, white clover can contribute up to 250kg N/ha, but to achieve this it is necessary to have at least 30% of clover in the total sward DM. The variety "Nesta" seems to be one of the better white clover varieties from the point of view of sustaining companion grass production. A problem with clover is that it can virtually disappear from the sward as the result of cold and wet winter weather. "Grasslands Demand" is a promising variety which combines good winter survival with good growth in spring and summer.

Bloat can also be a problem when hungry animals are turned into a clover field. This can occur with cows if they are returned to a grazing field after being milked without first being offered a buffer feed (see Section 2.3.3). The risk of bloat is also increased if the amount of herbage available is greatly in excess of the amount likely to be eaten and if the proportion of legumes in the herbage is high. Addition of poloxalene to the drinking water can reduce the incidence of bloat, but the risk of bloat can also be reduced, if not completely eliminated, by avoiding excessively rapid consumption of clover through daily or twice-daily buffer feeding.

2.2.8 *When to cut for silage*

A compromise has to be struck between quantity and quality. Infrequent cutting gives higher annual yield but lowers the feeding value. The depression in yield due to more frequent defoliation is greater in dry years than in wet years and greater at lower levels of fertiliser N than at higher levels. Thus it is possible, at least in wetter regions, to alleviate the reduction in annual grass production caused by frequent cutting by applying a greater total quantity of fertiliser N.

Traditionally, farmers sacrificed quality for quantity: grass was cut at a mature stage of growth, and at the most two cuts were taken per year. In the 1970s and 1980s fertiliser N was applied at very high rates to produce vast amounts of leafy, wet grass of high energy and protein content. Today farmers are turning increasingly to specialist silage crops like forage maize and whole-crop wheat. Consequently there is likely to be less pressure to produce vast quantities of grass silage, either by infrequent cutting of very mature crops, or by frequent cutting of very heavily fertilised grass. The timing of cutting for silage will then be determined by other considerations, such as the weather and the needs of the grazing animal.

The timing of silage cutting is also influenced by the need to have young grass available for grazing throughout the summer. Thus the farmer may decide to cut an area for silage to provide regrowth herbage in addition to that already allocated for grazing, to support animal performance in summer and autumn. The timing of the silage cut depends on the area of land grazed in spring. If a small area of land is grazed in spring, then an early cut for silage releases the extra regrowth area earlier in summer, when rainfall and grass growth can be low.

Early cutting for silage increases the likelihood of subsequent rapid regrowth because:

- Soil moisture levels are likely to be adequate to allow rapid regrowth. This is an important factor to take into account when planning aftermath (regrowth) grazing areas.

- The leaf bases of the grass plant are still green and capable of photosynthesis after the silage cut has been removed from the field, thus accelerating rate of regrowth.

- The plant has not lost the ability to produce new tillers, thus increasing the plant density of the regrowth.

An early start to silage making means that if the weather deteriorates subsequently, a pause can be taken without losing too much quality. Cutting a young crop, however, means that yield is lower at the first cut than for more mature crops.

2.3 Grazing strategies

Grazed grass is the cheapest feed for the dairy cow, so it is very important that its use is maximised as far as possible. This implies that a grazing strategy should be developed for a particular herd. The strategy adopted should reflect the site class, the layout of the fields on the farm, and the desired level of performance of the herd.

The main problem with grazing is variable feed intake leading to variable animal performance. In spring, cows turned out to pasture in late lactation or dry can gain weight rapidly and become over-fat by the time they calve. In autumn, insufficient herbage on offer coupled with shorter daylength and reduced grass quality can result in poor performance, especially in those cows which calve in summer and are at potential peak yield.

Many dairy farmers house their cows at the time of calving so that they can control nutrient intake. But this practice is more costly than grazing, increases labour and produces greater amounts of slurry for disposal.

The key to success in grazing is controlling daily herbage allowance per animal. This requires a flexible approach to stocking rate, since herbage growth fluctuates from very rapid in spring to zero in times of drought. Too much herbage on offer and, although intake may be high, grass is wasted, the quality of subsequent regrowth is reduced and feed intake is depressed later in the season (see Section 2.3.1). If too little herbage is on offer, intake is restricted (Figure 2.1).

Figure 2.1   Effect of sward height on herbage intake under continuous grazing (Hodgson, 1990)

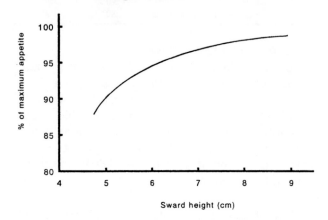

2.3.1 Sward height

Sward height is now accepted as the most practical way of assessing herbage availability and grazing pressure. Measured regularly by taking at least 25 measures at random with a ruler in both grazed and rejected areas across the field, the average sward height should then be compared with that in Table 2.6 and adjusted if necessary. Optimal intake is a compromise between too little grass on offer and too much (Figure 2.1). Ideally, sward height should be maintained within the critical range (see Table 2.6) for most of the season. If cows are grazed throughout the autumn period, then sward height should be allowed to increase to account for reductions in daylength, speed of grazing, pasture quality and herbage intake (Table 2.5). Thus target sward heights differ according to time of the season and the grazing system on the farm (Table 2.6).

Table 2.5   Effect of season on grazing behaviour and herbage intake (Leaver, 1983)

	Early season	Mid-season	Late season
Time spent grazing (h)	8	9	9
Herbage intake (kg DM/day)	16	14	11

Table 2.6   Target sward heights for rotational and continuous grazing

	Target sward height (cm)			
	Spring	Summer	Autumn	Winter
Rotational grazing	8	10	12	less than 5
Continuous grazing	6	8	10	less than 5

If sward height is too low, a buffer area or buffer feed should be offered (see Sections 2.3.2 and 2.3.3). If sward height is too high, the grazing area could be closed up for cutting and the animals moved to another area where sward height is lower. Alternatively, stocking rate may be increased on the current grazing area by closing off part of the field with an electric fence, or by drafting in additional animals.

The most important time of the year for tight control of sward height is the spring period when grass growth is at its most rapid. Farmers often waste grass in spring because they understock for fear of running out of grass later in the season. The consequences of this mistake are:

- Insufficient area cut for first-cut silage, and inadequate "clean" regrowth pasture.

- Too much grass rejected around dung and urine patches, which continues to grow and mature.

- Increased stem content in the grazed sward from July onwards, especially in previously rejected areas.

- Depressed herbage intake and reduced animal performance from July onwards.

It is vital that dung and urine patches should be grazed off as much as possible in spring, to reduce to the minimum the total area of rejected herbage in the sward, which inevitably increases with repeated grazings as the season progresses. Integrating cutting with grazing helps to avoid this accumulation of rubbish, and, in employing a system where sheep graze after cattle, also helps to maintain herbage intake in mid and late season.

2.3.2 Buffer grazing

Buffer grazing is a way of increasing stocking rate without running short of grass in mid-summer; it is not to be confused with buffer feeding (see Section 2.2.4). The technique is designed mainly for use in the early spring period, though it can also be used whenever grass growth is likely to exceed requirements. The procedure involves reserving about a third of the total area allocated to early spring grazing for first cut silage. If the weather is good for grazing the animals remain in the restricted area and the buffer area is the first to be cut for silage. If the weather is poor, either because of excessively cool or wet weather, the buffer area is grazed in sections by electric fence as necessary.

Adoption of the buffer grazing strategy produces:

- Tighter but flexible stocking in spring.

- Better control of sward height at a time of rapid grass growth.

- Rapid pasture regrowth if the buffer area is cut early.

- An early, clean aftermath if the buffer area is cut.

- The opportunity to maintain high herbage intakes through June and July.

- The prospect of increased yields of early-cut, high quality silage.

- Reduced worm burden in June and July.

The buffer grazing system was developed originally for beef calves. Tests of the system showed clearly that often the buffer area could be cut in spring because sward height remained optimal in the reduced early grazing area. Animal performance was improved in mid and late season, and when the buffer area was cut, stocking rate was higher because more silage was made.

The system illustrates well the principle outlined in Section 2.2.6 of tight grazing in spring producing benefits later in the season.

2.3.3   *Buffer feeding*

Buffer feeding is a useful tool for managing sward height. By offering the animals feeds which are not likely to be eaten in preference to grazed grass (hay, straw, or big bale silage) the buffer feed acts as a supplement to rather than as a replacement for grazed herbage. Cows offered a buffer feed after each milking for about half an hour can consume sufficient additional dry matter to rectify a shortage of pasture herbage. Delayed return to pasture after milking allows closure of the teat orifice which may help to reduce mastitis in summer. If grass and conserved grass are both in very short supply, then a mixture of 3 parts of wet brewers' grains to one part of alkali-treated straw on a fresh weight basis can be used as a buffer feed.

A particularly useful buffer feed in times of drought is urea-treated whole-crop wheat. The ammonia present in the material acts as a preservative to delay the process of aerobic spoilage, so the feed can be left in troughs or in ring feeders for several days at a time, even in hot weather.

Herbage intake declines progressively as the grazing season continues (Table 2.5). For this reason it is important that herbage allowance is increased and

that a daily buffer feed is also offered from mid to late summer onwards.

2.4   Assessing grassland productivity

The productivity of a field or farm can be assessed by calculating how much energy it supplies. Utilised metabolisable energy (UME) is a crude guide to grass energy output per hectare of land. It is approximate because it is derived indirectly from the input of energy in concentrates, it assumes a constant ME value for concentrates, and it is very sensitive to stocking rate. Errors in calculating stocking rate thus have a large impact on UME. The technique can be applied on a field by field basis, but only during the grazing season, and only when the weight and thus the maintenance energy requirement of the animals can be assessed.

UME is best suited to farms where the concentrate part of the diet comprises compounded cake of relatively constant energy value. The complication of feeding several different straights at the same time makes the calculation even less accurate.

The best approach to minimise errors is to estimate UME for the herd over the whole year. When calculated on an annual basis the technique can be used to assess relative efficiency, since there is a positive correlation between UME and gross margin per hectare.

UME is calculated as the difference between the total ME required and that supplied by concentrates (Figure 2.2).

Figure 2.2 Calculation of UME for a dairy herd

UME (GJ/ha) =

ME required/cow/annum = 25 (maintenance/cow/annum) + $\dfrac{\text{milk yield (litres/cow/annum) x 5}}{1000}$

less

ME from concentrates = $\dfrac{\text{concentrates (kg fresh weight/cow/annum)}}{1000}$ x 11

multiplied by stocking rate (cows/ha).

The target UME for good grass growing conditions is more than 100 GJ/ha. Achieving a high UME depends on having a high grass plant population, optimum fertiliser N, good grass growing conditions and a high proportion of grass being eaten or cut. A high UME does not necessarily mean low concentrate use, but it **does** mean efficient use of productive grass and forage crops. Similar UME can be achieved at quite different levels of concentrate input, provided appropriate adjustments are made to stocking rate. Often, as concentrate input is increased, there is little or no increase in stocking rate to take account of the reduced requirement of the animals for grass.

2.5 Silage

The main objective in silage making is to conserve nutrients as efficiently as possible for the winter period or for buffer feeding in times of inadequate herbage allowance or pasture quality. A secondary objective is to remove grass which is surplus to requirements for grazing. The first objective implies that there are losses in silage making which should be minimised as much as possible. The second objective implies that grazing takes precedence over silage making, which is now no longer the case on most dairy farms in developed countries.

There has been a steady increase in the amount of silage made in western Europe since the mid 1970s. In the UK alone about 15 million tonnes of dry matter (55 million tonnes fresh weight) is stored annually as silage. Big bale silage accounts for about 25% of total silage production (Wilkinson and Stark, 1992). This growth in the production of silage reflects the major role played by silage in the diet of the dairy cow. It also reflects the increasing importance in Europe and North America of specialist silage crops like forage maize (Section 2.6.2).

Figure 2.3 Fermentation in grass silage

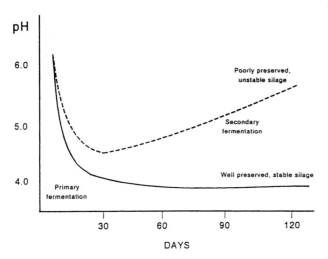

The objective in making silage is to create anaerobic conditions (no oxygen) for the fermentation of sugars to acids which lowers the pH and preserves or "pickles" the crop.

2.5.1 Fermentation in the silo

On entry to the silo, oxygen in the harvested, compacted crop mass is exhausted by plant respiration and by the growth of aerobic bacteria. Fermentation continues in the absence of oxygen, and this process is largely responsible for the acidification of the crop which characterises the stored silage.

The primary fermentation in the silo involves the production of lactic acid as the principal end-product. Secondary fermentation occurs when insufficient acid is produced by the primary fermentation to reduce the pH to below a critical level of about pH 4.5 (Figure 2.3). This may occur if the crop is too wet, or if the sugar content is too low, or if the buffering capacity of the crop is too high. The bacteria responsible for secondary fermentations are mainly the clostridia. These bacteria are strict anaerobes and may convert lactic acid to butyric, or they may degrade proteins, peptides and amino acids to amines and ammonia, depending on the particular strain of clostridia which develops. Clostridia thrive in wet conditions, so it is possible to have a stable, high pH value in a dry silage and yet have no evidence of secondary fermentation.

The consequences of secondary fermentations are a reduced proportion of amino acid N in the total N, an increased proportion of total N as ammonia N, smelly butyric silage, increased losses in the silo, reduced voluntary intake and reduced efficiency of utilisation of silage N by the cow.

Well-preserved silage contains lactic acid as the major product of the fermentation of the water soluble carbohydrates (WSCs or sugars) - principally fructose and glucose. Poorly-preserved silage contains a relatively low proportion of lactic acid and significant amounts of acetic, propionic and butyric acids. There is also greater degradation of plant proteins to non-protein nitrogenous compounds, including ammonia.

Fermentation is restricted by increasing the dry matter content of the crop or by direct acidification with an acid additive. Restricting the extent of fermentation produces a stable silage with a higher pH and lower free acidity than occurs in wetter crops which undergo more extensive fermentations and often reach pH values of less than 4.0.

The pattern and extent of the fermentation in the silo is influenced by many factors, but the main effects are those of the crop itself - principally dry matter content, buffering capacity and water soluble carbohydrate content.

Dry matter content. The dry matter content of the crop is increased by:

- advancing crop maturity, especially after the onset of flowering;

- dry weather, especially wind;

- field wilting, especially at low densities of crop per square metre of ground area.

and decreased by:

- rain and dew;

- an increased proportion of leaf in the crop;

- high rates of fertiliser N.

The effect of increasing crop dry matter content by field wilting in good weather on the fermentation of a crop of Italian ryegrass is shown in Table 2.7. In that case both wilted and unwilted silages were well-preserved, as indicated by the relatively low contents of volatile (ammonia) N and the absence of butyric acid. The main effects of wilting on the composition of the silage were:

- a restriction in the extent of fermentation;

- a reduction in the proportion of fermentation acids present as lactic acid;

- a large increase in the amount of residual, unfermented water soluble carbohydrate in the silage.

Table 2.7 **Effect of increasing dry matter content on the fermentation of Italian ryegrass (McDonald, 1976)**

	Direct cut	Wilted	
		1 day	2 days
Dry matter (g/kg)	159	336	469
pH	3.7	4.1	4.9
Volatile N (g/kg total N)	69	59	43
Lactic acid (g/kg DM)	121	54	17
Acetic acid (g/kg DM)	36	21	12
Butyric acid (g/kg DM)	0	0	0
WSC (g/kg DM)	17	117	164

Buffering capacity (or resistance to acidification). A buffered system resists change in pH; it comprises weak acids and their salts in equilibrium and operates in grasses and legumes mainly between pH 6 and pH 4. Buffering capacity is higher for crops with relatively high concentrations of organic acids (e.g. malic acid, succinic acid), mineral cations and protein. Legumes typically have relatively higher buffering capacities than the grasses (Table 2.8). It is notable that there is a general association between the buffering capacity of the crop and that of the silage made from it (Table 2.8). The very large increase in the buffering capacity of silage compared to the fresh crop is also important in relation to the neutralisation of silage acidity in the rumen - it takes a lot more alkali to neutralise the acidity of silage than the amount of acid to produce the low pH in the first place.

Table 2.8 **Typical range of buffering capacities of different fresh crop species and silages made from them (McDonald *et al.*, 1991)**

	Buffering capacity (meq/kg DM)	
	Fresh crop	Silage
Maize	200 to 250	900 to 1200
Ryegrass	250 to 350	1200 to 1500
Lucerne (legume)	500 to 550	1750 to 2500

The resistance to acidification of the fresh crop should ideally be as low as possible, as should the resistance to neutralisation of the resultant silage.

Water soluble carbohydrate content. The concentration of sugars (water-soluble carbohydrates or fermentable sugars) in the fresh crop is an indicator of the likely pattern and extent of fermentation. Grasses tend to assimilate WSC produced by photosynthesis into structural carbohydrates (growth) and store relatively little WSC during vegetative growth. Once the crop enters reproductive growth there is accumulation of WSC in the stem (as fructans), but the major factor affecting the concentration of WSC in the fresh crop is the content of water.

The higher the concentration of sugars in the fresh crop at harvesting the higher the probability of achieving a well-preserved silage. If the concentration of sugars has been increased in the crop by the rapid removal of water during field-wilting, it is likely that some of the original sugars will remain unfermented in the silage. This residual sugar content is very important as a source of readily available carbohydrate for the microbial population in the rumen, and thus is a major factor affecting the fermentable metabolisable energy (FME) content of the silage (Section 2.7.1).

There is a daily peak in the content of WSC in the fresh crop which occurs in late afternoon. WSC accumulated during the day decline at night as the result of plant respiration and conversion into new growth.

In wet, leafy grass crops the content of WSC may be as low as 10 g/kg fresh weight (100 g/kg DM), whilst in a high dry matter mature crop of ryegrass the WSC content may be as high as 50 g/kg fresh weight (170 g/kg DM). A five-fold increase in WSC in the fresh crop is accompanied by a proportionately smaller increase in the concentration of WSC in the DM.

High inputs of nitrogen fertiliser give rise to reduced levels of WSC, principally because of the stimulatory effect of N on the rate of leaf growth in immature grass crops.

As a general rule, a concentration of 30 g WSC/kg fresh weight is necessary to reduce the risk of secondary fermentation. A crude way of assessing sugar content is by squeezing grass juice on to a specially-calibrated refractometer; alternatively several laboratories offer a rapid analytical service for assessing WSC concentrations in grass samples.

2.5.2   *Preservability of different crops*

Crops which are very wet, have a low content of fermentable sugars or have a high buffering capacity (or all three) are at much greater risk of being poorly preserved than crops which are relatively dry, have a high sugar content and a low buffering capacity. Crops are ranked qualitatively from excellent preservability to very poor preservability in Table 2.9. Maize invariably ferments well without additive. Lucerne requires both wilting and an effective additive. The poorer the preservability, the higher the risk of poor quality fermentation, and the greater the need for an effective additive.

Table 2.9   Preservability of different crops

Excellent	Maize
↑	Whole-crop cereals
	Italian ryegrass
	Perennial ryegrass
	Timothy/meadow fescue
	Permanent grass
	Cocksfoot
	Arable silage (immature whole-crop cereals)
↓	Grass/clover mixtures
	Red clover
Very poor	Lucerne

2.5.3   *Crop scoring for preservability*

The type of crop itself is only one of many factors which influence the probability of achieving a well-preserved silage. Others include the stage of growth of the crop at harvest, the quantity of fertiliser N, the type of harvester and extent of chopping at harvest, the weather and the season.

A simple way of assessing the various factors that can influence preservability of crops, by directly or indirectly affecting dry matter content, WSC, buffering capacity and nitrate content is shown in Table 2.10.

Table 2.10 Crop scoring to assess risk of poor preservation (Wilkinson, 1990)

	Score				
	5	4	3	2	1
Crop	Italian ryegrass/ maize	Perennial ryegrass	Other grasses	Grass/ clover	Lucerne/ red clover
Stage of growth		Stemmy	Ear emergence	Leafy	
Fertiliser N (kg/ha/cut)			Less than 50	0 to 100	100
Harvester	Metered chop	Double chop	Flail, Big baler	Forage wagon	
Weather/ wilt	Sunny/ wilted		Cloudy/ wilted	Cloudy	Showery
Season			Spring & summer		Autumn

Crop scoring has been used in the UK since the mid-1960s. It is a useful indicator of the need for an acid additive to assist in achieving a well-preserved silage in difficult ensiling conditions. The value of the approach as a predictor of the need for inoculation is less well-established, since low crop scores imply wet crops with low concentrations of sugars. Since the bacteria in inoculants need an adequate supply of sugars to be effective, there is more chance of an inoculant failing and there is a higher risk of poor preservation when the crop score is low than when the crop score is high. Acid additives are most likely to be effective when crop scores are low (see Table 2.11).

2.5.4   *Mowing*

The main objective in mowing grass crops for silage is to avoid mowing material which is excessively wet. This means not mowing early in the day, especially when there is no wind and when there has been a heavy dew. The best time of the day to mow is in the afternoon, when both dry matter content and the concentration of sugars in the crop are likely to be at their highest levels.

The second objective is to produce a swath which will lose water as rapidly as possible. To achieve this objective, the maximum surface area of crop should be exposed to the atmosphere to intercept radiation from the sun and reflected from clouds. In practice heavy, wet swaths are often produced by wide mowers and it is hardly surprising that the only wilting which occurs is that on the top surface of the swath. This can have a deleterious effect on the quality of fermentation. The remainder of the swath stays wet and may deteriorate rapidly due to plant respiration and the action of undesirable micro-organisms. Consequently it is not advisable to put two or three rows into one at the time of mowing the crop.

Conditioners mounted on mowers which scratch the epidermal tissue of the crop can accelerate water loss from the swath. They are likely to be most effective when the crop is not too heavy or dense, and when there is no rain during the wilting period. The more aggressive the action of the conditioner on the crop, the faster the rate of water loss in good weather, but the greater the nutrient loss due to leaching when rain falls on the swath.

2.5.5   Field wilting

Wilting involves delaying the harvesting process and leaving the crop in the field for a period of time after mowing so that it can lose water. The optimal period of wilting is 24 hours with the aim to achieve a DM content of 30% for bunker silos and 40% for big bales and tower silos. Longer periods of wilting can result in greater losses of dry matter - mainly of sugars and proteins - whilst shorter periods of wilting are less likely to give significant increases in DM content.

A quick wilt in dry weather is beneficial because the weight of material to be harvested is less than with a direct-cut crop which is harvested immediately after being mown, less effluent is produced from the silo and the risk of secondary fermentation in the silo is reduced. In good weather the concentration of sugar in the fresh crop weight is increased by wilting because of the rapid evaporation of water from the crop. However, in humid or wet weather there may be little increase in sugar level because loss of sugars due to plant respiration may exceed the rate of water loss. There is little point, therefore, in prolonged field-wilting in poor weather. Short-range local weather forecasts should always be obtained whenever silage making is about to start, in order to increase the chances of mowing a dry crop and ensuring continued dry weather for the entire wilting period.

Rapid wilting is achieved by:

- **Spreading** the swath out over the entire ground area immediately after mowing.

- **Frequent tedding**, as in the Dutch system. Coupled with abrasion conditioning, tedded light leafy crops can be wilted to 30% dry matter in less than 5 hours.

- **Mat-making** involves macerating the crop and then squeezing the macerate through rollers to form a mat of pulverised grass. Resistance by the crop tissues to water loss is greatly reduced because the process of maceration destroys the integrity of the plant cells and makes much of the moisture available for evaporation from the mat as it lies on the stubble in the field. Wilting

to 30% DM in as short a period as 3 hours is possible with the technique, but nutrient losses following rain may be unacceptably high.

Prolonged wilting usually results in silage of reduced energy value as the result of relatively high respiration losses in the field. Feed intake is generally increased by wilting and this response tends to offset any reduction in digestibility so that animal performance is often similar for wilted compared to direct-cut silage.

Grass crops increase in DM content as they mature. Thus one way of achieving higher dry matter silage in a wet climate is to leave the crop to mature before mowing. Crops like whole-crop wheat and forage maize are harvested at an advanced stage of maturity and are relatively dry (normally more than 30% DM) even though they are harvested without being wilted.

2.5.6   Harvesting

The most common system of harvesting grass is to pick-up a mown swath by a metered-chop harvester. This type of harvester picks up the swath and feeds the crop at a predetermined rate into a chopping chamber before the material is blown out into a trailer.

Research in Northern Ireland (Gordon, 1988) has shown that maximum milk output per hectare is achieved with direct harvesting by flail harvester, with no separate mowing and subsequent pick-up and no field wilting. But there are drawbacks to this system of harvesting grass for silage. The main problems with direct harvesting are slow work rate and the probability of rapid effluent loss from the silo soon after harvest.

Large rakes are now available which will gather more than 8 metres width of crop, equivalent to 4 swaths, into a single row, increasing speed of harvesting substantially. The production of large swaths has been encouraged by the increased popularity of self-propelled harvesters capable of harvesting over 30 hectares per day.

2.5.7   Big bale silage

Big bales are increasing in popularity because less labour, less capital and less power is required to produce and store them than for conventional silage. Big bales are best suited to smaller farms where hay was made until recently. The attraction of the big bale, apart from lower labour requirements, is that there is no need for high capital investments to build a bunker silo. Since big bales are not classified officially as silos, and provided they are stored more than 10 metres from a water course, they do not come under current UK pollution controls.

Baled silage is usually wilted for longer than conventional silage in an attempt to achieve drier material at baling. Higher DM contents are desirable because of the need to avoid poor preservation and to reduce the risk of bales becoming deformed and losing their shape and their seal during storage. Sealing is rapid, and can occur immediately after baling. The crop is not chopped at harvest, so the speed of fermentation is slower than with conventional silage. The extent of fermentation is often less than with conventional silage, giving silage of higher pH than would otherwise occur.

Wrapping is now virtually universal for all big bale silage. Bagging still occurs on some small family units, but is more time-consuming. Wrapping should result in four layers covering the surface of the bale, with a 50% overlap between individual layers. It is better to wrap at the farm buildings within 24 hours of baling rather than in the field, and then to stack the wrapped bales immediately. Bales should be put in single layers if the crop is wet to avoid distorting bale shape and destroying the seal of the wrap, thereby introducing oxygen and initiating deterioration of the silage.

Two features of big bale silage are of special nutritional significance to the cow:

- **Restricted fermentations** in baled silages are desirable especially when the major source of silage on the farm is wet, very acid material. Intake is often increased by the provision of less-acid big bale silage alongside conventional silage.

- **Long fibre** can be crucial to the maintenance of a healthy rumen environment dominated by an acetate fermentation, especially in early lactation. If the fibre is digestible as well, the material is preferable to giving straw to animals in early lactation, because the energy content of the diet is not diluted to the same extent. Long fibre in well-preserved big bale silage can also be very useful in stimulating the development of the rumen in young calves.

Pre-chopping of the crop as it enters the baler is a compromise between the short chopping of conventional silage and the very long fibre of unchopped baled silage. The composition and feeding value of chopped baled silage are closer to that of bunker silage than to unchopped baled material. An additional advantage is that the increased density of chopped baled silage results in the crop being stored in fewer bales. Effluent loss is, however, likely to be greater for chopped than for unchopped bales.

2.5.8 Silage additives

The main objectives in using an additive are to improve the quality of the fermentation in the silo,

to reduce losses of nutrients, to increase voluntary intake and hence to improve animal performance. Many farmers use an additive as an insurance against making poorly-preserved silage. However it is often difficult to know by how much the additive actually improved the silage and, therefore, how cost-effective the product was. Thus it is important to know whether or not an individual product has a track record of efficacy under conditions similar to those likely to be encountered on the farm. There is little point in trusting research data collected on crops ensiled in a different climate or with different crops.

Several European countries operate approval schemes for silage additives. The UK now has a two-stage scheme involving registration of products followed by approval for one or more categories of efficacy, based on information supplied by the manufacturer. The UK categories are:

C   Good effects on fermentation quality and/or aerobic stability of silage.

B   Good effects on feed intake and digestibility.

A   Improved animal performance - liveweight gain and/or milk production.

There are many additive products available on the market. For example, in the UK alone there are some 120 individual products. This inevitably causes confusion, especially since some products look virtually identical to others and many have similar claims made for them.

The key criteria in choosing an additive are:

- **Efficacy**: Is the product likely to work on the farm? Does the product have reliable, independent data to support it? Were the data produced from crops similar to those to be ensiled on the farm? Are the claims made for the product justified by the efficacy data? Is the recommended rate of addition the same as that used in the data? Can the recommended rate of addition be achieved easily and consistently?

- **Safety**: Can the product be applied safely? Some products contain strong acids which pose a potential hazard to safety when handling the materials.

- **Uniformity**: Is the product the same now as it was when it was tested? Has it a specific shelf life and if so, is the shelf life adequate? Is the product likely to change during the storage period on the farm, and if so, is this likely to compromise its efficacy significantly?

The popularity of additives varies considerably from country to country. In Finland, for example, virtually all silage is made with the addition of acid

Feeding the Dairy Cow

or acid/formalin. In the Republic of Ireland, molasses is the most popular type of additive along with sulphuric acid. In England and France, inoculants have superceded acids as the most commonly-used type of additive. The popularity of acid-type additives reflects rainfall and the risk of secondary fermentations - thus in Scotland, in contrast to England, acids are used to a greater extent than inoculants (Wilkinson and Stark, 1992).

Silage additives may be divided into the following groups:

Acids. Products based on formic or sulphuric acid are most likely to have a proven track record of efficacy. The most important issue is whether or not the product contains sufficient active ingredient to produce well-preserved silage under extreme conditions, i.e. crops with low scores (Section 2.5.3). Generally, the higher the concentration of active ingredient the better. Some acid products can be difficult to handle safely especially by inexperienced operators; this has led to the reduced use of sulphuric acid in recent years. Sulphuric acid adds sulphur to the diet which may be a problem because of the reduction in the availability of dietary copper to the animal as the level of sulphur in the diet is increased (see Chapter 7, page 89).

Acid/formalin mixtures. Some products in this group are as effective as acids alone, and the value of the formalin (formaldehyde) component is debatable.

Salts. Additives based on salts of acids are generally less active, weight for weight, than the free acids themselves. Higher rates of application can overcome this disadvantage, but the cost of treatment may be increased as a result.

Sugars (molasses). Molasses is a well-established additive for silage. By providing additional fermentable carbohydrate fermentation quality is likely to be improved in wet crops of low sugar content. Molasses is safe to use, but the quantity of product needed to increase the concentration of sugar in the crop fresh weight is considerable - 15 litres per tonne is required to achieve an addition of 10 kg of sucrose per tonne of fresh crop and raise sugar concentration by 1 percentage unit.

Inoculants. These products act to drive the speed and pattern of the fermentation in a desired manner, namely the production of as much lactic acid as possible in a short period of time. The bacteria in the majority of inoculants are those which are homofermentative, that is they ferment sugars to produce lactic acid as the sole fermentation product.

As with acid additives, the key issue is whether or not the product contains sufficient active ingredient at the recommended rate of use. It is generally considered necessary to add at least 10^6 **live** bacteria, usually termed "colony-forming units (CFU)" per gram of fresh crop to influence the fermentation significantly. Clearly, the total **viable** count of colony-forming units is more important than the total number of bacteria, because some may be dead or of poor reproductive ability. Further, if the concentration of fermentable substrate is inadequate in the crop at the outset, it is asking a lot of an inoculant to prevent the development of secondary fermentations. Some products contain both bacteria and enzymes designed to generate extra fermentable sugar from plant cell wall material. Nevertheless, it is when crop and weather conditions are poor and the crop score is low that the efficacy of inoculants is most challenged.

Enzymes. The use of plant cell wall degrading enzymes in ensiling has theoretical attractions. Apart from generating more fermentable sugars from cell wall carbohydrates, there is the possibility that the enzyme might also produce an increase in the metabolisable energy content of the silage. In practice enzyme additions to silage can result in greater intensity of fermentation, presumably as the result of an increase in the amount of fermentable sugar in the material. But enzymes can also increase effluent loss. Furthermore, unless the enzyme can degrade material in the silo which is indigestible in the rumen, an increase in ME content is unlikely to be achieved.

Absorbents. These products are designed to reduce or eliminate the production of liquid effluent from the silo. The materials are usually pelleted mixtures of ground cereal grain, sugar beet pulp, straw and molasses. Pellet size is small (ca. 3 mm diameter) to maximise surface area for absorption. The recommended rate of addition often depends on the dry matter content of the crop at harvest, since higher rates are needed for wetter crops. For example, a rate of addition of 50 kg per tonne of fresh crop weight will result in a reduction in effluent loss from large bunkers by about 50 litres per tonne of fresh crop ensiled. The absorptive capacity of the product can be compromised by the high pressures exerted in larger silos. Conversely, the efficacy of absorbent products is highest in big bales, where the effect of packing density is much reduced compared to bunker silos.

Palatability enhancers. These products are not strictly silage additives but feed additives, since they are applied to silage at feeding time. Some materials comprise sodium bicarbonate to neutralise the acidity of silage; others contain sweeteners and "desirable" aromas to mask the unpleasant smell of butyric acid.

Different types of additive are best-suited to different crop scores (see Section 2.5.3). Acids are recommended when scores are low, whilst inoculants are suited to higher scores. Absorbents are designed for use with wet crops which also have low scores. The suitability of different types of additive for different crop scores is illustrated in Table 2.11.

Table 2.11 Types of additive and crop scores

	Dry matter content	
	Less than 25%	**More than 25%**
Crop score	**Recommended type of additive**	
Below 15	Acids and salts at higher rates Sugars at higher rates Absorbents	Acids and salts at lower rates Sugars at lower rates Enzymes
15 to 20	Acids and salts at lower rates Sugars at lower rates Absorbents	Inoculants with enzymes Enzymes
Above 20	Inoculants Absorbents	Inoculants Inoculants with enzymes Enzymes

2.5.9 Filling and sealing the silo

During the process of silo filling, consolidation of the forage should be constant and evenly carried out so that as much air as possible is excluded from the mass. This means filling in thin layers at a time, with each layer rolled as thoroughly as possible. Drier crops must be chopped short to facilitate consolidation.

The complete sealing of the silo is crucial to the establishment of acidic, anaerobic conditions and preservation of the crop. If warm air, produced by plant respiration and aerobic bacteria, is allowed to move out of the top of the silo in the hours immediately after filling the silo, then there is the risk that fresh cooler air may gain entry, introduce more oxygen, prolong aerobic conditions and delay acidification. Equally important is the movement of carbon dioxide downwards through the forage mass. If carbon dioxide is allowed to escape out of the silo at its base, then this encourages the influx of air higher up the silo, with a similar effect to that of the escape of warm air.

Complete sealing of the top, sides and base of the silo must be carried out as quickly as possible when filling the silo - even if the process of filling the silo is incomplete. This means that bunker silos must be covered overnight during filling, that the shoulders of the silo must have at least a double seal at the end of filling, that the sides must be properly sealed and that the plastic sheeting at the base of the silo must be fully secured to prevent air from escaping out and wind from entering.

2.5.10 Silage making technique

Research at the Institute for Grassland and Environmental Research, Hurley, highlighted the importance of paying attention to detail in silage making. In an experiment with dairy cows three silages were compared:

1. High digestibility (D-value), well made (HDG)

2. High D-value, deliberately poorly made (HDP)

3. Low D-value, well made (LDG)

Each silage was given *ad libitum* to cows together with a high energy (13 MJ/kg DM), 17% crude protein concentrate. Gross chemical composition (metabolisable energy content, pH, ammonia-N) of the two high D-value silages was similar. Silage intakes are shown in Figure 2.4.

Figure 2.4 Intake of well and poorly made silages when offered *ad libitum* to dairy cows fed different amounts of concentrate (Poole *et al.*, 1992)

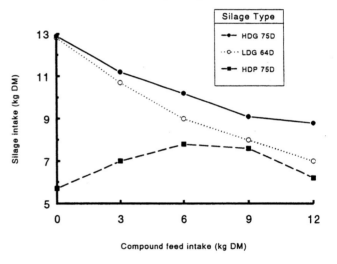

Milk yield differences between treatments were similar to those for intake. The main results and conclusions may be summarised as follows:

- When given as the sole feed, intake of well made silages were double that of poorly made silage.

- Intake of well made silages were reduced with increasing levels of concentrate, whilst intake of the poorly made silage was **increased** by concentrate feeding, up to 6 kg concentrate DM/day.

- Yields of milk fat and milk protein on the high D-value silages were maximised at 3 kg concentrate DM **less** per cow per day with the well made than the poorly made silage.

- Good silage making technique is more important than high D-value if high silage intakes are to be achieved, especially at low levels of concentrate feeding.

The essential elements of good silage making technique are:

- Mow in good weather in the afternoon, when sugars are at their highest concentration.

- Spread the crop as much as possible; avoid thick swaths.

- Wilt for 24 hours and for no longer than 48 hours, to a target DM content of 25 to 35%.

- Harvest and fill the silo as rapidly as possible.

- Consolidate evenly and consistently as the silo is filled.

- Seal the silo immediately and completely. Seal with a temporary seal overnight during filling.

- Use an effective additive to improve preservation quality and feeding value.

2.6   Specialist silage crops

Specialist silage crops are those which are not grazed but are grown specifically for ensiling. The most common specialist silage crop is maize, but in areas of Europe where maize cannot be relied upon to produce a consistently high yield whole-crop wheat is increasing in popularity.

2.6.1   *Characteristics*

Crops like maize and whole-crop cereals are attractive because they are harvested in one harvest a year, have relatively high dry matter contents pre-cutting, are harvested direct (i.e. without separate mowing and picking up), do not require wilting and need a third the quantity of fertiliser N per hectare than grass. They are also cheaper per unit of ME than grass silage, are easy to preserve well and have lower losses of DM in the silo than grass; but they are inherently unstable once the silo is opened for feed-out. Specialist silage crops reduce the pressure on grass yields and allow a more relaxed approach to first cut grass silage; if necessary first cut silage making can be delayed until the weather improves.

On the other hand, specialist silage crops can only be grown on land which is suitable for arable crops. Seed costs and the work required to produce a good seedbed can be high, especially for maize. Early harvest of whole-crop cereals allows time for new grass leys to be established before winter frosts occur.

Work at Reading, Wye College and elsewhere has shown clearly that intake and milk quality are enhanced by having a mixture of forage feeds in the diet, rather than having grass silage as the sole forage feed. In one trial with dairy cows grass silage was substituted by either maize silage, fermented whole-crop wheat, urea-treated whole-crop wheat (urea added at 4% of total forage dry matter), fodder beet or wet brewers' grains at 33% of the total forage dry matter of the diet. In addition, maize silage was included in the diet at 75% of the total forage dry matter. All cows received 6 kg of supplementary concentrate per day throughout the 16-week experiment. Average total diet dry matter intakes and milk yields are shown in Figures 2.5 and 2.6.

Figure 2.5   Effect of substituting grass silage by other forage feeds on average total dry matter intake (Browne *et al.*, 1995)

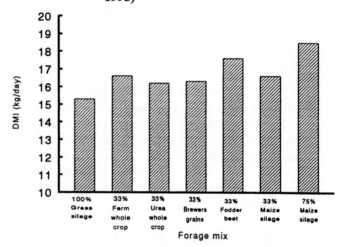

Figure 2.6   Effect of substituting grass silage by other forage feeds on milk yield (Browne *et al.*, 1995)

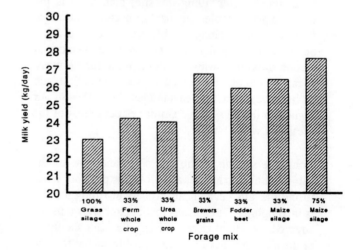

Grass silage alone gave the lowest level of feed intake and milk yield. The highest daily dry matter intakes and milk yields were achieved with maize silage at 75% of the total forage dry matter consumed; yields of milk fat and milk protein followed similar trends. At 33% inclusion in the total forage dry matter, urea-treated whole-crop wheat gave the lowest intakes and milk yields. Fodder beet gave the highest intake but brewers' grains gave the highest milk yield at this level of inclusion in the diet.

The main drawback to using whole-crop wheat in diets for dairy cows is its low ME content once crop maturity advances to a late stage and total crop dry matter content exceeds 40%. Prior to this point, ME value is likely to be similar to that of average quality grass silage (10.5 to 11.0 MJ ME/kg DM). Beyond 40% dry matter, even following treatment with urea at 4% of the dry matter, ME content is unlikely to exceed 10.5 MJ/kg DM. By harvesting the crop at a relatively high cutting height above ground level it may be possible to increase the ratio of grain to straw and improve the ME value, but yield per hectare is reduced.

There is also evidence that there is wastage of metabolisable energy in urea-treated whole-crop wheat silage. Nevertheless the inclusion of a limited amount of whole-crop wheat silage in the diet (3 to 5 kg of dry matter per cow per day) can result in improved milk composition, if not in milk yield itself. A positive response to whole-crop wheat is most likely to occur in situations where intake of grass silage is limited by poor fermentation quality, excess acidity or low dry matter content. Urea-treated whole-crop is relatively stable on feed-out from the silo and has a very useful role as a buffer feed in summer, when its stability and lack of mould development for several days in warm weather is a very valuable asset.

Maize silage and fodder beet, in contrast to whole-crop cereal silage, are high-energy crops which can produce good responses in both milk yield and milk compositional quality, especially in highly productive animals. Maize silage can be used as the sole forage feed with no detrimental effects to milk fat content or to herd health, but the overall content of protein and phosphorus in the diet must be maintained at an adequate level.

Typical analyses of maize and whole-crop cereals are shown in Table 2.12. Losses of dry matter in store and at feed out are shown for fermented (immature) whole-crop wheat and for urea-treated whole-crop wheat. The effect of urea in reducing losses is notable.

2.6.2 Maize silage

The area of land in Europe harvested as forage maize is almost the same as that harvested for grass silage (Wilkinson and Stark, 1992). In most countries the crop is grown for grain and for silage on the same farm, and both grain and silage are included in the diet of dairy cows. There has been much research effort into the maize crop, from breeding for

earliness of maturity and improved digestibility of the stover (stem and leaf) to optimal diets based on maize silage for high-yielding cows.

Table 2.12 Typical composition of maize and whole-crop cereal silages (Leaver, 1992)

	Forage maize	Fermented whole-crop wheat	Urea treated whole-crop wheat	Fermented whole-crop barley
DM (g/kg)	280	380	570	400
Ash (g/kg DM)	50	50	50	50
Crude protein (g/kg DM)	90	90	20	70
NDF (g/kg DM)	390	460	480	460
Starch (g/kg DM)	240	50	250	230
ME (MJ/kg DM)	11.0	9.2	9.3	8.3
pH	3.7	4.0	8.2	4.5
Ammonia N (% total N)	7	7	35	10
DM losses in store		11	4	
DM losses at feedout		16	2	

The key to the successful production of maize silage is to sow as early as possible, provided the soil is not too cold or too wet, so that the crop can develop early in the season and reach maturity before the weather deteriorates in the autumn. Soil compaction should be avoided at sowing time because it can reduce yield by up to 25%. If the soil is compacted, it should be sub-soiled before the next crop. At harvest the crop should be chopped short - to a target average length of 2 cm. All grain should be broken by fitting a grain cracker to the forage harvester. Harvest should occur between 30 and 35% total crop dry matter content. This stage is indicated when the milk line in the grain is about half-way between the tip of the grain and the base when the crop is harvested. The milk line represents the division in the grain between solid starch granules and liquid sugars in solution with granules of starch in suspension. The deposition of starch starts at the tip (the distal end) of the grain and proceeds to move slowly down the grain as it matures.

If forage maize is harvested too early, at less than 30% dry matter content, it is likely that the content of starch in the crop is lower and intake of digestible nutrients may be less than optimal. If the crop is harvested too mature, at more than 40% dry matter content, adequate consolidation in the silo is difficult to achieve and the crop is more likely to show mould development as a result. There is also the risk that the hard grains will not all be damaged during harvest, and their digestibility may be reduced.

Typical yields of maize silage are between 10 and 14 tonnes of dry matter per hectare, depending on topography and weather conditions during the growing season. Maize, being a sub-tropical grass, responds well at germination to warm soils and to warm weather thereafter. Deep loamy soils with good moisture retention are best-suited to maize, which is often grown continuously on the same fields on the farm.

Forage maize is relatively high in metabolisable energy, but low in crude protein and in major minerals (Table 2.12). It is therefore complementary in composition to grass and legume silages.

Ground ear maize is also used in some countries where a home-grown, high-energy feed of relatively high starch and digestible fibre content is needed for cows giving high milk yields. The maize ear is harvested in its entirety at about 50% dry matter content by forage harvester and the material ensiled as for forage maize. The remainder of the crop (the stover) is not harvested. Ground ear maize has an ME content in excess of 13 MJ/kg DM and is therefore of similar ME content to that of rolled barley. The ear of the maize plant represents 50 to 60% of the total crop dry matter, so there is a trade-off between reduced crop yield and increased energy content compared to forage maize.

2.6.3   Whole-crop cereals

The conservation of cereal crops as forages is not new. "Arable silage" has been made for many years on farms where both grass and cereal grain crops are produced. Often legumes, such as vetches, would be sown with a cereal crop like oats to increase yield and protein content.

Recently attention has focused on the harvesting of whole-crop wheat at a relatively mature stage of growth and ensiling the crop at 50% dry matter content with minimal fermentation in the silo. Addition of urea at harvest at 30 to 40 kg per tonne DM of whole-crop dry matter, with consequent hydrolysis of the urea to ammonia, ensures effective preservation with little or no mould development within the silo. A further benefit of the ammonia is that mould growth is restricted considerably after the silo is opened, thus reducing the problem of aerobic spoilage, which can be rapid and extensive in whole-crop cereal silages (including maize silage).

The main advantage of using wheat as a forage is its high total yield and high yield of grain compared to other cereals - up to 16 tonnes of total dry matter per hectare have been recorded on a field scale, which makes the cost of production low compared to other forage crops. A further advantage is that the crop can be grown as a grain crop, and the proportion

harvested as whole-crop can be determined in mid-season once first-cut grass silage yields are known. Whole-crop wheat can, therefore, be a tactical forage crop for use in years when grass yields are reduced by drought.

The energy value of whole-crop wheat is not as high as that of maize silage, but if harvested at an immature stage of growth whole-crop wheat silage can be comparable to grass silage. Like maize silage, the crude protein content of whole-crop wheat is low compared to that of most grass silages (see Table 2.12).

2.7   Assessing the composition of grass and silage

Analyses of samples of fresh grass to determine ME and crude protein are often ignored, partly because of the action of the grazing animal in selecting a diet which is usually of higher nutrient content than that of the crop as a whole and partly because cows are often expected to produce milk from grazed grass as the sole feed. Also the analysis of grass destined for silage may not reflect the composition of the crop which is eventually harvested and ensiled. However, if grazed herbage is to be supplemented by a buffer feed, or if feeds are to be purchased in spring for the following winter period, it is useful to have an idea of the composition of the grass which the animals are being offered at pasture, or are likely to be offered as silage in the future.

The analysis of grass silage has been revolutionised by the introduction of near infra-red reflectance spectroscopy (NIRs) and, in the case of silage, by the automatic electrometric titration of soluble components. These two developments have enabled analyses to be performed quickly and more comprehensively than hitherto, so that nutrient concentrations, pattern of fermentation and extent of fermentation can be described.

Both NIRs and electrometric titration are predictive techniques which are dependent on having adequate calibration of the equipment. This calibration must be done by wet chemistry, and must be comprehensive so that the full range of silages likely to be encountered in practice are assessed. It is useless to use a predictive technique, however rapid, if the samples being tested are outside the calibration range of the equipment.

NIR spectroscopy is now used routinely by all major laboratories in the UK. The latest development in technology is to use wet (i.e. fresh) samples of silage for both the wet chemistry and the NIRs scanning. This approach avoids the introduction of errors associated with the drying of samples and consequent losses of components such as ammonia and volatile fatty acids (VFA), or changes in cell wall components as the result of the drying process.

The electrometric titration technique involves acidifying a sample of juice extracted from silage with hydrochloric acid to pH 2.0, then progressively adding sodium hydroxide to raise the pH back to pH 12.0. Fermentation acids, soluble nitrogenous compounds and neutralising value are predicted from the amount of alkali required to raise the pH of the juice through specific pH ranges.

2.7.1 Analytical report for silage

The layout of an analytical report for silage based on the two new techniques of NIRs and titration described above, is illustrated in Table 2.13.

Table 2.13 An analytical report for silage

Determination	Result
Dry matter (g/kg)	205.0
pH	4.5
Crude protein (g/kg DM)	146.0
Soluble protein (g/kg DM)	82.6
Amino acid N (% Sol. N)	64.4
Ammonia (g N/kg TN)	121.0
NDF (g/kg DM)	585.0
ADF (g/kg DM)	344.0
Digestibility (DOMD) (%)	66.8
ME (MJ/kg DM)	10.7
Lactic acid (g/kg DM)	59.4
Formic acid (g/kg DM)	0.4
Acetic acid (g/kg DM)	78.4
Propionic acid (g/kg DM)	7.1
Butyric acid (g/kg DM)	6.2
Ethanol (g/kg DM)	25.7
Sugar (g/kg DM)	26.3
FME/ME	0.63

The analyses described in the report are as follows:

Dry matter. The assessment of dry matter content in forages which have not been fermented is relatively straightforward and comprises drying the sample in an oven. The residue is the dry matter. With fermented feeds the problem of volatile components has to be solved. Volatiles include acetic, propionic and butyric acids, ammonia and other nitrogenous compounds. Correction of silage dry matter for losses of volatiles is now accepted as necessary.

If an analysis sheet does not show dry matter values corrected for volatiles, then it may be assumed that dry matter is **underestimated**. This underestimation of dry matter leads to the ME value of silage also being underestimated, especially in extensively fermented wet grass silages. Distillation of silage with toluene captures most of the volatile products of the fermentation which are lost in oven drying and gives a truer dry matter value. Alternatively, the following formula can be applied:

$$CDM(\%) = ODM~(\%) \times 0.99 + 1.82$$

where: CDM = corrected dry matter content and
ODM = dry matter determined by oven drying.

The normal range of dry matter for all silages is between 15% and 60% of the fresh weight. The target corrected dry matter content for grass, maize and fermented whole-crop silage is 30 to 35%. The target dry matter content for urea-treated whole-crop is 50 to 55%.

pH. Most crops reach a stable low pH of around 4.0 if well preserved. Wilted silages, including most big bale silages, have restricted fermentations because of their lower available water content and thus stabilise at higher pH values than unwilted silages. If a wet silage has a high pH value of more than 4.5, the silage has undergone a secondary fermentation and is unstable, i.e. the pH value will increase with time and may eventually reach as high as pH 7.0. Target pH values for well preserved silages of different DM contents are shown in Figure 2.7. The pH value can be measured on the farm by using indicator paper or a portable pH meter.

Figure 2.7   Target values for the pH of well preserved silage of different dry matter contents (Wilkinson, 1990)

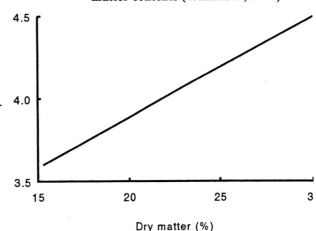

It is worth remembering that pH is a logarithmic scale. Thus a silage with a pH value of 3.5 has ten times as much free acidity as one with a pH value of 4.5, and a hundred times as much as one with a pH of 5.5. As the optimal rumen pH is about 6.5, most silages contain several hundred times more acid than rumen liquor and hence require considerable buffering by salivary bicarbonate and phosphate during chewing and rumination.

Crude protein. Crude protein, calculated from total N x 6.25, is what it implies. Essentially, its value lies as a general guide as to whether or not the silage is likely to supply enough ruminally-available protein (effective rumen-degradable protein, ERDP, see Chapter 6) to the rumen micro-organisms. The determination of crude protein indicates nothing about the extent to which the protein in the grass or the silage has been degraded or is likely to be degraded in the rumen.

The normal range of crude protein content in silage is from 70 g/kg DM in maize silage to 220 g/kg DM in young clover or young lucerne silage. Typically, the crude protein content of grass silages ranges from 120 to 180 g/kg DM. The lower the value, the more mature the silage is likely to be, since the content of crude protein is higher in the leaf than in the stem fraction of the plant. Low crude protein contents can be observed in grass crops growing rapidly in early spring, particularly Italian ryegrass.

DCP (digestible crude protein) is sometimes quoted in analytical reports, but this too is only a general guide to the nitrogen available to the animal and its ruminal microflora; it is of little use in current feeding systems.

Soluble protein, or soluble N. The soluble N is that proportion of the total N which is soluble in hot water. It consists mostly of small molecular weight non-protein nitrogen (NPN) compounds such as amino acids, amines, amides and ammonia. The proportion of the total N present as soluble N and the proportion of the soluble N which is present as amino acid N are both good indicators of the extent of degradation of true protein in the course of the fermentation in the silo. Both soluble N and amino acid N are related to the voluntary intake of silage and as such are important parameters in silage analysis.

The proportion of soluble N in the total N should be as low as possible, but it can comprise up to 0.75 of the total N. It is likely to be higher in extensively fermented silages than in those which have undergone a restricted fermentation. Soluble N is also elevated in silages which have undergone secondary fermentations, especially those in which proteolytic clostridia have been active and in which the content of ammonia-N is high. The target proportion of total N present as soluble N in silages is 0.3 to 0.5.

Amino acid N. The proportion of the soluble N present as amino acid N should be as high as possible, though in poorly preserved silages much of the amino acid fraction is further degraded to amide, amine and ammonia-N. The target proportion of the soluble N present as amino acid N in silages is more than 0.75.

Ammonia-N. Ammonia-N is an indicator of the proportion of the total N which has been completely degraded during the fermentation in the silo. It is the best indicator of secondary fermentation and for many years was used as a general indicator of the fermentation quality and intake potential of the silage (Table 2.14).

Table 2.14 Ammonia-N and quality of silage preservation

Quality of fermentation	Ammonia-N (g/kg total N)
Excellent	Less than 50
Good	50 to 100
Moderate	100 to 150
Poor	150 to 200
Very poor	More than 200

Silages with high contents of ammonia-N also have reduced ME contents, since secondary fermentations are also associated with losses of energy from the silo.

The normal range of ammonia-N in silages is 50 to 150g NH_3-N/kg total N. The target value for NH_3-N is less than 50 g/kg total N. In the case of urea-treated whole-crop silage the range is much greater (100 to 500 g NH_3-N/kg total N) and a typical value is 300 g NH_3-N/kg total N.

Neutral detergent fibre (NDF). The extraction of material soluble in neutral detergent separates plant material into two fractions - cell contents (soluble) and cell wall (insoluble). This division is extremely important because it distinguishes between the material which is digested rapidly in the rumen and that which is digested slowly (cell wall or fibre). The NDF residue includes hemicellulose, cellulose and lignin. Work in the USA (Mertens, 1973), has shown that the NDF content of unfermented forages is related to voluntary intake, with forages of lower NDF contents having higher intakes than more mature forages of higher NDF content. With silages, however, the products of fermentation can dominate NDF in determining the level of intake, so the value of NDF measurement is diminished accordingly. NDF is used in diet formulation to assess the total fibre content of the diet, fibre intake and the efficiency of rumen function.

The normal range of values for the content of NDF of silages is from 450 for maize silages to 650 for legume silages, with grass silages in the middle. A target NDF value for a high-quality grass silage is 500 g NDF/kg DM.

Acid detergent fibre (ADF). The proportion of the dry matter insoluble in acid detergent is an estimation of the cellulose and lignin in the material. ADF is more closely related to digestibility than to intake, so the parameter can give an indication of energy value. The normal range of ADF is from 250 to 450 g/kg DM. The target ADF content for a high-quality grass silage is 350 g ADF/kg DM.

The proportion of the total N which is insoluble in acid detergent gives an estimation of the indigestible N in the material. This parameter, known as ADIN (acid detergent insoluble nitrogen), should be as low as possible since heat-damaged protein and the products of Maillard reactions are insoluble in acid detergent. The range of ADIN in silages is from 50 to 150 g ADIN /kg total N and the target ADIN value is less than 75 g ADIN/kg total N. The role of ADIN in the Metabolisable Protein System is discussed in Chapter 6.

Modified acid detergent fibre (MADF). Modified acid detergent fibre, otherwise known as MAD fibre, has been used extensively as a predictor of ME content. This method of predicting ME is now outmoded in favour of digestibility of organic matter (OMD) determined with sheep.

The problem with MADF as a predictor of ME is that less than half of predicted ME values lie within 0.5 MJ ME of the value determined with the animal (Table 2.15).

Organic Matter Digestibility (OMD). Organic matter digestibility (OMD) determined with sheep was accepted in the UK in May 1993 by the advisory services (ADAS, SAC) and by several feed companies as a uniform basis for the prediction of ME by NIR spectroscopy.

The use of OMD as the predictor of ME is superior to MADF, as shown in Table 2.15, based on estimation by NIRs and the standard errors of prediction.

Table 2.15 Errors associated with using MADF or OMD by NIRs as predictors of the ME of silage (Offer, 1993)

	% of samples meeting tolerance of:	
Method	±0.5 MJ ME	±1.0 MJ ME
MADF by NIRs (19 Filter machine)	47	79
OMD by NIRs (19 Filter machine)	68	95
OMD by NIRs (Scanning machine)	81	99

Digestible organic matter (DOMD). DOMD, or D-value is the content of digestible organic matter in the dry matter. DOMD may be expressed on an oven dry matter basis ($DOMD_o$) or corrected for volatile losses during oven drying ($DOMD_c$).

The higher the DOMD the higher the ME of the silage. The normal range of DOMD values is from 450 to 800 g/kg DM, with most grass and maize silages lying between 550 and 750 g DOMD/kg DM.

Metabolisable energy (ME). The normal range in the ME content of silages is from 7.0 to 13.0 MJ/kg DM. Clearly, values at the extreme ends of this range are rare, and most silages are likely to have ME contents between 10.0 and 12.0 MJ ME/kg DM.

Given the tolerances in Table 2.15, it is crucial that ME is assessed as accurately as possible; diet formulation may be very inaccurate if a silage with a real ME of 11.0 is assessed as having an ME of only 10.0 MJ ME/kg DM.

Fermentation acids. The principal fermentation acid in silage is lactic acid, which is sweet-smelling and indicative of an efficient fermentation in the silo. It is the strongest acid in silage and is produced by the most acid-tolerant bacteria and is therefore associated with relatively low pH values in silage. The range in lactic acid contents can be very great - from as little as 20 g/kg DM in silages of high DM content which have restricted fermentations, or poorly preserved silages in which lactic acid has been fermented to other acids, to as much as 200 g/kg DM in wet silages which have undergone very extensive fermentations. Typical values for well preserved silages of 25 to 35% DM are 80 to 120 g/kg DM.

The volatile fatty acids (VFA) comprise acetic acid (the most common), propionic acid, butyric acid and other acids. The production of these acids is a reflection of an inefficient fermentation or of secondary fermentation of lactic to butyric acid and degradation of amino acids to ammonia with the production of acetic acid from the carbon skeleton of the amino acid. Ideally, VFA in silage should account for less than 0.20 of total fermentation acids.

Residual sugars. The content of residual sugars in silage is important because unfermented water-soluble carbohydrate (WSC) is a valuable source of readily-available energy for the rumen microflora. The extent of fermentation can be restricted substantially in wilted crops and in those treated with acid additive. Inoculated crops can also show elevated levels of residual sugar through the action of the additive in accelerating fermentation and reducing losses of sugar via plant respiration or less efficient fermentation pathways. Many silages, especially wet grass silage and legume silages, show no residual sugars at all - the fermentation has continued to exhaustion. The range in residual sugars in silages is from zero to 200 g/kg DM. The target should be to achieve a content of residual sugars in excess of 100 g/kg DM.

Fermentable metabolisable energy (FME). The Metabolisable Protein system considers that not all the ME of the feed is able to support microbial fermentation. The fraction that is able to supply energy to the rumen microbes is termed Fermentable Metabolisable Energy (FME). The amount of FME in silages is related to the extent of fermentation in the silo, as assessed by the content of fermentation acids.

Silages should have as a high a fermentability in the rumen as possible, so that as much of the readily-available nitrogen can be used by the microbes as possible. The proportion of the total ME which is fermentable ME should exceed 0.70.

The key factors in the production of silage of high fermentability are:

• grow a high sugar crop

• wilt as rapidly as possible to more than 25% dry matter

• restrict fermentation with acid additives, promote a lactic fermentation with an effective inoculant or add molasses

• seal the silo quickly and completely

2.8   The ideal silage

The targets listed above can be combined into an overall specification for the ideal grass or grass/legume silage for lactating dairy cows. Essentially, the material should be well preserved, of high ME and FME, and have a restricted fermentation. The specification is shown in Table 2.16.

Table 2.16 The ideal silage

Dry matter	More than 300 g/kg
ME	More than 11.0
FME/ME	More than 0.70
CP	150 to 175 g/kg DM
pH	4.0 to 4.5
NDF	500 to 550 g/kg DM
NH_3-N	Less than 50 g/kg total N
Amino acid N	More than 750 g/kg total soluble N
Residual sugars	More than 100 g/kg DM
Total fermentation acids	100 to 150 g/kg DM
Lactic acid	80 to 120 g/kg DM
Volatile fatty acids	Less than 0.20 of total acids

2.9   Silage and health

Silage has a reasonably clean health record, considering what might go wrong during storage and during the feed-out period. Listeriosis in sheep and cattle is a disease which is often linked to the feeding of animals on silage, especially big bale silage, which has been incompletely sealed. *Listeria monocytogenes*, a soil-borne bacterium is associated with aerobically-deteriorated silage. If visibly spoilt silage is thrown away, the risk of listeriosis is greatly reduced. Iritis (inflammation of the iris of the eye) in animals given stemmy baled silage in ring feeders can be caused by contaminated stems poking into the eye and thereby introducing listeria.

Moulds in spoiled silage, especially *Aspergillus*, can cause abortion in cattle and sheep. **All** visibly spoilt silage should be thrown away, and not given to animals.

Contamination of silage by soil and manure may prove fatal. Cases of botulism were reported in 1994 in cattle on several different farms in Cheshire and north Wales. The common factor was that the animals had been given silages made from grass to which poultry manure, which apparently contained carcasses of dead birds, had been applied. *Clostridium botulinum* had survived and presumably multiplied in the silos during the storage period.

High ammonia levels in silage are thought to be associated with lameness and scouring in dairy cows. In a recent epidemiological study of lameness in dairy herds in the north west of England, an inverse relationship was found between the dry matter content of silage and the incidence of lameness.

Wet, highly acid silages predispose to low intakes, especially in late winter when animals have been given silage for long periods. The feeding of excess-ively fermented silages, as can occur with high sugar, wet grass ensiled with an effective inoculant, can result in clinical symptoms of acidosis (i.e. cows ceasing to eat), especially in animals given large amounts of high energy supplements.

CHAPTER 3

SUPPLEMENTARY FEEDS

3.1   The need for supplements

3.2   Forages and concentrates

3.3   Chemical assessment of supplements
      3.3.1   *Dry matter*
      3.3.2   *Fibre*
      3.3.3   *Sugar and starch*
      3.3.4   *Fat and oils*

3.4   Classification of feeds

3.5   Compounds and blends
      3.5.1   *Predicting the ME of compounds*

3.6   Selecting supplements
      3.6.1   *Relative economic value of feeds*

3.1   The need for supplements

Dairy cows existed traditionally on forages as their sole diet. In summer grass was grazed and in winter hay and/or straw was offered. However, milk yields were low, especially in winter. As the demand for higher levels of milk production increased, the need for more "concentrated" sources of energy and protein to supplement low-quality hays and straws in the winter diet became apparent. So the concept evolved of giving forage feeds - known at the time as "roughages" because of their very high fibre content - for maintenance of body functions. Con-contorted supplements were given for the production of milk according to yield; the higher the yield, the more supplementary feed was given.

With the advent of silage-making at the end of the nineteenth century, and the recognition several decades later of the factors affecting the digestibility of forages, the nutritive quality of the so-called "roughage" feeds gradually increased. Roughages still comprised predominantly fibre (albeit more digestible fibre than hitherto), digestion was still relatively slow and intake was limited as a result. So the need for "concentrate" supplements remained, especially in higher-yielding herds, as a way of increasing total feed intake. Even if the supplement virtually replaced the roughage on a dry matter basis (which rarely happened), total nutrient intake was increased as a result, because the supplement contained more nutrients per unit weight and was digested more rapidly than the roughage. Nowadays, the high-yielding cow requires supplementary nutrients to meet her requirements, above those supplied by even the highest quality forage feeds eaten *ad libitum*. These nutrients are supplied by a wide range of raw materials, often pre-processed into compounded feeds or blends according to the farmer's individual specification.

3.2   Forages and concentrates

The conventional division of feeds into "concentrate" supplements and "forages" or "roughages" is a crude way of distinguishing between those feeds that contain mainly plant cell wall ("cellulosic") material and those which contain mainly starch, sugar, or protein ("non-cellulosic") material.

Dividing feeds into the categories of "cellulosic" and "non-cellulosic" feeds recognises the fact that cell contents, especially starch, sugars and proteins, are fermented rapidly in the rumen and tend to be highly digestible in the whole digestive tract, whilst cell wall components, hemicellulose, cellulose and lignin, are fermented at a slower rate in the rumen and are digested less completely in the whole tract (Table 3.1). This division into quickly and slowly digested feeds is important as it indicates the likely level of feed intake by the animal, the proportion likely to be digested, the likely end-products of digestion and the possible consequences for milk output and composition. In general, the faster the fermentation in the rumen, the higher the possible intake and the greater the proportion digested.

Table 3.1   Digestibility and speed of digestion of some common feeds (from Ørskov, 1987)

	Digestibility (%)	Speed of digestion (hours)
"Cellulosic" feeds - more than 500g NDF/kg DM		
Straw	40	45 to 55
Poor hay	55	30 to 40
Good grass	70	18 to 24
"Non-cellulosic" feeds - less than 500g NDF/kg DM		
Good clover	70	12 to 18
Grains	80	12 to 14
Beet and turnips	85	2 to 6
Molasses	95	0.5

The distinction between quickly and slowly digested feeds is usually made on the basis of the content of neutral detergent fibre (NDF) in the feed dry matter (Section 3.3.2). However, the division is somewhat arbitrary; some forage feeds, for example young grass and maize silage, contain less than 500 g NDF/kg DM

(Tables 3.2 and 20.21). Other feeds, like brewers' grains, contain more than 500 g NDF/ kg DM, yet fibre length is short and lignin content is low, so digestion can be quite rapid as a result.

Table 3.2   Some common "Cellulosic" and "Non-cellulosic" feeds

Cellulosic (more than 500 g NDF/kg DM)	Non-cellulosic (less than 500g NDF/kg DM)
Straw	Fat
Hay	Molasses
Grass (except very young)	Immature grass
Silage (except maize)	Maize silage
Brewers' grains	Cereal grains
Unmolassed beet pulp	Molassed beet pulp
Pectin-extracted fruit	Fodder beet, turnips
Wheatfeed	Maize gluten feed
Palm kernel meal	Soyabean meal

The lower the digestibility of a feed, the more chewing and rumination is required and the longer it takes for the digestible material to be broken down and solubilised in the rumen.

The lower the cell wall (NDF) content, the lower the ratio of acetate to propionate produced in the rumen, and the greater the likelihood of reduced milk fat content. Over-feeding of "non-cellulosic" feeds can cause acidosis and rumen stasis, known in the beef industry as "feedlot bloat".

"Non-cellulosic" feeds are essential for high milk protein content because it is thought that they spare gluconeogenesis (breakdown) of amino acids in the liver when the cow is deficient in energy early in lactation, thereby leaving more amino acid available for milk protein synthesis.

In summary, **"non-cellulosic"** feeds are used to:

- boost total feed intake;

- increase the energy or protein content of a diet;

- rectify specific nutrient deficiencies in a forage.

"Cellulosic" feeds are used to:

- stimulate rumination and production of saliva;

- produce acetic acid in the rumen;

- buffer acidity in the rumen;

- reduce feed intake, reduce weight gain, encourage weight loss, e.g. during the dry period;

- reduce feed costs;

The ratio of cellulosic to non-cellulosic feeds in the diet is a better way of describing the proportion of rapidly-digested feeds and the likely pattern of fermentation in the rumen than the traditional forage to concentrate ratio which is too crude and now outdated (see below).

Maize silage typically contains only 400 g NDF/kg DM because of the relatively high proportion of grain in the total dry matter. Thus although it is a forage, maize silage is classified as a "non-cellulosic" feed. The starch in maize silage is digested more rapidly than fibre in the rumen, and therefore the feed is termed "non-cellulosic". However, in a cool year the starch content of immature maize silage may be as low as 100 g/kg DM. In this situation the feed would be considered to be "cellulosic" because its NDF content would be more than 500g/kg DM.

Forage to concentrate ratio. The ratio of forages to concentrates is often considered to be important in diet formulation. It is, however, clear from the above discussion of "cellulosic" and "non-cellulosic" feeds that it cannot be assumed that starch and sugars are always from concentrates and fibre always supplied by forages and/or straws. Thus the forage:concentrate ratio of a diet must be interpreted with care, recognising that a feed may not be entirely "forage" or entirely "concentrate". Maize silage, for example, may be considered to be 30% "concentrate" and 70% "forage". Young grass, molassed sugar beet pulp, fodder beet and other roots crops, are other examples of feeds and supplements which typically contain less than half their dry matter as fibre (Table 20.21), and therefore behave more like concentrates in the rumen.

In dairy cow rationing it is better to use the single measure of fibre than to use the forage:concentrate ratio. In this way the contribution of fibre of each feed is recognised, however large or small. The question then arises: which assessment of fibre is most useful? Neutral detergent fibre is the most logical component to use, though it does not take into account the digestibility of the cell wall fraction.

3.3   Chemical assessment of supplements

The chemical composition of some common feeds is shown in Table 3.3 and in more detail in Table 20.21. Energy is described as gross energy (GE), metabolisable energy (ME) and as fermentable metabolisable energy (FME), protein as crude protein (CP), fat and oil as fat, major minerals as calcium (Ca), phosphorus (P) and magnesium (Mg) and fibre as neutral detergent fibre (NDF), which has now largely replaced crude fibre in diet formulations.

Table 3.3 Principal nutrient composition of common feeds (AFRC, 1993; MAFF 1992; MAFF, 1986)

Feed name	DM	GE	ME	FME	CP	Ca	Mg	P	NDF	Fat
	%	——MJ/kg DM——			——————g/kg DM——————					
Brewers' grains (ensiled)	28	21.5	11.7	9.0	245	3.3	1.5	4.1	572	77
Fishmeal white	92	19.7	14.2	11.4	694	56.2	2.3	38.1	0	75
Grass D 65-70	21	18.6	10.7	10.0	121	4.6	1.4	2.7	610	20
Grass silage	26	19.0	10.9	8.3	168	6.4	1.7	3.2	582	43
Hay average	87	18.5	8.8	8.2	107	5.2	1.4	2.6	657	17
Maize gluten feed	89	19.0	12.7	11.5	232	2.8	14.3	10.0	390	34
Maize silage	30	18.5	11.5	9.0	88	3.9	2.4	1.8	390	30
Palm kernel meal	86	20.4	11.6	10.4	170	2.4	3.0	6.9	693	83
Rapeseed meal	90	19.5	12.0	11.2	418	7.8	4.5	12.0	279	23
Soyabean meal	88	19.7	13.4	12.8	507	4.5	2.9	7.6	154	16
Wheat grain	87	18.2	13.6	12.9	128	0.6	1.1	3.4	166	19
Wheat straw	87	18.1	6.1	5.6	38	3.8	0.8	0.7	805	13

3.3.1 Dry matter

It is tempting to assume that so-called "dry" feeds, dry concentrates, compounds and blends, are 100% dry matter. In fact, the dry matter of dry feeds is usually significantly less than 100% (see Table 3.3), especially in the case of liquid supplements like molasses where dry matter content may be as low as 75%. Most other "dry" feeds contain between 86% and 90% dry matter. Meals, including blends, may absorb slightly more moisture from the surrounding air than pelleted feeds. It is always worthwhile checking the dry matter content of all diet ingredients; if feeds which are supposed to be "dry" contain more than 15% moisture (i.e. less than 85% dry matter), mould development is likely during storage.

The chemical composition and inclusion of "dry" feeds is sometimes quoted on an "as-fed", i.e. fresh weight basis, whilst that of "wet" feeds like silage, roots and brewers' grains may be quoted on a dry matter basis. Correction should therefore be made for the moisture in the "dry" feeds in calculating rations.

3.3.2 Fibre

Crude fibre. Crude fibre was used traditionally as the parameter which approximates to indigestible cellulose + lignin. The estimation of crude fibre did not, however, take into account the **digestible** fibre which is nutritionally useful to the animal, both as a source of metabolisable energy in the diet and as a substrate for the acetate-producing bacteria in the rumen. Crude fibre has now been superseded by detergent extraction methods which distinguish between cell wall material (fibre) which is slowly digested in the rumen and cell contents which are digested rapidly once the cell wall is ruptured by eating, by rumination or by microbial action.

Neutral detergent fibre (NDF). The material which is insoluble in neutral detergent is the cell wall part of the plant comprised of hemicellulose, cellulose and lignin. NDF is the best single measure of slowly-digested material across a very wide range of feeds (Table 3.3). NDF is inversely related to the voluntary feed intake, i.e. the higher the content of NDF in the diet the lower the intake. Too much NDF and intake is less than optimal; too little and there is a risk of depressed milk fat and/or acidosis. Diet formulation for cows should include a check that the overall content of NDF in the diet is optimal (see Chapter 18, page 173).

Acid detergent fibre (ADF or MADF). Acid detergent fibre (ADF) is cellulose and lignin. It is a measure of the cell wall which is likely to be digested very slowly or not at all. ADF is inversely related to digestibility and hence to derived ME value.

Acid detergent insoluble nitrogen (ADIN). The nitrogen which is insoluble in acid detergent (known as acid detergent insoluble nitrogen, or ADIN) is an estimate of the amount of the total N which has undergone heat damage, or as a result of Maillard reactions in which proteins are complexed with sugars, and is virtually indigestible as a result.

Feeds with high concentrations of ADIN are usually darker than expected and give lower than expected animal responses. Dark maize gluten, for example, has a lower protein digestibility than beige-coloured material. The digestibility of the protein in distillers' dark grains is also suspected to be relatively low. Less than 50 g ADIN/kg total N is considered to indicate little heat damage, 50 to 100 g/kg moderate, and more than 100 g/kg is associated with excessive heat damage.

It is possible to protect protein from degradation in the rumen to a greater extent than normal, but so that it is still digestible in the abomasum and small intestine. For example, "protected" soyabean meal, in which the protein has been treated with form-aldehyde or by controlled heating, is now sold as a supplement for situations where there is a specific need for extra undegraded protein in the diet.

Lignin. This is material which is insoluble in acid detergent and boiling 72% sulphuric acid and which is almost completely indigestible in the cow. Lignin, a complex substance containing polymers of phenolic acids, is cross-linked with hemicellulose and with cellulose to confer structural rigidity on the plant cell wall. Its presence restricts the access of bacteria and their enzymes to the cellulose and hemicellulose in the cell wall, reducing both rate and extent of cell wall digestion in the rumen so that the more mature structural parts of the plant are poorly digested compared to leaf or seed.

3.3.3   Sugar and starch

Of equal importance to fibre is the total content of rapidly-digested carbohydrate, or non-structural carbohydrate. This is normally measured in the laboratory by enzymatic techniques to hydrolyse starch to glucose, which is then measured. The water-soluble carbohydrate fraction (free sugars) is also assessed without hydrolysis, and the contents of starch is estimated as the difference between the total and the water-soluble fractions. The total content of sugar and starch in feeds is an important consideration in diet formulation: too much and the diet is likely to be digested too quickly with the risk of acidosis; too little and the rumen microbes are likely to be short of readily-fermentable energy. In crops destined for silage the content of water-soluble carbohydrate is a guide to the amount of fermentable sugars and to the likely pattern and extent of fermentation during conservation.

3.3.4   Fat and oils

The fat or oil content of feeds is measured by extraction with ether. Fats and oils are important as feed for two reasons. First, oil has a very high energy content (33 MJ ME/kg DM) - almost three times that of cereal grain. So feeds with a high oil content are desirable to boost the overall con-centration of energy in the diet. Second, the concen-tration of oil in feeds can depress digestion of fibre. The oil acts to reduce the hydrophilic nature of fibre particles in the rumen and therefore bacteria cannot attach as easily to the fibre surface. Too much fat in the diet, and rumen function can be impaired. The role of fats and oils in the diet is further discussed in Chapter 5 (page 51).

3.4   Classification of feeds

The greater the proportion of the organic matter of a feed fermented in the rumen (FME), the higher the microbial requirement for nitrogen (ERDP). This relationship is shown diagrammatically in Figure 3.1. and discussed in more detail in Chapter 6. The relationship can also be described in terms of FME and ERDP (Figures 3.2 and 3.3). In Figures 3.2 and 3.3, the metabolisable energy of feeds which is available for fermentation (digestion) in the rumen (FME) is plotted against the protein available to the rumen microflora (ERDP) for common forage and concentrate feeds if they are given to high-yielding dairy cows. The solid line represents the optimal balance for a high-yielding dairy cow (11g ERDP/MJ FME). Feeds above the line supply more available protein than available energy. Feeds below the line supply an excess of energy relative to their available protein.

Clearly, if a feed is deficient either in digestible organic matter or in degradable protein, then the rate and extent of digestion in the rumen will be reduced. The key to success in using supplements, therefore, is to know the energy (ME) and the ERDP of each raw material so that imbalances can be corrected by including feeds which complement each other in the diet.

Figure 3.1   Effect of proportion of organic matter digested in the rumen on microbial requirement for nitrogen. The solid line represents the optimal balance for the high-yielding cow (from Ørskov, 1989).

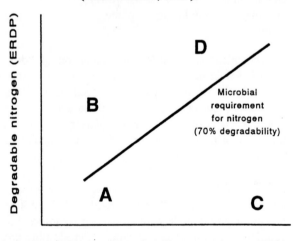

Organic matter fermented in rumen (FME)

Feeds of low energy and low nitrogen (A). Feeds in this category include straws, husks, pods and haulms. Digestion of these feeds in the rumen is usually slow, and supplementary N is required to increase the rate of digestion. As residence time and contents of indigestible material are high, intake of these feeds is generally low.

Figure 3.2   Fermentable metabolisable energy (FME) and effective rumen-degradable protein (ERDP) in some common forage feeds when given to high-yielding cows. The solid line represents the optimal balance for microbial digestion in such cows.

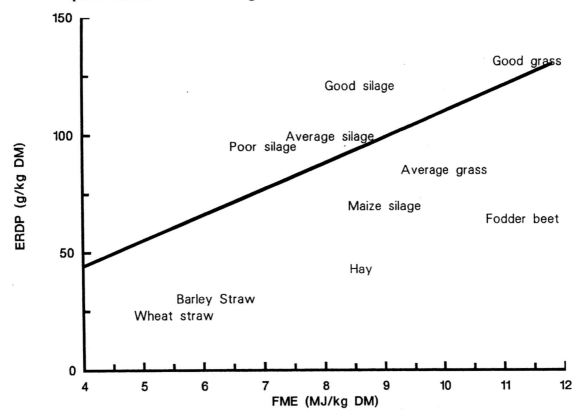

Figure 3.3   Fermentable metabolisable energy (FME) and effective rumen-degradable protein (ERDP) in some common concentrate feeds when given to high-yielding dairy cows. The solid line represents the optimal balance for microbial activity in such cows.

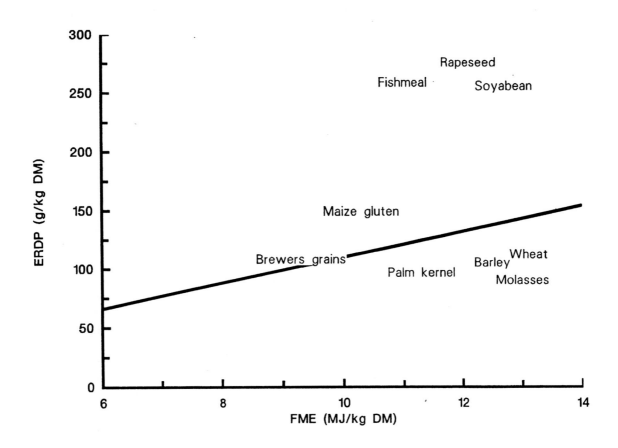

Feeds of low energy and high nitrogen (B). Some by-products of the food industry, for example coffee residues, grape pulp and cocoa meal, are in this category. Animal excreta also have an excess of nitrogen in relation to FME. Urea is the extreme example of feeds in this group because it is very high in nitrogen (46%) but provides no energy to the rumen. Feeds in this category are useful supplements to feeds in Category C, especially for low-producing animals and dry cows when the need is for low-energy diets to prevent weight gain or induce weight loss.

Feeds of high energy and low nitrogen (C). Molasses, cereal grains, potatoes and beet pulp are typical feeds of this category. Their rapid rate of digestion means that there is usually a substantial need for supplementary ERDP to balance the readily-available energy in the feeds. Heat-treated protein feeds, like distillers' dried grains, are not the best supplements to balance the feeds in this group as too much of their protein content by-passes the rumen microbes. Urea, grass silage and legume silage are the most cost-effective supplements.

Feeds of high energy and high nitrogen content (D). Feeds in this category include fishmeal, skim milk, distillers' solubles, oil seed meals and vegetable wastes. Many of these feeds, especially those which are leafy or which are not dried, are liable to deteriorate rapidly and must be consumed close to the source of their production or processed carefully. The feeds in this group are often used in conjunction with feeds in Category A.

The range in the composition of some feeds discussed above is illustrated in Figures 3.2 and 3.3 for forage feeds and concentrates, respectively.

The nutritive quality of raw materials varies to a greater or lesser degree within and between supplies, however carefully they are selected. In practice it is becoming increasingly important to identify the more consistent and reliable supplies and avoid those which exhibit marked and unpredictable variation. Descriptions of some of the more commonly used straights, as well as maximum recommended levels of inclusion in the total diet and possible problems associated with their use, are shown in Table 3.4.

3.5   Compounds and blends

Compounded feeds are mixtures of ground raw materials, whilst blends are usually made from unmilled materials. Compounds are usually pelleted prior to delivery to the farm. Both compounds and blends are formulated to detailed specifications for ME, crude protein, degradable and digestible undegraded protein (DUP), minerals and vitamins. In other words, the complicated nutrition is performed by the staff of the animal feed company, and the end product is, or should be, completely balanced to meet the full nutrient requirements of the animal when combined with forages.

Compounds and blends are formulated on a least-cost basis, subject to various constraints to prevent low-cost ingredients from being included at too high a proportion of the total mix. Thus cereal grains, the principal starch-containing ingredients of compounds, are sometimes replaced when their cost is high by imported sources of starch such as cassava (manioc), or by sources of highly digestible fibre such as citrus pulp. Feed wheat is a major cereal ingredient which has recently replaced barley on cost per MJ of ME. Cereal grains rarely account for more than 50% of ruminant compounds, though with increasing emphasis in dairy cow nutrition on the importance of starch in the diet, the amount of cereal grain in compounds for dairy cows is likely to increase.

Home-produced proteins feature more prominently today than in the past, especially rapeseed meal, linseed meal, hydrolysed feather meal, field beans and peas, which tend to replace imported sources of protein such as soyabean meal, sunflower meal and cottonseed meal.

Protected fats have gained in popularity recently, probably because other feeds of low digestibility, such as rice bran, are being used to a greater extent than hitherto. It is theoretically possible to produce two compounds of the same specification; one comprising "conventional" feeds consisting of cereal grains and high quality proteins; the other containing by-products of high energy content, such as fat, mixed with poor quality fibre sources and lower-quality proteins or urea. Obviously, cows given the latter compound will have a lower performance compared to animals given the former.

Compounds and blends for dairy cows are sold on the basis of the crude protein content in the fresh weight, not on a dry matter basis. High-energy compounds are available at most levels of crude protein. A typical 18% crude protein dairy compound contains 11.2 MJ ME/kg fresh weight (12.5 MJ/kg DM) and 210g CP/kg DM. Some companies produce very high protein compounds and blends (34% protein) specifically to feed at a low rate with silage. The protein is digestible, but relatively undegradable (50%) in the rumen. Other companies attempt to match the composition of their compounds to the fermentation characteristics of the silage. Thus a well-fermented silage with residual sugars is matched by a compound relatively low in rapidly-digested starch and sugar and relatively high in digestible fibre. A poorly-fermented silage is matched by a compound containing more starch and sugar.

Table 3.4 **Description and composition of some common raw material feeds. Maximum inclusions are for the total diet, so to obtain maximum inclusion levels in concentrates double the values given here.**

Feed	ME MJ/kg DM	CP g/kg DM	NDF g/kg DM	Max. inclusion (%)	Description	Comments and possible problems
Apple pomace	9.1	69	489	10 to 15	Residue from juice extraction. Porridge-like consistency (200 to 280 g DM/kg).	High pectin content can cause problems in younger animals.
Barley	13.3	129	201	25	Lower in energy and higher in fibre than wheat; needs to be £7/tonne cheaper to be competitive with wheat.	Acidosis.
Beans	13.1	267	167	8	Spring beans have a better analysis than winter beans.	Tannins can reduce protein digestibility. High in phosphorus (8.6 g/kg) and starch (395 g/kg).
Brewers' grains	11.7	245	572	-	Barley residues after hot water extraction of sugars from 'mash'. Usually sold wet. More available in the summer than winter so often ensiled.	Highly palatable wet feed. High in protein and digestible fibre. Can be fed fresh or ensiled. If ensiled DM should be over 30% to prevent excessive effluent losses.
Citrus pulp pellets	12.6	72	228	5 kg	By-product of citrus juice industry. Containing varying proportions of orange, lemon, lime and grapefruit. High oils (>22 g/kg) indicate inclusion of seeds.	Mouldy samples can cause haemorrhaging in cattle. Characteristic smell can be used to mask other ingredients. Seeds contain limonin which is toxic to pigs and poultry but not ruminants.
Copra expeller	12.9	198	517	-	Residue from the oil extraction of dried coconut flesh.	Highly palatable but can go rancid. High in saturated oils and low in essential amino-acids.
Cotton seed meal or cake	11.1	375	385	-	By-product meal from cotton industry. Woody and yellow in colour.	Contains gossypol which can reduce appetite in animals other than mature ruminants. Needs an aflatoxin guarantee.
Distillers' dark grains (barley)	12.2	275	420	13	Produced during manufacture of whisky.	Lower in energy and higher in fibre than the other distillers grains. Copper content can be high.
Distillers' dark grains (maize)	14.7	317	342	13	Produced from the manufacture of whisky and alcohol.	High unsaturated fat profile may depress forage intake. Protein can be indigestible. Copper content can be high.
Distillers' dark grains (wheat)	12.4	322	335	13	Produced by distillery industry.	High in protein and energy. The digestibility of the protein in dark samples may be limited.
Fishmeal	14.2	694	0	4	Either the dried offals and trimmings or purpose-caught small fish.	Milk taint can be a problem in high oil samples. High in calcium (56 g/kg DM) and phosphorus (38 g/kg DM).
Fodder beet	11.9	63	136	25 kg fresh	Grown in colder climates where maize cannot be grown.	Highly palatable but soil contamination and possible milk taint can be problems. Must be washed to control soil intake.
Groundnut meal (decorticated + extracted)	13.7	495	180	10	Peanuts. Fibrous hulls removed and oil extracted.	Can contain aflatoxin and imports were banned in 1981 because of this. Since 1988 limited imports possible with guaranteed aflatoxin contents.
Linseed meal	13.0	391	192	10	Residue after linseed oil extraction by expelling.	High unsaturated fat profile, depressed forage intake. Contains linamarin and linase but high temperature processing usually inactivates the latter.
Maize gluten feed	12.7	232	390	15	A mixture of maize fibre, maize germ and corn steep liquor after the wet processing of maize grain.	Poor amino acid profile and variable protein digestibility. Lighter samples (straw coloured) have better protein digestibility.
Maize gluten meal (prairie meal)	17.5	666	84	1 kg	Residue after maize grain has been stripped of outer layer and germ and starch removed.	Excessive use may soften fat and give it a yellow tinge. Poor amino acid profile.
Maize germ meal					Maize germ extracted after wet milling either with oil extracted or expelled to high oil (120 g/kg DM) or low oil (40 g/kg DM) sample.	In large quantities high oil samples can give soft fat in slaughter animals. Poor amino acid balance. High DUP supply with low Ca content.
High oil	14.51	115	223	2 kg		
Low oil	3.0	250	224	2 kg		

Table 3.4 (continued)

Feed	ME MJ/kg DM	CP g/kg DM	NDF g/kg DM	Max inclusi-on (%)	Description	Comments and possible problems
Malt culms	11.0	283	463	-	Dried rootlets from malting barley.	Can be bitter.
Malt residual pellets	11.5	220	463	10	By-product of the malting industry. Roots of chitted barley and barley husks. Unlike culms contains broken grains so starch content is higher (175 g/kg DM).	Can be bitter.
Manioc (cassava)	12.6	28	114	20	Starch-rich (680 g/kg DM) roots of tropical shrub.	Contains linamarin which is enzymatically hydrolysed to toxic hydrocyanic acid. EU regulations limit linamarin content.
Molasses (cane)	12.7	41	0	10 to 15	Imported as by-product from sugar cane industry. Sugar beet molasses is rarely available.	No fibre and high in potassium - can cause scours, do not feed in marginal Mg situations.
Oats	12.1	105	310	-	Higher fibre and lower energy than other cereals.	Rarely cost-effective in ruminant diets.
Palm kernel	11.6	170	693	5	Imported from Far East - needs an aflatoxin guarantee.	Presence of aflatoxin can be a problem. Poorly ground samples can cause foreign body lameness. Low palatability if fed alone.
Peas	13.5	261	116	10		Tannins can reduce protein digestibility. High inclusions can cause problems in milling.
Pot ale syrup	15.4	374	6	4 kg	Produced from evaporating the liquid remaining after producing whisky. High transport costs limit distribution and localise use.	High potassium may cause scouring, do not feed in marginal Mg situations.
Potatoes	13.4	108	73	15 kg fresh	Either processing rejects or surplus ware potatoes; the latter are marked with an edible dye to prevent human consumption.	High starch induces acidosis and reduced forage digestion. Always feed from the floor or chopped to avoid choking.
Rapeseed meal	12.0	418	279	15		Palatability has been a problem but improved with double zero varieties.
Rice bran	7.1	165	451	5	The outer layer of rice (the brown bit in brown rice). If crude fibre is over 200 g/kg or ash above 160 g/kg then husk has been added.	High initial oil content (>20 g/kg) means that oil must be extracted to prevent feed going rancid.
Soyabean (whole)	15.5	408	122	15	May be processed to reduce protein degradation and oil release in the rumen.	High oil (200 g/kg DM)
Soyabean meal (44)	13.4	507	154	-	By-product of soya crushing industry. Expelled soyabean meal tends to have a higher oil content than extracted.	A high quality palatable protein supplement. The one against which all others are judged!
Hi-pro soyabean meal (48)	13.3	520	130	-	Unlike soyabean meal the soya hulls are not added back giving a higher protein content.	
Sugar beet feed (molassed)	12.5	129	294	15	By product of sugar beet industry. Available in molassed or unmolassed form.	Unmolassed form is very dense pellet and can be unpalatable. Molassed form highly palatable.
Sunflower meal	9.6	335	473	10	Byproduct from sunflower seed crushing. Variable amounts of hull are added back.	Can have a variable fibre content - NDF should be below 400 g/kg DM. High oil samples can go rancid with storage.
Wheat bran	10.8	178	475	-	The husk and outer layers of the grain. Low in starch (196 g/kg).	Highly palatable but widely used in human and horse diets so rarely available.
Wheat grain	13.6	123	166	20	Energy and CP can vary according to season and hectolitre weight.	Danger of acidosis. High in gluten; large inclusions can result in 'dough-balls' forming in the rumen.
Wheat (caustic wheat)	12.6	118	114	25	Wheat is treated with sodium hydroxide and water to damage outer husk and improve digestibility.	Danger of acidosis. Excessive sodium intake.
Wheatfeed	11.9	181	364	15	By-product of the milling industry.	Surprisingly high in starch, up to 30%, but variable analysis depending on mill of origin.

Declaration of ingredients is either "open", i.e. by individual ingredient with percentage inclusion, or "closed", by product group. The problem with product group is that it tells you little about the likely ME or protein quality of the product. Thus extracted rice bran (7 MJ ME/kg DM) and wheat grain (13.7 MJ ME/kg DM) are in the same group of cereals and cereal by-products.

Although the exact formulation of individual compounds is a commercial secret, reputable companies should be expected to disclose their formulation to *bona fide* customers, so that a judgement as to what their animals are receiving and how well the compound balances the forages in the diet can be made.

3.5.1   *Predicting the ME of compounds*

A prediction equation (Equation E3, Thomas *et al.*, 1988), developed from limited feeding trials with dairy cows, is used for predicting the ME of compounds from chemical analyses.

The ME content predicted by the E3 equation may be quoted on the label on the feed bag. The error associated with the prediction is plus or minus 0.7 MJ of ME, so although the equation was developed from animal experiments rather than from laboratory analyses of compounds, there is still some way to go before the actual ME of a compound can be predicted accurately.

3.6   Selecting supplements

The energy and protein characteristics of the raw material feeds described above are the essential starting point in the selection of supplements for diets. Other characteristics, such as the presence of toxins or imbalances of major minerals play a greater or lesser role, depending on the raw material concerned and the level of inclusion in the diet which is desired.

Another way of selecting supplements is to decide what specific nutrient(s) are required to balance the forage feeds in the diet, and to choose from within the categories accordingly. Feeds are listed in Table 3.5. on the basis of their contents of ME, FME, ERDP or DUP. It is notable that some feeds, like fishmeal and soyabean meal, feature in all four categories. This is because protein has a high gross (and therefore metabolisable) energy content. Production responses to the inclusion of these feeds in the diet may not simply reflect extra protein, but also extra energy.

Table 3.5   Supplements ranked in order of ME, FME, ERDP or DUP content

High ME	High FME
Fat	Wheat and barley grain
Wheat and barley grain	Molasses
Molasses	Molassed sugar beet pulp
Maize gluten feed	Maize gluten feed
Molassed sugar beet pulp	Fodder beet
Young grass	Young grass
Fodder Beet	Soyabean meal
Maize silage	Fishmeal
Fishmeal	Rapeseed meal
Soyabean meal	Palm kernel

High ERDP	High DUP
Fishmeal	Fishmeal
Soyabean meal	Protected soya
Sunflower seed cake	Soyabean meal
Rapeseed meal	Rapeseed meal
Cottonseed meal	Sunflower cake
Brewers' grains	Cottonseed
Young grass	Brewers' grains
Maize gluten feed	Maize gluten feed
Palm kernel	Palm kernel
Grass silage	Young grass

3.6.1   *Relative economic value of feeds*

Selection of feeds and supplements is first carried out on the basis of their nutrient composition, then the most economic source of the desired nutrient is found; finally the constraints (if any) on their inclusion in the diet are considered.

The relative value of a range of different feeds compared to wheat, soyabean meal and urea is shown in Table 3.6. Feed prices are compared to wheat at £100/tonne, soyabean meal at £160/tonne, and urea at £280/tonne. Level of production and hence rumen outflow rate are used to determine the ERDP and DUP content. The price of the combination of reference feeds needed to match the feed composition is the total value of the feed which can be compared to the cost. The final three columns show the value of the feed when used to supply a single nutrient.

To determine the relative value of a feed the level of animal production and hence the rate of rumen outflow must be known to determine effective degradability. The level of production used here is 3 times maintenance, giving an outflow rate of about 8% per hour, and is applicable to a cow giving 30 to 40 litres of milk a day. From the effective degradability the ERDP and DUP content of each feed can be calculated. This analysis is then matched using a combination of wheat, soyabean meal and urea to make up for any ERDP shortfall and from this the value of the feed is determined, which can be compared with its price to see if it represents good value for money or not as a supplier of a particular nutrient.

The columns in Table 3.6. show the relative value of a feed if it were to be used to supply only a single nutrient to a ration. For example, brewers' grains are worth £38/tonne overall against a purchase price of £20/tonne, and if considered solely as an energy source they are still worth £30/tonne. It should be noted that this method of comparing feeds takes no account of the relative nutrient densities. For example wheat straw at £50/tonne is a cheaper energy source than wheat grain at £110/tonne, but its low energy density will preclude its use in many diets for cows where intake is a constraint.

As the level of animal production falls, rumen outflow declines and hence the degradability of protein increases. The change in the value of the protein in the feed depends on the change in its degradability and that of the reference feed.

Table 3.6   The relative values (£/tonne fresh weight) of feeds

Feed name	Price (£/t)	Total value	Energy value	ERDP value	DUP value
Grass hay	50	79	69	4	30
W wheat straw	20	51	50	2	7
Grass average	10	22	21	0	1
Silage average	20	28	26	1	1
Maize silage	25	33	33	1	1
Wheat grain	110	110	110	8	9
Brewers' grains	20	38	30	1	7
Fishmeal white	335	200	121	25	225
Maize gluten feed	100	123	105	14	25
Palm kernel feed	85	130	107	8	71
Rapeseed meal	130	152	101	24	62
Soyabean meal extr.	160	209	110	22	141

PART 2

ANIMAL REQUIREMENTS

CHAPTER 4

VOLUNTARY FEED INTAKE

4.1 Why is intake important?

4.2 Definition

4.3 Factors controlling voluntary feed intake

4.4 Practical assessment of diet quality

4.5 The role of saliva

4.6 Diet presentation
     4.6.1   Total mixed rations

4.7 Other factors affecting voluntary feed intake

4.8 Predicting the voluntary intake of silage
     4.8.1   Dry matter content and free acidity
     4.8.2   Effect of protein and protein degradation products
             on intake
     4.8.3   Effect of fermentation products on intake

4.9 Conclusions

4.1   Why is intake important?

Predicting voluntary feed intake is the most difficult component of feeding the dairy cow because it is affected by many different factors and is therefore difficult to predict with confidence. The forage component of the diet is often offered *ad libitum*, so research has focused attention on predicting forage intake, sometimes ignoring the interactions between forages and concentrates. Achieving a high intake of forage feeds is accepted as being desirable because forages are considered to be less costly than concentrates. High forage intakes are usually reflected in high total feed intakes and improved profitability of the dairy enterprise.

Take for example a cow with a requirement of ME of 220 MJ a day (a cow giving about 30 litres of milk). The effect of different levels of total daily feed intake on the overall energy density of the diet required to supply that amount of ME can be considerable (Table 4.1). The range of feed intakes shown in the table is seen on farms. The lower end of the range applies to cows in very early or very late lactation or animals given low-quality forages, or self-feed silage, and two meals of concentrates at milking. The higher end of the range is more typical of animals given complete diets (total mixed rations).

Table 4.1   Effect of feed intake on the energy density of the diet required to supply a dairy cow with 220 MJ ME/day

Total ME required (MJ/day)	Feed intake (kg DM/day)	Energy density required in total diet (MJ/kg DM)
220	17.0	13.0
220	19.0	11.5
220	21.0	10.5
220	23.0	9.5

At lower voluntary feed intake, the energy density of the diet must be increased if energy intake is to be sufficient to sustain a high output of milk. Concentrates usually contain a higher energy density than forages, so the need for a high proportion of concentrates in the diet is greater the lower the voluntary feed intake. At higher voluntary feed intake, the proportion of feeds of relatively lower energy content may be increased. In practice, what happens at higher levels of feed intake is that the energy density of the diet is usually maintained at a reasonably high level, and either milk output is greater or the cows gain weight.

In this chapter some of the factors which control feed intake in cows are discussed. Specific attributes of diets which might affect feed intake are described, with particular emphasis on silage and on total mixed rations. The prediction of feed intake is considered in Chapter 8.

4.2   Definition

Voluntary feed intake is usually defined as the amount of feed which will be consumed when the animal has access to the feed for most or all of the time. Continuous access to feed, with about 10% of the amount offered being refused and removed daily is termed access *ad libitum* (literally, free access or free-choice), or intake *ad libitum*.

Voluntary feed intake is usually expressed as **dry matter**, but other definitions, such as fresh weight intake, cell wall intake, metabolisable energy intake or sodium intake, may be equally valid. The period of time over which intake is measured is usually 24 hours, particularly when cows are fed once daily. In other situations, such as buffer feeding, when the time of access to the buffer feed is restricted, the amount consumed in a much shorter period of time (e.g. one hour) may be more relevant than intake per day.

4.3   Factors controlling voluntary feed intake

Although larger animals eat more than smaller animals, other factors modify the general relationship between body size and feed intake. For example, at similar body weights high-yielding cows eat more feed than lower-yielding cows. In other words, they eat more **per unit of liveweight.** This suggests that cows eat to satisfy their demand for energy. Thinner animals also tend to eat more per unit of liveweight than fatter animals. There is no evidence that ruminants eat for any other nutrient, except for sodium.

If there is a long term control (homeostatic) mechanism for feed intake and body weight in the dairy cow, the mechanism is imprecise as the cow is able to gain or lose considerable amounts of body-weight over a relatively short period, i.e. a single lactation.

Control of appetite is via the area of the brain known as the hypothalamus. Signals are received in the hypothalamus from the gut, liver, blood and body energy stores. Fat-soluble hormones may also be involved in modulating the balance between signals indicating satiety (full up) and those indicating hunger. Satiety may be signalled via metabolites in blood or liver and by receptors in the gut wall. Hunger may also be signalled via receptors in the wall of the gut, as well as by physical removal of feed from the tract as digestion proceeds.

Signals to the hypothalamus are thought to be determined by the animal's ability to metabolise nutrients. Thus bovine growth hormone (BST, bovine somatotropin) increases the intake of high-energy diets, where the end products of digestion may limit feed intake, but not of low-energy diets where the physical bulk of the feed in the gut and its rate of breakdown may limit intake.

The intensity of the satiety or hunger signals received in the brain may reflect the characteristics of the diet or of specific feeds as much as the animal's physiological or productive status. In diets of a lower concentration of energy, the physical bulk or "fill" is considered to limit intake. Animal factors and/or end products of digestion probably assume relatively greater importance as the energy concentration of the ration is increased (Figure 4.1). The net effect is for dry matter intake to **increase** with increasing energy concentration of the diet up to a point, beyond which it **decreases** (Figure 4.1). The changeover marks the end of physical limitations to dry matter intake and the start of physiological and/or metabolic control of voluntary intake.

Figure 4.1   Relationships between voluntary dry matter intake (kg/day) and animal and feed characteristics (from Forbes, 1983)

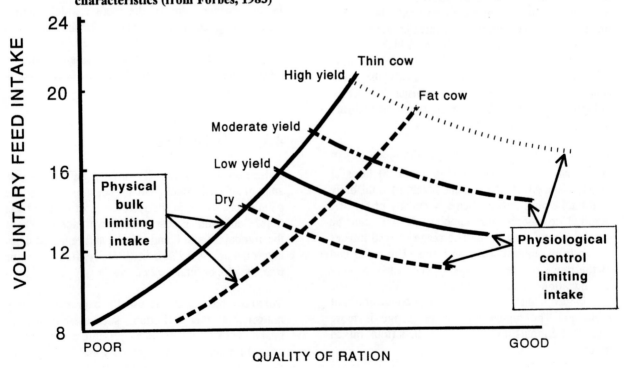

Several mechanisms have been suggested to attempt to explain why the physical bulk of feed limits the intake of lower quality feeds. The most popular theory is the "hotel" theory: you cannot have your room until I have moved out of it. Feed particles occupy space in the rumen and until their size is reduced to a small enough size that they can pass on down the digestive tract, the animal feels full and is unwilling to eat more. Since the particles of interest are the slowly digested cellulose and hemicellulose polymers present as cell wall fibres (NDF), cows should eat a constant amount of cell wall irrespective of the cell wall content of the feed. Put another way, dry matter intake is lower the higher the cell wall content of a feed (Figure 4.2).

Figure 4.2 Relationship between voluntary dry matter intake of forages by sheep and cell wall content (from Mertens, 1973, quoted by van Soest, 1982)

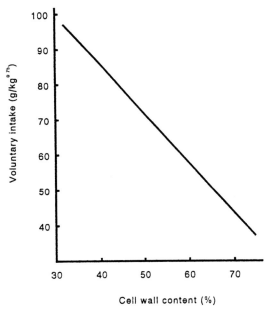

Unfortunately there is considerable variation in dry matter intake at the same cell wall content. The R^2, or the proportion of the variation in intake accounted for by forage cell wall content, in the data used to derive Figure 4.2 was only 0.58. This suggests that not all cell wall is the same and therefore the effect on intake is not the same for all cell wall types. The degree of lignification, structural geometry and fibre length interact to influence rate, and extent, of particle size reduction in the rumen.

The rate of fibre breakdown may also be important in determining feed intake in addition to the amount of slowly digested cell wall in a feed. However, the overall rate of digestion of a feed not only reflects the structure and composition of the cell wall, but also the proportion of non-structural components of the feed, especially sugars, proteins, and - in the case of silages - fermentation products such as acids and non-protein nitrogenous components.

Three feeds with the same theoretical extent of digestion, or potential digestibility, but with different rates of degradation in the rumen are shown in Figure 4.3. If there is no metabolic control of intake the animal will eat most of Feed 1 and least of Feed 3. In other words, the faster the potentially digestible material is digested, the quicker the rumen is likely to be re-filled by another meal, and the greater the rate (and the amount) of feed intake per day.

Figure 4.3 Three feeds with the same potential digestibility but different speeds of digestion (from Ørskov, 1987)

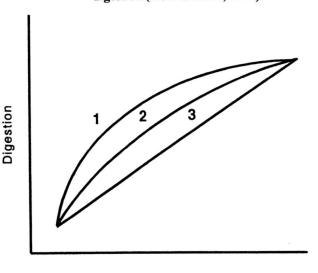

The non-structural materials in feeds (cell contents) are digested at a faster rate than the cell wall fraction (see Chapter 3). So feeds with a relatively low content of cell wall should be eaten at faster rates and in greater amounts than feeds with high cell wall contents. This is true, at least up to the point where nutrient requirements and metabolites from digestion predominate over feed factors in determining the amount eaten (Figure 4.1).

4.4 Practical assessment of diet quality

We have seen already that the main factors affecting the intake of forages appear to be cell wall content (Figure 4.2) and rate of cell wall digestion (Figure 4.3). Most diets for dairy cows, however, are mixtures of forages and concentrates, with silage as the main forage feed in winter and grazed grass in the summer. We have also seen (Figure 4.1) that feed dry matter intake can decrease with diets containing high levels of high-quality feeds as requirements for nutrients and feed metabolites increasingly control the animal's feeding behaviour.

It follows that ME, although a good indicator of feed quality from the viewpoint of the likely supply of useful energy to the animal, is not a good indicator of the likely level of feed intake. D-value or digestibility can be useful to predict intake, but is unlikely to be of use in high-concentrate diets.

At low levels of concentrates in the diet, a major problem in feeding the dairy cow is to achieve a high voluntary intake. At high levels of concentrates, the risk of digestive upsets is increased. Cell wall, or NDF, is required to maintain a healthy rumen (see below) but too much fibre and feed intake is likely to be depressed. So a balance is required between having too much fibre in the diet and too little. The content of cell wall, or neutral detergent fibre, can be used as a single (though relatively crude) unifying component of feed ingredients in diet formulation.

If the importance of NDF in determining the dry matter intake of forage-based diets is accepted, then diets may be formulated with varying contents of NDF to meet the need for high dry matter intakes in highly productive animals and lower intakes in unproductive ones. Furthermore, since the ME of cell contents is usually higher than that of cell wall, formulating to a given concentration of NDF in the dry matter will produce diets of higher ME content at lower contents of NDF and *vice versa*. As the intake of the dairy cow is limited in early lactation (see Chapter 15), it is useful to have a relatively low cell wall content to reduce the "hotel" or "fill" effect as much as possible at this stage, and to maximise the density of nutrients and the speed of digestion of the diet so that intake is as high as possible.

Research has shown that dry matter intake decreases as the total NDF content in the diet is increased, in the range 310 to 390 g NDF/kg DM, from 20.2 kg/day at the lowest level of NDF to 18.6 kg/day at the higher level of NDF. In addition, milk yield and milk protein also decreased with increased content of NDF in the diet.

The suggested values for the optimal content of NDF in the whole diet dry matter for a range of milk yields are shown in Table 4.2.

Table 4.2   Suggested contents of NDF in the total diet DM of dairy cows

Milk Yield (litres/day)	Optimal NDF (g/kg DM)
Non-lactating	600
< 15	500
15 to 20	450
20 to 30	400
30 to 40	350
>40	300

4.5   The role of saliva

The rate of saliva production is approximately constant in cattle and aids swallowing of feed during eating and rumination. Fibrous feeds with long particles require more chewing than pelleted feeds which have been mechanically milled to reduce particle size, so more saliva is added per unit of fibrous feeds eaten than per unit of pelleted feeds (Table 4.3). It therefore follows that the least buffering of acids (formed by fermentation of feed in the rumen) by saliva is when pelleted feeds are eaten. Since pelleted concentrates often contain rapidly fermentable starch and sugar, the accumulation of free acidity in the rumen is likely be much greater than with hay or dried grass, which have more saliva mixed with them during eating and are fermented at a slower rate. Depression of the pH of the rumen liquour results in a reduced rate of fibre digestion as the bacteria responsible for fibre digestion are more sensitive to acidity than those which digest starch and sugar.

Table 4.3   Effect of type of feed on rate of eating and on saliva production (from Bailey, 1959)

Feed	Eating rate (g/minute)	Saliva production	
		(ml/minute)	(ml/g of feed)
Pelleted feed	357	243	0.68
Fresh grass	283	266	0.94
Silage	248	280	1.13
Dried grass (long)	83	270	3.25
Hay	70	254	3.63

The data in Table 4.3. show that silage had less saliva mixed with it per unit of feed eaten than either dried grass or hay, and a similar amount to that for fresh grass, indicating that wetter long forages require less lubrication to aid swallowing than dry long forages. Unfortunately silage is acidic, so the relatively low level of buffering by saliva of silage implies that either more rumination is required per unit of silage eaten than for other forage feeds, or more buffering is required in the rumen itself to prevent rumen pH from being depressed below the normal range of pH 6.5 to 7.0. Both these factors may restrict total daily consumption of silage.

Adding a small amount of water to dry diets can increase intake as it augments saliva production. For example, moist grain is usually eaten in greater amounts than dry grain. However, too much water in a diet can limit intake, especially if the water is within plant cells rather than extra-cellular. Very wet silages can have low intakes not only because of their excessive wetness, but also because of their excessive acidity. The optimal dry matter content of the whole diet is 40 to 55% (see Chapter 12, page 128).

4.6 Diet presentation

Voluntary intake is usually elevated by the frequency the diet or feed is offered to the animal. At pasture, when the feed is on offer continually, the cow has four or five major periods of grazing per day. Housed animals also eat in discrete meals, but the distribution of fresh feed is an extra stimulus to eating.

Feed intake can also be depressed by inadequate access to the feed trough, especially when the diet is not on offer all the time. The optimum length of trough for a total mixed ration on continuous offer is 0.45 metres per cow.

The presence of electrified wire or metal bar placed between the animal and a self-feed silage face can very effectively restrict feed intake. The wire or bar is intended to restrict access to the silage, and as a result the animal eats less than if the same silage was on unrestricted access. The more timid animals in the herd, especially the younger heifers, can suffer from relatively greater deprivation than the established members of the herd which have become more used to the risk of receiving an electric shock at the feed face. Intake of silage may be increased by up to 25% by replacing an electrified wire by a solid barrier at the self-feed silo face.

Short chopping of forages increases intake; in the case of silages a reasonable target average particle length is 5 cm, though responses in intake have been recorded in silage chopped as short as 7 mm particle length.

4.6.1 Total mixed rations
Complete diets, or total mixed rations, are usually eaten in greater amounts than when the major components - forages and concentrates - are offered separately. Voluntary intake may be up to 30% higher than normal in dairy cows given total mixed rations. The most likely explanation for the response in intake is that large meals of rapidly digested concentrates are avoided in complete diets. Rate of fibre digestion is likely to be faster compared to twice daily concentrates with silage offered separately *ad libitum*, partly because rumen pH may be held higher for longer, and partly because the supply of fermentable metabolisable energy (FME) and protein (ERDP) to the rumen microbial population is improved compared to separate feeding of silage and concentrates. The inclusion of a sweet feed ingredient such as molasses not only

provides supplementary FME but also assists in masking the sour taste of silage.

Figure 4.4 **Diagrammatic representation of the effects on rumen pH and on digestion of cellulose of low and high levels of concentrate given as two separate feeds daily or in a complete diet (from Ørskov, 1987)**

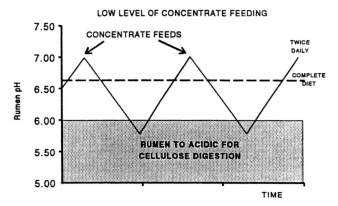

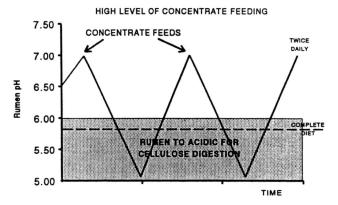

Possible effects in the rumen of separate feeds compared to twice daily feeds of concentrate, at high and low levels of feeding, are shown diagrammatically in Figure 4.4. Rapidly-digested feeds result in depressed pH levels in the rumen, which in turn adversely affect the rate of digestion of cell wall. The extreme situation, known as "feed-lot bloat", occurs with chronic rumen acidosis and rumen stasis. The bloat may be caused by giving too large a meal of concentrates along with an inadequate supply of fibre, or inadequate buffers, in a high-energy diet.

Some complete diets contain inadequate long fibre mixed with a high proportion of rapidly-fermented starch and sugar, with the result that the rumen is too acidic for too long a period of time (Figure 4.4). The importance of including some long fibre which is not itself acidic and which will promote rumination, such as high dry matter big bale silage, hay or haylage, or straw, in diets for high-yielding cows cannot be overstressed.

4.7 Silage

Silage is the most important ingredient of the diet of housed dairy cattle, yet its voluntary intake cannot be predicted with accuracy. The problem lies with the over-riding influence on intake of the extent and pattern of fermentation in the silage and its assessment. The prediction of silage intake is further complicated when mixtures of silages are given to cows together with concentrates in varying proportions. It is therefore very important that actual intakes of silage should be assessed on the farm, rather than attempting to predict silage intake from an analysis of its composition. Guidelines for assessing silage intake on-farm are given in Chapter 12 (page 123).

In the following sections some of the more significant features of silage which are considered to influence intake are reviewed so that where an analysis report is available, the results can be interpreted as an aid to diagnosing possible causes of intake problems.

4.7.1 *Dry matter content and free acidity*

Well-preserved silages with lower free acid contents (higher pH) are likely to be eaten at a faster rate per meal than those of higher acidity, and that total time spent both eating and ruminating is relatively constant. Thus the faster the rate of ingestion during a meal, the more time is available for rumination, with the possibility of greater grinding of feed particles and more saliva added per unit of feed during rumination.

Bicarbonate and other buffering agents can alleviate the lack of salivary bicarbonate and the depressing effect on intake of excess acidity, either from silage or from too much rapidly fermented feed in the diet. Recommended levels of sodium bicarbonate are 0.1 to 0.35 kg/cow/day or 0.7 to 1.0 kg sodium bentonite/cow/day. However, these rates of inclusion are not normally sufficient to make a large contribution to the total supply of buffering agents to the rumen.

Buffers are often included in early lactation diets, or in situations where the concentration of dietary NDF is too low. Increases in milk production of between 4 and 10%, and in milk fat of 0.2 to 0.4% units have been recorded following inclusion of buffers in the diet.

4.7.2 *Effect of protein and protein degradation products on intake*

Recent work at the Scottish Agricultural College (Offer *et al.*, 1994) has highlighted the importance of protein breakdown products on the intake of silage by dairy cattle. The best predictors of silage DM intake by cows were true dry matter content (i.e. dry matter corrected for volatile fermentation products, see Chapter 2, page 27), the content of digestible organic matter in the dry matter (D-value or DOMD) and the proportion of soluble protein in the crude protein. Amino acid N as a proportion of total soluble N is a good indicator of the extent of degradation of the small molecular weight nitrogenous material in silage. At least 70% of soluble N should be amino acid N - the higher the proportion the better. Amines are also thought to depress silage intake, especially in poorly preserved material.

4.7.3 *Effect of fermentation products on intake*

Apart from degraded protein, fermentation acids influence silage intake. Work at the Scottish Agricultural College (SAC) has identified four main types of grass silage, characterised by extent and pattern of fermentation. The main features of the four SAC clusters are in Table 4.4.

Table 4.4 SAC Cluster Index for silages (from Offer *et al.*, 1993)

	Cluster index			
	1	2	3	4
Fermentation	Bad	Moderate	Good	Very good
Residual sugar	Zero	Low	Low	High
Lactic acid	Low	High	High	Low
VFA	High	Moderate	Low	Low
Amino-N % total soluble N	Low	Moderate	Moderate	High
Neutralising value	Low	High	Moderate	Low

Animal feed companies have adopted similar classification systems for silages, and some are using the approach in an attempt to assess the potential intake of silage and to match the type of cake to the type of silage.

The SAC Cluster Index accounted for considerably more of the variation in silage intake by sheep than did ammonia-N, which has been used for many years as the single best indicator of the preservation quality of silages (Figures 4.5 and 4.6). The real problem with ammonia N is that it fails to distinguish between silages with less than 100 g ammonia-N per kg total N.

4.8 Other factors affecting voluntary feed intake

Feed intake can be increased in winter by increasing day length up to 16 hours per 24 hours. High ambient temperatures and inadequate water supply depress feed intake. Voluntary intake is known to be stimulated by behavioural factors, such as the presence of other animals, previous experience of feeds, having a variety of different feeds in the diet and the inclusion of sweet feeds in the diet. Research into the taste preferences of cows has shown that total mixed rations offered with different additives were ranked by cows in the following order: sweet (sucrose added at 1.5% of diet DM) > no additive > bitter (urea added at 1% of diet DM) > salt (NaCl at 4% of DM) > sour (HCl at 1.25% of DM). Intake was 13% higher for the sweet diet compared to the second placed control diet (Nombekela and Murphy, 1992).

4.9 Conclusions

Voluntary feed intake is difficult to predict with accuracy, so it is very important that intake is assessed on the farm. A great benefit of total mixed rations is that often intake is known, so animal performance can be related to nutrient supply in the practical situation. Changes in voluntary intake can be recorded and related to changes in individual feeds or to the formulation of the diet. Management practices under the control of the farmer, like silage making technique, can be linked to changes in intake and performance, and to profit. If diets are not weighed out to the animals, indirect methods of assessing intake have to be used on the farm. Some ways of estimating feed intake indirectly are described in Chapter 12. The prediction of feed intake is considered in more detail together with tables of likely levels of intake for lactating and dry cows in Chapter 8.

Figure 4.5 **Relationship between ammonia-N and intake of 28 Scottish silages by sheep (Offer *et al.*, 1993)**

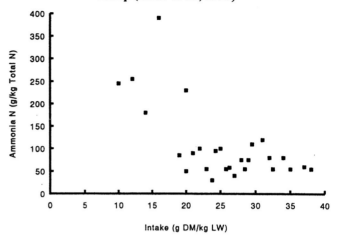

Figure 4.6 **Relationship between Cluster Index and intake of 28 Scottish silages by sheep (Offer *et al.*, 1993)**

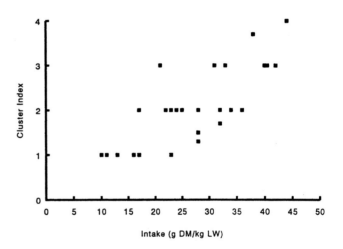

CHAPTER 5

ENERGY

5.1   Introduction

5.2   Units of measurement

5.3   Sources of energy
      5.3.1   *Carbohydrates*
      5.3.2   *Fats and oils*
      5.3.3   *Proteins*

5.4   Sites of energy digestion

5.5   Optimising microbial growth in the rumen

5.6   Energy digestion
      5.6.1   *Gross energy*
      5.6.2   *Digestible and metabolisable energy*
      5.6.3   *Net energy*

5.7   Products of energy digestion

5.8   Estimating energy requirements
      5.8.1   *What are the most sensible units?*
      5.8.2   *Efficiency of conversion of ME to NE*

5.9   Practical aspects of energy nutrition
      5.9.1   *Rate of energy release and acidosis*
      5.9.2   *Fibre requirements*
      5.9.3   *Low milk fat syndrome*
      5.9.4   *Ketosis due to dietary energy deficiency*
      5.9.5   *Fatty liver*

5.10 Beyond metabolisable energy
      5.10.1 *Rumen-resistant starch*

5.11 Fat
      5.11.1 *Digestion of fat*
      5.11.2 *Inclusion of fat in diets*
      5.11.3 *Protected fats*
      5.11.4 *Health problems with high-fat diets*

5.1   Introduction

Energy is the major nutrient required by dairy cows and is second only to dry matter intake in terms of its importance in ration formulation. Under-supply of energy is one of the major reasons for under-performance by the animal. The principles of the current metabolisable energy system used in this country were laid down in the 1960s by the late Sir Kenneth Blaxter. Recent changes in the system have merely been a natural progression of the original ideas, made possible by new research results and the wider availability of computers.

This chapter is concerned with the principles of energy metabolism and the energy requirements of dairy cows; the calculation of metabolisable energy requirements is considered in Chapter 9.

5.2   Units of measurement

The currently accepted unit for measuring energy is the joule. Previously it was the calorie (still used in America) which is equivalent to 4.2 joules. The joule is defined as the amount of heat required to raise one cubic centimetre of water by one degree centigrade. Given the size of dairy cows and their products the joule is too small a unit for the formulation of rations and therefore the kilojoule (KJ = 1000 joules) and the megajoule (MJ = 1000 KJ) are more commonly used. To put these units into perspective, a four-bar Kit-Kat contains about a 1 MJ of energy, so that a dairy cow giving 30 litres of milk requires the equivalent of about 220 Kit-Kats. Alternatively a 3-bar electric fire would need to burn for 20 hours to use up the same amount of energy.

5.3   Sources of energy

5.3.1   *Carbohydrates*

Like all mammals dairy cows can utilise simple sugars and starch as a source of energy. These are rapidly broken down in the rumen principally into lactic acid. High levels of lactic acid in the rumen alter the pH and microbial flora, leading to reduced efficiency of fibre degradation, acidosis, indigestion and the low milk fat syndrome (see Section 5.9.3 for further details). Therefore starchy foods should be fed with care. However it is now becoming apparent that some starch and sugars are needed in rations to match the rapidly released nitrogen found in feeds such as grass silage. A recommended overall ration content for a typical milking cow is about 120 to 200 g sugar and starch/kg DM but is higher at higher yields.

The digestion of the different carbohydrate sources is shown in Figure 5.1 (page 50). The speed of digestion is slowest for cellulose and fastest for simple sugars such as glucose and they are all broken down, through a variety of intermediate compounds, to glucose. Glucose is rapidly converted to pyruvate which is converted into the various end-products and carbon dioxide. The major products of digestion are the volatile fatty acids (VFA) - acetic acid (2 carbons), propionic acid (3 carbons) and butyric acid (4 carbons) - which are absorbed through the rumen wall.

As the fermentation is anaerobic the rumen microbes must obtain their oxygen for metabolism from the compounds they degrade. Therefore a certain amount of carbohydrate (on average 8%; range 5 to 12%) is converted into methane to give up its oxygen. The methane collects in the top of the rumen and is periodically belched up.

Figure 5.1   The breakdown of carbohydrates in the rumen (adapted from McDonald *et al.*, 1988)

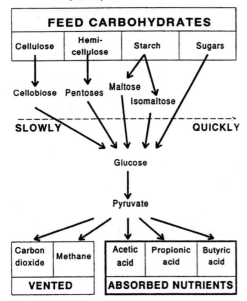

5.3.2   *Fats and oils*

Fats and oils are concentrated sources of energy compared to carbohydrates. Fats are, however, only of practical value in diets for high-yielding cows when feed intake may be inadequate to meet the animal's requirement for energy and a more concentrated source of energy is essential to maintain energy intake. Unless fat is protected from the rumen microbes, inclusion rates above about 60 g/kg DM (depending on fat type) can result in reduced microbial function, depressed feed intake and lower synthesis of milk fat. See Section 5.11 for further details.

5.3.3   *Proteins*

Like all mammals, ruminants can use amino acids as sources of energy. To use proteins in this way the cow must deaminate them in the liver. If this process becomes excessive, the metabolic load on the liver reduces its ability to achieve other functions.

Rations containing more than 200 g crude protein/kg DM have been reported to result in reduced fertility (see Chapter 16, page 155) and even very high-yielding cows, giving more than 50 litres of milk a day, should not need more than 190 g CP/kg DM.

5.4   Sites of energy digestion

In ruminants the majority of carbohydrates are digested in the rumen and fats are digested in the small intestine. Almost all of the digestible carbo-

hydrate is converted to volatile fatty acids (VFA) in the rumen and very little passes into the small intestine to be absorbed as glucose. Therefore the milking cow has to synthesise large quantities of glucose (up to 2 kg/day) in the liver. It is, however, becoming apparent that varying amounts of starch escape the actions of the rumen microbes and are digested in the small intestine to be absorbed as glucose. This seems to be beneficial as it promotes higher milk protein contents (see Chapter 13, page 131).

5.5   Optimising microbial growth in the rumen

The population of microbes in the rumen comprises a wide range of organisms, chiefly bacteria, protozoa and fungi. The bacteria are mainly responsible for cellulose digestion and in some instances ruminal efficiency can be improved by killing off the protozoa (for example by including monensin in the diet). However, protozoa do seem to have a valuable function in maintaining the stability and flexibility of the rumen microflora. Optimal digestion of cellulose will only take place if all the microbial requirements are met. The major requirements are:

- **Warmth.** Like many bacteria the rumen microbes function best at about 37°C. The heat of fermentation, the body heat produced by the cow and the insulation of the cow's skin maintain the rumen at a steady 37°C even in very cold climates.

- **Water.** The microbes work best if suspended in a "soup" of water and food. If cattle are deprived of water then the rumen can dry out with consequential reduction in cellulose digestion.

- **Anaerobic conditions.** The major rumen microbes are anaerobes in that they can grow without oxygen. The healthy rumen is anaerobic.

- **Mildly acidic pH.** The microbial population in the rumen functions best in neutral mildly acidic conditions (pH 6.0 to 7.0, see Table 5.1). If the pH falls too much below pH 6.0, this discriminates against the volatile fatty acid (VFA) forming microbes and favours those that produce lactic acid.

- **Energy** or a source of carbon. The microbes can utilise a wide range of carbon sources for energy and can break down cellulose and hemicellulose to produce energy to fuel their metabolism.

- **Nitrogen.** The microbes require a certain amount of nitrogen to synthesise proteins; they can either degrade dietary protein or use non-protein nitrogen (see Chapter 6, page 64). In general the microbes require a minimum of about 1% nitrogen in the diet dry matter to maintain their own population and to break down the plant material. Rations based on feeds such as straw that contain less than 1% nitrogen (6.25% protein) will result in a reduced microbial metabolism which will reduce the rate of cellulose digestion leading to increased rumen retention times and reduced dry matter intake.

- **Sulphur.** This is required to synthesise the sulphur-containing amino acids methionine and cysteine.

- **Numerous trace elements.** Like all life forms the rumen microbes require a wide range of trace elements for the synthesis of enzymes and other proteins (see Chapter 7). One element of major importance is cobalt. Ruminants do not need dietary vitamin B_{12} because the microbes synthesis it but in order to synthesis vitamin B_{12} a supply of cobalt is needed.

Table 5.1 Optimum pH range for different ruminal microbial reactions (from McCullough, 1973)

Reaction	pH
Cellulose digestion	6.0 to 6.8
Formation of volatile fatty acids	6.2 to 6.6
Synthesis of protein	6.3 to 7.4
Lactate production	5.9 to 6.2

It should be emphasised that for maximal activity the rumen microbes require their nutrients in a balanced form. This is currently of significance in terms of the energy:nitrogen ratio of the diet. Too little degradable nitrogen and the rate of digestion of cellulose is reduced. Too much energy and lactic acid production in the rumen is increased (Table 5.1) and acidosis may develop. It is hoped that in the

future we will be able to predict the rate at which nitrogen is released and the rate of dry matter disappearance in the rumen, which, when combined with a knowledge of the amounts of sugars, starch and fibre in the diet, should allow the energy and nitrogen release to be far better-matched. At the moment, however, our current methods of assessing the rate of feed degradation appear to be inadequate for this purpose.

Traditionally it has been assumed that all the energy in a feed has been available to rumen microbes. However, the AFRC Metabolisable Protein System (1992) recognises that certain energy sources such as the VFA and fats yield little energy to the rumen microbes and hence are not significant supporters of microbial growth. Fermentable metabolisable energy (FME) is defined as the metabolisable energy minus the energy in the fat and fermentation products. FME is taken as the amount of energy available to the microbes. This will be dealt with in greater detail when protein is considered in Chapter 6.

5.6   Energy digestion

5.6.1   Gross energy

The gross energy (GE) of a feed (Figure 5.2) is the total amount of energy the feed contains. Gross energy is usually measured by burning a sample of the feed in oxygen and measuring the heat produced.

Figure 5.2   Pathways of energy digestion in the dairy cow

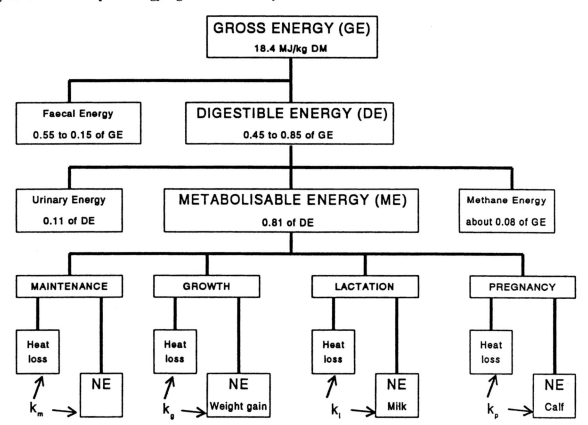

Carbohydrates, the major component of most feeds, contain about 17.5 MJ GE/kg DM, protein about 26 MJ and fat about 44 MJ.

Feeds that contain principally carbohydrate, such as forages, have a relatively constant GE of about 18.5 MJ/kg dry matter. Silages have a slightly higher GE due to the fermentation acids. Protein and fat supplements have higher values for GE (Table 5.2).

Table 5.2　The gross energy content of some common feeds (MAFF, 1990)

Feed	Gross energy (MJ/kg DM)
Straw	18.3
Fresh grass	18.7
Wheat grain	18.4
Grass silage	19.0
Soyabean meal	19.7
Rapeseed meal	19.7
Fishmeal	19.9
Fat	35.0

5.6.2　Digestible and metabolisable energy

Not all the gross energy in a feed is digestible and a varying amount passes out in the faeces. The fraction which is digested is called the Digestible Energy (DE) and varies from about 45% of the gross energy for poor feeds such as straw to about 85% for good quality feeds such as barley (see Figure 5.2). Further losses of energy occur in the rumen as methane. Some of the waste products of metabolism, excreted in urine, also contain energy and for simplicity such energy is regarded as being unavailable to the animal and is considered together with the methane energy. The digestible energy of the feed minus the losses in methane and urine is therefore the energy available to the cow and is called Metabolisable Energy (ME); it is about 81% of the DE.

5.6.3　Net energy

The ME content of a feed represents the amount of energy that can be used to support the various body functions. However the conversion of the energy sources from the form in which they are absorbed (mainly as VFA) into forms that the body tissues use, such as glucose, lactose and fat, involves several biochemical steps and some of the absorbed energy is lost as heat during these transformations. The heat produced is lost into the environment and the remaining energy which is converted into a useful form is called Net Energy (NE). NE can be used for maintenance of body functions, milk production, body tissue growth and foetal tissue growth. The efficiency with which ME is converted to NE is referred to as k which may be suffixed to indicate the fate of the NE, for example k_l represents the efficiency of converting ME to NE for lactation (Figure 5.2).

An example of the calculations required to determine the different energy fractions in a diet is shown in Table 5.3. In this instance the feed was a grass hay and it was fed on its own to a sheep at maintenance.

The sheep consumed 19.1 MJ of gross energy and by capturing all the faeces it was determined that they contained 7.4 MJ of energy. Urine contained a further 0.7 MJ and by housing the animal in a sealed insulated chamber it was possible to measure that 3.8 MJ of energy was given off as heat and 1.3 MJ as methane. These figures can then be used to determine the different energy fractions of the feed. As it was the only feed consumed then the ME content of the diet (9.7) is the ME content of that feed.

Many feeds cannot be used alone, either because the animal will not eat them (e.g. urea, fat or fishmeal) or the feed would cause severe metabolic disturbances (e.g. wheat would cause acidosis). In such circumstances, a series of trials must be carried out with different inclusions of the test feed and then the results extrapolated to see what would happen if it were offered as the sole feed. Similarly because the sheep was neither growing, giving milk nor pregnant the efficiency of converting metabolisable energy to net energy can be taken as the efficiency with which ME is used for maintenance (k_m). When one of the other conversion efficiencies needs to be measured then it is necessary to separate out the use of energy for the production purpose, say milk production from that required for maintenance. This can be resolved by looking at the overall efficiencies for different milk yields and separating the effects by relating the change in k to changes in milk yield.

Table 5.3　Energy digestion by a mature sheep fed on grass hay (adapted from Wainman et al., 1971)

Energy measurements	MJ
Energy intake	19.1
Faecal energy	7.4
Urinary energy	0.7
Methane energy	1.3
Heat loss	3.8
Energy calculations	**MJ**
Gross energy	19.1
Digestible energy	19.1 - 7.4 = 11.7
Metabolisable energy	11.7 - 0.7 - 1.3 = 9.7
Net energy	9.7 - 3.8 = 5.9
k_m	5.9 / 9.7 = 0.61

5.7　Products of energy digestion

The principle products of energy digestion are the volatile fatty acids absorbed in the rumen with a small but variable amount of glucose being absorbed in the small intestine. However, dairy cows require considerable amounts of glucose for the udder (milk), brain and foetus. Glucose is synthesised via oxaloacetic acid (OAA) from propionate. Low blood glucose and low levels of OAA can cause problems as will be discussed later when ketosis is considered (Section 5.9.4). VFA are metabolised in the liver to acetyl CoA, and, via the Krebs Cycle, to oxaloacetic acid and then to glucose (Figure 5.7).

5.8   Estimating energy requirements

5.8.1   *What are the most sensible units?*

Looking at Figure 5.2, it might appear that net energy is the unit of choice because it is this which concerns the animal. The amount of NE available will determine how much milk can be produced or body tissues lain down. Such a system forms the basis of the American and Dutch energy systems. Using a NE system makes it very easy to determine how much energy a cow requires to meet her nutritional obligations; one determines the energy content of all the products and adds this on to an allowance for maintenance. However it is not so easy to determine how much energy the diet is supplying.

The amount of metabolisable energy in a feed is considered to be solely dependent on the feed and not on the animal. The efficiency with which the cow converts absorbed metabolisable energy into net energy depends, however, on how the energy is used. For example, the efficiency for using absorbed energy for maintenance is about 70% whereas it is more likely to be 50% for weight gain. The result of this variation in efficiency of usage is that it is impossible to quote a single NE value for a feed as it depends on what the animal uses the energy for. The American system gets around this by quoting three NE values for any feed, one NE value for if the feed energy is used for maintenance, another for use to support growth and a third if the energy is used to support milk production. This increases the assessments that need to be made on a feed and the data that need to be collected for any feeds used.

An alternative system would be to consider how much energy a feed would yield that is available for metabolism (ME). This is the basis of the UK system. The advantage of this system is that farmers and their advisors need only remember one energy value for feeds and all the complex mathematics of converting ME to NE requirements can be left to a computer. However given the increasing awareness of the number of factors affecting the efficiency of converting ME to NE (see below) the two systems are tending to become the same and indeed one national feed company called the new UK energy system a Net Energy system and no-one complained! The rest of this chapter and subsequent chapters will only be concerned with the Metabolisable Energy system (AFRC, 1990).

5.8.2   *Efficiency of conversion of ME to NE*

If we are to be able to calculate what a cow can produce on a given ration and hence from a given ME intake, we need to have a better understanding of what affects the efficiency of conversion of ME to NE, i.e. what factors influence the value of k. Our current understanding is that the efficiency of conversion of ME to NE is not constant and is affected by three main factors:

The fate of energy in the body. For a given animal on a given diet there is considerable variation between the different k values, with the biologically more important functions having higher values for k (i.e. you must stay alive first (maintenance) before you can consider growth, pregnancy or milk production). ME used for maintenance is converted to NE with an efficiency of about 0.72 (k_m); energy for lactation with an efficiency of about 0.62 (k_l); energy for growth with an efficiency of about 0.53 (k_g) and pregnancy 0.133 (k_p). Note that for pregnancy the efficiency with which ME is retained in the foetus is low as much of the energy supplied to the foetus is used in its own maintenance.

Figure 5.3   The change in k values with changing ration quality (q)

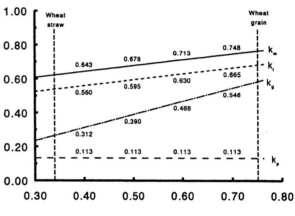

Quality of the ration (q) (ME/GE)

K varies with the quality of the energy in the diet. As the quality of a diet falls the efficiency of conversion of ME to NE falls. For example if a cow is given poor feeds such as straw her digestive tract has to work hard (increased chewing, rumination, faecal excretion) to extract the energy from the feed whereas if she is given the same amount of energy in a high-quality feed such as rolled barley the effort and therefore energy required to extract the nutritive value would be less. As less energy is used during digestion, the efficiency of converting ME to NE will be higher resulting in a higher k value. Therefore k increases as the quality of the feed increases. There are various ways of measuring feed quality but one method, which uses feed measurements already available in many feed tables, is to look at the metabolisability (usually called q) which is defined as the proportion of the gross energy that is metabolisable energy:

q   =   Metabolisable Energy / Gross Energy

For example wheat straw has a GE of 18.1 and an ME of 6.1 giving a q of 0.34 (6.1/18.1=0.34), whereas wheat grain has a similar GE and an ME of 13.6 so q is 0.75.

Figure 5.3 shows the change in k as the quality of the ration increases from 0.3 to 0.75. Note that q has a greater effect on k_g than for maintenance (k_m) and lactation (k_l). This is because as the quality of the feed changes the proportions of the different VFA produced in the rumen changes and this alters the supply of the precursors for fat synthesis. The value of k_p is generally considered to be constant even though it is well known that it will change with q. However in most practical situations changes to k_p will have very little effect on overall requirements for energy or on the diet formulated.

Level of production. It is generally considered that the efficiency of digestion and metabolism falls as the level of production increases. The reasons for this are twofold. Firstly, as the level of production increases so does voluntary intake (see Chapter 4, page 42) and, as the cow remains the same size, the rate at which feed passes through the cow must increase. This causes the digestibility of feed to fall as it is exposed to the effects of microbial and enzymatic digestion for less time and hence k is considered to fall. Secondly, ruminant production, like all biological processes, is subject to the law of diminishing returns. This is partially due to the fact that all biological processes have a finite capacity (i.e. an udder can only synthesis so much lactose and casein) and partially because high-yielding animals require to eat more feed, digest more, excrete more faeces and urine etc., all of which put an increasing energy demand on the animal.

Whilst such declines in efficiency have been recognised and understood since the 1960s it is only recently that it has become possible (through the use of computers) to incorporate them in feeding standards. The traditional method of determining energy requirements whereby the requirements of each activity (maintenance, lactation, pregnancy, growth and exercise) were calculated separately and then summed with no consideration for interactions has progressively been superceded.

If the efficiency of the use of ME falls with increasing production, the cow giving 30 litres milk and gaining 500 g/day is working harder than the animal giving the same yield but loosing 500 g/day and therefore will be less efficient. Being less efficient the former cow will require more energy to produce milk, but exactly how much can only be determined when all the other activities and their energy requirements are known. The feeding standards (AFRC, 1990) include complex equations as to how to determine the corrected ME requirements from the NE requirements and the appropriate k values. However, such corrections can also be applied to the total ME requirements as calculated by considering each production activity separately and so a factorial approach can still be used when formulating rations manually.

To correct for level of production (C_L) it is first necessary to quantify the level of production. This is done by expressing the total energy requirements as multiples of the animal's maintenance requirements and is referred to as the Animal Production Level (APL). A dairy cow requiring 140 MJ ME/day to produce 25 litre of milk and 70 MJ ME/day for maintenance will have an APL of (140+70)/70=3.0. Figure 5.4. shows how the correction factor (C_L) is determined from the APL. As production increases above maintenance the APL rises and the correction factor rises above 1.0, and the animal will require more energy than predicted. For example the 25 litre cow with an APL of 3.0 will have a C_L of 1.036 and will require 1.036 x (140+70)=218 MJ ME/day rather than 210 MJ ME/day (140+70). Such increases may seem small but, as it is often difficult to meet the energy requirements of high yielders, in practice the extra few megajoules per day are important. The exact methods of calculating energy requirements are considered in Chapter 9.

Figure 5.4 **Changes in correction for level of production (C_L) with increasing level of animal production (APL)**

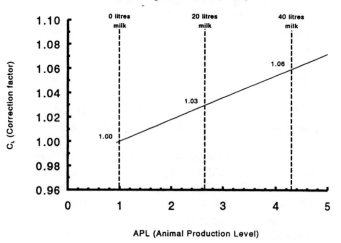

5.9 Practical aspects of energy nutrition

5.9.1 *Rate of energy release and acidosis*

As mentioned previously, energy is released at differing rates from the different carbohydrate sources. In general soluble sugars are released very rapidly from ingested feeds, starch quite rapidly and energy from cellulose is released slowly (see Figure 5.1). If ruminants are fed high levels of feeds from which the starch can be rapidly released acidosis may develop. Such feeds usually stimulate little chewing and so saliva production is reduced (Figure 5.5) and the rumen pH falls as the volatile fatty acids are less buffered. The fall in pH depresses the growth of the VFA-forming bacteria (see Table 5.1) and favours lactic acid bacteria, hence the pH falls further and rate of VFA production drops.

As the pH of the rumen falls there is a shift away from acetate and butyrate production and milk fat content may be depressed as a result. The increasingly acidic rumen may also make the animal uncomfortable and restless with indigestion. The reduction in microbial activity also reduces the rate at which plant material is broken down and can leave the rumen and therefore intake falls. Once intake falls then the energy balance is disturbed and ketosis may develop (see Section 5.9.4). Ultimately, rumen contractions cease, the animal cannot belch and bloat develops which, unless treated quickly, is fatal.

Figure 5.5   The development of acidosis in the rumen (van Soest, 1994)

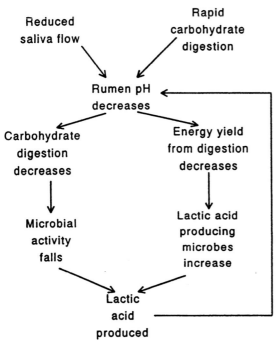

Table 5.4   The development of acidosis in a sheep (from Ryan, 1964)

Day	Time	Rumen pH	Comment	Acetic acid	Propionic acid	Lactic acid
				\% of total acids		
1	9:30	6.8	Forage diet	69	18	1.5
1	9:45	-	given 1.5 kg wheat			
1	12:00	6.0		58	20	7.7
1	16:00	6.0		57	18	7.5
1	20:30	5.9		53	18	3.7
2	9.00	6.3		47	21	5.3
2	9:30	-	Given 1.5 kg wheat			
2	13:00	5.7	Faeces soft	35	9	47.1
2	16:00	5.0	Rumen contents very fluid			
3	10:00	4.7	Rumen stasis	9	4	85.0
3	12:15	4.3	Profuse diarrhoea	0	0	96.0
4	8:00		Dead			

Table 5.4 shows how acidosis developed in a sheep given large amounts of ground wheat. The first feeding (equivalent to about 9 kg of wheat given to a Holstein cow) reduced the pH slightly and increased the proportion of lactic acid in the rumen, but the animal appeared to be coping in that the pH remained around 6.0 for the next 24 hours and the proportion of lactic acid did not increase. The wheat passed on through the intestines and it was probably the first dose that caused the soft faeces on Day 2. Giving another 1.5 kg of wheat on the second day was too much for the rumen's homeostatic control and the pH decreased further, the proportion of lactic acid increased rapidly until the animal died on Day 4.

In practice the main cause of acidosis in dairy cows is the feeding of high levels of concentrates. Animals under these feeding systems are quite likely to be continually in the same situation as the sheep on Day 1 with a pH about 6.0. It can be seen that it takes very little to drive the animal into the situation found on Day 2. The problem of acidosis can be addressed by either dietary monitoring or dietary modification.

Dietary monitoring
Ratio of forage to concentrate. With the assumption that starch and sugar are mainly in concentrates and cellulose in forages, the ratio between concentrate and forage (in dry matter terms) can be used to assess the level of intake of the rapidly-fermented components of the diet. In general, a 50:50 ratio of concentrates to forage is considered to be the upper limit. However, the energy requirements of many high-yielding dairy cows are such that diets based a 50:50 ratio contain insufficient energy. If the measures mentioned below (diet modifications) are used then the ratio can go to 40:60 forage to concentrates, however even using all the possible measures outlined below a ratio of 35:65 is about the upper limit. One of the major criticisms of this method of assessment is that with the increasing use of straights and the production of very leafy precision chopped silages the boundary between what is a forage and what is a concentrate is becoming unclear. For example brewers' grains are a by-product of barley but contain a high content of fibre (about 600 g NDF/kg DM) but the particle size of the fibre is short and does not promote chewing or saliva flow, so it may be considered to be a concentrate. On the other hand maize silage, a forage crop, contains significant amounts of starch (250 g/kg DM) so it is really not all forage.

The content of NDF in the diet. This reflects the amount of slowly digestible cell wall in the feed. A recommended lower limit is 35% to 40% of the total diet DM. In many diets for high-yielding cows (over 40 litres/day) this lower limit cannot be maintained and many 10,000 litre cows are given diets containing only 30% NDF during much of the lactation. It must be remembered that the cow does not know what NDF is, and whilst this measurement is a good assessment of the fibre content of a ration it says nothing about the physical properties of the fibre. Long stemmy material will promote more rumination than a leafy precision-chopped silage and will often alleviate a sub-clinical acidosis and stimulate intake. Evidence of this can often be seen when cows are given the choice of "poor" (low energy) big bale silage and "good" high energy clamp silage. Intake of the big bale silage is often considerable and although, in theory, energy intake falls, milk quality and production often increases as the cows eat more total feed.

The content of starch and sugars in the diet. The total content of starch and sugar reflects the amount of rapidly digestible organic matter in the diet. A recommended upper limit is 20 to 25% of the total diet DM, but this may be increased to 30% in well-managed diets for high-yielding cows. However, measuring the content of starch in feeds in the laboratory is difficult and is not always performed on a routine basis. As a result the feed database is patchy.

Dietary modification
- **Include sodium bicarbonate**. The rumen pH is depressed by the lactic acid because the amount of acid produced exceeds the buffering capacity. The main buffers in the rumen are sodium bicarbonate and phosphates from the saliva. With rations containing high levels of compound feeds and low fibre levels chewing and rumination times are reduced (see Chapter 4, page 44), which reduces the amount of saliva and hence the buffering capacity of the rumen fluid. Adding sodium bicarbonate to the ration can augment the salivary bicarbonate and increase the rumen buffering capacity. An alternative, which is physiologically better, is to add long fibre to the ration and hence stimulate chewing and saliva flow.

- **Include starch in a less rapidly-released form**. Rumen pH is depressed by the rapid release of a large amount of starch (Table 5.4). If the starchy feeds are offered in a form where the starch is released at a slower rate, then the rumen pH will not be so depressed. For sheep this means the feeding of whole uncrushed grains, and for cattle the grains need only be lightly bruised rather than heavily rolled or crushed. Treatment of grain with sodium hydroxide also slows down the release of starch as the grains are still whole when fed but their outer husk has been damaged by the caustic action of the treatment. On the other hand it has been shown that the less aggressive chemical reaction that takes place when whole-crop wheat is treated with urea can be insufficient and many grains can pass straight through the cow without releasing their starch.

- **Feed starchy feeds little and often**. The amount of lactic acid produced is related to the amount of starch released at any one time. This can be reduced by limiting the amount of starchy concentrates eaten at any one time. High-yielding dairy cows may be receiving 12 to 14 kg of concentrates a day. If all the concentrate is given in the

parlour then this is 6 to 7 kg in a 5 to 10 minute period of milking which can amount to 2 to 3 kg of starch. To overcome this rapid intake of large amounts of starch, out-of-parlour feeders have been developed which allow cows to receive their concentrates throughout the day in several small feeds. Complete diet feeding is another application of this principle.

Note   All the above recommendations assume that farmers want to maintain or boost milk fat. In the future, due to quota constraints and changing market demands, farmers will often want to depress milk fat. Whilst this is quite easy to do, by ignoring the above recommendations, achieving low fat without impairing intake, milk protein and cow health has not received the attention it deserves - see Chapter 13 for further details.

5.9.2   *Fibre requirements*
For "safe" and efficient rumen function the animal has a need for a certain amount of fibre. This fibre is required to ensure that the animal chews the cud enough and therefore salivates. The length and structure of fibre in the feed is important as this will determine how much a food needs chewing which therefore affects saliva flow. Thus fine chopped straw is far less effective than unprocessed straw or hay with fibres 10 to 20 cm long in stimulating saliva production.

Fibre can be measured in several ways; the simplest of which is the amount of fibrous materials fed. This is a subjective judgement but does allow consideration of the length of fibre particles. It has been suggested that 2 kg a day of forage longer than 10 cm length supplies adequate fibre to a cow, but this is very subjective.

Forage to concentrate ratio can be used as an indication of the fibre content of a feed. However, if the type of forage is not known, the ratio is of little use in assessing levels of fibre intake. This is because there is a wide range in content of fibre of different forages. For example, barley straw will promote far more chewing and rumination than will the same amount of precision-chopped, early cut, leafy grass silage.

A more objective way is to use a chemical estimation of the feed such as neutral detergent fibre (NDF) to reflect its fibre content in conjunction with a physical assessment of fibre particle size. It is considered that the diet should contain 35 to 40% NDF with 75% of this coming from forage and that the average forage particle length should exceed 1.5 cm.

5.9.3   *Low milk fat syndrome*
Low milk fat syndrome can be a manifestation of sub-clinical acidosis seen in high-yielding cows given high levels of concentrates together with high-energy

forages such as leafy silage (see Figure 5.6). Such forages are often low in fibre and so chewing and rumination are reduced, leading to a fall in rumen pH. As the pH falls the pattern of fermentation shifts towards producing more propionate and less acetate and butyrate. Approximately 50% of milk fat is synthesised from acetate and butyrate, so milk fat drops. The problem can be overcome by manipulating the way the high-starch concentrates are fed and by manipulating the fibre content of the ration.

Figure 5.6   The development of low milk fat syndrome in dairy cows

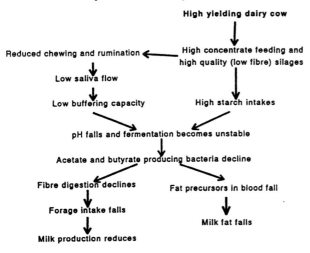

5.9.4   Ketosis due to dietary energy deficiency

Ketosis is seen commonly in high-yielding dairy cows particularly just after calving. In order to understand and therefore prevent the disorder it is necessary to consider the biochemistry of energy metabolism (Figure 5.7). As mentioned previously the main sources of energy to the dairy cow are the volatile fatty acids that are absorbed from the rumen. Acetate and butyrate are converted to acetyl CoA and to energy via the Krebs Cycle in the liver. On entering the cycle, acetyl CoA combines with oxaloacetic acid (OAA) to form citrate. Citrate passes through a series of intermediate steps to become OAA again during which energy is released and two molecules of carbon dioxide are produced. Most tissues can use a range of energy sources, but the udder, brain and foetus require glucose. As mentioned previously very little glucose is absorbed from the intestines and therefore it must be synthesised in the liver from propionate using OAA as an intermediate compound.

Ketosis can develop when demand for glucose is high and intake of dietary energy is inadequate to meet requirements. Two things occur in this situation. Firstly, as the concentration of blood glucose falls the concentration of OAA is reduced and this slows the Krebs Cycle as acetyl CoA cannot be incorporated to form citrate. Secondly, as intake of energy is inadequate, energy reserves are mobilised and deposits of fat are converted to free fatty acids (FFA; also called non-esterified fatty acids, NEFA). The FFA would be converted to acetyl CoA and enter the Krebs Cycle but as OAA is limiting they accumulate in the blood and liver. Accumulated acetyl CoA is converted into aceto-acetate and beta-hydroxy-butyrate (βHB) which are collectively called ketones, hence the name of the disorder, ketosis.

Clinical signs of ketosis. The initial clinical signs of ketosis are due to the low glucose supply to the brain. Cows usually become dull and lethargic but a small proportion (10%) can show aggressive nervous signs. The reduced glucose supply also limits milk production. If mobilised fatty acids cannot be con-

Figure 5.7   Energy metabolism in the dairy cow

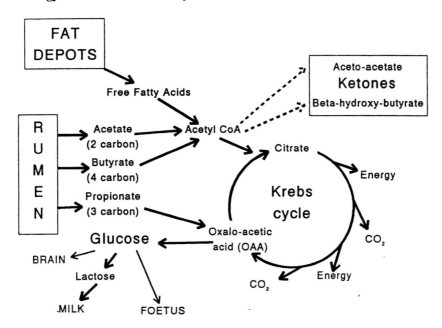

verted into acetyl CoA or ketone bodies they accumulate in the blood and liver and can result in severe fatty deposits (fatty liver).

Diagnosis. Diagnosis is initially on clinical grounds; a freshly calved cow which is slightly off-colour, dull and lethargic and with a depressed milk yield. Further diagnosis depends on detecting the ketones and fatty acids. Aceto-acetate has a typical "pear-drop" smell and many people can smell this on an affected cow's breath. Ketones can also be detected in the milk using "Rotheras" powders and βHB, FFA and NEFA can all be measured in the blood. Such blood tests are central to the metabolic profile and will be considered further in Chapter 17.

Treatment. In dairy cows many mild cases are self-limiting in that as milk yield falls the demand for glucose falls to match production. More severe cases can be treated in various ways. The drain of glucose can be reduced by restricting milking or aborting pregnant animals. Glucose (or glucose precursors such as glycerol) can be given by mouth to increase supply. As glucose is synthesised in the liver, drugs that stimulate liver function are very useful. The anabolic steroids were an excellent treatment in this respect but have now been banned. Other steroids such as cortisone will also stimulate the liver but they have unfortunate side effects of making the cow more prone to infectious diseases and causing abortion.

Prevention. Many high-yielding cows are likely to suffer sub-clinical ketosis and it is sadly regarded as an occupational hazard. But, as with most nutritional disorders, it is important to control the problem so it does not economically impair production. Cows should not be "steamed up" in the dry period nor given large amounts of concentrates immediately post-calving as this stimulates milk production and glucose demand. Every effort should be made to maximise intake post-calving (see Chapters 4 and 15) so that energy consumption better matches output.

Cows should not be too fat at calving as they are more likely to succumb to ketosis than thinner cows for two reasons. Firstly, fat cows have more fat depots to mobilise and therefore will do so more readily and in such quantities as to "flood" the Krebs Cycle. Secondly they eat less than "fit" cows (see Chapter 15) and therefore intake of energy in early lactation is likely to be less than that of thinner cows. Fat reserves are often assessed using condition scoring in which cows are scored from 1 (emaciated) to 5 (obese) (see Chapter 17 for more details) and the target should be for cows to calve at score 3.0.

5.9.5 *Fatty liver*

Fatty liver was first detected in the herds at the Institute of Animal Health at Compton, Berkshire, in the 1980s (Morrow, 1976). The disease was common in all of the Institute herds and was the subject of considerable research interest as it appeared to be the root of many of the causes of poor performance in newly-calved cows. Subsequent work in commercial herds has failed to identify it as a routine herd problem, but it is still seen in individuals and very occasionally on a herd basis. Cows in good condition at calving and in negative energy balance mobilise fat deposits as a source of energy. As blood glucose levels are low the concentration of OAA in the liver also falls which slows the Krebs Cycle (Figure 5.7). Acetyl CoA can not be converted into energy and so there is a "back-damming" of free fatty acids (FFA) and non-esterified fatty acids (NEFA). If the energy deficit and subsequent mobilisation of body reserves is large then the FFA circulating in the blood stream are deposited in the liver and, to a lesser extent, in other tissues. If the build up of fatty acids in the liver is too great then their physical presence can hamper hepatic function.

Clinical signs. The clinical history of cows susceptible to fatty liver is one of over-fatness at calving, being in major energy deficit and mobilising excessive amounts of weight (often in excess of 1 kg/day). The signs of impaired hepatic function are more difficult to detect but are thought to predispose the cow to the many problems that can occur at calving (milk fever, mastitis, metritis etc.) and to reduce the response to treatment and slow clinical recovery.

Diagnosis. The clinical history of over-fat cows at calving losing a lot of weight is highly suggestive of this disorder. Final diagnosis can be made by examining a liver biopsy. A large (1 g) sample of liver tissue is taken and histologically stained for fat. Microscopic examination of the biopsy tissue is used to determine the proportion of fat in a cross-section of the tissue. If more than 20 % of the cross-sectional area is occupied by fat then a definitive diagnosis can be made. If liver infiltration is severe, raised concentrations of the liver specific enzymes will increase in blood samples.

Treatment. Treatment is not easy as there are no drugs specific for liver damage. Much of the treatment is similar to that given for ketosis; energy-rich foods can be given to reduce the energy deficit and steroids to stimulate liver function.

Most of the stored body reserves are in the form of fat and thus the animal has more energy reserves to mobilise than protein reserves. The result is that the amount of production achieved by the mobilised reserves is limited by their protein content. For example, a kilogram of weight loss will supply sufficient energy for about 6.5 litres of milk but will only supply enough protein for about 3.5 litres. Protein mobilisation therefore restricts the use of energy mobilised and, not having anywhere else to go, FFA accumulate in the blood and then in the liver. It follows that if additional protein were supplied then the mobilised FFA could be utilised for milk production. However, a source of DUP must be used as a supplement not ERDP. If ERDP is used there will be insufficient FME for the microbes to convert it into microbial protein and hence it will be lost to the urine as urea.

Prevention. Prevention is centred around preventing animals being too fat at calving. Fat cows have lower feed intakes and are therefore more prone to mobilise their body reserves. As mentioned in Section 5.9.4, cows should be in a condition score of about 3.0 at calving. If previous management has resulted in over-fat cows then the feeding of high-DUP supplements in the period immediately post-calving should minimise the likelihood of fatty liver.

5.10   Beyond metabolisable energy

Throughout the development of the ME system it has been shown that the system works well for cows with average and low milk yields (<6,000 l/year) but there is a growing realisation that it is not sufficient for the fine tuning of the high-yielding dairy cow. This is not surprising when one considers how crude an assessment metabolisable energy is of the energy content of a feed. Energy sources in a feed can come from a range of chemical substances and they are digested very differently in the cow (Table 5.5).

Table 5.5   Fate of various feed components when used as sources of energy by the dairy cow

Source of energy	Fate in dairy cow
Sugars and starch	Broken down rapidly in the rumen to VFA
Fibre	Broken down slowly in rumen and large intestine to VFA
Fats	Absorbed in small intestine but can impair rumen activity
Protein	Either broken down in rumen to ammonia and VFA, or converted in the liver to energy
Silage acids	Absorbed directly in the rumen making little or no contribution to microbial metabolism

Many nutritionists are now considering the different feed components separately and some guidelines as to rate of inclusion are beginning to emerge (Table 5.6). Too much starch (or too little NDF) will result in rapid fermentation, an unstable rumen, do-mination of *lactobacilli* and the formation of lactic acid and a pH depression. Too little starch in the diet, particularly in conjunction with high silage fermentation acid content, will result in reduced microbial activity due to a lack of available energy for the microbial population in the rumen. Reduced microbial activity will increase requirements for by-pass protein in the diet and decrease appetite. Too much protein in the diet will result in excessive de-amination in the liver, reduce liver function and possibly limit fertility. Too much fat can depress appetite and alter milk composition, but the extent

to which these effects occur depends on the type of fat used. Too much NDF will depress intake, but this will rarely be reached in diets for high-yielding cows. The lower limit of crude protein will be determined by the animal's protein requirements.

Table 5.6   Suggested optimal levels of inclusion for dietary sources of energy

Nutrient	Lower limit	Upper limit
	% of total diet DM	
Starch and sugar	12	22
NDF	32	50
Oil	0	6
Crude protein	12	19

5.10.1   Rumen-resistant starch

As mentioned earlier it has been recognised that, in some diets, considerable amounts of starch escape microbial degradation and pass undigested into the small intestine. Here the starch is broken down and absorbed and may form a valuable source of glucose. Table 5.7 shows some results obtained from feeding high-starch diets to steers. As starch intake increased from 1.9 to 2.7 kg/day the proportion degraded in the rumen declined and the proportion digested in the small intestine increased which presumable resulted in a similar increase in glucose absorption. However, it is worth noting that these diets used very high levels of maize grain, far higher levels than are likely to be used in the UK. The diets were also being fed to steers which would either have been at mainten-ance or a low level of production. Rate of rumen outflow will have been slower than in the high-yielding dairy cow and hence rumen degradation of starch may have be higher than in a dairy cow.

Table 5.7   Partition of starch digestion between different sections of the intestines for ground maize diets fed to steers (Kara *et al.*, 1966)

	Diet		
Ground maize (g/kg)	400	600	800
Lucerne hay (g/kg)	530	310	75
Starch (g/day)			
Consumed	1948	2438	2684
Entering small intestine	544	778	982
Leaving small intestine	81	169	358
In faeces	19	39	62
Starch digestion (g/kg intake)			
Ruminal	721	681	634
Small intestine	238	250	336
Large intestine	32	53	110
Undigested	10	16	23

Paradoxically, an increase in starch supply usually causes an increase in milk protein rather than yield or milk fat. The explanation for this is thought to lie in the small intestine. The small intestine is a very active organ with considerable tissue turn-over and hence high energy requirements. Rather than drawing energy from the arterial blood supply (as other tissues do) the intestinal tissues merely draw upon nutrients passing through from the gut contents to the blood vessels. On traditional high-fibre diets, there is very little glucose in the absorbed nutrients and therefore amino acids are deaminated and used as energy sources. This results in a decreased supply of amino acids to the liver and hence the udder.

It is thought that increasing the supply of starch, and hence glucose, to the small intestine spares amino acids from deamination here and in the liver and therefore increases amino acid supply to the udder and hence increases milk protein production. Not all starch sources appear to behave in the same way. Maize starch seems to be the most resistant to microbial degradation and hence the effect of starch on milk protein content is seen mainly on diets which contain maize silage and ground-ear maize. If highly degradable starches are eaten increases in propionate production in the rumen and hence increased glucose synthesis in the liver can be observed. If this glucose is not used by the udder to produce lactose and milk fat, then the increased insulin production in response to elevated blood glucose is likely to trigger fat deposition and body weight gain.

The above results have lead to the concept of "rumen-resistant starch" (RRS). It is, however, very difficult to measure the actual rate of starch degradation, hence RRS tends to be a static measurement unrelated to rumen retention time and outflow rate.

5.11   Fat

High-yielding dairy cows in early lactation have a high energy requirement (a cow yielding 40 litres a day requires about 270 MJ ME/day) but may have an intake of less than 20 kg DM in the few weeks after calving. A 20 kg DM intake requires an energy density of 13.5 MJ ME/kg DM and with wheat at about 13.7 MJ and good silage at about 11 MJ ME/kg DM, the diet will have to contain large amounts of wheat to satisfy the animal's energy requirements. Too much wheat in a diet results in starch overload and the development of acidosis, indigestion, low milk fat and poor performance. Fats typically contain 35 MJ ME/kg DM and their use in such rations is very attractive as it allows the total amount of concentrate to be reduced, which results in more silage being eaten. Thus the fibre content of the diet is increased and starch intake is reduced accordingly. There may also be a reduction in cost, since fat is often cheaper per unit of ME than cereal grain. However most fats are not inert in the rumen and care must be taken to ensure that they do not interfere with or impede microbial activity. The fat content of feeds traditionally used in ruminant rations varies from about 20 to 50 g/kg DM (Table 5.8) and diets that have not been deliberately supplemented with high-fat feeds typically contain 30 to 50 g fat/kg DM.

5.11.1   Digestion of fat

Whilst fats contribute energy to the ruminant, they are not available as a source of energy to the rumen microbes to use to fix protein (see Chapter 6) and are therefore not part of the fermentable metabolisable energy (FME) of a ration. When supplementary fats are fed to a dairy cow two things happen to them in the rumen. Firstly the fatty acids are saturated. As the rumen is anaerobic there is a surplus of hydrogen and any "sink" for hydrogen ions is fully exploited by the microbial population. The normal "sink" is to attach four hydrogen atoms to a carbon atom to form methane but if any unsaturated fats are present then the double bonds are split to accommodate two hydrogen atoms. Table 5.9 shows how fat is processed in the rumen.

Table 5.8   Typical fat content of some common feeds

	Fat content (g/kg DM)
Grasses and silages	20 to 40
Grains	20 to 40
Grain by-products	50 to 80
Solvent extracted protein meals	20 to 40
Expelled protein meals	40 to 80

Table 5.9   Digestion of fat in the rumen

	Total fat (g)	C18 Oleic acid (saturated)	C18.2 Linoleic acid (unsaturated)	C18.3 Linolenic acid (unsaturated)
Feed	112	4	48	15
Duodenum	136	81	5	0.7

There is higher concentration of fat in the duodenum than in the feed because the rumen microbes have synthesised some fat. As the fat has been modified in the rumen the amount of fully-saturated eighteen carbon-chained fatty acid (C18) has increased and the amount with two (C18.2) and three (C18.3) double bonds has decreased. As a result virtually all the fat leaving the rumen is completely saturated and hence all dairy cow products are high in saturated fatty acids but low in unsaturated fatty acids. Saturated fatty acids are considered to be harmful to human health and are also solid at refrigerator temperature whereas most unsaturated fatty acids are liquids. This explains why butter will not spread straight from the fridge whereas margarine will!

Secondly, fats are adsorbed on to feed particles and on the surface of the microbes themselves which impairs microbial digestion. This results in a reduction in the rate of degradation of plant material and hence a fall in intake and reduced utilisation of protein (nitrogen) in the rumen. The production of VFA is reduced and the pattern changes; acetic and butyric acid production from fibre degradation declines whilst propionic acid production increases. The increased supply of dietary long-chain fatty acids (LCFA) in the udder inhibit acetic/butyric conversion to short-chained fatty acids and hence in some

Figure 5.8   Schematic diagram of the digestion of fat by the ruminant

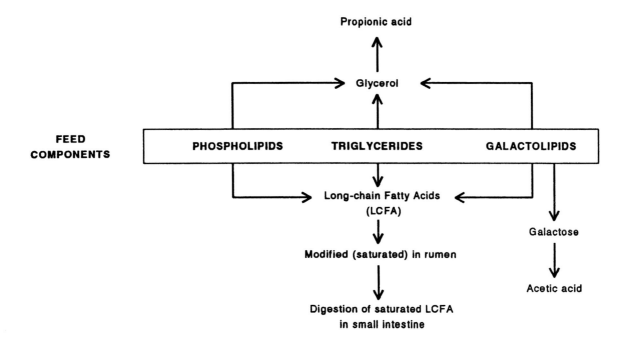

instances milk fat production can decline. The only possible beneficial effect of all this is that the rumen protozoa may be killed which may increase the efficiency of energy use in the rumen.

5.11.2   Inclusion of fat in diets
Fats are used in rations for two reasons; to increase the energy density of the diet and to increase the output of milk fat.

Increasing energy intake. Figure 5.8 summarises the digestion of fats in the ruminant. It can be seen that as well as supplying long-chain fatty acids they also supply smaller amounts of propionic and acetic acid.

The response in milk production to fat depends on the type and the amount of fat in the diet (Figure 5.9). The response to unprotected fat peaks at about 40 to 50 g fat/kg DM intake and then decreases. Given that the fat content of many common feeds ranges from 20 to 40 g/kg DM (Table 5.8) there is little scope for supplementation with unprotected fats. Where such fats are used, it is often for other reasons. For example, coating pelleted feeds with fat helps them to flow better through pellet presses, storage bins and conveyors.

Protection of fat allows much higher inclusions of up to 130 g/kg DM with a continual increase in milk production (Figure 5.9).

Increasing milk fat. Milk fat contains a wide range of fatty acids ranging in length from four to eighteen carbons (Table 5.10). The shorter carbon chains can be synthesised by the cow but the longer ones (more than 14 carbons) must come from dietary sources. It

Figure 5.9   Milk production responses to supplementary fat in experimental trials (Naylor and Ralson, 1991)

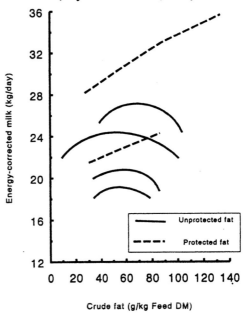

would therefore be logical to assume that increasing the intake of longer-chain fatty acids would increase milk fat production. However, the responses seen from including fats in dairy cow rations have been very variable (see Chapter 13, page 134). The reason for the variable response may be seen from looking at Figure 5.10. Whilst dietary fat is required for the synthesis of the milk fat, a source of glucose and energy are also required to form triglycerides. The rest of the fatty acids (the shorter chains) are synthesised from acetate and butyrate and are dependent on a good supply from the rumen fermentation process. The net effect of adding fat to the diet depends on the stimulation of the upper synthesis route without the depression of the lower route (Figure 5.10). All too often the dietary fat has such a large effect on microbial activity that the depression of acetate and butyrate production outweighs the increased supply of fatty acids.

Table 5.10 Fatty acid composition of milk from cows

Fatty acid carbon chain length	g/kg total milk fat	
C4	30	
C6	25	
C8	15	Cow can
C10	30	synthesis
C12	38	these molecules
C14	125	
C16	340	
C18	117	These molecules
C18.1	218	must come from
C18.2	27	the diet

Figure 5.10   Pathways of milk fat synthesis

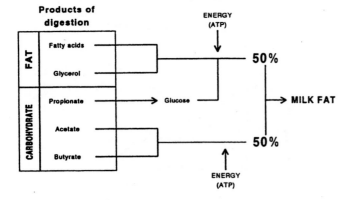

5.11.3   *Protected Fats*
Given the potential benefits of fats in terms of increased energy and fatty acid intake and the beneficial effects of inclusions of protected fats (Figure 5.9), there has been considerable interest in their development. The protection has two aims: Firstly, protection of the rumen microflora so that higher fat levels can be fed without causing digestive upsets. Secondly, and less importantly, protection of the fat from the actions of the rumen microbes so that milk produced would contain unsaturated fatty acids which would be healthier and produce butter that is easier to spread. Whilst there has been a lot of research on protecting fats it should be emphasised that not all protection techniques are equal and that there are considerable differences between different processes that use the same tech-

nique. Most people therefore refer to specific protected fats rather than a generic group produced by one technique. The methods of protection can be divided into four categories:

Fat coated with protein. The aim is to coat the fat particle with a layer of treated protein that is resistant to microbial activity but will be digested together with the fat in the small intestine. The proteins used have been blood meal (prior to the BSE ban) and soya flour, heated or treated with formaldehyde to reduce degradability in the rumen. Although there is good experimental evidence that such protected fats are effective, they are not widely used at present for financial reasons.

Whole oil seeds. If small oil seeds are fed whole they may escape rupture through chewing and their small size and density should cause them to sink to the bottom of the rumen and pass on into the abomasum and small intestine where the seed would be digested and the oil released. It is possible, however, that if the seed does not get broken in the mouth or in the rumen, it will pass straight through the animal and no oil will be released at all - as can happen with whole wheat and barley grains. The technique is very price-sensitive and is only worthwhile when world vegetable oil prices are low.

Spray-cooled fatty acids. Fatty acids such as palmate have a high melting point so may not disperse in the rumen and hence present a smaller surface area to the microbes. Saturated long-chain fatty acids such as palmitic and stearic acids (C16 and C18) are insoluble in the rumen and therefore do not interfere with microbial activity.

Calcium salts of fatty acids. The calcium reduces the effects on rumen microbes as the calcium salt is insoluble in rumen liquor, but dissociates to free calcium and free fatty acid in the abomasum. In addition, careful selection of the fatty acid can reduce the extent to which it is likely to disperse in the rumen.

5.11.4   *Health problems with high-fat diets*
Many of the animal health problems which can arise from the effect of fats on rumen microbes are associated with inappetence, ketosis or indigestion. Increases in hypocalcaemia and hypomagnesaemia have also been observed, attributed to the binding of free fatty acids by calcium and magnesium in the rumen and small intestine. To compensate for the reduced availability of calcium, the Americans recommend raising the calcium content of the ration by 0.1% when fats are included. Vitamins A, D, and E are fat-soluble, so increasing dietary fat can decrease the absorption of these vitamins.

CHAPTER 6

PROTEIN

6.1   Introduction

6.2   Units of measurement

6.3   Protein digestion
   6.3.1   Sources of protein
   6.3.2   Sites of protein digestion
   6.3.3   Functions of rumen microbes

6.4   The Metabolisable Protein system
   6.4.1   Variable degradability of feeds
   6.4.2   Digestibility of protein not degraded in the rumen
   6.4.3   Value of degraded protein to the microbes in the rumen
   6.4.4   Availability of energy to the microbes in the rumen
   6.4.5   The amount of microbial protein synthesised per MJ FME supplied
   6.4.6   Absorbed protein
   6.4.7   The Metabolisable Protein (MP) system

6.5   The industry's position regarding the MP system

6.6   Limitations of the MP system
   6.6.1   Assessment of degradability
   6.6.2   ADIN
   6.6.3   QDP
   6.6.4   FME
   6.6.5   Appraisal of the MP system

6.7   Beyond the MP system

6.8   Amino acids
   6.8.1   Responses to amino acid supplements

6.9   Response to feeding high protein rations

6.10 Practical aspects of protein digestion
   6.10.1 Matching the release of nitrogen and carbohydrate in the rumen
   6.10.2 Matching type of protein to requirements
   6.10.3 Matching levels of protein to requirements

6.1   Introduction

Protein is the third most important limiting factor in dairy cow nutrition after voluntary intake and energy. This is particularly so with high-yielding dairy cows, as their milk has a much higher protein: energy ratio than any other ruminant product. Our understanding of protein digestion in ruminants has progressed considerably over the past twenty years and is now markedly more sophisticated than the metabolisable energy system. Since 1992 a new set of feeding standards that incorporate the Metabolisable Protein system have been in use in the United Kingdom. Whilst most countries in the Developed World use either the metabolisable or net energy systems they all have their own protein standards. The different systems all have their merits, but one thing is certain: the large number of systems in use means that none of them are correct! Further research into new feeding standards will be expensive and, for reasons that will be discussed later, may not be very fruitful.

This chapter is concerned with the principles of protein digestion and metabolism. The calculation of requirements and dietary supply is discussed in Chapter 10.

6.2   Units of measurement

The protein content of a feed is measured as crude protein (CP) which is calculated from the chemical determination of the nitrogen content of the feed. It is then assumed that all the nitrogen in the feed comes from protein and that the protein contains 16% nitrogen. Therefore the CP content is the nitrogen content divided by 0.16 or multiplied by 6.25 (1/0.16 = 6.25). This is a very crude measurement of protein and it was soon realised that the crude protein of some feeds was more digestible than that of others. In general, feeds of high metabolisability (q) have high protein digestibilities and feeds of low metabolisability have low protein digestibilities. To recognise the value of the protein to the animal a new measurement, digestible crude protein (DCP), was used in diet formulation. This was an improvement over crude protein, but inconsistencies occurred when feeds containing high levels of non-protein nitrogen (NPN) were used. For example, urea contains 2,875 g of "digestible crude protein" per kilogram, yet its inclusion in diets at high levels can result in inefficient use by the animal compared to that of true proteins.

During the 1970s it was recognised that some dietary protein was broken down (degraded) in the rumen into ammonia and carbon fragments. The ammonia released was used by the microbes for protein synthesis. A smaller fraction of protein passed undigested into the abomasum and small intestines. The degradability of protein varied considerably from feed to feed. This led to the development of the theory that some protein was degraded in the rumen (rumen-degradable protein, RDP) whilst a smaller fraction was undegraded in the rumen (undegraded dietary protein, UDP) and passed into the abomasum.

It was only in the 1980s that sufficient data were available for this theory to be used in ration formulation. Under this system an animal's requirements for protein were expressed, initially, in terms of the net tissue protein (NP) required for the bodily processes. Then, by linking this to the energy supplied, the NP requirements were converted into RDP and UDP requirements. Feed analyses were given in terms of total crude protein content (CP) and the protein degradability (dg), from which the feed RDP and UDP content could be determined.

In 1992 the metabolisable protein system was published. This was a natural progression from the previous RDP/UDP system and incorporates various modifications relating to the breakdown of proteins and the availability of energy in the rumen.

6.3   Protein digestion

6.3.1   Sources of protein

Like all mammals, dairy cows can digest a wide variety of proteins from both animal and vegetable sources. However, the ruminants are also able to make use of nitrogen from non–protein sources (NPN) such as urea and ammonia. The microbes in the rumen assimilate the NPN into microbial protein and surplus and dead microbes pass on down the alimentary tract where their protein is broken down into amino acids and absorbed. However, about 25% of the nitrogen in the microbes is in non–protein molecules such as nucleic acids and therefore this is an inefficient way of digesting dietary protein.

6.3.2   Sites of protein digestion

A proportion of the dietary protein eaten by the cow is broken down by the microbes in the rumen into ammonia, energy and carbon fragments. This portion is called the Rumen-Degradable Protein (RDP). A smaller fraction of the protein (Undegradable Protein, UDP) passes intact into the abomasum. Some of the free ammonia in the rumen can be absorbed by the microbes and assimilated into microbial protein, part of which passes into the abomasum. The abomasum, therefore, contains protein of a dietary source as well as microbial protein. In the abomasum pepsin secreted by the gastric glands starts to digest the protein outflow from the rumen, breaking it down into peptide chains and eventually to individual amino acids. The breakdown into separate amino acids continues in the small intestine where they are absorbed into the blood stream.

6.3.3   Functions of rumen microbes

The protein requirements of the dairy cow must be considered both in terms of the animal's needs and the microbes' requirements. The animal's needs are linked to requirements for protein at the tissue level and will be dealt with later. The requirement for protein, or more correctly for nitrogen, by the microbial population of the rumen is linked to the amount of energy in the diet. As mentioned in the previous chapter, the majority of energy digestion (except fat and some starch) takes place within the rumen. The microbes can only convert dietary energy into VFA if they have sufficient nitrogen (and other elements such as sulphur and potassium) to meet their metabolic requirements. Therefore the RDP requirement of the ruminant is linked to energy intake and not to net tissue protein (NP) requirement. This means that animals at maintenance or at low levels of production require more RDP than is needed to supply TP requirements solely to ensure that the ruminal fermentation is optimal. The following points also arise from the fact that much of the ruminant's protein needs are met by microbial synthesis.

Non-essential amino acids. Microbially-synthesised protein is of a very high quality in that the balance of essential amino acids is very close to the dairy cow's requirements (Table 6.1). It is only in diets where a considerable amount of the dietary protein is in the form of by-pass protein that certain amino acids may become essential. Specific amino acid deficiencies (i.e. responses to supplementary amino acids) are generally limited to low–protein diets such as those based on maize silage. French workers have gone so far as to suggest specific amino acid requirements for ruminants but many English workers have failed to identify any response to specific amino acids and are questioning whether there is a specific requirement for amino acids. The subject of amino acid requirements will be considered in more detail in Section 6.8.

Non-protein nitrogen. Much of the protein eaten by the cow is degraded in the rumen to ammonia and it is possible to include non-protein nitrogen, such as urea, in diets in place of the RDP.

UDP requirements. Requirements for RDP and microbial protein synthesis are linked to energy intake, therefore the amount of microbial protein produced may fail to meet the requirements for net tissue protein if an animal is producing large amounts of high protein products, such as milk or lean tissue. In these cases the diet must contain a source of UDP. However, for the UDP source to be of any use it must be digestible. In the 1980s a considerable amount of UDP was used in rations, but as will be seen later, the new Metabolisable Protein (MP) system does not call for as much UDP in the diet and most rations do not need supplementing in this way. Despite this shift in rationing there are still a wide range of high-UDP supplements on the market.

Table 6.1 Essential amino acid composition (g/100 g CP) of cattle muscle, milk, rumen microbes and some common protein sources. Figures in brackets are an expression of amino acid composition as a proportion of cow's milk (van Soest, 1994)

	Cattle muscle	Cow's milk	Rumen bacteria	Rumen protozoa	Maize gluten	Brewers' grains	Soyabean meal
Arginine	7.7	3.7	9.1 (2.46)	9.0 (2.43)	3.2 (0.86)	2.6 (0.70)	8.4 (2.27)
Histidine	3.3	2.7	2.3 (0.85)	2.0 (0.74)	2.4 (0.89)	1.5 (0.56)	2.4 (0.89)
Isoleucine	6.0	6.0	6.4 (1.07)	7.0 (1.17)	4.3 (0.72)	3.5 (0.58)	4.2 (0.70)
Leucine	8.0	9.8	7.3 (0.74)	8.2 (0.84)	16.2 (1.65)	8.5 (0.87)	6.7 (0.68)
Lysine	10.0	8.2	9.3 (1.13)	9.9 (1.21)	1.2 (0.15)	2.1 (0.26)	5.7 (0.70)
Methionine	3.2	2.6	2.6 (1.00)	2.1 (0.81)	2.1 (0.81)	1.3 (0.50)	0.8 (0.31)
Phenylalanine	5.0	5.1	5.1 (1.00)	6.1 (1.20)	6.5 (1.27)	4.8 (0.94)	4.4 (0.86)
Threonine	5.0	4.6	5.5 (1.20)	4.9 (1.07)	2.9 (0.63)	2.8 (0.61)	3.3 (0.72)
Tryptophan	1.4	1.4	n/a	n/a	n/a	n/a	1.3 (0.93)
Valine	5.5	6.7	6.6 (0.99)	5.3 (0.79)	n/a	3.9 (0.58)	3.8 (0.57)

The digestion of protein is summarised in Figure 6.1. This was the basis of the RDP/UDP system proposed in 1980 and was used widely in the industry although it was never officially adopted in the UK. RDP which is surplus to microbial requirements is converted to ammonia and absorbed through the rumen wall into the blood and converted to urea in the liver before being excreted through the kidneys or recycled to the rumen in saliva. The undegradable portion of the feed protein (UDP) passes into the abomasum and lower intestines together with the microbial protein, where it is digested and absorbed.

Figure 6.1 Digestion of protein in the ruminant

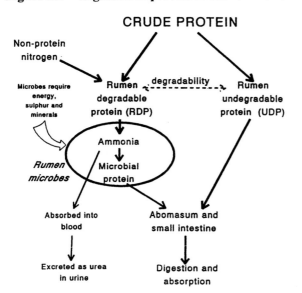

It is important to understand the digestive pathways shown in Figure 6.1 as they form the basis of the new metabolisable protein system. The MP system is a direct development of the RDP/UDP system but the two protein fractions are further subdivided and the description of the degradability of feeds and the supply of energy have been redefined.

6.4 The Metabolisable Protein system

Ever since the RDP/UDP system was first proposed there have been concerns about some of its shortcomings. In 1980 an expert group was set up to reconsider the protein rationing systems in the UK. Their proposals, a new protein system called the Metabolisable Protein system, were adopted rapidly by the advisory services and the UK animal feed industry. The new developments in the MP system are as follows.

6.4.1 Variable degradability of feeds

The RDP/UDP system assumed the degradability of a given feed in the rumen was constant (Figure 6.1). This is an over-simplification for the following reason; high-yielding cows eat more feed, therefore the feed passes faster through the rumen than in lower-yielding cows. The faster the feed passes through the rumen the less time it is exposed to the microbial population and a smaller proportion is degraded. For some feeds, such as soyabean meal, the retention time of the feed in the rumen alters the degradability of protein considerably. Thus for high-yielding dairy cows with short retention times a large proportion of the protein escapes degradation whereas in low-producing and dry cows most of the soyabean meal protein is degraded. Other feeds such as fishmeal are less affected in this way (see Figure 6.2).

In the high-yielding dairy cow during the short period of time the feed is retained in the rumen the proportion of the protein degraded by the microbes is about the same for both feeds at 0.4 g/g (Figure 6.2). However, for the lower-yielding animal with a longer feed retention time, the degradability of the soyabean meal has increased considerably to about 0.85 g/g whereas that for fishmeal has changed only slightly to 0.55 g/g. However, if such concepts of variable degradability are to be used on a routine basis there must be a method of measuring the degradability and converting it into a mathematical format that can be incorporated easily into computer programs.

Figure 6.2   The effect of rumen retention time on the proportion of protein degraded in soyabean meal and fishmeal

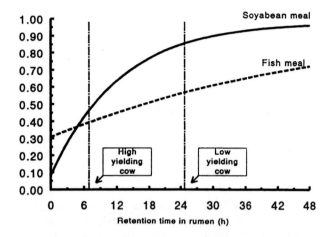

Measurement of protein degradability. The method currently used for measuring degradability was first proposed in the 1970s and has been used in research centres worldwide ever since. Although there have been many criticisms as to the value and repeatability of the technique to date nothing has replaced it. A known amount of feed is placed in a small bag made of a finely woven synthetic fibre which will not be digested in the rumen and has a pore diameter of about 0.05 mm. The bag is sealed and then placed in the rumen of a sheep or cow and weighed down to hold it in the rumen liquor. After a given incubation time the bag is removed, washed thoroughly, dried and then the amount of dry matter and nitrogen lost from the bag is determined. A range of different incubation times (for instance 3, 6, 12, 24 and 48 hours) are used to construct a graph similar to that shown in Figure 6.3.

Figure 6.3   Degradation of protein in the rumen

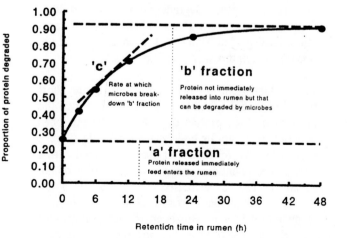

The losses at zero hours are determined by washing the bag without placing it in the rumen. The curve is described mathematically by three parameters generally referred to as "a", "b" and "c". The "a" fraction is that which is lost from the bag which was not placed in the rumen but washed, and represents the immediate losses when a feed enters the rumen. The "b" fraction is the difference between "a" and the maximum amount of feed that is degraded if the feed is left in the rumen for a long time (up to 100 hours) and represents the portion of the feed that could potentially be degraded if the microbes had long enough to do so. The final parameter "c" describes how quickly the "b" fraction is degraded by the microbes. Typical values for soyabean meal and fishmeal are shown in Table 6.2.

Table 6.2   Typical degradability parameters for soyabean meal and fishmeal

	"a" (g/g)	"b" (g/g)	"c" (/h)
Soyabean meal	0.08	0.89	0.081
Fishmeal	0.29	0.63	0.019

The low value of the "a" fraction for soyabean meal means very little is lost on washing and thus the losses at 0 h are low whereas the higher value for fishmeal indicates a higher loss from the washed bag. For both feeds "a" + "b" approach 1.0, indicating that, given enough time, the microbes could break down most of the protein. This is the case for most proteins as there is such a wide range of microbes and enzymes in the rumen. If protein cannot ultimately be broken down in the rumen it is unlikely to be capable of being broken down in the small intestines. The "c" value (rate of degradation) for soyabean meal is faster than for fishmeal. This can be seen graphically in Figure 6.2.

The next stage in using variable degradability data in routine ration formulation is to be able to relate the retention time of the feed to animal parameters and then to predict the retention time for a given animal. Experimentally, it is easier to measure the rate at which rumen contents leaves the rumen rather than retention time of feeds. Rate of outflow of feed from the rumen can be related mathematically to retention time and therefore the "a", "b" and "c" parameters can be used to predict degradation of the feed from a given rate of outflow. It is more difficult to predict the rate of outflow of a feed for a given class of animal. There are very little data on this subject but it is possible to relate outflow rate to level of production (Animal Production Level, APL) which is the total energy requirements divided by maintenance requirements (Chapter 5, page 54). (Thus a cow yielding 25 litres of milk daily, with a total energy requirement of 210 MJ and a maintenance energy requirement of 70 MJ, has APL of 3.0.) Figure 6.4 shows the relationship between APL and rumen outflow rate. It can be seen that for animals at maintenance the outflow rate is 0.02 or 2% of the rumen contents per hour. This rises to about 7% for cows giving about 20 litres of milk and 10% for animals giving 40 litres of milk. However, it should be emphasised that there is very little experimental evidence to support this graph!

Figure 6.4   Relationship between level of production (APL) and predicted rumen outflow rate (AFRC, 1992)

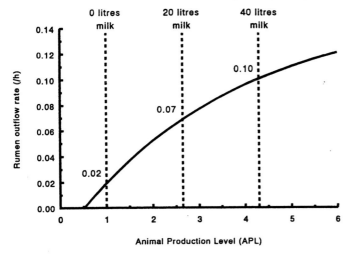

Figure 6.5 shows the effective degradability of soyabean meal and fishmeal plotted against level of production. At APL = 1.0 (which is an animal at maintenance) the feeds stay in the rumen for a long time and hence most of the protein is degraded for both feeds. As the level of production (APL) increases the degradability falls for both feeds, but above an APL of 2.0 it falls faster for soyabean meal than for fishmeal as soyabean meal has the faster rate of degradability and is more sensitive to rumen retention time. The effective degradability of a given feed therefore depends on the level of production, and hence on rate of outflow as well as the specific degradability pattern for that feed.

Figure 6.5   Changes in degradability of soyabean meal and fishmeal with level of production (APL)

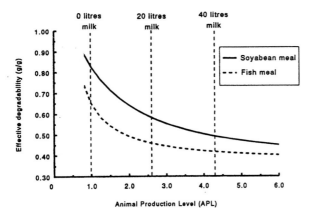

6.4.2   Digestibility of protein not degraded in the rumen

The RDP/UDP system (Figure 6.1) assumed that all protein that escaped ruminal degradation was digested in the small intestine or at least that the indigestible part was a constant fraction. When the system was used in practice farmers reported that they got a poor response to some UDP sources and in particular dark coloured feeds such as maize gluten and dark distillers' grains. These feeds are generally dark because they have been overheated and some of the protein has reacted with sugars in the feed to form an insoluble, indigestible product (Maillard compounds). When this occurs the undegradable protein is indigestible in the small intestine and passes out in the faeces. This indigestible protein behaves chemically rather like lignin and so the content of heat-damaged protein can usually be estimated by measuring the amount of nitrogen in the acid detergent fibre (ADF) fraction and is referred to as acid detergent insoluble nitrogen (ADIN). Table 6.3 gives ADIN values for some common feeds. ADIN is a measurement of nitrogen and therefore to use it in the MP system it is necessary to convert it to the protein equivalent "ADIP" by it multiplying by 6.25.

Table 6.3   Contents of ADIN and indigestible crude protein ("ADIP") in some common feeds (ADAS Feed Evaluation Unit, 1989)

	ADIN (g/kg DM)	"ADIP" (g/kg DM)	"ADIP" range (g/kg DM)	
			Min	Max
Grass hay	1.23	7.7	0.0	10.0
Barley straw	0.99	6.2	0.6	9.3
Fresh grass	1.05	6.6	1.9	35.6
Grass silage	1.30	8.1	1.9	13.7
Barley	0.37	2.3	1.2	3.1
Maize gluten feed	1.37	8.6	3.1	18.1
Wheat	0.25	1.6	1.2	1.9
Palm kernel meal	2.95	18.4	13.1	25.0
Rapeseed meal	3.63	22.7	18.7	29.3
Soyabean meal	2.15	13.4	5.0	16.3
Sunflower seed	2.02	12.6	9.4	14.3

It can be seen that some of the processed by-product feeds contain large amounts of ADIN and this can account for up to 10% of the total crude protein content of the feed. In practice most diets contain about 100 to 150 g of heat-damaged protein ("ADIP") per kg of dry matter. The Metabolisable Protein system discounts the amount of undegradable protein (UDP) that bypasses the rumen microbes by deducting the amount of "ADIP" in the feed from the total UDP to give the amount of protein that escapes microbial degradation, but which is digested and absorbed into the blood stream in the small intestine: it is known as Digestible Undegradable Protein (DUP).

6.4.3 Value of degraded protein to the microbes in the rumen

In the model of protein digestion in Figure 6.1 it was assumed that all the protein released in the rumen is of equal value to the rumen microbes. Most evidence suggests that, because the microbes break down dietary protein to ammonia, all nitrogen sources are of equal biological value in the synthesis of microbial protein. There are, however, considerable differences in the pattern of release of nitrogen in the rumen. As can be seen in Figure 6.2, the size of the "a" fraction (the intercept on the vertical axis) and the rate of protein degradation ("c") differ between feeds. The "a" fraction can range from 0.08 for soyabean meal to over 0.65 in grass silages. The rapid release of large amounts of nitrogen in the "a" fraction from feeds such as grass silage can exceed the microbes' capacity for nitrogen assimilation. Rumen ammonia concentrations rise and exceed the concentration in the blood, at which point ammonia diffuses across the rumen wall to be converted to urea in the liver and excreted via the kidney. This loss of nitrogen was first noted by farmers and advisers who commented that when they rationed to the RDP/UDP system they did not get such good results with grass silage as they did with other feeds such as fresh grass and hay.

The Metabolisable Protein System takes account of the pattern of release of the nitrogen in feeds by subdividing RDP into a quickly degraded protein (QDP) fraction which corresponds to the "a" fraction, and a slowly-degraded protein fraction (SDP) which is the difference between the "a" fraction and the total RDP at a specified rate of outflow. Only 80% of the QDP is considered to be available to the microbes with the other 20% being lost to the blood supply. The summed combination of the discounted QDP and the SDP is known as the "Effective Rumen Degradable Protein" (ERDP) and is the amount of protein, or nitrogen, available for microbial metabolism and growth.

6.4.4 Availability of energy to the microbes in the rumen

As mentioned previously the amount of ERDP the microbes can fix is dependent on the amount of energy available to them in the rumen. In the previous protein system the energy supply was considered as the amount of ME in the diet. However this is an over–simplification as certain metabolisable energy sources such as fat and volatile fatty acids are not used by the microbes as major sources of energy. The energy in fat (approximately 35 MJ/kg) is discounted as are the lactic and volatile fatty acids in silages. The energy available to the microbes is called the Fermentable Metabolisable Energy (FME) and is defined as the metabolisable energy minus the gross energy

content of the fermentation acids and the gross energy of the oil in the feed.

Oils are measured in the laboratory as ether extract. The major fermentation acids in silage are lactic, acetic, propionic and butyric acid. Whilst this is not a precise definition of which chemical components do not contribute to the energy supply in the rumen it is a suitable approximation (see below).

Table 6.4 gives an indication of the range in the content of oil and fermentation acids in first-cut grass silages. The total content of fermentation acids varies from almost zero to more than 200 g/kg DM, whilst the oil content varies from 8 to 47 g/kg. Such variations produce a wide variation in FME content and when this is expressed as a percentage of the ME content it can be seen that between 48 and 90% of the energy in the silage is available for microbial metabolism.

Table 6.4   Content of total fermentation acids, oil and energy of 93 first cut grass silages (Chamberlain *et al.*, 1993)

	Average	Minimum	Maximu
Dry Matter (%)	24	13.8	40.6
Lactic acid (g/kg DM)	68	Trace	193
Total fermentation acids (g/kg DM)	99	Trace	214
Oil (g/kg DM) (Ether Extract)	32	8.2	46.8
ME (MJ/kg DM) (From MADF)	10.3	8.8	11.8
FME (MJ/kg DM)	7.5	4.4	9.7
Fermentability (%) (FME/ME)	73	48	90

Total fermentation acids and the content of ether extract in silages can be predicted by Near Infra-red Reflectance spectroscopy (NIRs) with reasonable accuracy, so it is now possible to determine the FME content and the fermentability (FME/ME) of silages on a routine basis. The higher the fermentability, the larger the microbial population is likely to be in the rumen.

The wide range of energy availability in silages has several important implications for rations formulated to meet ME requirements. Silages with a high content of FME will have a reduced need for protein supplementation as there will be more energy to support the production of microbial protein from the nitrogen in the silage. Silages with low contents of FME will require supplementing with additional sources of FME, which in practice is usually starch. Therefore high FME silages will have a reduced need for starchy supplements and thus less risk of digestive upsets and acidosis. The more energy and nitrogen that can be supplied to the microbes in a balanced manner, the greater the microbial population and hence the faster plant material will be degraded and intake will be higher. Overall therefore a high-FME silage is likely to give rise to cheaper, nutritionally better rations.

Silages of low fermentability tend to be wetter and to have higher total acid contents and lower concentrations of residual sugars, whereas silages with high fermentability tend to be drier, lower in total acid content and to have higher concentrations of residual sugars. Table 6.5 shows the effects of using two silages that differ only in their fermentability in the formulation of rations for a dairy cow giving 30 litres of milk a day. The lower FME silage requires an additional 500 g of soyabean meal to make up for the reduced microbial protein synthesis. An alternative would be to supply more FME by including more of an energy feed (wheat). Of the two methods of supplementing a low fermentability silage the latter is preferable as the energy feed promotes a larger microbial population, faster feed degradation and higher feed intakes. However, care must be taken that total ME intake does not exceed requirements otherwise the animal will put on weight. In practice it has to be accepted that rations that contain a large proportion of extensively fermented silage will have excess ERDP and hence a deficiency of FME.

Table 6.5   Effect of fermentability in the rumen of silage on supplements needed for 30 litres of milk

Fermentability of silage	Low	High
Silage characteristics		
Dry matter (g/kg)	Low (less than 250)	High (more than 250)
Acid content (g/kg DM)	High (more than 100)	Low (less than 100)
Residual sugars	Low	High
Silage composition		
ME (MJ /kg DM)	11.1	11.1
FME (MJ /kg DM)	7.3	9.5
Fermentability	0.66	0.86
Crude protein (g/kg DM)	160	160
Supplements needed for 30 litres milk (kg)		
Energy feed (wheat)	4.0	4.0
Protein feed (soyabean meal)	0.7	0.2

The increased understanding of energy supply to the microbes and the cow is likely to have as much effect on ruminant nutrition as any other aspect of the MP system.

6.4.5   The amount of microbial protein synthesised per MJ FME supplied

In Figure 6.1 the activity of the rumen microbes and the amount of protein they synthesise is dependent on either the amount of nitrogen, energy, sulphur or other minerals available. In practice nitrogen or energy usually limit microbial protein production but sulphur may become important as emissions from industry decline (see Chapter 7, page 87). The metabolisable protein system takes into account the energy and protein supplied to determine the amount

of microbial crude protein (MCP) produced. If the supply of protein (nitrogen) is limiting then the amount of MCP produced equals the supply of ERDP. If energy is limiting then the amount of MCP synthesised depends on the amount of energy available and the yield of MCP per MJ of FME. The yield of MCP per megajoule of FME, known as Y, is shown in Figure 6.6. Y is not a constant value but is considered to increase with increasing animal production level. At lower levels of production the outflow rate from the rumen is lower (see Figure 6.4) and hence the digesta spend more time in the rumen. The lifespan of a rumen microbe is not very long. Dead microbes are digested by living ones and their protein is used to synthesise new microbial protein. Although the nitrogen is reused, energy is required so additional FME has to be supplied. The lower the level of production the more microbial nitrogen is recycled in the rumen and the less total MCP is produced per MJ of FME.

Figure 6.6   The relationship between animal production level (APL) and the predicted yield of microbial crude protein (MCP) per MJ of FME (Y)

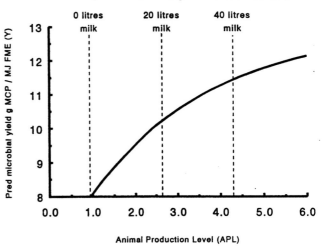

6.4.6   Absorbed protein

In the previous protein feeding standards, the efficiency of conversion of absorbed amino acids to tissue protein was assumed to be constant across all end uses. This is not the case for energy in the metabolisable energy system and is unlikely to be true for protein either. Body functions such as maintenance require the synthesis of a wide range of proteins and therefore a wide range of amino acids are needed. All the absorbed amino acids can be used in the synthesis of proteins and therefore little is likely to be wasted. When protein is used to meet a specific productive process, such as deposition of muscle tissue or production of milk protein which have specific protein profiles, it is likely that not all of the amino acids are utilised and some are surplus to requirements. The efficiency of use of the absorbed amino acids is therefore less than 1.00, and

Figure 6.7   The UK Metabolisable Protein system (see text for details of acronyms)

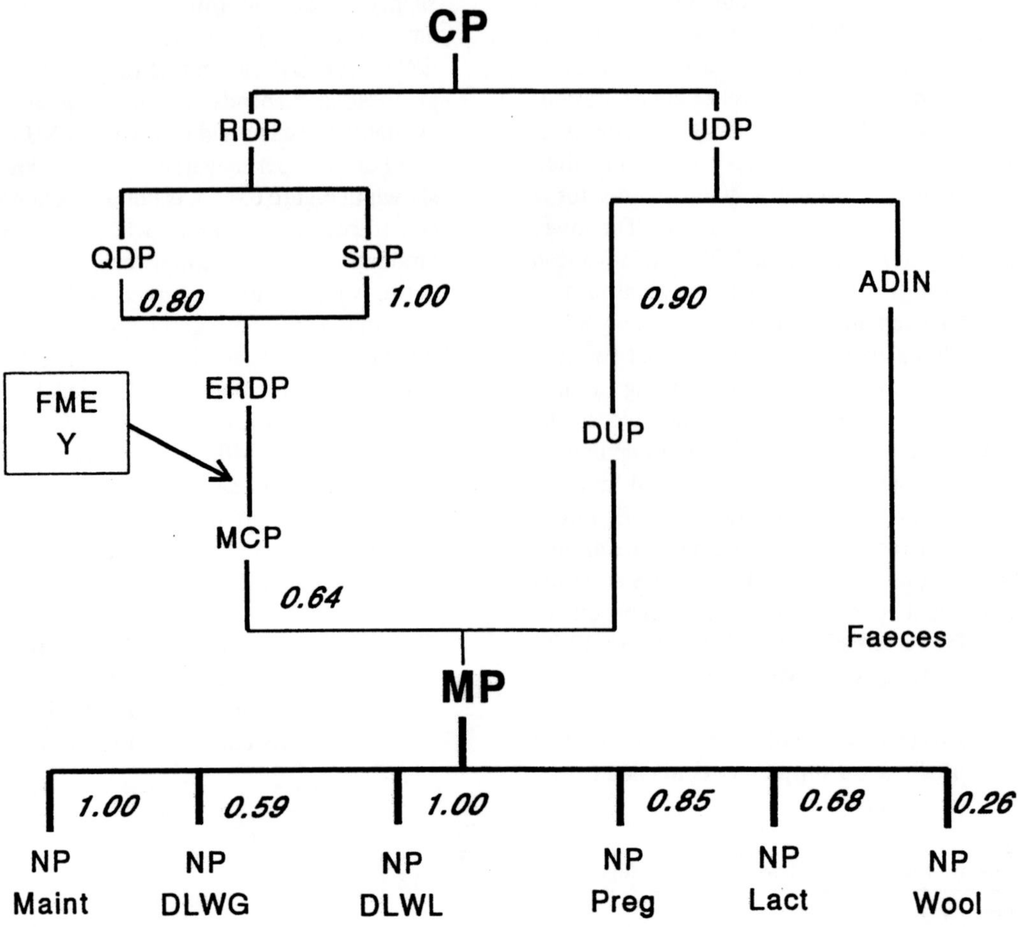

varies from 0.85 for pregnancy to 0.26 for hair and wool production. The variable efficiency of use of absorbed amino acids for different end uses is an extension of the concept of metabolisable protein to net protein, the proportion of the dietary crude protein which is actually used by a specific purpose.

6.4.7   The Metabolisable Protein (MP) system

The UK metabolisable protein (MP) system (AFRC, 1992) is summarised in Figure 6.7. Crude protein (CP) can still be considered as being divided into a fraction that is degraded in the rumen (RDP) and that which is undegraded in the rumen (UDP) although these two terms are not actually included in the formal MP system. The rumen degraded protein is divided into the quickly degraded protein fraction (QDP) and the slowly degraded fraction (SDP). The QDP corresponds to the "a" fraction in Figure 6.3 where the degradability curve crosses the vertical axis and is considered to be constant for a particular feed, irrespective of other dietary and animal factors. Because QDP is released as soon as the feed enters the rumen some will escape uptake by the microbes and will be lost to the blood stream; the MP system considers that 0.8 of the QDP will be available to the microbes irrespective of the other dietary or animal factors.

The slowly degraded protein fraction (SDP) is the difference between the "a" fraction and the degradation of the protein (Figure 6.8). The extent of protein degradation varies according to the time the feed stays in the rumen and therefore the SDP content will be higher in low-yielding cows with a low rate of rumen outflow and decline with increasing animal production level (Figure 6.5). The sum of 0.8 of the QDP and the SDP is considered to be the total amount of protein (or more correctly nitrogen) that is available to the rumen microbes (ERDP). The amount converted into microbial crude protein depends on the supply of FME and the value of Y for that level of production (Figure 6.6). Either protein or energy supply limits the synthesis of microbial crude protein (MCP) and consideration of both is required to determine how much MCP leaves the rumen and passes into the abomasum for digestion and absorption as amino acids in the small intestine.

Microbial crude protein (MCP) is, as the name implies, a crude measurement actually based on the nitrogen content of the rumen microbes. In fact not all the nitrogen is associated with amino acids with some being found in nucleic acids (Table 6.6). The MP system considers that only 0.75 of the microbial crude protein is actually made up of amino acids and then states that only 0.85 of the amino acids in the microbial protein are absorbed into the blood in the small intestine so that only 0.64 (0.85 x 0.75) of the MCP is absorbed.

Figure 6.8   QDP, SDP, DUP and "ADIP" in a feed at different levels of production

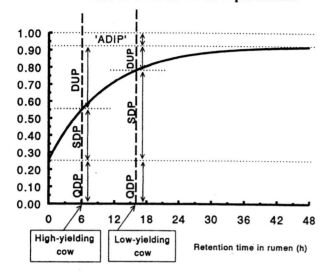

Table 6.6   Composition (g/100 g DM) of rumen microbes (van Soest, 1994)

True protein	47.5
RNA	24.2
DNA	3.4
Peptidoglycans	2.0
Polysaccharides	11.5
Lipid	7.0
Other	4.4

The portion of protein that is undegraded in the rumen (UDP) is considered to be made up of two fractions. Part of the protein ("ADIP") is considered to be totally indigestible and therefore can be represented as the difference between the maximal degradation and total protein content (Figure 6.8). As it is totally undegradable, the content of "ADIP" will not vary with animal or dietary changes. The other fraction of the UDP is protein which is digestible but undegraded in the rumen (DUP). For a given feed the content of DUP is the difference between the maximal degradation and the actual degradation in the rumen at a given retention time. The DUP content will therefore vary with rate of rumen outflow and hence animal production level (Figure 6.8). DUP is considered to be 90% digestible. The 90% of the DUP and the 64% of the MCP that are absorbed into the blood stream are considered as metabolisable protein which is analogous to metabolisable energy and represents the amount available in the blood stream to meet the animal's requirements.

Metabolisable protein is converted to net protein (NP) with differing efficiencies for different end uses (Figure 6.7). The wide range of amino acids required for maintenance allow MP to be used with an efficiency of 1.00 for maintenance. Weight loss (DLWL) is assumed to be used to support maintenance and therefore such mobilised protein is used with an efficiency of 1.00. Weight gain (DLWG) is assumed to use metabolisable protein with an efficiency of 0.59, pregnancy 0.85, milk production 0.68 and hair and wool production 0.26.

6.5   The industry's position regarding the MP system

In general everyone is in agreement that the MP system is an improvement over the old system, in that it closes up several of loopholes and explains animal performance on certain diets far better. However there is considerable doubt if all the numbers are correct and concern whether some of the concepts need further refinement. UK animal feed companies have been using the system for several years in the field as have the advisory services. However, given the complexity of the new system and the limited research to validate results as well as inadequate data for feed characterisation, its uptake at farm level has unfortunately been slow.

6.6   Limitations of the MP system

6.6.1   Assessment of degradability
A serious concern regarding the MP system (and most of the current generation of feeding standards) is that the model system requires complex data which are very difficult to obtain accurately. For instance, the "a", "b" and "c" parameters that define the degradability of protein of a feed are only available for a limited number of samples of feed, are difficult to measure and handle mathematically, and show considerable variation between laboratories. Furthermore, the estimation of degradability requires surgically modified animals which may not be acceptable to the general public.

Others have questioned whether the microbial digestion taking place in the small bags used for assessment of feed degradation is representative of what is happening in the whole rumen. For example the rate of degradation of high-oil fishmeals is very slow but the amount of fat within the bag makes it a far more hostile environment for the microbes than if a small amount of fishmeal (500 to 700 g) were mixed throughout the rumen. Such concerns have been supported by laboratory work but the complexity of designing suitable animal experiments makes this concern hard to investigate further.

6.6.2   ADIN
ADIN (or "ADIP") is difficult to measure as the acid detergent fibre (ADF) residues can easily be

contaminated with nitrogen from the detergent. Secondly, the small residue left after extraction contains low levels of nitrogen which makes subsequent nitrogen determinations difficult. This problem has been considered to be so great that many laboratories have been refusing to carry out estimations of ADIN as they had no faith in the quality of the results obtained! Formulae have been proposed for predicting the content of ADIN of a feed from protein and fibre (MADF) content but these appear only to work for forages and give too high a result for many supplementary feeds. A further complication is that about half of the heat–induced ADIN (found in many by-products) has been shown to be digestible in the small intestine.

6.6.3   QDP

The acknowledgement that not all of the quickly degraded protein will be available to the microbes is a considerable advance and allows better prediction of performance of grass silage based diets. However, it is unlikely that the efficiency of uptake will always be 0.8; the efficiency of uptake will depend on the amount of QDP in the diet and the daily feeding pattern of both the QDP and feeds high in FME. Such considerations lead to the concept of synchronisation of energy and protein release (Section 6.10.1).

6.6.4   FME

Whilst the concept of FME is an improvement on using ME as the unit of ruminally available energy there are several problems. Firstly, FME is a static measurement in that it does not take into account the rate of outflow from the rumen. At higher levels of production one would expect the rate of energy release in the rumen and hence FME to be lower. Secondly, FME is derived from ME which is a whole animal measurement not a rumen–based measurement. It seems erroneous to discount FME for the energy in urine and methane as both have been available to the rumen microbes. As stated previously FME is obtained by discounting ME for its content of oil and fermentation acids. Whilst it is safe to assume the microbes can get very little energy from acetic acid in silage (as this is an end-product of their fermentation) laboratory work (Chamberlain, 1994) suggests that they obtain some energy from lactic acid, which can be a major source of energy in silages. Finally, FME is a derived measurement based on analyses commonly available; it is not based on any animal observations. The limitations of the FME concept can be demonstrated by considering maize grain. It is high in ME and contains little oil and no starch so is high in FME but it is also considered to be high in rumen-resistant starch (RRS) (Chapter 5, page 59) which implies that much of the energy escapes fermentation in the rumen and so is not a source of FME. Having said that, it is difficult to envisage how any animal-based observations could be obtained. Whilst it will be difficult to resolve these problems with FME it does represent a considerable improvement over the older ME based predictions.

6.6.5   Appraisal of the MP system

Shortly after the MP system was published in 1992 a three-year dairy cow trial was commissioned to assess the new proposals. The results suggest that the MP system underpredicts the animals requirements by about 10%. There may be several reasons for this.

Firstly, because the MP system is so closely linked to the energy nutrition of the cow, errors in the energy system impair the MP system as well. The prediction of the energy content of feeds is usually only to within 7% and if energy intake is overestimated by 7% this will lead to an over-prediction of MCP production. However the prediction of the energy content of feeds is simply poor rather than biased and so one would not expect this limitation to cause an under-prediction across three years of trials.

Secondly, the calculation of MP requirements may be incorrect. The maintenance requirements for protein predicted by the MP system are considerably lower than that of other European systems and the efficiency of converting MP into milk protein (68%) may be an over-estimate. Furthermore, the efficiency of converting MP to NP for lactation is assumed to be constant with increasing milk yield which is contrary to the situation in the ME system where k_l is considered to fall with increasing output. All of these errors would result in MP requirements being under-estimated and the cow responding to additional protein. However if the error is in estimating maintenance requirements the errors would be larger at lower yields when maintenance is a greater proportion of the total whereas if the error is in estimating lactation requirements the under-estimation would increase with increasing milk yield as milk protein production became more dominant. Unfortunately the results released to date do not allow such analyses to be performed.

Finally, the supply of MCP and hence MP may be over-estimated. As mentioned above, FME cannot be measured directly and is derived from ME assessments. The calculation of FME does not take into account outflow rate and it is likely that in milking cows the high outflow rates restrict the fermentation of the FME fraction and hence FME supply and MCP production are over-predicted. If the failure to relate the ruminally available energy supply to level of production and outflow rate is the cause of the under-prediction then the errors would again be greatest for high-yielding cows and also for feeds high in rumen-resistant starch such as maize silage.

Such errors could be reduced by correcting FME supply or MCP production for level of production (as for energy - C_L), hence reducing MP supply.

6.7   Beyond the MP system

Even before it was widely adopted the MP system was being criticised by some research workers. This is inevitable and possibly one of the functions of any set of feeding standards in that it acts as a high tide mark from which further research work can proceed. The MP system was published after continental systems such as the French PDI system and therefore is more sophisticated; for instance it relates outflow rate, degradability and microbial protein yield (Y) to level of production.   In the United States a new system has been published since the MP system which is referred to as the Cornell Net Protein system and this has found favour with some nutritionists in the UK, but for applied use it has limitations. It is a progression of the MP system and considers five protein fractions rather than four. However, determining the rate of degradation of these fractions is even more difficult than determining the overall degradability of a feed and, as with the MP system, acquisition of the necessary data will be very slow.

Future progress in the development of new feeding systems will be limited by several factors. Firstly, the need to be able to obtain input data for the models proposed. New systems may well use more sophisticated methods of feed assessment; these often have larger errors and are usually more difficult to perform on a routine basis. Secondly, more sophisticated models will require more sophisticated experiments in their development and validation, and the funding of such large projects is uncertain.

It is likely that any future system will be based on an understanding of the nutrients the animal requires. Feeds will be characterised in terms of specific nutrients (e.g. glucose, amino acids) rather than by conventional laboratory analyses (e.g. CP, ME, NDF). The objective would be to use such models in a predictive manner rather than just as a planning tool. Such models ought to be able to predict animal responses to additional nutrients and similarly allow nutritionists to predict how to achieve given types of performance. The models would need to be dynamic and would model responses over time to allow users to determine the likely time scale of responses to current inputs.

There are several concerns regarding the development of such models; if they are to work at the level of specific nutrients and blood components the role of the controlling hormones will have to be considered. Hormonal responses differ considerably between animals; for example consider the lability of the adrenergic flight/fight response in cows. Some cows are remarkably placid and presumably rarely secrete adrenaline whilst other cows react to the slightest stimulus and must frequently be under the influence of adrenaline. Even if all the metabolic control mechanisms can be elucidated it is likely that the model that emerges will be extremely complex. Models of similar complexity have been developed in the field of meteorology and workers in this field have come to recognise they have very finite limits. Given the complexity of meteorological models and the time scale over which they must be run (15 minutes between dynamic steps) it is still very difficult to predict the weather 7 days in advance and it is generally regarded that it is impossible to predict 14 days ahead in any detail. Such limits are linked to a inability to define the input parameters (pressure, temperature) with sufficient precision and the accumulation of the imprecision as the model makes its predictions over time.

Extrapolating the meteorologists' experiences to nutritional models two things are clear. Firstly the model inputs must be very precise; currently estimates of such things as rumen microbial protein outflows can only be measured to within 20% of their true value. Secondly the useful time horizon of a model is linked to the time scale used in the iterations. Meteorologists use a time scale of about 5 to 15 minutes to model what most people consider to be a slowly change entity. Given the speed at which hormonally-induced changes take place in mammals a likely time-step for a mammalian model is seconds rather than minutes and it follows that such models would struggle to predict events 3 to 12 hours ahead and be unable to work 24 hours ahead.

6.8   Amino acids

Just as metabolisable energy is an aggregated over-simplification of the range of different energy containing nutrients required by the dairy cow so the metabolisable protein requirements are also an over-simplification. As mentioned previously the cow requires specific amino acids rather than just general protein to meet the requirements of her protein metabolism. In previous sections it has been stated that most dairy cows do not have a requirement for specific amino acids. However, the success and importance of recognising the specific amino acid requirements in pigs and poultry has lead many workers to consider specific amino acid requirements in dairy cows.

In pig and poultry nutrition the amino acids are divided into two groups according to whether or not the animal can synthesise the amino acid to make up for any shortage in the diet. There are ten or eleven amino acids that are considered "essential" and if any of these are insufficient to meet a given level of production then production is limited.

The rumen microorganisms can synthesise all the essential amino acids and therefore it is difficult to determine when a ruminant's performance is limited by the supply of a specific amino acid. However, it is likely that the dairy cow herself is unable to synthesise the same range of 10 or 11 amino acids that are essential to pigs and poultry. In high-yielding dairy cattle as much as 40% of the protein absorbed in the small intestine may be of dietary rather than of microbial origin and will have the same amino acid profile as that of the parent feed. Any major imbalance in the essential amino acids in the feeds offered may therefore limit the supply to the animal and limit production.

The amino acid profile of the protein in milk and muscle, rumen microbes and several common feeds is shown previously in Table 6.1 (page 65). Microbial protein is fairly well-balanced in essential amino acids, so milk production in low-yielding cows should not be limited by any amino acid deficiencies. In higher-yielding cows there may be deficiencies in some amino acids, with methionine and lysine being the most obvious.

Table 6.7   Disappearance of selected amino acids in fishmeal. Mean of three samples of herring meal incubated for 24 hours in rumen (adapted from Pike *et al.*, 1994)

	Content (g/100g protein)		Disappearance
	Before	After	(% of average)
Arginine	9.2	8.5	92
Alanine	6.0	6.2	103
Aspartic acid	9.0	10.0	111
Glycine	6.0	5.2	87
Histidine	1.4	1.8	129
Hydroxy–Proline	0.9	0.5	56
Isoleucine	4.3	5.4	126
Leucine	7.0	8.1	116
Lysine	7.8	8.1	104
Methionine	2.9	3.2	110
Phenylalanine	3.8	4.6	121
Proline	3.7	4.1	111
Serine	4.1	4.8	117
Threonine	3.9	4.9	126
Tyrosine	3.1	4.1	132
Valine	4.7	5.6	119

If requirements for essential amino acid are to be used in routine dairy cow rationing, it will be necessary to determine the disappearance of individual amino acids in feeds to determine the amino acid profile of the dietary protein residues being digested and absorbed in the small intestine. Such data are not widely available but the results for three assessments of herring fishmeal after 24 hours degradation in the rumen are shown in Table 6.7. Amino acid contents are shown for the fishmeal and for the residue, and this can be used to determine the disappearance of each amino acid relative to overall protein. It can be seen that the relative disappearance ranges from 56% to 132%. It is therefore not possible to say that the supply of dietary amino acids is proportional to protein degradability. It is also likely that different amino acids have different patterns of disappearance such that the ratios shown in Table 6.7 are not valid for different incubation times. Given such difficulties and the need to derive such data for the range of commonly used feeds it will be a long time before sufficient data are available for the amino acid supply of diets to be determined.

6.8.1   *Responses to amino acid supplements*

Supplementation with essential amino acids is likely to be expensive and therefore it is important that they are not used simply as a source of microbial nitrogen. Because of this most products on the market are protected by some means from microbial degradation.

The reported responses to rumen protected amino acids are variable. For example one group of American workers (Donkin *et al.*, 1989) reported that the addition of rumen protected methionine and lysine to a maize based diet increased milk protein content from 3.15 to 3.25% and daily milk protein yield from 0.799 to 0.863 kg. However another group (Nalsen *et al.*, 1987) gave concentrates based on maize and wheat with or without supplementation with protected lysine and methionine. They found that milk yields, milk fat and milk protein were not significantly affected by diet.

More recent work in France (Chillard *et al.*, 1995) showed that supplementation of a grass silage (160 g CP/kg DM) and concentrate-based ration significantly increased milk protein composition from 30.9 to 32.1 g/kg milk but, because of changes in milk yield, did not have a significant effect on milk protein yield (641 vs 614 g protein/day). Other workers in Ireland (Younge *et al.*, 1995) showed that methionine supplementation increased milk protein content but the response was dependent on the type of basal concentrate. In many cases using alternative ingredients in the compound feed may be more cost effective. In neither experiment were milk yields high (20 and 23 kg/day respectively) and the response in higher yielders is still uncertain.

In general, responses to supplementation of diets with protected amino acids are only seen on maize-based diets, since maize silage is relatively low in protein content and also low in methionine. Responses are rarely seen from diets based on grass silage because rumen microbial activity is usually high, so MCP production is also high and this has a good amino acid profile (Table 6.1). In addition, such diets usually have a high overall CP content resulting in high specific amino acid contents; therefore the amino acids with lowest concentrations are unlikely to be limiting. However some farmers are reporting responses to protected methionine with diets based on grass or mixed silages. Recent work in France has suggested that protected methionine can increase milk protein by 0.1 to 0.2% when fed against a range of forages and with soyabean meal as a supplement. However the cost of such supplementation is about 12p/cow/day and therefore a good response in high yielders is required to make it economically justifiable.

More recently workers at Reading University have shown that infusions of specific amino acids have the potential to raise milk protein by 0.5% over a range of yields. Whilst such results are very exciting, the work is still in the initial stages and it will take 3 to 4 years to determine if a commercial feed supplement can be developed with the same potential.

6.9 Responses to high-protein diets

Recently farmers and their advisors have been using rations that contain far more protein than is indicated by the MP system, and which may contain in excess of 200 g CP/kg DM. The history behind this development is that in the late 1980s it was widely accepted that the old RDP/UDP system under-predicted protein requirements and an animal response was usually seen if requirements were exceeded. The reasons for this were two-fold. Firstly, high-protein supplements tend to lift the intake of grass silage with a consequent increase in energy intake and hence milk production. Secondly, absorbed amino acids do not always have to be used for protein synthesis. Where protein intake is in excess relative to energy intake, amino acids can be deaminated in the liver and used as an energy source. In such situations absorbed amino acids are used both as an energy and a protein source for milk production and yields are greater than predicted. Because some of the amino acids are diverted to replace energy sources, the conversion of MP to milk protein is low at around 30% (cf. the usual value of 68%).

When protein supplements such as maize gluten feed and rapeseed meal are cheap relative to energy

feeds it is financially advantageous to feed a higher CP diet than indicated by the MP system; the milk yield response is worth more than the cost of the additional supplements. However, at high protein intakes (over 200 g CP/kg DM) the amounts of protein being deaminated in the liver are considerable and this can impair other functions of the liver sufficiently to reduce fertility (see Chapter 16, page 155).

6.10 Practical aspects of protein digestion

As mentioned in Section 6.6.5 the initial evaluation of the MP system suggested that it under-predicts requirements by about 10%. Given the relatively low cost of many sources of feed protein and the likely response by the cow to extra total protein in the diet, it may be prudent to allow a surplus of 100 to 200 g of MP in routine diet formulation. However, if penalties for using excess protein or producing excess nitrogen in manure increase due to environmental pressures, then it may be necessary to reappraise a strategy which involves deliberately over-supplying MP to the animal.

Many nutritionists include different protein systems when devising diets for cows. Thus some nutritionists are unwilling to formulate diets for any milking cows with less than 16% crude protein. Others, after comparing the different systems around the world for assessing protein requirements, have concluded that the content of crude protein in the total diet dry matter is as good a guide to tissue protein supply and milk production response as any other nitrogen or protein fraction.

Recommended concentrations of crude protein in diets for dairy cows are shown in Table 6.8. They are not absolute levels and should be taken as a general guide when designing diets and when making diagnoses of the possible causes of problems

Table 6.8 Recommended contents of crude protein in diets for cows

Milk yield (litres/day)	Crude protein (g/kg DM)
0	135 to 145
10	145 to 155
20	155 to 165
30	165 to 175
40	175 to 180
50	180 to 190

The conclusion that sophisticated systems of assessing and meeting protein requirements are no better than crude protein begs the question: have the comparisons between systems been made at high yields and at low yields, or simply at moderate yields? The answer is that most comparisons have been made at below 30 litres of milk yield and above 15 litres. Thus the real test of the system – its ability to meet high requirements adequately and to enable savings to be made at low requirements has not been carried out.

6.10.1 Matching the release of nitrogen and carbohydrate in the rumen

As mentioned in Chapter 5, the rate at which carbohydrate is released from feeds is variable with starch being released rapidly especially if the grain is crushed. The release of ERDP from feeds shows a similar degree of variability, with dry feeds such as hay having a relatively slow release rate and silages having a more rapid rate of release. The released ERDP is rapidly converted to ammonia by the microbes and if it is not utilised within a short time and assimilated into microbial protein, the free ammonia moves across the rumen wall and into the blood stream. In the liver it is converted into urea and though some will be recycled via the saliva much will be lost to the urine.

In order for the microbes to assimilate the ERDP–derived ammonia they must have a suitable energy source available at the same time. Therefore when feeds such as silage are used, they should be offered together with a feed such as rolled barley which has a similar rate of carbohydrate release, resulting in optimal ammonia uptake rates and maximal microbial protein synthesis. Conversely, a feed like grass hay has a slow rate of energy release from the cellulose and a similarly slow rate of release of ERDP (Figure 6.9).

Figure 6.9   Relative rates of production of ammonia (NH_3) and VFA in the rumen after feeding

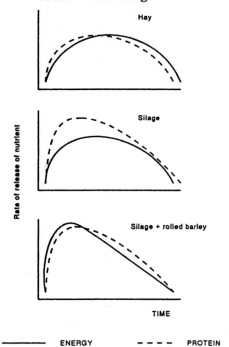

The graphs in Figure 6.9 are diagrammatic and are intended to illustrate the balance between nitrogen and energy release. Although the MP system takes more account of the rate of release of nitrogen from feeds in the rumen, by subdividing ERDP into QDP and SDP, it does not take into account the need for suitable sources of energy. It is likely that the rate of digestion of the energy sources in the diet affect the 80% efficiency of utilisation of QDP for microbial protein production.

The possible impact of the pattern of energy and protein release in the rumen has lead to the consideration of synchrony i.e. the formulation of diets such that energy and protein are released at compatible rates throughout the day ensuring that neither is in excess and minimising wastage and hence maximising rumen efficiency. It has been proposed that this is one of the reasons that complete diets work better than feeding the ingredients individually. Workers in the UK have looked at experimental diets formulated to be at the two extremes of synchrony (the widest difference they could get experimentally). They detected differences in microbial efficiency in that more MCP was being formed per unit of FME in the synchronous diet. However it is not certain how far apart the energy and nitrogen release patterns have to be before efficiency falls off. If such a concept is to be used in practice either daily feeding patterns will require very tight definition or complete mixed diet feeding will be required. Other workers have compared the daily fluctuations of VFA and ammonia production in sheep fed diets of differing synchronies with the patterns that would be predicted from the degradability data obtained from Dacron bag studies. The results indicated that the current measurement techniques are inadequate in their prediction of the dynamics of degradation and better feed characterisation will be required before synchrony becomes a practical component within formal feeding standards.

At a more practical level American workers (Herrera-Saldana and Huber, 1987) fed diets containing a rapidly degraded source of energy (barley) or a slowly degraded source (milo) with a rapidly degraded source of protein (cottonseed meal) or a slowly degraded form (dried brewers grains) (Table 6.9). The rapidly degraded synchrony produced the most milk but when it was corrected to 3.5% fat content then it can be seen that the two synchronous diets were more productive than the asynchronous diets. Such results suggest that if the release of energy and protein in the rumen can be balanced then there will be increased microbial activity and protein supply giving increased production. However, it should be noted that the milk quality reported in this American trial would not be acceptable to most UK farmers and this difference between the two countries means that great care must be taken when adopting feeding recommendations that originate from America.

Table 6.9 Animal performance results from diets with fast or slowly degrading sources of energy and protein (Herrera-Saldana and Huber, 1987)

	Diet degradability			
Energy	Fast	Fast	Slow	Slow
Protein	Fast	Slow	Fast	Slow
Milk (kg/day)	37.4	34.9	34.2	34.6
3.5% FCM (kg/day)	34.3	31.4	33.6	34.8
Fat (%)	3.1	2.9	3.4	3.6
Milk protein (%)	2.9	3.0	3.0	2.8

6.10.2 Matching type of protein to requirements

The metabolisable protein system has concentrated attention on the fermentation in the rumen and the requirement of the microbial population for fermentable energy and for degradable protein. The widespread use of silages of relatively high degradable protein means that for most diets containing grass and legume silage the most limiting major nutrient to the rumen bacteria is FME. Responses to urea and other sources of degradable N have therefore generally been non-existent.

However, when diets are formulated which are high in maize silage, or when the protein content of grass silage or hay is low because of delayed harvest or reduced fertiliser use, deficiencies in ERDP are likely to occur. In this situation urea can be a very cost–effective supplement (see Chapter 3). Urea can be added to raise dietary crude protein from 120 to 150 or 160 g/kg DM, but the total amount of urea should be limited to a maximum of 150 or 160 g per day if given in a concentrate supplement, or 250 to 300 g/day if mixed uniformly into the total ration.

At the other extreme, fishmeal and other sources of undegraded protein have given responses in production in situations where dietary crude protein and metabolisable protein supply are adequate. Requirements for tissue protein have usually been relatively high, and the possibility exists that the animal, or its ruminal microflora, is responding to specific amino acids or peptides in the protein supplement. Alternatively, the extra protein may simply be used for gluconeogensis in the liver and is supplying additional energy to the body, leading in turn to the production response.

6.10.3 Matching level of protein to requirements

Many apparent responses to the feeding of supplementary protein above theoretical protein requirements are responses to additional energy. When energy is adequate, the response to extra MP is likely to be small and uneconomic, as shown in a recent test of the metabolisable protein system with four diets based on grass and maize silages (Table 6.10). There was an increase in milk yield reflecting an increased intake of silage (and hence of ME) at the two higher protein diets. There was also a small increase in milk protein content and in milk protein yield, but the requirements for MP, based on actual performance, agreed closest to intake of MP with the diet which supplied MP closest to recommendations. The conclusion was that the MP system offered the prospect of achieving the optimal level of protein in the diet in relation to requirements.

Table 6.10 Effect of increasing MP supply (as DUP) above recommendations on intake and milk production (Mansbridge et al., 1994)

	Target supply of MP above recommendations			
	1.1	1.2	1.3	1.4
ERDP intake	1810	1873	1893	1847
DUP intake (g/day)	440	613	759	941
MP intake (g/day)	1597	1806	1962	2182
Intake of silage DM (kg/day)	10.7	10.7	11.6	11.5
Milk yield (kg/day)	26.5	26.5	28.3	28.3
Milk fat (%)	4.26	4.17	4.30	4.08
Milk protein (%)	2.92	3.04	3.07	3.12
MP requirement from performance (g/day)	1374	1430	1500	1586
Actual MP intake/MP requirement	1.16	1.26	1.32	1.37

CHAPTER 7

MINERALS AND VITAMINS

7.1   Introduction

7.2   Calcium
        7.2.1   *Calcium metabolism*
        7.2.2   *Calcium deficiency*
        7.2.3   *Clinical signs of calcium deficiency*
        7.2.4   *Diagnosing calcium deficiency*
        7.2.5   *Interactions*
        7.2.6   *Treatment of calcium deficiency*
        7.2.7   *Preventive measures*
        7.2.8   *Calcium toxicity*

7.3   Magnesium
        7.3.1   *Clinical signs of magnesium deficiency*
        7.3.2   *Diagnosis of magnesium deficiency*
        7.3.3   *Treatment of magnesium deficiency*
        7.3.4   *Availability of dietary magnesium*
        7.3.5   *Preventive measures*

7.4   Phosphorus

7.5   Sodium

7.6   Sulphur
        7.6.1   *Requirements for sulphur*
        7.6.2   *Sources of sulphur*

7.7   Trace elements
        7.7.1   *Copper*
        7.7.2   *Selenium*
        7.7.3   *Cobalt*
        7.7.4   *Zinc*
        7.7.5   *Iodine*
        7.7.6   *Iron*
        7.7.7   *Summary*

7.8   Vitamins
        7.8.1   *Vitamin A (retinol)*
        7.8.2   *Vitamin B*
        7.8.3   *Vitamin C (ascorbic acid)*
        7.8.4   *Vitamin D_3*
        7.8.5   *Vitamin E*
        7.8.6   *Vitamin K*
        7.8.7   *Vitamin H (biotin)*
        7.8.8   *Summary*

7.1   Introduction

Mineral and trace element deficiencies are the cause of some of the major metabolic disorders which affect productive dairy cattle. These disorders are all associated with short or long term imbalances between the "inputs", "throughputs" and "outputs" of essential nutrients. The inputs are the animal's feed and water, which vary both in quantity and quality and may contain other minerals that interfere with absorption. The outputs are the unavoidable losses in urine and faeces and the productive outputs to calf, milk and meat. The throughputs are the animal's body reserves, which vary in size and the extent with which they may be used to compensate for imbalances between the dietary inputs and the animal's outputs. In the long term, inputs and outputs must balance to maintain an animal's health. If short term outputs exceed inputs, the animal mobilises body reserves. Conversely, if the inputs exceed outputs the excess must be stored or excreted, or uptake from the diet reduced. Whether or not metabolic disorders are avoided depends upon the animal's ability to cope with imbalances between inputs and outputs, the size and mobility of body reserves and the animal's ability to alter the amount absorbed from the diet.

For the majority of minerals (except calcium), trace elements and vitamins control and regulation is remarkably uncontrolled with the animal dependent on absorbing sufficient from the diet by passive uptake to meet requirements. Excess intake is stored in the body but the control and regulation is usually limited. Excess storage can therefore occur and cause problems of toxicity.

There has been considerable controversy over the mineral requirements of ruminants in the past decade resulting in changes in requirements and allowances. The changes have had a particularly large impact on phosphorus, which is also the most expensive of the major minerals to supplement and therefore has led to considerable debate within the industry. Little reference will be made in this chapter to blood or tissue concentrations. These often differ between laboratories according to the methods used in the assay and the wide range of units reported in the literature leads to a confusing number of normal ranges. Any reputable laboratory will supply details of their normal range when they report their results and these should be used as the basis of any interpretation.

In this chapter the major minerals (calcium, magnesium, phosphorus, sodium and sulphur) are discussed first, followed by the more important trace elements (copper, selenium, cobalt, zinc, iodine and iron) and then the vitamins. Allowances for the major minerals are outlined in greater detail in Chapter 11.

7.2   Calcium

Calcium is the most common mineral of the body and the major extra-cellular divalent cation. The majority of the calcium (99%) is in the bones with the rest being distributed between the other tissues and blood. Calcium is involved in blood clotting and in a wide range of enzymatic actions including the contraction of muscles and the transmission of nerve impulses. It is the loss of this last function that gives rise to the clinical signs of milk fever and is ultimately responsible for death. Whilst the bones contain several kilograms of calcium only a small proportion of this is available as only recently lain down bone can be mobilised. As the extent of bone remodelling declines with age the amount that can be mobilised also falls; this is the reason why milk fever is more common in older cows.

Figure 7.1   Calcium fluxes (g/day) for a 600 kg cow in the last week of pregnancy (plain text) or giving 20 litres milk a day (italics)

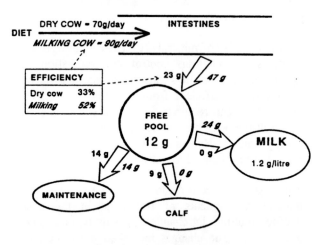

Figure 7.1 shows the daily calcium fluxes for a dry cow one week before calving and for a cow yielding 20 litres of milk a day. Requirements for maintenance are the same in both cases and the major increase in demand is the switch from foetal to lactation requirements. The amount required during lactation is twice that required during the last week of pregnancy but typically dietary supply only increases by a factor of about 1.3. The major change occurring is the efficiency with which calcium has to be absorbed from the intestines and it is the sudden change from 33% to over 50% efficiency that can cause the problems at calving that lead to hypocalcaemia and milk fever.

7.2.1   Calcium metabolism

Calcium metabolism is under close control in the cow and blood concentrations are usually maintained within a narrow band. Such tight control is in contrast to that of all the other minerals considered in this chapter and, ironically, is the root of much of the problems that occur with milk fever.

Calcium is under the direct control of three hormones: calcitonin, parathyroid hormone (PTH)

and vitamin D_3 (also called cholecalciferol). Calcitonin is secreted from the thyroid gland in the neck in response to high concentrations of calcium in the blood and it suppresses resorption of calcium from the bones and absorption from the intestines. High concentration of calcium in the blood are rarely a problem in dairy cows and so this will not be considered further. Parathyroid hormone (PTH) is produced by the parathyroid gland which is located in the neck in close proximity to the larynx and the thyroid gland. Production of PTH is stimulated by low concentration of calcium in the blood and is depressed as concentrations of calcium rise. Vitamin D_3 may be obtained from dietary sources or can be synthesised in the skin. In this form, it is relatively inactive in controlling calcium metabolism and needs to undergo two chemical transformations to become active (see Figure 7.2). In the liver it is converted to 25-hydroxy-Vit D_3 and then it undergoes further transformation into the active form in the kidney to 1-25-dihydroxy-Vit D_3. The latter conversion is regulated by PTH whilst the former is regulated by magnesium and may be depressed if blood magnesium concentration falls.

Figure 7.2 Pathways for synthesis and activation of vitamin D_3

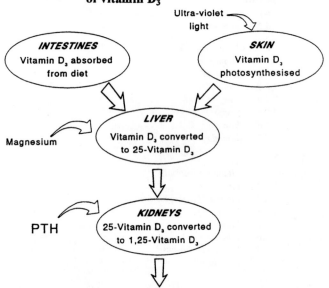

Figure 7.3 shows how the concentration of calcium in the blood is regulated by the action of PTH and the active form of vitamin D_3. When the cow calves and starts to produce milk calcium output increases dramatically (Figure 7.1) and concentration of calcium in the blood falls. The reduction stimulates the secretion of PTH which stimulates the conversion of 25-hydroxy-Vitamin D_3 to the active form 1-25-dihydroxy-Vit D_3. Mobilisation of calcium from the bone is stimulated by both PTH and vitamin D_3, whereas absorption from the intestines is only under the control of vitamin D_3. About 24 hours of intestinal stimulation by vitamin D_3 is required before calcium absorption increases significantly. The bone takes about 48 hours to respond. It

is these delays and the remorseless drain of calcium into the milk that cause hypocalcaemia and milk fever.

Figure 7.3 **The control of concentration of calcium in blood by the action of PTH and vitamin D₃**

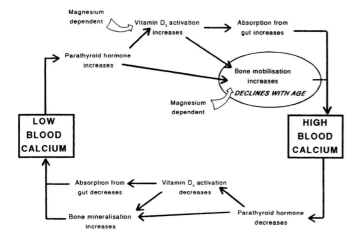

7.2.2 Calcium deficiency

Although the clinical disorder caused by low concentration of calcium in the blood is known as "milk fever", a raised temperature is rarely found. The incidence of milk fever in dairy cows is about 10%, but varies widely from year to year and from farm to farm. Most cases occur in the period immediately around calving (see Table 7.1) and the incidence increases with age from around 0.2% in heifers to a maximum of 18% in older animals.

Table 7.1 **Timing of milk fever in relation to calving (% of cases)**

Before calving	21
Within 24h of calving	61
Within 24 to 48 h of calving	15
More than 48 h after calving	3

At term, the calf takes about 0.4 g of calcium per hour across the placenta. Once the calf is born this drain ceases but is replaced by the greater demand for milk of about 1g/h. These changes in demand can be accommodated by the regulatory mechanisms (Figure 7.3), but this takes 24 to 48 hours. It is the delay in adjustments that causes the clinical problems and all efforts at treatment are merely an attempt to "buy time" whilst the animal's own control mechanisms adjust to the new situation. However care must be taken to ensure that any treatments do not worsen the situation by delaying the animal's ability to adjust.

7.2.3 Clinical signs of calcium deficiency

There are three clinical stages of hypocalcaemia or milk fever. The first stage is a brief period of hyper-

excitement and hypersensitivity with muscle tremors and twitching. This stage is not often observed but leads to the second stage in which the cow becomes recumbent in the normal sternal position. Muscle activity is reduced and the animal does not dung or urinate, fails to ruminate and her breathing is shallow with a slow heart rate. Unless treated this progresses to the third, terminal stage. Muscle activity is weakened further, the head may go around to lie on the flank, bloat will develop and the heart beat become fainter. The reduced heart activity reduces circulation to the tissues and the animal becomes hypothermic. Death follows, usually caused by the progressive bloat eventually stopping respiratory activity, or by heart activity becoming too weak. In addition, cows with low concentrations of calcium in the blood are three to four times more likely to develop left displaced abomasum in early lactation, irrespective of whether the low calcium results in clinical milk fever (Massey *et al.*, 1993). Although the cause of left displaced abomasum is not known it is thought that reduced muscle tone may be involved and this would occur in cows with a low blood calcium.

7.2.4 Diagnosing calcium deficiency

Diagnosis is relatively simple. Firstly, most (uncomplicated) cases respond to intravenous infusions of calcium borogluconate, and secondly concentration of calcium in the blood is below the normal range. Calcium circulates in the blood both as free calcium ions and bound to blood proteins such as albumin. Roughly half the blood calcium is in the ionic form and it is only this fraction that is metabolically active. Measuring ionic calcium is tedious and, as long as blood albumin concentrations remain within the normal range, total calcium is just as useful a measurement.

7.2.5 Interactions

Age. Older cows are more prone to milk fever as both the intestine and the bone are less responsive to vitamin D₃ than young animals. The intestine has fewer receptor sites for vitamin D₃ and therefore there is less response to a given dose. Calcium can only be released from bone that is being actively remodelled and as animals grow older the amount of bone remodelling declines and hence less calcium can be mobilised. As a result heifers generally have an adequate concentration of calcium in the blood concentration irrespective of the calcium content of their diet (Shappell *et al.*, 1987) and rarely succumb to milk fever.

Sodium. The uptake of calcium from the intestines is an active process dependent on sodium and to a lesser extent potassium. Many spring pastures are low in sodium (see Section 7.5) and the Dutch have shown that supplementation of pasture with sodium reduces the incidence of milk fever and hypomagnesaemia (grass staggers). In practice if the concentration of sodium in herbage is below 3 g/kg DM, supplementation is warranted. Up to 110 kg sodium/ha can be applied without scorching, except in very dry weather but 32 kg Na/ha is usually adequate.

7.2.6   Treatment of calcium deficiency

The conventional treatment is to administer 400 ml of a 20% or 40% w/w solution of calcium boro-gluconate, either under the skin or directly into a vein to provide 6 g or 12 g of calcium. Given that the losses of calcium to the milk are 1.2 g/litre, or 24 g for a cow yielding 20 litres a day, it can be seen that the amounts administered only substitute for normal sources for a few hours, and the homeostatic mechanisms must respond to give a longer term solution.

7.2.7   Preventive measures

A range of preventive methods has been developed which may reduce the problem, depending on how bad the situation was before. It should be realised that no one solution will eliminate the problem in all cases and it will usually take some combination of one or more methods to control a herd problem.

Control strategies can be divided into two categories:

1.   Manipulate the homeostatic control of calcium metabolism

a) Increase efficiency of absorption of calcium in dry cows. As discussed above, calcium requirement increases more than supply at calving and therefore the efficiency of absorption needs to increase by about 20% (see Figure 7.1). If the intake of calcium in the dry cow could be restricted then the efficiency of absorption would rise and the change in efficiency required at calving would be less.

In an American trial (Shappell *et al.*, 1987) two groups of heifers and cows (third or greater pregnancy) were given diets high (12 g Ca/kg DM) or low (5 g Ca/kg DM) in calcium for four weeks prior to calving at 1.4% of body weight (approximately 9 kg/day). After calving all animals received the same diet. Cows, but not the heifers, on the high calcium diet developed severe milk fever whereas none of the animals given the low-calcium diet were affected.

Animals given the low-calcium diet showed a lower concentration of calcium in the blood before calving than those given the high-calcium diet (Figure 7.4) which triggered increased PTH production. Thus efficiency of absorption of calcium was increased in the animals given the low-calcium diet. Immediately prior to calving the concentration of calcium in the

blood fell in both groups, triggering an increase in PTH. In the cows given the low calcium diet the introduction of the high-calcium milking diet (11 g Ca/kg DM) combined with the higher efficiency of calcium absorption rapidly returned blood calcium levels to normal and blood concentration of PTH fell.

Figure 7.4   Changes in concentrations of blood calcium and PTH before and after calving in cows given diets differing in calcium content pre-calving (adapted from Shappell *et al.*, 1987)

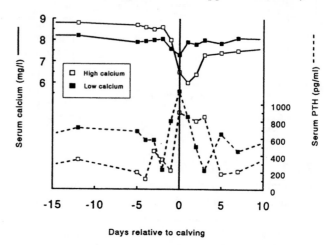

In the cows on the high-calcium diet, the increase in calcium available from the milking ration was insufficient to correct the blood calcium deficit because PTH levels had been low prior to calving and hence absorption efficiency was poor. It took 48 hours for the increased PTH concentration to elevate calcium absorption and mobilisation and only after this time did blood calcium return to normal and PTH concentration fall. Furthermore, the cows on the low calcium diet gave about 5 kg more milk a day during the first three weeks of lactation.

b) High doses of vitamin D₃. Increased concen-trations of vitamin D_3 in blood increase the mobilisation of calcium from bone and absorption from the intestines. Preparations of synthetic vitamin D_3 on the market are designed for use in the last few days of pregnancy. Unlike earlier prepara-tions, they do not cause excessively high concentra-tions of calcium in the blood and calcification of blood vessels, but they still have their drawbacks. Both preparations increase the concentration of vitamin D_3 in the blood which then increases calcium concentration. If the cow does not calve soon after the rise in the concentration of calcium in the blood, the supplementary vitamin D_3 can have an inhibitory effect on the parathyroid and can depress PTH production and the activation of endogenous vitamin D_3. In time, therefore, absorp-tion and mobilisation of calcium falls rather than increases. The time scale of these changes is several days and therefore it is necessary to predict calving date to within a few days, which in practice is not always feasible. It is possible to repeat the vitamin D_3 injection to hold absorption and mobilisation artificially high but the cost makes this unattractive.

c) Supplementary magnesium. Many dry cows have a marginal status of magnesium. Magnesium deficiency, even in a mild sub-clinical form, can predispose the animal to milk fever. Magnesium stimulates mobilisation of bone calcium (Braak *et al.*, 1987) (Figure 7.3) and is involved in the activation of vitamin D_3 (Figure 7.2). However, care must be taken not to over-supplement with magnesium as it will increase gut transit times and, at high doses, may even compete directly with calcium to be absorbed from the gut, all of which will worsen any calcium deficiency problems. In practice, mineral supplements for dry cows are usually formulated to contain little or no calcium and sufficient magnesium to meet the cow's requirements.

d) Reverse-ratio dry cow minerals. The closer the calcium:phosphorus (Ca:P) ratio is to 1:2, the better calcium is absorbed from the intestines. As most dry cow diets have ratios of Ca:P of about 2:1 and requirements are almost 1:1, supplementation with phosphorus and a reduction in calcium intake increases absorption of calcium. However, phosphorus is an expensive mineral to include in rations and to achieve a Ca:P ratio of 1:2 it has to be supplied in excess of requirements. To minimise the amounts of supplementary phosphorus required, intakes of calcium also need to be minimised and some benefit will be obtained by merely reducing the calcium content of the dry cow diet without increasing phosphorus supplementation.

e) Acidic salts in the dry cow ration (DCAB). American work (Beede, 1992) has suggested that acidification of the diet for 3 to 5 weeks before calving increases calcium uptake from the intestines and this has been related to dietary cation-anion balance (DCAB). The DCAB of a diet is calculated as follows:

DCAB (mEq/kg DM) =
(43.5 x sodium) + (25.6 x potassium) -
(28.2 x chlorine) - (62.5 x sulphur)

with all minerals measured as g/kg DM.

The high concentration of potassium and, to a lesser extent, sodium in the dry cow diet keep the cow mildly alkalotic. Addition of sulphur and chlorine to the diet reduces alkalosis and possibly makes the cow mildly acidotic. It has been shown that in alkalotic cows the kidney and bone are less responsive to PTH but their response to PTH is increased when the cow is acidotic. The more negative the DCAB, the less likely the cow is to suffer from milk fever. In one trial changing the DCAB from +978 to -228 meq/kg DM reduced milk fever in a group of 47 Jerseys from 26% to 4%. Animals given diets with negative DCAB went on to have less problems with retained placenta, better fertility and increased milk yields (300 to 400 litres/cow).

Unfortunately to calculate the DCAB, special analyses of the dry cow ration are needed for potassium, sodium, sulphur and chlorine as these can vary considerably between different forages and are not carried out as routine analyses. The target DCAB is between -100 and -200 meq/kg DMI which can be achieved using the following steps:

* Remove all supplementary sources of sodium and potassium: watch out for minerals containing salt and sodium bicarbonate.

* If the DCAB is greater than + 200 meq/kg DM, try to reformulate the diet to use forages with lower contents of potassium or sodium.

* Use ammonium chloride, ammonium sulphate or magnesium sulphate (Epsom salts) to lower the DCAB. To avoid the risk of ammonia toxicity mix the ammonium and magnesium salts in a ratio of 1:1 but limit their intake to 100 g/day as magnesium sulphate is bitter and is likely to affect feed intake.

2. Alter the balance between calcium supply and demand

a) Reduce calcium outflow. This is the oldest preventive measure but it should not be overlooked. The calcium content of milk is similar regardless of calcium intake (Shappell *et al.*, 1987), indicating that the cow has no control over her calcium output. Calcium output is therefore linked to milk production and if it can be restricted in the first few days after calving the output of calcium will be reduced. However, the benefits of incomplete milking-out should be balanced against the increased risks of mastitis during a high risk time for this disease.

b) Calcium fluids. Solutions of calcium borogluconate, with or without added magnesium, can be given sub-cutaneously to all cows after calving. However, excessive or repeated use will artificially raise concentrations of calcium in the blood and prevent any increase in PTH to stimulate increased calcium absorption and mobilisation. The ethics of injecting all cows routinely should also be questioned.

7.2.8   Calcium toxicity

Magnesium and calcium appear to be absorbed from the intestines through similar routes and it has been shown in sheep that high calcium diets will impair magnesium uptake and *vice versa*.

7.3   Magnesium

Magnesium is the major intra-cellular divalent cation. It is an important activator of enzymes and is involved in the control of nerve impulses, ensuring that excessive transmission activity is restricted. The total amount of magnesium in an adult cow is about 200 g but about 70% of this is locked into the bone structure and is unavailable to the animal. A further 28% lies within the various soft tissues of the body leaving only 2%, or 4 g, circulating in the body fluids and available in times of shortage (Figure 7.5).

Figure 7.5   Magnesium fluxes in a 600 kg dairy cow

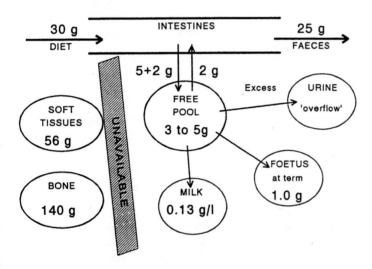

Milk is a considerable drain of magnesium (0.13g Mg/l). The secretion of 2 g/day of magnesium into the intestines is obligatory and any excess absorbed magnesium is excreted via the urine. Unlike calcium there is no hormonal control over the concentration of magnesium in the blood. The cow requires a continuous supply in the diet since the magnesium already within the free pool will only buffer a severe dietary deficit for a few hours.

The major site of absorption of magnesium is the rumen. Dietary availability is only 15 to 30% (whereas calcium is 30 to 70%) is highly variable and totally uncontrolled.

7.3.1   Clinical signs of magnesium deficiency

Clinical magnesium deficiency (staggers) is seen in two forms:

i)   *Rapid development in spring*. Animals grazing on highly fertilised, rapidly growing pastures in the spring have a lower intake of magnesium than when given winter diets. The magnesium from herbage is less available in the intestines and travels through the animal faster then that in other feeds. Also, there is often insufficient sodium for maximal absorption of magnesium (see below). Concentration of magnesium in the blood falls rapidly and clinical disease is seen within days of the animal being introduced to the pastures.

ii)   *Slow development in autumn.* Autumn pastures often have low concentrations of magnesium and with time the cow also becomes depleted. If the animal stops eating, absorption of magnesium falls and the limited free pool (3 to 5 g) can soon be depleted. Sometimes simply handling the cows is sufficient to trigger clinical disease. On other occasions stresses such as bad weather can stop the cow eating and precipitate staggers.

The rapid progression of staggers (hypo-magnesaemia) is such that in most cases affected cows are found dead. In fact the disease is one of the commonest causes of sudden death in dairy cows and it must be remembered that Anthrax causes similar signs and must be tested for by law. Where clinical signs are observed, these start as a hyper-excitability and an over-reaction to being touched or driven. The cow soon becomes recumbent and there is considerable uncoordinated flailing of the legs. Such leg motions are very strong and mark the ground on which the cow lies, which can aid the diagnosis once the cow has died. However such flailing also makes treatment difficult and cows are often given sedatives to facilitate the setting up of a drip and to prevent injury.

7.3.2   Diagnosis of magnesium deficiency

In the living animal the diagnosis of magnesium deficiency is relatively simple. Concentrations of magnesium in the blood are usually below the normal range and the animal responds to slow infusions of magnesium. However, in the dead animal a positive diagnosis is more difficult. After death magnesium diffuses out of the cells into the inter-cellular fluid and the plasma; so, even if a blood sample can be obtained, it is of limited value. The concentration of magnesium in the aqueous humor of the eye has been suggested as an alter-native site for sampling but this again is of little use. At the *post-mortem*, (which can only be carried out once a negative Anthrax test result has been obtained), cerebro-spinal fluid may be collected for magnesium assay. In freshly dead animals, assay of the fluid can be of value but samples are difficult to obtain in field situations.

If intake of magnesium is greater than that used by the body the excess is excreted via the urine, and therefore examination of a urine sample may be useful. Magnesium in the urine indicates the cow was absorbing excess magnesium from her diet, but a negative finding may indicate either a finely balanced intake or a deficiency. In practice, though, all too often the final tetanic struggles immediately prior to death include a contraction of the bladder and at *post-mortem* it is all too often empty!

7.3.3 Treatment of magnesium deficiency

Treatment is not difficult in terms of choice of drug; infusion of magnesium will reduce the deficiency and clinical signs will abate. The difficulty is in finding cows with clinical symptoms of staggers and being able to treat them before they die. Intravenous infusions of magnesium sulphate (25% w/w) give a faster response than injection under the skin, but great care must be taken to infuse the magnesium slowly otherwise the animal may be killed (rapid infusion of magnesium is a recognised method of putting cows down).

7.3.4 Availability of dietary magnesium

The principle problem in magnesium metabolism is the very variable availability of magnesium in the diet, which can be affected by the following factors:

- Low concentration of magnesium in the feed, for example herbage from pasture in spring, especially those that have been selected for rapid early growth, or have had high applications of nitrogen fertiliser. The content of magnesium can also be marginal during the autumn flush of growth.

- Availability of magnesium is lower in fresh grass than in the same grass conserved either as hay or silage and therefore staggers is normally seen in grazing animals.

- Fast-growing ryegrasses are poorer at assimilating magnesium from soil than clovers and other broad-leaved plants.

- The application of potassium to pastures in the spring reduces the availability of magnesium. If fertiliser nitrogen is replaced by spring dressings of animal manure, the risk of reduced availability of magnesium is likely to be increased significantly. High doses of potassium to pastures have three effects:

  ° High potassium content (6 to 7 g/kg DM) reduces the plants' ability to take up magnesium.

  ° Plants have a "luxury" uptake of potassium in excess of their requirements so that the grazing animal consumes forage with high concentrations of potassium. This reduces magnesium absorption.

° Sodium uptake in the plant is reduced. Absorption of magnesium from the intestines is a sodium-linked process, and if sodium content of herbage falls below 3 g/kg DM the rate of absorption of magnesium is decreased. Low sodium intakes also result in a substitution of sodium salts for potassium salts in the saliva thus further worsening any potassium excess.

- Spring grass is generally low in fibre which results in increased rate of passage of the feed through the intestines, reduced retention of digesta and hence reduced absorption of magnesium.

- Plants high in nitrogen or in degradable protein increase the concentration of ammonia in the rumen liquour which may result in the magnesium precipitating out from the rumen contents, thus reducing its absorption.

- The form and preparation of the magnesium supplement affects its availability. Mineral sources obtained from different countries have different availabilities and recent American work (Xin *et al.*, 1989) has shown that reducing the particle size of magnesium oxide from 324 to 237 microns made the magnesium more available.

7.3.5 Preventive measures

Magnesium does not seem to be under any form of homeostatic control, so it cannot be manipulated as can calcium. Control measures can be divided into two categories; those to increase magnesium supply and those designed to rectify the pasture and dietary factors that reduce availability.

1. Increase magnesium supply

a) Inclusion of supplementary magnesium in concentrates. Traditionally, spring-calving cows were given large amounts of concentrates and therefore this was an ideal route for supplementation with magnesium. Feed compounders formulate a winter ration to contain 2 oz of calcined magnesite per 20 lb to 12 lb of cake (their units not mine - equivalent to 6 to 10 g/kg DM). In the spring this will be increased to between 2 oz in 8 lb to 2 oz in 2 lb (16 to 62 g/kg DM), but at the higher inclusions palatability is impaired and molasses or spices must be added to maintain high intakes. With the shift towards late summer calving, many cows are giving little milk at turnout and consequentially are given little or no concentrates, so this supplementation route is of limited value. Even where animals receive adequate supplementation this method is not always reliable due to differences in the availability of magnesium between different sources.

b) Magnesium bullets. Magnesium "bullets" (one or two) can be given using a balling gun. They lie in the cranial part of the rumen and slowly dissolve in the rumen liquor. However bullets are unlikely to release more than about 1 g magnesium/day and this is often inadequate in the face of severe deficiencies. Furthermore, as the magnesium is released in the rumen, its absorption is affected by the levels of nitrogen, potassium and sodium in the diet. Bullets may be useful for dry cows to ensure that calcium absorption and mobilisation is optimal and may provide sufficient magnesium in cases of chronic deficiency. Regurgitation of the bullet can occur.

c) Magnesium-rich licks. Magnesium salts can be included in licks but are generally bitter in taste and require masking with molasses. Whilst this route can supply sufficient magnesium, intakes of such "free access" minerals by individual animals can be very variable, and some animals in a group can succumb to staggers whilst others have severe scours due to consuming too much magnesium.

d) Addition of magnesium to the water supply. Supplementing the water is better than using licks, as intake of water is more consistent and intake is linked to milk production which in turn is linked to magnesium requirements (see Chapter 11). Magnesium acetate or magnesium chloride can be used, with the latter being more palatable. However, cows can detect both in the water and therefore no untreated water sources (e.g. streams or ditches) should be available. Low-yielding animals on low dry matter forages may drink very little water, therefore intakes of magnesium might be low.

e) Pasture dressing. Dressing the pasture with calcined magnesite (35 kg/hectare) is used to good effect in New Zealand. It should be noted that the magnesium is actually consumed directly by the cow and not via increased uptake of magnesium by the grass. Showers of rain or heavy dew will wash the supplement off the grass and re-application will be necessary. Again, the source of the magnesite, the fineness of grinding and the presence of other elements in the diet will affect the availability of magnesium.

f) Use magnesium-rich plants. Many plants, for instance chicory, plantain and ribgrass, contain considerably more magnesium and other trace elements than the highly selected, fast growing ryegrasses. Inclusion of such plants in grazing pastures may be of benefit but they are slow growing in the spring and may be forced out of pastures following high applications of fertiliser N.

2. Increase magnesium availability

a) Fertiliser policy. As potassium reduces magnesium uptake by the plant and absorption of magnesium by the animal, it should not be applied to pasture in the spring. Potassium is far more stable in soils than nitrogen and so can be applied in the preceding autumn for utilisation during spring growth. To maximise the availability of magnesium, nitrogen applications should be minimised, but this will impair the extent and timeliness of spring growth and so a balance must be struck.

b) Supply sodium licks. Many pastures are deficient in sodium. Dairy cows have a pica for sodium and will actively seek it out. Supplying ample sodium licks may be of benefit to redress this deficiency. Whilst there is little direct experimental evidence that licks are effective, they are cheap, easy to use and unlikely to cause any problems in grazing cattle.

7.4   Phosphorus

Phosphorus is present in a wide variety of essential substances in the body such as the nucleic acids and in energy-rich compounds such as adenosine tri-phosphate (ATP) and creatine phosphate. Deficiencies of phosphorus manifest as general poor performance with low growth rates and ill-thrift. Primary phosphorus deficiency is not common in dairy cows. When it is detected it is usually secondary to a calcium deficiency and is resolved when the calcium deficiency is resolved. The existence of deficiency can be easily confirmed by the measurement of the concentration of phosphorus in blood.

Phosphorus is found in feeds as simple inorganic phosphates and in complex organic molecules called phytates with the latter being the predominant form in most ruminant feeds. Pigs and poultry can only utilise simple phosphates but ruminants, through the action of ruminal enzymes, can break down phytates and therefore potentially have access to all the phosphorus in feeds. For the lactating cow the recommended allowance of phosphorus is approximately 80% of that of calcium but, on average, grass contains only 50% as much phosphorus as calcium. An all-grass diet can therefore be deficient in phosphorus, especially if the grass is mature, because the concentration of phosphorus declines with maturity. Cereal seeds are rich in phosphorus and therefore animals given grains usually receive an adequate dietary phosphorus supply. Maize is deficient in phosphorus and therefore needs careful supplementation.

7.5 Sodium

Sodium is the major cation in blood and other body fluids and helps maintain the volume of these fluids as well as being involved in the acid-base balance of the blood. It is also involved in the transmission of nerve impulses and in the absorption of nutrients (especially sugars) across the gut wall and into other cells in the body. Such a widespread range of functions means that deficiency results in general underperformance and slow growth rates rather than any specific clinical sign. The requirement for sodium may increase considerably if mastitis occurs because the excretion of sodium into milk is increased.

Primary clinical deficiency of sodium is rare in dairy cattle in the UK, but it is becoming apparent that many cows on heavily fertilised pastures do not receive sufficient sodium in their diet. Pastures should contain in excess of 3 g sodium/kg DM to ensure adequate intakes. Many spring pastures, however, are deficient in sodium, with surveys showing that between 11% and 25% of UK grassland contain less than 1.5 g sodium/kg DM. Deficiency is particularly common if the pastures have received large doses of potassium fertiliser as this increases potassium and decreases sodium uptake by the plant.

In a trial in Wales (Table 7.2), addition of 32 kg of sodium per hectare per year increased the sodium content and decreased the potassium content of herbage whilst calcium and magnesium content rose slightly. The content of water-soluble carbohydrates (sugars) increased considerably whilst non-protein nitrogen content fell, suggesting that plant metabolism had improved.

Table 7.2 Effects of the application of sodium to pasture on grass composition, rumen characteristics and animal production (Phillips *et al.*, 1994)

	No sodium	32 kg sodium/ha/year
Herbage composition (g/kg DM)		
Na	3.5	4.2
K	16.2	14.5
Mg	1.8	2.0
Ca	4.5	4.9
DM digestibility	716	719
Water-soluble carbohydrates	190	319
Non-protein nitrogen	74	67
Rumen characteristics		
Fluid turnover/h	0.065	0.078
DM degraded in rumen (g/kg)	677	731
Rumen pH	6.6	7.3
Cow production		
Milk yield (kg/day)	18.1	20.0
Milk fat content (g/kg)	37.3	38.8
Milk protein content (g/kg)	33.6	33.3
Liveweight change (kg/day)	0.02	0.21

Cows ate and drank more water, so fluid outflow and degradability of dry matter were increased whilst overall diet digestibility was unaffected. The increased intake of sodium raised salivary sodium content and rumen pH, which was reflected in a raised ratio of acetate to propionate in rumen fluid, and an increased milk fat content was reported. Milk yield was also increased.

The increase in the concentration of magnesium and sodium, and the reduction in potassium and in non-protein nitrogen is likely to increase the availability of magnesium in spring pastures. The improved pasture composition and cow performance after supplementation with sodium suggests that both were sodium-deficient and the maintenance of adequate content of sodium in the herbage would seem advantageous in ensuring optimal animal productivity and good herd health.

American workers (Olson *et al.*, 1989) observed that sodium deficiency caused decreased production in commercial herds. In an experiment to look at the importance of sodium deficiency two groups of cows (past peak lactation) were fed a ration either unsupplemented or supplemented with sodium to 7.5 g Na/kg DM. Milk yields declined to a lesser extent (25.1 to 22.7 kg) than in the unsupplemented group (18.8 to 13.3 kg) during the experimental period. Urinary sodium below 20 meq/l and faecal sodium below 2 g/kg DM were indicative of deficiency. Sampling of 5 high-yielding cows is recommended since they would be at greatest risk of deficiency.

7.6 Sulphur

Sulphur, like nitrogen and carbon, is an essential nutrient for the ruminal micro-organisms. The microbes require the sulphur for the synthesis of the sulphur-containing amino acids, methionine and cysteine. Therefore to get the optimal rate of fermentation and hence maximal intakes and energy digestion the microbes must receive adequate sulphur. In past decades there have been considerable depositions from sulphur emitted into the atmosphere from power stations and other industrial processes. As pollution controls became more rigorous, depositions declined and sulphur deficiencies have appeared in crops - especially in the brassicas. In New Zealand, with its low industrial emissions, sulphur is applied routinely to grassland and in due course deficiencies may become a problem in grassland, and hence in dairy cows, in the UK.

7.6.1 Requirements for sulphur

Sulphur is required for microbial protein synthesis and therefore animal requirements are linked to the amount of effective rumen degradable protein (ERDP) that is fixed by the rumen microbial population. Note that this is the amount of ERDP fixed in the rumen not the amount contained in the diet. Some diets can appear to be deficient when the ratio of S to N in the feeds is checked, but because the diet contains excess ERDP the sulphur supplied is adequate to meet the microbes' requirements.

The high sulphur to nitrogen ratio of wool (Table 7.3) means that sheep which have rapid rates of fleece growth may require additional sulphur. The same applies to Angora goats if they are given feeds low in protein and high in NPN.

Dietary requirements for sulphur usually work out at between 1.1 g and 1.6 g sulphur per kg DM depending on the concentration of protein in the diet, the digestibility of the diet and the level of animal production.

7.6.2　Sources of sulphur

Supplementary sulphur can be supplied by molasses or sodium sulphate (the anhydrous form contains 22.5% sulphur) but elemental sulphur (flowers of sulphur) should not be used as it is not readily assimilated. If elemental sulphur must be used, it should be added at twice the rate of the sulphur in sodium sulphate to achieve the same level of available sulphur in the diet. To meet the requirement of the microbial population for sulphur, each gram of ERDP in the diet requires 0.0112g of sulphur.

Most feed protein sources contain a similar ratio of sulphur to nitrogen as that of animal products (Table 7.3), so as long as the protein sources are "normal" then intakes of sulphur are likely to be adequate. However, if the diet contains high levels of NPN then it is possible that it is deficient in sulphur, and supplementation may be required.

Table 7.3　Typical ratio of sulphur to nitrogen of animal products and some common feeds (ARC, 1980)

Product / Feed	Ratio of S to N
Beef	0.065 : 1
Cow's milk	0.055
Fleece	0.200
Coconut	0.082
Cottonseed	0.068
Linseed	0.078
Groundnut	0.055
Wheat	0.082
Oats	0.105
Barley	0.102
Maize	0.091
Maize silage	0.063
Oat straw	0.167
Barley straw	0.238

It follows therefore that sulphur deficiency will be rare, even in high-yielding dairy cows. The typical UK dairy cow yielding 30 litres milk and given a diet based on grass silage will be receiving most, if not all, of her protein requirements as microbial protein and the grass silage will usually ensure an excess of ERDP. Therefore although the dietary nitrogen to sulphur ratio may be low the cow will usually be receiving adequate sulphur for microbial needs.

7.7　Trace elements

Trace elements are a group of nutrients that are required in small quantities throughout the animal's life. They are usually involved in enzymes or enzyme co-factors within the body and a very wide range of elements have been identified as being essential. In practice the vast majority are never a problem and the following section is limited to those that can cause problems in dairy cows. There are a large number of interactions between different trace elements (see later sections) and these alter the availability of minerals in the intestine and their absorption. For example the availability of copper in the diet is influenced by the concentration of dietary molybdenum, sulphur and iron.

Trace element deficiencies are seen in the dairy cow, but are more common in the young growing animal. There are several reasons for this difference. Firstly trace element requirements for lactation (relative to the requirements for the major minerals, energy and protein) are small in comparison to the requirements for growth, and secondly the dairy cow often receives a concentrate ration containing many ingredients which often originate from many different areas of the world and from a wide range of soil types. In contrast, the growing animal eats home-produced forage with a trace element composition derived from the local soil. However, the increasingly common practice of relying only on home-grown pasture for dairy cows during the summer and of reducing the usage of concentrates during winter increases the likelihood of mineral and trace element deficiencies if the soil is deficient.

The signs of sub-clinical trace element deficiency are not distinctive; similar symptoms can be caused by other problems. For example, low selenium status can result in poor fertility and low copper and cobalt status can reduce growth rates. Great care must be taken not to link the clinical signs directly with a deficiency without considering all the other possible causes. Usually poor performance is not due to a mineral deficiency but a failure in management or nutrition, and these factors must be investigated and corrected first before trace element problems are considered. All too often, mineral supplementation is used in an attempt to correct problems in herds when deficiency is not the primary cause of the problem.

7.7.1 Copper

Copper is involved in the uptake of iron from the diet, its incorporation into haemoglobin and in the oxygen metabolism in the red blood cell as well as being involved in many other enzyme systems. It has a role in the production of many pigments in hair, fur and wool, hence the classical signs of severe copper deficiency are lack of pigmentation, with a lightening of coat colour - particularly around the eyes which leads to a "spectacled" appearance. However such signs are only seen in severe cases and more often changes in coat colour are associated with other factors such as seasonal moulting. However, copper deficiency has a serious economic impact well before the classical signs are observed; in dairy cattle these are reduced fertility and anoestrus and in young animals ill-thrift and reduced growth.

Copper deficiency can be either primary, where there is an absolute lack of copper in the soil and hence the pasture, or secondary, when there is adequate copper in the soil but its uptake is blocked by other soil minerals. Primary deficiency is not common in the United Kingdom but can be seen on sandy soils and other types of soils which do not retain minerals. Secondary copper deficiency is more common and is often called "teart". Copper metabolism is inhibited by a range of minerals; in descending order of importance these are molybdenum, sulphur, iron, calcium, zinc and selenium. High concentrations of molybdenum in the soil are the greatest problem and interfere with copper metabolism at various levels including copper availability in the feed, uptake of copper and the metabolism of copper within the body. In the gut copper reacts with the molybdenum and sulphate to form thiomolybdates which are not absorbed by the animal and are excreted in faeces.

Copper deficiency occurs in various circumstances. Firstly where animals are highly dependent on home-grown feeds for all their nutrient requirements, a primary deficiency or mild "teart" problem can lead to inadequate absorption of copper and hence deficiency. Calves are particularly susceptible to copper deficiency as milk is a poor source of copper but a good source of molybdenum.

Secondly, in severe "teart" areas, such as Somerset, even normal supplementation with copper is inadequate to overcome the high concentrations of molybdenum in soils and plants. Such problems have been referred to as molybdenum toxicity as it is the excess of this mineral that causes the problems rather than a copper deficiency. In areas where "teart" occurs but is rare the additional use of supplementary sulphur and other trace elements may be sufficient to put animals into a deficiency state. For example the use of sulphuric acid as a silage additive has been reported to change a marginal copper status into a deficiency. Similarly, excessively high intakes of calcium, zinc, iron or selenium may cause problems.

Improving pastures often exacerbates a copper deficiency problem as lime (calcium carbonate) is frequently used. The conservation of grass generally increases the availability of copper by breaking down the thiomolybdate complex, so the risk of copper deficiency is greatest in the summer. However on many farms in "teart" areas the deficiency is so great that problems occur throughout the year.

Definitive diagnosis of copper deficiency is difficult. The best method is actually to observe a response to supplementation but this is slow, ideally requires an untested control group, and could lead to toxicity if the original supposition was incorrect. Blood, or more correctly plasma, total copper levels are well correlated with the biologically-active form of copper - cerulo-plasmin. It should be noted, however, that plasma copper concentrations are about 15% higher than serum, as copper is removed when the blood clot forms. Furthermore the bio-availablity of copper in the blood falls with increasing intake of iron and molybdenum, making interpretation of the results difficult. Furthermore, the concentration of copper in blood plasma remains within the normal range over a wide range of dietary intakes and so is of little value in the diagnosis of marginal deficiency.

Copper is stored in the liver and during periods of deficiency the concentration of copper in the blood are maintained by drawing on liver reserves. Therefore any period of copper deficiency depletes liver concentrations and liver biopsy may be more useful in the assessment of sub-clinical deficiency. However, many laboratories require in excess of 1 g of liver tissue so a 3 to 5 mm core must be obtained; whilst this can be carried out with little risk to the cow it is a far greater undertaking than obtaining a simple blood sample.

The measurement of copper-containing enzymes such as super-oxide dismutase (SOD) in red blood cells has been suggested as a way of diagnosing deficiency. However, this reflects the copper status of the animal when the red blood cell was produced and therefore is only an indication of copper status several weeks previously. Similarly the copper in the hair is closely related to concentration of copper in the plasma but again reflects the status of the animal when the hair was lain down and not at the time of sampling.

Despite all the above considerations copper deficiency is usually investigated in practice via plasma copper assays; if concentrations are low then the animal is definitely deficient. If they are within the normal range, and copper deficiency is still suspected, then a liver biopsy should be taken.

Supplementation with copper. Pasture dressing of 5 to 7 kg copper sulphate/hectare usually increases the concentration of copper in herbage for 2 to 3 years. Licks and others supplements can be used, but uptake of copper will be inhibited by any molybdenum or sulphur in the diet. Copper proteinates seem to give better responses than the oxide or the sulphate in "teart" areas and can be used to replace about 33 to 50% of the copper in an oral supplement. Proteinates are far more expensive than the oxide or the sulphate form and therefore should only be used on farms with severe problems. Gelatine boluses containing copper oxide needles can be given by mouth. The needles lodge in the folds of the reticulum and slowly dissolve over 12 months. Another form of oral supplementation are boluses made of a special formulation of glass rich in copper, cobalt and selenium that dissolve over a period of months.

Injections of copper overcome the problems of impaired absorption from the alimentary tract, but the problem is the narrow therapeutic range for copper. Most injectable preparations release the copper quickly, hence initial absorption is high and then rapidly trails off. If too large a dose is injected the initial peak release results in toxicity; if too little is given the benefit gained is limited (Figure 7.6). The limited amount of copper that can be given at any one time restricts the duration of the benefit gained.

Figure 7.6   Copper status of an animal after a small or large dose of injectable copper preparation

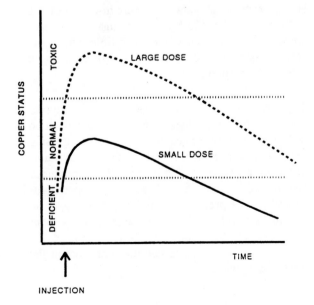

Three preparations can be used in injectable form; copper calcium EDTA, copper sodium EDTA and copper glycinate. Copper calcium EDTA is released more slowly that copper sodium EDTA but neither can be used in sheep as their rate of release is too rapid. Release from copper glycinate is slower, but its use is associated with abscesses at the site of injection.

7.7.2   Selenium

Selenium and vitamin E are often considered together as they have a similar function in the animal as antioxidants, guarding cells against the potentially destructive free radical compounds formed during cellular metabolism. Deficiency in either can result in cellular damage and death. Severe cases manifest as white muscle disease where cells in the locomotor muscles are damaged and appear white and dry on *post-mortem*. If the heart muscle cells are affected sudden death occurs. However, of greater economic importance is subclinical deficiency. Growing animals show signs of muscle weakness, poor growth rates and potentially mortality. In the dairy cow deficiencies have been linked with increased mastitis, metritis (retained infected placenta) and impaired disease resistance. It is important to remember that there are other, more common, causes of these diseases and great care must be taken to exclude these before suspecting selenium deficiency.

Supplementation of selenium-deficient dairy cows has been shown to increase first service conception rates (McClure *et al.*, 1986). With regard to retained foetal membranes, benefits have only been seen where deficient herds (<0.06 mg Se/kg DM) are supplemented and where the incidence is greater than 20% (Olson, 1994). The results of supplementing two selenium-deficient herds with 0.1 ppm selenium in their diets are shown in Table 7.4.

Table 7.4   Effect of supplementation with 0.1 ppm of selenium on cow fertility (adapted from Cortese, 1988)

	Herd A		Herd B	
	Before Supplementation	After	Before Supplementation	After
Number of services per conception	2.34	2.10	2.82	1.81
Days open (calving to conception)	136	116	168	98
Calving interval	421	401	453	383
Blood selenium concentration (ppm)				
-immediately after calving	0.038	0.081	0.021	0.073
-at peak lactation	0.053	0.088	0.047	0.076

Work in the 1980s showed that supplementation of selenium deficient animals reduced the incidence and severity of environmental mastitis (Olson, 1994). American work investigated the selenium status of 16 herds with a high somatic cell count (SCC, >700,000 cells/ml) and 16 herds with a low SCC (<150,000) and found that both selenium and vitamin E were significantly higher in the herds with low SCC. The herds with high SCC had predominantly *Streptococcus agalactia* and *Staphlococcus aureus* mastitis but other trials showed less of an effect on staphylococcal mastitis (Olson, 1994).

Diagnosing selenium deficiency. The blood enzyme glutathione peroxidase (GSPx) is highly correlated with selenium status and can be measured in most laboratories. Therefore, unlike copper and cobalt, a definite diagnosis can be made. But unfortunately concentrations of GSPx in the blood in normal animals vary widely, and animals that respond to supplementation may show values for GSPx which actually lie within the normal range. It is preferable to measure serum GSPx as this stabilises within 1 to 3 weeks of changes in selenium status whereas red blood cell GSPx will take several months to stabilise due to the long lifespan of the red blood cells.

Supplementation with selenium can usually be carried out via the feed, but care must be taken as the difference between beneficial and toxic supplementation is small. Selenium can be added to the compound feed for dairy cattle or given via slow release glass boluses for growing stock.

7.7.3 Cobalt

Cobalt is required in the rumen for the synthesis of vitamin B_{12}. Deficiency leads to poor growth and ill thrift in young stock and makes them more susceptible to internal parasitism. In dairy cows ketosis and weight loss are the usual clinical signs of cobalt deficiency. In its acute and severe form cobalt deficiency is limited to well defined geographical areas. Signs of disease vary from unthriftiness to severe emaciation and death.

Diagnosis is made by measuring vitamin B_{12} concentration in blood. Unfortunately total vitamin B_{12} measurement is of little value because not all of it is biologically active in the blood and the relative proportions are not constant. Biologically active vitamin B_{12} can be measured but the assay takes a long time and is not very reliable. Methylmalonic acid (MMA) has been shown to be a better assay with high levels indicating a cobalt deficiency, but at the moment few laboratories can measure MMA, so in practice diagnosis is usually made by observing a response to supplementation.

7.7.4 Zinc

Deficiencies cause anorexia, skin lesions, ill-thrift and possibly lameness. Baggot *et al.* (1988) demonstrated lower levels of zinc in the hoof horn of lame cows compared to normal animals. Italian workers have suggested that zinc may play an important part in the aetiology of sole ulcer in dairy cattle. However, no significant reduction in the incidence of lameness in cows given 4.5 g zinc methionine per cow for two 4-month periods has been found (Dermertzis *et al.*, 1973). Bonomi *et al.* (1988) reported a beneficial effect of zinc on the healing of soft tissue lesions associated with foul-in-the-foot whereas Mortellaro (1986) found no association between zinc status and susceptibility to digital dermatitis.

Zinc affects the properties of hoof keratin by its action on synthesis rather than by incorporation in the protein structure. Any effect of deficiency would be that of faulty keratin synthesis and would almost certainly be reflected in other deficiency symptoms. It is unlikely that a simple trace element deficiency such as that of zinc could alone be responsible for the high incidence of lesions such as white line disease or sole ulcer in a herd. Given the large amounts of galvanised steel on most farms it is also unlikely that zinc deficiency will be a problem in practical situations. However, some producers seem to find the idea of a panacea attractive and it appears sectors of the feed industry are ready and willing to meet that demand.

7.7.5 Iodine

Iodine is involved in the formation of the thyroid hormones thyroxine and tri-iodothyronine which regulate metabolic rate. Deficiency may arise either as a primary deficiency due to the low iodine content of soil, water and feeds, or as a secondary deficiency induced by the presence of goitrogens in the diet. Common sources of goitrogens are kale, cabbage and certain clovers. These compounds increase the iodine requirements of animals because they prevent the incorporation of absorbed iodine into the thyroid hormones.

Iodine deficiency can impair reproductive efficiency and cause stunted growth. Foetal development may be arrested at any stage with the result that weak or hairless calves are stillborn or born alive with low birth weights, poor growth and low survival rates. In lactating cattle, iodine deficiency reduces milk yield and may also cause irregular or suppressed oestrus.

Diagnosing iodine deficiency. Measuring thyroxine and tri-iodothyronine in blood plasma is of little value in cattle. Only where a representative sample of cattle has been taken and the results can be assessed together with dietary information can a reliable interpretation be given. Measuring plasma iodine content directly is more useful but also more difficult. Concentrations of iodine may also be measured in the urine and milk. Diagnosis at *postmortem* is best done by examining the thyroid. The thyroid must be carefully dissected out of a fresh calf carcass, taking care not to include any other tissues. The weight of a clean thyroid should be less than 0.0375% of the calf body weight (15 g for a 40 kg calf); a heavier weight than this suggests hypertrophy in response to low iodine supply.

Herd problems with stillborn calves are slow to develop and slow to respond to treatment. Supplementation midway through an outbreak will not resolve the problem immediately and problems may persist for some time before a response is seen. The currently recommended dietary iodine concentration for all stock, including pregnant and lactating animals, is 0.5 mg iodine/kg DM (ARC, 1980).

Many grasses contain considerably less iodine than the recommended concentration and clovers contain only 0.06 to 0.17 mg iodine/kg DM. It is therefore important that supplementary iodine is provided when herbage is used as a major part of the diet, particularly during the winter months when the iodine requirement increases. However, excessive iodine supplementation can increase the iodine concentration of milk. For instance an increase in dietary intake from 16 to 164 mg iodine/day can increase milk iodine from 370 to 2160 µg/kg. As the daily human requirement is between 40 and 150 µg/day, elevated levels of iodine in milk should be avoided.

7.7.6 *Iron*
Iron is involved in the formation of haemoglobin and deficient animals show signs of anaemia and weakness. Most soils contain sufficient iron to meet the requirement of the animal, so only those housed and given an all-milk diet are likely to become deficient. Excessive iron in the diet impairs the uptake

and metabolism of other trace elements and can decrease concentrations of copper in the liver and plasma and also decrease the activity of copper-containing enzymes. Where supplements are used, diets should not contain more than 500 mg iron/kg DM.

7.7.7 *Summary*
A summary of the role of major and trace elements in dairy cows is given in Table 7.5.

7.8 Vitamins

Vitamins are essential organic molecules required by the body but which it cannot synthesise. The original definition referred to humans, and several (B, C and K) can in fact be synthesised by ruminants. The vitamins frequently act as hormones, enzymes or co-enzymes in a variety of metabolic pathways. In general they are absorbed from the small intestine but are only required in small amounts as they are recycled within the body. Vitamin requirements can be calculated for specific classes of animals at specific production levels; however, this is rarely done in practice. More commonly rations are supplemented with the vitamins known to be required by the cow, usually vitamin A, D and E. The level of supplementation is usually generous so that all classes of animal are covered and it is assumed that highly productive animals will be given more of the supplemented feed and therefore receive sufficient vitamins. In a few instances (see below) other dietary factors can reduce the availability or uptake of vitamins, in which case specific additional supplementation is required.

Table 7.5 Summary of role of minerals and trace elements in dairy cows and possible interactions (McCullough, 1986)

Mineral	Primary use or effect	Interactions
Calcium (Ca)	Bone growth, milk production, enzyme systems and muscle function	Phosphorus, vitamin D_3, iron, lipids in feeds, manganese, zinc
Phosphorus (P)	Bone growth, milk production, appetite, reproduction, carbohydrate metabolism	Calcium, vitamin D_3, iron, manganese
Magnesium (Mg)	Milk, bone formation, enzymes, muscle and nerve function	Potassium, calcium, phosphorus, zinc, nitrogen (in plants)
Potassium (K)	Water balance, nervous system, milk production, acid-base balance, feed intake, hair gloss	Magnesium, sodium
Sodium (Na)	Water balance, milk production, appetite, hair coat	Potassium
Sulphur (S)	Necessary for sulphur containing amino acids in rumen, inappetence	Copper, selenium
Iron (Fe)	Cellular respiration, haemoglobin (anaemia)	Cobalt, copper, calcium, phosphorus
Copper (Cu)	Bone formation, energy metabolism, nerve network, reproduction, retained placentas, colour change in hair and around eyes	Zinc, sulphur, molybdenum, iron, lead
Zinc (Zn)	Component or co-factor of many enzyme systems, reproduction, rumen function	Calcium, copper, iron, phosphorus, lead, magnesium.
Cobalt (Co)	Rumen production of Vitamin B_{12}, prevention of anaemia, nerve function	Iron, iodine
Selenium (Se)	Reproduction, retained placentas, muscle dystrophy, liver necrosis, stiff joints	Vitamin E, sulphur, fats, proteins
Manganese (Mn)	Bone formation, muscle development, delayed oestrus periods, growth	Calcium, phosphorus, iron

7.8.1 Vitamin A (retinol)

Although plant materials do not contain any vitamin A they are rich in carotenoids which are precursors of vitamin A. Carotenoids are associated with chlorophyll in plants and are therefore abundant in most green feeds and rarely in deficit in diets based on grass. Carotenoids are absorbed intact across the gut of the cow (and horse) and can be responsible for the yellow tinge to milk and fat depots.

Vitamin A is involved in the maintenance of simple epithelial surfaces such as the lining of the alimentary, respiratory and urogenital tracts and in the maintenance of vision. Deficiency results in a disordered change to these surfaces.

Supplementation with vitamin A is safe with up to 100 times the recommended dose failing to produce signs of toxicity. As a result most compound feeds are supplemented routinely. However, vitamin A degrades over time, particularly in damp conditions in the presence of sunlight and therefore inclusion levels are only guaranteed for a limited period. Responses to vitamin A have been recorded with diets based on maize silage.

7.8.2 Vitamin B

Vitamin B is in fact a range of different vitamins known as the vitamin B complex. They are involved as co-enzymes in various biochemical reactions but are generally well conserved in the body and deficiencies rarely occur. Ruminants synthesise their own B vitamins via the rumen microbial population and then absorb them in the small intestine. The microbes require cobalt for this and therefore vitamin B deficiency manifests itself as cobalt deficiency (see Section 7.7.3).

Secondary deficiency of thiamine (vitamin B_1) can occur through the activity of thiaminase. Typically this is seen in young animals (less than 2 years old) given diets high in sugars and starch which result in ruminal acidosis which favours thiaminase activity. It also occurs in animals given diets rich in sulphite. Thiamine deficiency causes cerebro-cortical necrosis (CCN) with destruction of neurones and oedema and haemorrhage in the cerebral cortex of the brain resulting in blindness. Sub-clinical deficiency usually occurs in the herdmates of CCN affected animals and results in depressed growth rates. The disease usually responds to thiamine injections which are virtually non-toxic at any dose. Deficiencies of the other vitamin B compounds have not been reported in ruminants.

7.8.3 Vitamin C (ascorbic acid)

Most animals can synthesise vitamin C and therefore deficiencies are never seen. Only humans and guinea pigs are unable to synthesise vitamin C.

7.8.4 Vitamin D_3

Vitamin D_3 is involved in the regulation of the concentration of calcium in the blood (see Section 7.2.1). It is either absorbed from sun-cured forage or it can be synthesised in the skin through the action of ultraviolet light. Most animals can synthesise sufficient vitamin D_3 in the skin, so eating sun-cured forage is not essential. Vitamin D_3 then undergoes two conversions, one in the liver and the second in the kidney, to become 1-25 dihydroxy-Vitamin D_3 which is the form active in the regulation of calcium metabolism (Figure 7.2). Deficiency manifests itself as rickets in young animals due to poor bone formation. Toxicity is seen occasionally, usually through the erroneous use of vitamin D_3 injections to prevent milk fever. Excessive vitamin D_3 results in calcium deposition in the soft tissues and deposits in the heart muscles lead to weakness, recumbency and finally death.

7.8.5 Vitamin E

Together with selenium, vitamin E acts as an antioxidant, preventing the cell from being damaged by the products of cellular metabolism. The functions of selenium and vitamin E are similar, therefore clinical signs of deficiency are also similar. Vitamin E is found in fresh green feeds and therefore body reserves increase during the grazing season, but can decline over the winter. Severe clinical cases are therefore most often seen at the time of turn-out to pasture. Clinical signs are due to oxidative damage and death of muscle cells. In young animals the heart muscles are affected and therefore sudden death is seen. In older animals the locomotor muscles are affected and cases show as white muscle disease. In adult cows, vitamin E deficiency may increase the incidence of metritis, retained afterbirths and mastitis, but it must be remembered that many other factors also predispose to these diseases and they are usually more common. Supplementation can be either vitamin E or selenium. Vitamin E is stable in dry feeds but is reduced in moist feeds so that inclusion levels are usually only guaranteed for a limited period of time. Vitamin E is destroyed in moist grain treated with propionic acid. High-fat diets need increased vitamin E supplementation, especially where the fats are unsaturated.

7.8.6 Vitamin K

Vitamin K is synthesised by the rumen bacteria and is involved in the regulation of the blood clotting mechanism. Primary deficiency is rare but secondary deficiency can occur when poorly conserved (moist) sweet clover hays (an American forage feed) are eaten. Such feeds contain warfarin (rat poison) and this blocks the clotting mechanism.

7.8.7 *Vitamin H (biotin)*

Biotin deficiency has been reported in pigs which develop soft friable hooves and an increased incidence of lameness. This has also been noted in horses, but despite a high incidence of lameness in dairy cattle due to other causes nobody has yet been able to demonstrate a biotin deficiency.

7.8.8 *Summary*

A summary of the role of vitamins in dairy cows and their possible interactions is given in Table 7.6.

Table 7.6 Summary of role of vitamins in dairy cows and possible interactions (McCullough, 1986)

Vitamin	Primary use or effect	Interactions
Vitamin A	Normal epithelium, prevents night blindness, milk production, reproduction, growth	Nitrates, stress
Vitamin D_3	Bone formation, growth, calcium and phosphorus utilisation	Calcium, phosphorus
Vitamin E	Reproduction, muscle dystrophy, prevention of oxidised flavour in milk	Selenium, fats
Vitamin K	Blood clotting	Mycotoxins, dicoumarol
Niacin (B_3)	Milk production, ketosis, rumen fermentation	None
Thiamine (B_1)	Nervous system, polioencephalomalacia (CCN)	High grain rations, thiaminase in feeds
Other B vitamins	Needed by young calves and adults during anorexia	

PART 3

DIET FORMULATION

CHAPTER 8

PREDICTING FEED INTAKE

8.1   Introduction

8.2   Factors affecting intake
       8.2.1   Body weight
       8.2.2   Milk yield
       8.2.3   Quality of the ration
       8.2.4   Stage of lactation
       8.2.5   Stage of pregnancy

8.3   Predicting feed intake
       8.3.1   Milking cows
       8.3.2   Dry cows

8.4   Modifying intake

8.5   Examples

8.6   Manual exercises

8.7   Computer exercises

8.1   Introduction

The ability to predict voluntary intake accurately is crucial to successful diet formulation, but achieving accuracy has eluded research workers for many years. Recent work has resulted in a series of equations being derived that use a range of different parameters to predict intake. Some of the better predictions come from equations that either predict the intake of the silage on its own, or require the amount of concentrate fed to be known to make the prediction. Whilst such equations are valid in experimental situations where the supplementary feeds are offered as a compounded pellet along with a single forage, in practice there may be more than one forage on offer (e.g. grass silage, maize silage and straw) and it may be difficult to determine which feeds should be regarded as concentrates and which as forages (e.g. high-starch maize silage, high-fibre brewers' grains and sugar beet pulp). This chapter and those that follow do not use equations where the intake of concentrate is required or which predict silage intake.

Other equations for predicting intake are based on a better characterisation of grass silage (ammonia nitrogen, VFA content etc.). However, as such analyses are not available for all feeds (e.g. ensiled brewers grains can contain both ammonia nitrogen and VFA), these equations are disregarded to ensure that sensible predictions can be derived in all farm circumstances. The unfortunate corollary to the two constraints outlined above is that most of the equations that can be used are based on data from the 1970s or earlier.

A major parameter in the early published equations is body weight. It is assumed that body weight is related to rumen and intestinal capacity. However the dairy cow has changed considerably over the intervening decades with the increasing influence of Holstein blood. This has resulted in a larger cow that carries less flesh but has a deeper abdomen and presumably a larger rumen and greater intestinal capacity. Such animals are likely to eat more feed relative to their body weight than their predecessors and these differences can be seen in results such as those shown in Figure 8.1.

Figure 8.1   Intake and milk production of 650 kg cows over the first 30 days of lactation (from Zamet *et al.*, 1979)

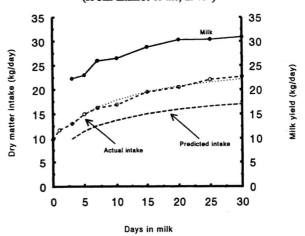

The intake predicted using the relationships outlined in this chapter (the dashed line in Figure 8.1) follows the shape of the actual measured intake well over the first 30 days of lactation but needs to be increased by approximately 20% to match the amounts actually eaten.

The main factors affecting voluntary dry matter intake considered in the following sections are body weight, milk production (yield or yield corrected for energy content), ration quality, stage of lactation and stage of pregnancy. From the arguments presented in Chapter 4 it can be seen that this approach omits many other factors that are known to influence voluntary intake. Voluntary intake is therefore the least well predicted mechanism of all those considered, which is very unfortunate in that only with a valid estimate of intake can any sensible assessment be made about the adequacy of the energy, protein and mineral supply. This limitation must always be borne in mind when formulating rations and two actions in particular should be taken:

- Always, but always, assess voluntary intake on the farm. With a little ingenuity intake can usually be estimated with some accuracy. Supplementary feeding is usually controlled in some way and this can be used to assess intake (with suitable checks and caution over calibration of the measurements).

- Assessment of voluntary intake of forages is more difficult, especially in the grazing situation. When conserved feeds are used it is possible to measure how fast the feed leaves the silo, or to weigh blocks of silage. It is also possible to fit weight detectors to the hydraulics of material handling equipment or load cells to forage and mixer wagons. In all cases some estimate of intake should be made and this compared to, and allowed to override, the predictions.

- Be prepared to modify predicted voluntary dry matter intakes. Given the many factors known to influence intake it is important that any ration calculation procedure allows the users to modify intake. This may be regarded as "fudging" but time will usually tell if estimates are correct and animals perform as required. Such "fudging" is acceptable as most of the factors mentioned in Chapter 4 that influence intake can sensibly be assessed by the farmer and their advisers.

8.2   Factors affecting intake

As mentioned in Chapter 4, the water content of feeds does not usually exert a major influence on voluntary intake. Intake is therefore expressed as dry matter per day in the following sections. All feeds contain some water (compound feeds are typically 14% water, silage 75% water) so voluntary intake of fresh feeds on the farm will need to be corrected for their water content before comparisons of actual intake are made with predictions.

The factors considered to affect voluntary intake and used in making the predictions will now be considered in order of importance and brief tables presented of predicted dry matter intake. The final part of this chapter contains a series of examples and exercises related to the prediction of intake from the tables. More detailed versions of the tables will be found in Chapter 20.

8.2.1   Body weight

Body weight is the major factor determining intake (Figure 8.2) to such an extent that a simple rule of thumb - intake is 3% of body weight - gives a very valuable first estimate across all types of dairy cattle.

The great advantage of the relationship in Figure 8.2 is that it is simple enough to be applied on-farm whilst inspecting the cows and their diets and so it is usually the first estimate used. This simple approach does

however have some limitations due to the inherent assumption that body weight is a suitable indicator of gut capacity. As mentioned above, the relationship has changed with the increasing influence of Holstein cattle such that the gut capacity per kilogram body weight has increased. It also assumes all animals have the same degree of fat cover. In fact it is likely that fatter cows will eat less as they are likely to make use of the stored energy reserves (Chapter 16). When assessing body weight it is therefore important to estimate what the cow would weigh at condition score 2.5 (and barren - see later) rather than her exact weight.

Figure 8.2   The prediction of dry matter intake from body weight (MAFF, 1984)

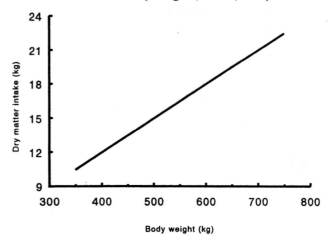

8.2.2   Milk yield

A milking cow eats more than the same cow on the same diet when not giving any milk. There has been considerable debate as to whether intake stimulates milk production or *vice versa*, but experiments with bovine somatotrophin (Chapter 15) have shown that milk yield increases first and intake rises a few weeks after. Figure 8.3 shows how intake increases with milk yield in a 600 kg cow.

Figure 8.3   Predicted dry matter intake for different milk yields in a 600 kg cow (MAFF, 1984)

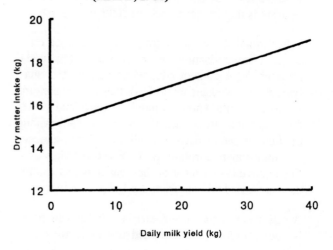

Note that dry matter intake is 18 kg when 30 kg of milk is produced. The accuracy of the equation is sufficiently poor that it does not matter if you use litres or kilograms to measure milk production. Given that milk yield seems to stimulate voluntary intake it is probable that milk quality also influences intake. Milk of high solids content from Jersey cows may have a greater stimulatory effect on intake than lower quality milk. Some predictions take this into account by correcting milk yield to a constant milk fat composition of 4% - called Fat Corrected Milk (FCM) - whilst others do not.

8.2.3 Quality of the ration

As mentioned in Chapter 4, voluntary intake is influenced by the quality of the diet and the needs of the animal. Feed of lower quality stays in the rumen for a longer time to be degraded by the microbes and only when particles have been degraded and have passed out of the rumen can more feed be consumed. On higher quality diets voluntary intake is not limited by rate of digestion and the cow eats to meet her nutritional commitments and usually also gains weight. However, with lower quality feeds such as hays and straws, the physical limitation to intake must be taken into account.

The quality of a diet can be assessed by a variety of methods but the metabolisability or q (ME/GE) is often used as this is also required to calculate energy requirements and is based on ME and GE of the feed, which are both normally available (see Chapters 5 and 20). Figure 8.4 shows how predicted voluntary intake increases with q. From a voluntary intake of about 19 kg DM on a ration with a q of 0.55 (an average silage) there is a decline to about 10 kg DM when q is 0.35 (straw).

Figure 8.4   Predicted dry matter intake for a 600 kg cow giving 30 kg of milk of 4% fat and given diets of differing quality (q) (ARC, 1980)

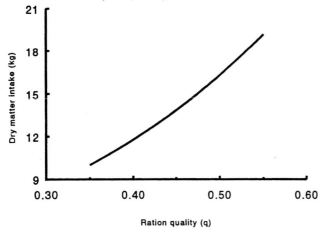

8.2.4   Stage of lactation

Freshly-calved cows do not eat as much as would be predicted. Figure 8.1 shows the intake in a group of

cows (650 kg) on a diet of silage and concentrates in the first 30 days of lactation. Milk yields are over 25 kg/day but intakes are well below 3% of body weight (19.5 kg) for the first three weeks. Cows probably do not feel much like eating just after calving, but there are additional reasons for the low intakes. Firstly, much of the abdomen in the heavily pregnant cow is occupied by the uterus and foetus, so the rumen is smaller as a result and can take several days to adjust in size after calving. Secondly, there is a major change in the type of diet at calving from a high-forage to a high-concentrate mix. Both the rumen wall and the microbial population need to adapt to the feed being consumed and this can take 10 to 14 days.

8.2.5   Stage of pregnancy

The size of the foetus and the depression in voluntary intake is small in the first two thirds of pregnancy and it is normal to ignore the effects of pregnancy on voluntary intake until the final two months of gestation. As mentioned already, the volume of the rumen is likely to decline in late pregnancy as the uterus enlarges and hence voluntary intake is lower than expected at this time. Figure 8.5 shows the pattern of voluntary intake of cows and heifers on two trials conducted in America (Zamet *et al.*, 1979 and Saun *et al.*, 1993). It can be seen that throughout the last month voluntary intake was low at 1.5 to 1.7% of body weight, despite a reasonably good quality ration being offered. In the last few days of pregnancy intake declined considerably so that at calving animals were eating only 7 to 9 kg DM/day.

Figure 8.5   Actual dry matter intake of 650 kg cows and 565 kg heifers in the in the last 25 days of gestation (from Zamet et al., 1979 and Saun et al., 1993)

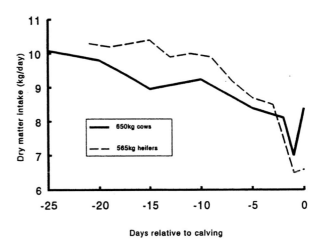

8.3   Predicting feed intake

As can be seen from the figures in the above section there is a range of possible predictions for intake and each will give a slightly different answer. For example consider a 600 kg cow giving 20 litres of milk on a ration with a q of 0.50. If body weight alone is used to predict intake then the value obtained is 18 kg (Figure 8.2). If milk yield is also included the intake is 17 kg (Figure 8.3) and if the quality of the ration is taken into account the intake is predicted as 14.6 kg (Figure 8.4). Clearly the quality of the ration is having a big effect on predicted intake and the value to use in further ration assessments should be 14.6 kg.

In general, when calculating voluntary intake from published predictive equations it is necessary to consider the full range of factors appropriate to the animal in question, to determine which gives the lowest answer and then to use that. This procedure involves a lot of calculation much of which is eventually not necessary. To eliminate this tedium, the following tables are derived from a combination of the different predictive equations with only the lowest, most limiting value being given.

8.3.1   Milking cows (see Chapter 20, Table 20.1)

To predict the dry matter intake of a milking cow the following information is required:

- Body weight (at condition score 2.5 and not in calf)
- Milk yield
- Ration quality (q)
- Days into lactation

Table 8.1   Predicted dry matter intake of milking cows according to diet quality (q), body weight (kg) and milk yield (litres or kg) (from MAFF 1984)

q = 0.50	Milk yield		
Body weight	0	10	20
500	9.4	11.1	12.8
550	10.3	12.0	13.7
600	11.2	12.9	14.6
650	12.1	13.8	15.5
700	12.9	14.6	16.3

q ≥ 0.60	Milk yield				
Body weight	0	10	20	30	40
500	12.5	13.5	14.5	15.0	16.5
550	13.8	14.8	15.8	16.5	17.8
600	15.0	16.0	17.0	18.0	19.0
650	16.3	17.3	18.3	19.3	20.3
700	17.5	18.5	19.5	20.5	21.5

Table 8.1 shows how voluntary intake varies with changing milk yield, body weight and ration quality. The table is divided into two sections - one for ration qualities (q) of 0.5 which corresponds to a diet of poor silage as might be given to a low-yielding cow. The other section corresponds to diets with q greater than or equal to 0.60 which would be typical of diets given to higher-yielding animals. Within each section the rows are for different cow weights, ranging from 500 to 700 kg and the columns correspond to different milk yields, ranging from

zero to 40 litres. If we consider a 600 kg cow giving 20 litres of milk a day given a diet with a q of 0.5, then she is predicted to be able to eat 14.6 kg dry matter a day and this rises to 17.0 kg when q is 0.6.

The intakes given in Table 8.1 are predicted appetites and say nothing about the adequacy of such rations to support milk production. In many cases intake is too low for the animal to consume sufficient energy and protein. Diet quality has a large influence on intake, particularly at low milk yields and it may be necessary to estimate intakes for intermediate values of q. A fuller version of this table that considers more weight and milk yields is given in Chapter 20 (Table 20.1, page 204).

Figure 8.6 shows the recommended correction factors for week of lactation. For example a 600 kg cow yielding 30 litres of milk and given a diet with q > 0.60 is predicted to eat 18 kg of DM (Table 8.1). In her 4th week of lactation she has a correction factor of 0.88 and her corrected intake is 18 x 0.88 = 15.8 kg DM. A table giving correction factors for each week is presented in Chapter 20 (Table 20.2).

Figure 8.6   Correction factors for dry matter intake in relation to week of lactation (adapted from Vadiveloo and Holmes, 1979)

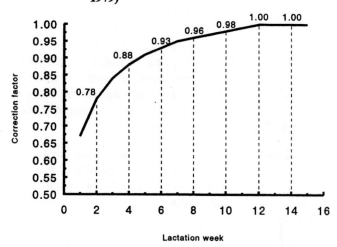

8.3.2   Dry cows (see Chapter 20, Table 20.4)

To predict the dry matter intake of a dry cow the following information is required:

- Body weight (at condition score 2.5 and not in calf)
- Ration quality

Table 8.2   Predicted dry matter intake of dry cows according to ration quality (q) and animal body weight (kg)

	q value of diet		
Body weight (kg)	0.40	0.50	0.60
450	6.1	8.5	11.6
500	6.8	9.4	12.9
550	7.5	10.3	14.2
600	8.1	11.2	15.5
650	8.7	12.1	16.7

Table 8.2 shows the predicted dry matter intake of dry pregnant dairy cows. The rows relate to different body weights and the columns to different ration qualities. For example, a 600 kg cow on a diet with a q value of 0.5 is predicted to eat 11.2 kg dry matter. It is difficult to make predictions about voluntary intake in the last two weeks of pregnancy but they are likely to fall a further 1 to 2 kg (see Figure 8.5).

8.4   Modifying intake

A wide range of factors can influence intake in addition to those discussed in Section 8.2, but they are difficult to quantify in terms that can be included in predictions. Most nutritionists tend to modify intake according to their own experience and the farm situation. Some of the possible correction factors that have been suggested are shown in Table 8.3, but care should be taken not to end up overestimating or inflating voluntary intake as a high intake is usually able to solve most nutritional problems.

The modified voluntary dry matter intake should be calculated by multiplying the predicted intake (Section 8.3) by the appropriate correction factor. For example if a 600 kg cow giving 30 litres of milk has a predicted dry matter intake of 18 kg and is given a complete diet, the appropriate correction factor would be 1.2 to give a modified dry matter intake of 18 x 1.2 = 21.6 kg DM.

Table 8.3   Possible correction factors for dry matter intake

Reason	Correction factor	Comments
Complete diet	1.2 to 1.3	Depends on the quality of the original diet
Out-of-parlour feeders	1.05 to 1.1	Depends on the quality of the original diet
Mixed forages	1.0 to 1.05	Depends on "fit" of blend of forages
Heifers grouped with cows	0.9 to 0.95	Intake of heifers lower than that of cows
Self-feed silage	0.9 to 0.95	Depends on width of silo face
Electric fence at silage face	0.8 to 0.9	Greatest depression in short-necked animals
Poorly-preserved silage	0.7 to 0.9	Depends on proportion in total diet and silage
Week of lactation	0.66 to 1.00	See Figure 8.6
Holstein	1.1 to 1.2	Larger frame and gut size.

8.5   Examples

Example 1
How much will a 650 kg cow giving 20 litres of milk in the second week of lactation eat if she is fed a ration with a q of 0.6? If two weeks later she is giving 30 litres of milk and is still on the same diet what will her predicted intake be then? If the farmer increases the amount of supplements offered and the ration quality rises to 0.65 how will this change her intake?

Dry matter intakes of milking cows are given in Table 8.1 and the second section relates to rations with a q of 0.6 and above. A 650 kg cow giving 20 litres of milk has a basic predicted intake of 18.3 kg. Figure 8.6 shows that intake in the second week of lactation is only 0.78 of the basic predicted figure giving a final prediction of intake of 18.3 x 0.78 = 14.3 kg DM (the exact answer is 14.27 but given the wide range of other factors that affect intake it is only really sensible to predict to the nearest 0.1 kg or 100 g).

The same cow giving 30 litres of milk will have a basic predicted intake of 19.3 kg and the correction factor for four weeks post-calving (Figure 8.6) is 0.88, giving a final prediction of 17.0 kg DM.

If the ration quality (q) increases to 0.65 then the basic predicted intake will still be 19.3 and the correction factor 0.88, so the final prediction is still 17.0 kg DM.

Example 2
How much will a 550 kg dry cow eat in the 34th week of pregnancy if she is fed on a ration with a q of 0.5? If four weeks later the farmer has started feeding a pre-calving compound feed which raises the q of the overall ration to 0.6 how much will the cow eat then?

Table 8.2 gives the intakes for pregnant dry cows. A 550 kg cow on a diet with q of 0.5 is predicted to eat 10.3 kg DM.

Four weeks later she will be 38 weeks pregnant. The predicted intake with a ration q of 0.6 will be 14.2 kg DM.

Example 3
Consider a 600 kg cow in the fifth week of lactation giving 20 litres of milk and being fed the ration shown below. Calculate her predicted intake and compare it to the intake of feeds offered to check that she can eat the ration being offered. At the moment the silage is fed in a forage box and the compound feed in the parlour. Would you alter your opinion if the farmer said that it would be possible to change to feeding the ration mixed in a complete diet?

	Intake (kg fresh)	DM (%)	ME (MJ/kg DM)	GE (MJ/kg DM)
Silage	46	25	10.4	19.0
Compound	6	86	13.3	18.4

This final example is more realistic of the problems met on farm but therefore more complicated! In previous examples q has been given and therefore before we can calculate the intake we need to calculate q for the ration. This is the quality of the entire ration and we need to know the total ME content and the total GE content. Both the ME and the GE of the feeds are given in MJ/ kg DM, so the first step is to determine the dry matter intake of each feed whilst remembering that the dry matters were given as percentages.

Silage DMI   =   46 x (25/100) =   11.5 kg DM
Compound DMI =   6 x (86/100) =   5.16 kg DM
Total DMI   = 16.66 kg DM

Next we need to calculate the amount of ME and GE in the ration from each feed and hence the total.

Total silage ME   11.5 x 10.4 = 119.6
Total silage GE   11.5 x 19.0 = 218.5

Total compound ME   5.16 x 13.3   =   68.6
Total compound GE   5.16 x 18.4   =   94.9

Total ration ME   = 119.6 + 68.6 = 188.2
Total ration GE   = 218.5 + 94.9 = 313.4

The q of a ration is the ME divided by the GE which is

188.2 / 313.4   =   0.60

We now have the information required to determine the predicted intake.

Milking cow rations with a q value of 0.60 and over are considered in the second section of Table 8.1. A 600 kg cow giving 20 litres of milk has a basic predicted intake of 17.0 kg DM. The cow is in the fourth week of lactation and therefore will eat 0.88 of the basic predicted amount (Figure 8.6) to give a final intake of 15.0 kg DM. The total DM offered was 16.6 kg DM and this is greater than predicted by 1.6 kg. In such situations the cow will probably eat all the cake but eat about 6 kg (1.6/0.25) less silage fresh weight.

From Table 8.3 it can be seen that placing the feed ingredients in a complete mix diet will increase intake by a factor of 1.2 to 1.3 which would increase the predicted intake to between 18 and 19.5 kg.

NOTES
- It is incorrect to calculate the ration q as the average q value for the different ration ingredients as this fails to take into account the different amounts of the different ingredients in the diet.

- Whilst it is sensible to give the final intake to the nearest 100 g all intermediate calculations should be carried out with all the precision possible otherwise rounding errors can combine to have a large effect.

8.6   Manual exercises

These exercises will require you to use Tables 20.1 to 20.4 in Chapter 20 on pages 204 to 205. In some instances the exact animal description will not be in the tables and you will have to determine the intermediate values required. The answers to these exercises can be found in Chapter 19 on pages 179 to 180.

Exercise 1
A 625 kg cow is being fed a ration with a q of 0.65. If she is giving 30 litres of milk in the third week of lactation how much will she eat? If she peaks at 45 litres milk/day in the 10 week of lactation how much will she be eating then? If the ration is made up of cake and silage with the silage being fed behind an electric fence off the silo face how will this alter the predicted intake?

Exercise 2
A barren, stale milker weighing 575 kg is giving 15 litres of milk in the 35th week of her lactation. She is being fed a silage with a q of 0.60 and no supplementary feeds. How much will she eat? How much will she be eating the week before she is dried off (Week 43) when she is giving 10 litres of milk?

Exercise 3
A dry is on a straw-based diet with a q of 0.4. If she weighed 625 kg when in condition score 2.5 and barren how much will she eat? How much will she eat after the farmer has started feeding a ration with a q of 0.55? How would you expect her intake to change if she was carrying twins rather than one calf?

Exercise 4
A 700 kg cow giving 35 litres of milk in the 5th week of lactation is being fed the diet given below. The cake is fed in the parlour twice a day and silage is fed in troughs with the sugar beet pulp sprinkled over the top as a midday feed.

	Intake (kg fresh)	DM (%)	ME (MJ/kg DM)	GE (MJ/kg DM)
Grass silage	36	25	10.8	19.4
Sugar beet feed	3	86	12.5	17.1
Compound feed	9	87	12.5	20.5

Will she eat the ration offered and if not what can the farmer do to ensure she does?

8.7   Computer exercises

The objective of the computer exercises is to allow the user to see how voluntary intake is affected by various factors in practical situations and to assess the relative importance of the differing factors considered in Chapters 4 and 8. These and subsequent computer exercises assume familiarity with the computer program distributed with the book and readers are advised to work their way through Section 19.1 before carrying out these exercises. The exercises look at the effects of body weight, milk yield, stage of lactation, ration quality and subjective assessment of intake on milking cows' intake and are given with the solutions in Chapter 19 (page 181 to 182).

CHAPTER 9

CALCULATING METABOLISABLE ENERGY SUPPLY AND REQUIREMENTS

9.1   Introduction

9.2   Calculating ME supply

9.3   Calculating ME required by the animal
  9.3.1   Safety margins
  9.3.2   Maintenance
  9.3.3   Lactation
  9.3.4   Pregnancy
  9.3.5   Changes in body weight
  9.3.6   Activity
  9.3.7   Level of production

9.4   Examples

9.5   Manual exercises

9.6   Computer exercises

9.1   Introduction

When assessing the energy status of an animal two sets of calculations have to be carried out. Firstly, the amount of energy supplied by the diet, and secondly, how much energy the animal needs to meet its different commitments such as maintenance, lactation and pregnancy. When the two calculations are complete a comparison allows one to determine the adequacy of a ration. The UK feeding system uses Metabolisable Energy (ME) to make the comparisons and therefore we must convert energy supply and requirement into these units.

9.2   Calculating ME supply

The ME system makes it possible to express the metabolisable energy of a feed without consideration of the animal to which the feed will be given. Calculating the energy supplied is therefore just a matter of determining the dry matter intake of each feed in the ration and multiplying it by its predicted ME content (determined by analysis or by consulting standard tables) to give the quantity of ME from each feed and hence the total energy supplied by the diet.

9.3   Calculating ME required by the animal

A dairy cow's requirements for energy are actually cited as net energy, as this is the amount of energy that she commits to each bodily function and, for milk, is the amount of energy that leaves the body (see Figure 5.2 page 52). Requirements for net energy are therefore calculated for maintenance and for each productive process, but they then need to be converted to metabolisable energy before they can be compared to the supply from the diet.

As discussed in Chapter 5 (page 52), the efficiency of conversion of ME to NE is referred to as k and this is affected by the use to which the animal puts the energy, the quality of the ration and the overall level of production. Traditionally an animal's requirements are considered one–by–one and then summed to give the total. Given the quality of the ration, the individual ME requirements can be determined for each end-use but must be summed before they can be corrected for level of production.

The steps involved in determining an animal's requirements for ME are therefore:

- Determine total intake of gross energy (GE) and of ME, and then calculate q (ME/GE) as outlined in Chapter 8 (page 97).

- Determine requirement for ME of each of the animal's functions according to the ration quality (q). The functions usually considered are:

  ° Maintenance
  ° Lactation
  ° Pregnancy
  ° Weight change
  ° Activity

- Determine the sum of the various ME requirements.

- Correct for level of production to give the total ME required which can then be compared to dietary ME supply.

9.3.1   Safety margins
The equations behind the prediction of an animal's requirement for energy are based on experimental results from small numbers of animals and should be regarded as the minimum requirements. It is recognised that there will be considerable variation within a group of cows on a farm and in order to ensure that, on average, they receive sufficient

energy it is recommended that a 5% safety margin be added. Such a safety margin will ensure that 50% of a group of animals will be correctly or overfed but some individuals will be underfed. It should be emphasised that this will give a sensible prediction of the energy requirements for the average cow in the group but that individual requirements may vary. All the tables and graphs in this chapter and in Chapter 20 include the 5% safety margin.

9.3.2 Maintenance (Chapter 20, Table 20.5, page 206)

The maintenance requirements of the animal are defined as the amount of energy required when the cow is doing absolutely nothing. This means no walking, eating, digesting, defaecating as well as no growth or milk production, and is therefore difficult to measure. Such measurements are performed in insulated, sealed chambers with the animal confined in a stall or a small pen. This gives both the net energy required and also a measure of the ME required for maintenance, because the heat, methane and urine energy losses are determined.

In practice, dairy cows are not confined in small pens or stalls but are kept in small paddocks or suitable housing and are required to walk between milking, feeding, drinking and lying, all of which requires additional energy. It is possible to calculate how much energy is required for a given activity, but in practice this can be taken as a constant amount for the total amount of activity. A constant allowance is therefore added on to the basic maintenance requirements.

Figure 9.1 shows how daily maintenance ME requirement changes with increasing body weight and ration quality (see Table 20.5, page 206, for a fuller numerical prediction). The major effect on maintenance requirement is body weight and over the range of weights found in adult dairy cows the increase is virtually linear. As ration quality (q) declines energy requirement increases (Chapter 5, page 54).

Figure 9.1   Effect of body weight (kg) and ration quality (q) on maintenance energy requirements (AFRC, 1992)

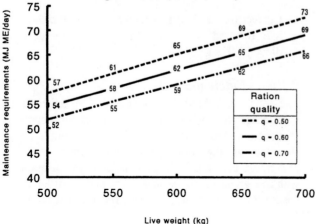

Live weight (kg)

9.3.3 Lactation (Chapter 20, Table 20.6, page 207)

The net energy requirement for lactation is affected by the amount of milk produced and its composition in terms of fat, protein and lactose. In practice only fat and protein need to be considered as milk lactose varies little from a value of 4.6%. As with maintenance, the amount of ME required to meet NE requirements is affected by the quality of the ration (q) and increases as quality declines. Table 9.1 shows the ME requirements for milk of differing composition and different ration quality. A fuller version considering a wider range of milk composition and ration quality is given in Chapter 20 on page 207 (Table 20.6).

Table 9.1   Metabolisable energy requirements (MJ/litre) for milk of differing fat (%) and protein (%) contents at two ration qualities (q) and assuming constant lactose of 4.6% (AFRC, 1992)

Milk fat (%)	Milk protein (%)			
	2.80	3.00	3.20	3.40
q = 0.6				
3.00	4.32	4.39	4.47	4.54
3.50	4.64	4.71	4.79	4.86
4.00	4.96	5.03	5.11	5.18
4.50	5.28	5.35	5.43	5.50
5.00	5.60	5.67	5.75	5.82
q = 0.7				
3.00	4.09	4.16	4.23	4.30
3.50	4.40	4.47	4.54	4.61
4.00	4.70	4.77	4.84	4.91
4.50	5.00	5.07	5.14	5.21
5.00	5.30	5.38	5.45	5.52

9.3.4 Pregnancy (Chapter 20, Table 20.7, page 208)

Foetal growth is not constant; most of the tissue growth and increase in size occurs in the last third of pregnancy. Figure 9.2 shows the energy requirement of a 40 kg calf through pregnancy. For the first half requirements are negligible and in practice it is only necessary to allow for the energy requirement of the foetus in the dry cow. Different foetal weights can be accommodated via direct linear scaling. For example for a 55 kg Charolais calf the energy requirements for pregnancy are scaled up by a factor of 55/40 = 1.375. Table 9.2 gives average birth weights for calves born in dairy herds according to the common breeds of sire.

9.3.5 Changes in body weight (Chapter 20, Table 20.8, page 208)

The energy required for growth will depend on the NE content of the tissue laid down and also on the efficiency of converting ME to NE. A kilogram of lean tissue deposition requires 5 MJ energy whereas a kilogram of fat deposition requires 39 MJ energy, which is an eightfold difference in energy content. Therefore in growing animals it is important to predict the likely composition of the weight gain. In mature dairy cows, however, the weight lost and gained during lactation is assumed to be of a relatively constant composition and therefore a single figure can be taken for its net energy content.

Table 9.2   Average calf birth weight (kg) for common breeds of sire used in dairy herds (AFRC, 1992)

Breed of sire	Bull calf	Heifer calf	Average
Angus	27	25	26
Ayrshire	35	33	34
Charolais	44	41	43
Friesian	39	36	38
Guernsey	33	31	32
Hereford	36	34	35
Holstein	45	42	43
Jersey	26	24	25
Limousin	39	36	38
Simmental	44	41	43

Figure 9.2   Energy requirement (MJ ME/day) for pregnancy (40 kg calf) (AFRC, 1992)

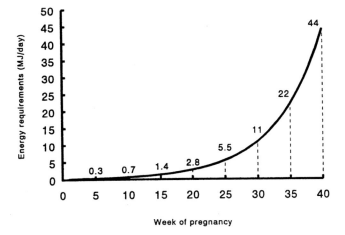

When a dairy cow gains weight the ME required depends only on the quality of the diet (q). However, when she loses weight the ME value of that weight loss (the amount by which her total requirements are reduced) will depend on how the energy is used and how ration quality affects the conversion of ME to NE in that end-use. In practice dairy cows usually lose weight during early lactation and it is safe to assume that most of the mobilised energy will be used for milk production. If weight is lost during the dry period it is assumed that this is used to support pregnancy. Table 9.3 gives the energy value of weight change for dry and milking cows given rations of different qualities.

Table 9.3   Metabolisable energy value (MJ ME) of weight change in milking and pregnant dry cows on rations of differing qualities (q)

	Liveweight change (kg/day)			
	-1.00	**-0.50**	**0.50**	**1.00**
q		*Lactating cow*		
0.50	-23.3	-11.6	19.4	38.8
0.60	-22.0	-11.0	18.3	36.7
0.70	-20.8	-10.4	17.4	34.7
		Pregnant / dry cow		
0.40	-24.8	-12.4	34.5	69.0
0.50	-24.8	-12.4	27.7	55.4

9.3.6   Activity (Chapter 20, Table 20.9, page 209)

As mentioned in Section 9.3.2 above, the maintenance energy allowances include a constant allowance for the exercise that will take place when the cows are housed or in small paddocks. If the amount of walking is greater than this, then additional allowances should be made.

Figure 9.3 shows suggested energy allowances for animals undertaking moderate or extensive exercise. Moderate exercise may be considered as walking long distances on level ground, as may occur when cows graze distant pastures or have access to a large number of paddocks. Extensive exercise is walking long distances on hilly ground, as may occur when dry cows are turned out onto moorland or uplands.

Figure 9.3   Energy allowances (MJ ME/day) for moderate and extensive exercise

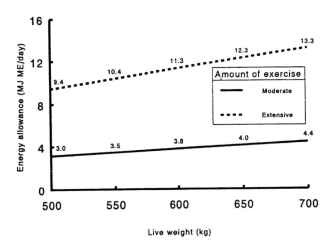

The allowances made for exercise in Figure 9.3 and in Table 20.9 in Chapter 20 (page 209) are for milking cows. The current feeding standards use a slightly different allowance for dry cows but the difference is only about 2 MJ/day and may be ignored in manual calculations.

9.3.7   Level of production (Chapter 20, Table 20.10, page 209)

As discussed in Chapter 5 (page 54) the high-producing animal is less efficient at using energy than the low-producing animal. A correction for level of production (C_L) can only be calculated once all the energy allowances have been calculated. The level of production is expressed as the Animal Production Level (APL) and is the total energy allowance divided by the allowance for maintenance. The APL is used to determine the correction factor (C_L) as shown in Figure 9.4. The correction factor C_L is multiplied by the total energy required, as calculated from the sections above, i.e. maintenance plus milk production plus pregnancy (if appropriate) to give the final estimate of total ME requirement.

Figure 9.4   Relationship between animal production level (APL) and correction factor for level of production (C_L)

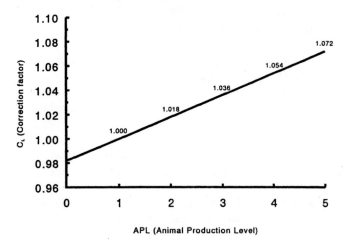

APL (Animal Production Level)

A table relating APL to C_L is given in Chapter 20, Table 20.10, page 209.

Consider, for example, a 600 kg cow giving 30 litres of milk with no weight change and not pregnant, with the following ME requirements.

ME_{maint} = 63 MJ
ME_{lact} = 142 MJ

Then:

$$APL = ME_{Total} / ME_{Maint}$$
$$= (63 + 142) / 63$$
$$= 3.25$$

$$C_L = 1.04$$

$$ME_{total} = 1.04 \times (63 + 142)$$
$$= \textbf{213 MJ}$$

9.4   Examples

Example 1

A Friesian dairy cow weighing 550 kg is giving 22 litre of milk with a fat content of 4.0% and a protein content of 3.2%. If she is given a ration with a q of 0.6 what are her energy requirements?

Maintenance (Figure 9.1)
550 kg cow for q = 0.6 = 58 MJ ME

Lactation (Table 9.1)
4.0% fat, 3.2% protein
q = 0.6
5.11 MJ ME/litre
22 litres = 22 x 5.11 = 112.4 MJ ME

Correction for level of production
APL = (58 + 112.4) / 58 = 2.94
C_L (Table 20.10, Chapter 20, page 209) ≈ 1.035

Total ME requirement
(58 + 112.4) x 1.035 = 176 MJ ME/day

Example 2

What are the energy requirements of a 650 kg Holstein cow when she is giving 42 litres milk (3.5% fat and 3.2% protein) and losing 500 g weigh a day on a ration with a q of 0.7?

Maintenance (Figure 9.1)
650 kg cow for q = 0.7 = 62 MJ ME

Lactation (Table 9.1)
3.5% fat, 3.2% protein,
q = 0.7
4.54 MJ ME
42 litres = 42 x 4.54 = 190.7 MJ ME

Weight change (Table 9.3)
0.5 kg loss at q = 0.7 = -10.4 MJ ME

Correction for level of production
APL = (62 + 190.7 - 10.4) / 62 = 3.91
C_L (Table 20.10, Chapter 20, page 209) ≈ 1.052

Total ME requirement
(62 + 190.7 - 10.4) x 1.052 = 255 MJ ME/day

Example 3

What are the energy requirements of a 550 kg Holstein heifer in the 40th week of pregnancy on a ration of q = 0.5 if she is in calf (of unknown sex) to a Holstein bull. How would this change if she were in calf to a Limousin bull?

Maintenance (Figure 9.1)
550 kg cow for q = 0.5 = 61 MJ ME

Pregnancy (Figure (9.2)
40 weeks pregnant = 44 MJ ME

Calf weight (Table 9.2)
Holstein calf = 43 kg
Corrected for calf weight (43 / 40) x 44 MJ (Figure 9.2)
= 47.3 MJ ME

Correction for level of production
APL = (61 + 47.3) / 61 = 1.78
C_L (Table 20.10, Chapter 20, page 209) = 1.014

Total ME requirement
(61 + 47.3) x 1.014 = 110 MJ ME/day

For a Limousin calf:

Calf weight (Table 9.2)
Limousin calf = 38 kg
Corrected for calf weight (38 / 40) x 44 = 41.8 MJ ME

Correction for level of production
APL = (61 + 41.8) / 61 =1.68
C_L (Table 20.10, Chapter 20, page 209) =1.013

Total ME requirement
(61 + 41.8) x 1.013=104 MJ ME/day

Example 4

A 650 kg Holstein cow giving 25 litres milk (fat = 4.0%, protein = 3.2%) and 10 weeks pregnant (in calf to a Holstein bull) and gaining 0.5 kg/day is being fed on the following ration.

	Fresh weight	DM	ME	GE
	(kg/day)	(%)	MJ/kg DM	
Grass silage	36	27	10.8	19.6
Caustic wheat	3	77	12.6	18.7
Soyabean meal	1	88	13.4	19.7
Compound	6	87	13.5	20.9

Will this ration meet her energy requirements?

The first thing to do is to calculate the ration quality (q) for which we need the dry matter intakes (DMI) of each feed from which we can calculate ME and GE intakes for each feed and then the ration totals.

Grass silage DMI = 36 x (27/100)= 9.72 kg DM
Caustic wheat DMI = 3 x (77/100) = 2.31 kg DM
Soyabean meal DMI = 1 x (88/100) = 0.88 kg DM
Compound DMI = 6 x (87/100) = 5.22 kg DM
Total DMI = 18.1 kg DM

Calculate the amount of ME and GE in the ration from each feed and hence the total.

Total silage ME 9.72 x 10.8 = 104.98
Total wheat ME 2.31 x 12.6 = 29.11
Total soya ME 0.88 x 13.4 = 11.79
Total compound ME 5.22 x 13.5 = 70.47
Total ration ME = 216.35

Total silage GE 9.72 x 19.6 = 190.51
Total wheat GE 2.31 x 18.7 = 43.20
Total soya GE 0.88 x 19.7 = 17.34
Total compound GE 5.22 x 20.9 = 109.10
Total ration GE = 360.15

The q of a ration is the ME divided by the GE which is:
216.35 / 360.15 = 0.60

Maintenance (Figure 9.1)
650 kg cow for q = 0.6 = 65 MJ ME

Lactation (Table 9.1)
4.0% fat, 3.2% protein
q = 0.6
5.11 MJ ME
25 litres = 25 x 5.11 = 127.8 MJ ME

Pregnancy (Figure 9.2)
10 weeks pregnant. Basic requirement = 0.7 MJ ME

Calf weight (Table 9.2)
Holstein calf = 43 kg
Corrected for calf weight (43 / 40) x 0.7 = 0.75 MJ ME

Weight change (Table 9.3)
0.5 kg gain at q = 0.6 = 18.3 MJ ME

Correction for level of production
APL = (65 + 127.8 + 0.75 + 18.3) / 65 = 3.26
C_L (Table 20.10, Chapter 20, page 209) ≈ 1.041

Total ME requirement
(65 + 127.8 + 0.75 + 18.3) x 1.041 = 221 MJ ME/day

This ration will therefore not quite meet the animal's requirement (216 MJ supplied cf. 221 MJ required). Given the stage of pregnancy, the cow may not put on weight as fast as predicted.

9.5 Manual exercises

These exercises require you to use Tables 20.5 to 20.10 in Chapter 20 on pages 206 to 209. In some instances the exact animal description will not be in the tables and you will have to determine the intermediate values required. The answers to these exercises can be found in Chapter 19 on pages 182 to 184.

Exercise 1

What are the energy requirements of a 600 kg cow, not pregnant, giving 25 litres of milk containing 4.0% fat and 3.2% protein when given a ration with a q of 0.6?

Exercise 2

What are the energy requirements of a 650 kg cow, not pregnant, giving 43 litres of milk containing 3.75% fat and 3.3% protein and losing 0.75 kg/day when given a ration with a q of 0.7?

Exercise 3

What are the energy requirements of a 600 kg dairy cow be the week after she is dried off if she is 35 weeks pregnant to a Charolais bull, losing 0.5 kg a day and on a straw-based ration with q = 0.4?

weeks pregnant to a Charolais bull, losing 0.5 kg a day and on a straw-based ration with q = 0.4?

Exercise 4

Consider a 640 kg Friesian dairy cow on silage with the following analysis:

Dry matter: 25%
q: 0.6
ME content: 11.5 MJ / kg DM

Calculate her energy requirements for maintenance. Calculate the required dry matter intake of silage to supply this amount of energy and hence the amount of silage to feed daily to meet her maintenance requirements.

Now calculate her requirements for lactation, assuming that the cow is giving 15 litres of milk a day with the following analysis:

Fat: 4.0%
Protein: 3.2%
Lactose: 4.6%

Calculate the total ME requirements per day and hence the required silage intake. Is this a realistic figure?

Exercise 5

A 650 kg Holstein cow giving 28 litres of milk (Fat = 3.75%, Protein = 3.4%) and 10 weeks pregnant (in calf to a Holstein bull) and losing 0.5 kg/day is given the following ration:

	Fresh weight	DM	ME	GE
	kg/day	(%)	MJ/kg DM	
Grass silage good	36.0	27	10.8	19.8
Caustic wheat	3.0	77	12.6	18.8
Soyabean meal Ext	1.0	88	13.4	20.0
Compound 18% CP	6.0	87	12.5	21.5

Will this ration meet her energy requirements?

9.6   Computer exercises

The objective of the computer exercises is to show the relative importance of the different metabolic commitments and to look at some of the interactions between feeds and requirements. The figures calculated on the computer for the requirements for each metabolic activity (such as maintenance and lactation) differ from those obtained in manual exercises even when the precise value of q has been taken into account. This is because the computer corrects each requirement for the level of production (C_L) so that the numbers on the screen add up to the total shown. The exercises look at the effects of body weight, milk yield, weight change, pregnancy and the effects of different feeds on energy requirements and are given with the solutions in Chapter 19 (pages 184 to 186).

CHAPTER 10

CALCULATING METABOLISABLE PROTEIN SUPPLY AND REQUIREMENTS

10.1 Introduction

10.2 Calculating MP supplied
    10.2.1 ERDP and DUP
    10.2.2 MP supplied by ERDP
    10.2.3 MP supplied by DUP
    10.3.4 Total MP

10.3 MP required by the animal
    10.3.1 Maintenance
    10.3.2 Lactation
    10.3.3 Pregnancy
    10.3.4 Weight change
    10.3.5 Activity

10.4 Examples

10.5 Manual exercises

10.6 Computer exercises

Appendix: Calculating ERDP and DUP supply
         from degradation figures

10.1 Introduction

As mentioned in Chapter 6, protein is the third most important consideration in dairy cow rations after dry matter intake and energy. However, because of the high ratio of milk protein to maintenance protein requirements and our rapidly progressing, but still incomplete, understanding of protein metabolism, protein nutrition is often a major problem in dairy cows as a result of incorrect diet formulation.

Two sets of calculations need to be performed to assess the protein status of an animal. Firstly, to determine the amount of protein supplied by the diet and secondly, the amount required by the animal. As feed protein content is expressed in different units to the animal's requirements (crude protein, ADIN and degradability, cf. metabolisable protein) more calculations are needed to determine the amount of protein a ration supplies than are needed when calculating the supply of metabolisable energy. This is shown in Figure 6.7 (page 70), where it can be seen that it is necessary to calculate the amounts of four different protein fractions (QDP, SDP, DUP and ADIN) in order to determine the MP supplied by the diet. As mentioned in Chapter 6 (page 65) the amount of SDP and DUP in a ration will depend not only on the type of feed but also on the type of animal – or more correctly the level of production.

Also, the amount of microbial crude protein produced in the rumen is related to the amount of energy available for nitrogen fixation. As the animal is characterised in terms of its requirement for energy, protein supply and requirements are normally calculated after those for metabolisable energy.

This chapter is divided into two sections. In the first section the amount of MP supplied is determined from the crude protein content and degradability of crude protein of the feeds in the ration. This can be simplified from the methods published in AFRC (1992) but it still requires that the ERDP and DUP supply be determined and that the ERDP and FME supply are compared to determine the amount of MCP produced, after which the total supply of MP can be calculated. The second section considers how the MP requirement of an animal is determined according to her active processes and this has a similar structure to that used in Chapter 9 whereby maintenance, lactation, pregnancy and weight change are each considered in turn.

10.2 Calculating MP supplied

10.2.1 ERDP and DUP (Table 20.22, pages 220 to 223)

As can be seen from Figure 6.7, degradable protein in the feed (RDP) is made up of the quickly degradable protein (QDP) and slowly degradable protein (SDP). The QDP is considered to be released so quickly that only 80% is available to the microbes and the amount of protein available to the microbes is the sum of the discounted QDP and the SDP which is called the effective rumen degradable protein (ERDP). The amount of QDP in a feed is constant irrespective of the animal it is being fed to (see Figure 6.8), but the amount of SDP declines with increasing level of production due to the reduced time the protein is retained in the rumen.

It is possible to calculate the amounts of QDP and SDP in a feed and hence determine the total supply of ERDP from the degradability parameters ("a", "b", "c"), the content of CP and ADIN in the feeds. An example of the calculation is shown in the appendix on page 114 at the end of the chapter, as in some instances only this information will be available.

However, feed tables can be generated from which the ERDP supply of a feed can be determined once the animal production level is known. Table 10.1 shows the ERDP and DUP supply of some common feeds at different levels of production. The level of production is defined as the APL which is the total requirements for ME divided by the maintenance requirements for energy (see Chapter 5, page 54).

The first rows in Table 10.1 relate the yield of microbial crude protein per MJ of ME (Y) to the rumen outflow rate, which will be considered in the next section. Beneath this are two rows for each feed (see Table 20.22, Chapter 20, pages 220 to 223 for more feeds). The first of the rows shows the dry matter (DM), CP, ME and FME and then the ERDP supply (g/kg DM) of the feed at different animal production levels. The second row gives the DUP (g/kg DM) supplied by that feed which will be considered in a later section. For example, if an animal with an APL of 2.0 is being fed a diet of grass (65 to 70D) and wheat grain then each kilogram dry matter of grass will supply 87.2 g ERDP and 28.0 g DUP and each kilogram dry matter of the wheat will supply 103.5 g ERDP and 10.0 g DUP. As the level of production increases (going across the page), the amount of ERDP supplied by a feed declines and the amount of DUP increases such that when APL = 4.0 the grass will only be supplying 76.0 g of ERDP but 38.1 g of DUP.

As an example consider a dairy cow with a maintenance ME requirement of 65 MJ ME producing 26 litres of milk, for which she requires 130 MJ ME on a ration of 75 kg of fresh grass (65 to 70D). The first step is to calculate the APL for this cow:

$$APL = ME_{total} / ME_{maint} = (65 + 130) / 65 = 3.0$$

From Table 10.1 it can be seen that at an animal production level of 3.0 Grass 65 to 70D will supply 80.1 g ERDP/kg DM and that it has a dry matter content of 20%. The dry matter intake of grass will be:

$$75 \times 20/100 \quad = 15.0 \text{ kg DM}$$

The total ERDP supply from the diet is

$$15 \times 80.1 = 1201.5 \text{ g ERDP}$$

This is the total amount of protein available to the microbes and the next stage is to determine if there is sufficient FME in the ration to allow the microbes to fix all this protein.

10.2.2   MP supplied by ERDP

As mentioned in Chapter 6, the amount of microbial crude protein (MCP) produced in the rumen is affected by the amount of protein available and the amount of FME. One or the other will be in short supply and this will limit the output of MCP. To determine how much MCP will be produced we there-

Table 10.1 ERDP, DUP and FME supply of some common feeds at different animal production levels (APL) (adapted from AFRC, 1993 and other sources)

						Level of Production (APL)							
						≤1.0	1.5	2.0	2.5	3.0	3.5	4.0	≥4.5
Microbial Yield (Y) (g MCP/MJ FME)						8.8	9.5	10.0	10.5	10.9	11.2	11.5	11.8
Feed Name	**DM (%)**	**CP (g/kg DM)**	**ME**	**FME (MJ/kg DM)**		Protein Supply (g/kg DM)							
Grass 55 to 60D	20	97	7.5	6.9	ERDP	56.9	50.2	45.8	42.8	40.5	38.8	37.5	36.5
					DUP	29.4	35.4	39.3	42.1	44.1	45.6	46.8	47.7
Grass 65 to 70D	21	121	10.7	10.0	ERDP	101.1	92.9	87.2	83.2	80.1	77.8	76.0	74.5
					DUP	15.5	22.9	28.0	31.6	34.4	36.5	38.1	39.5
Grass silage 65D	25	140	10.3	7.6	ERDP	102.5	99.3	97.1	95.3	94.0	93.0	92.1	91.5
					DUP	10.5	13.4	15.5	17.0	18.2	19.1	19.9	20.5
Grass silage 70D	25	174	11.7	8.6	ERDP	125.6	122.4	120.0	118.2	116.7	115.6	114.7	113.9
					DUP	16.9	19.7	21.9	23.5	24.8	25.8	26.7	27.4
Maize silage	30	88	11.5	9.0	ERDP	68.7	67.5	66.5	65.8	65.2	64.7	64.3	64.0
					DUP	9.1	10.2	11.1	11.7	12.3	12.7	13.0	13.3
Wheat grain	87	123	13.6	12.9	ERDP	108.2	105.6	103.5	101.7	100.3	99.2	98.2	97.4
					DUP	5.8	8.1	10.0	11.6	12.8	13.9	14.8	15.5
Sugar beet feed - molassed	86	129	12.5	12.4	ERDP	73.1	64.1	59.4	56.5	54.6	53.2	52.2	51.4
					DUP	12.6	20.7	24.9	27.5	29.2	30.5	31.4	32.1
Maize gluten feed	89	232	12.7	11.5	ERDP	162.3	153.8	148.1	144.1	141.1	138.8	137.0	135.6
					DUP	9.6	17.3	22.4	26.0	28.7	30.7	32.4	33.6
Fishmeal	92	694	14.2	11.4	ERDP	388.3	319.9	287.4	268.6	256.5	248.0	241.9	237.2
					DUP	209.6	271.1	300.3	317.2	328.2	335.8	341.3	345.5
Rapeseed meal	90	418	12.0	11.2	ERDP	320.0	300.5	286.3	275.4	266.9	260.2	254.8	250.4
					DUP	25.4	42.9	55.7	65.5	73.1	79.1	84.0	88.0
Soyabean meal	88	507	13.4	12.8	ERDP	399.6	344.4	308.2	282.9	264.4	250.4	239.5	230.9
					DUP	68.1	117.8	150.4	173.1	189.8	202.4	212.2	220.0

fore need to calculate how much can be synthesised from the energy available and how much can be synthesised from the protein available. The lesser figure will then show which nutrient is limiting and how much MCP can be produced. If ERDP is limiting the amount of MCP produced is equal to the amount of ERDP so:

$$MCP_{\text{(protein limited)}} = ERDP = 1201.5 \text{ g}$$

If the energy is limiting the amount of MCP produced will be determined by the fermentable metabolisable energy (FME) supply and the yield of MCP per MJ of FME. The FME content of the grass is 10.0 (Table 10.1) and so the total intake of FME will be:

$$10.0 \times 15.0 = 150 \text{ MJ FME}$$

At an APL of 3.0 the microbial yield (Y) (top lines of Table 10.1) will be 10.9. So the amount of MCP synthesised if energy is limiting is:

$$\begin{aligned} MCP_{\text{(energy limited)}} &= FME \times Y \\ &= 150 \times 10.9 \\ &= 1635 \text{ g} \end{aligned}$$

The smaller value of the two is the one where protein in limiting MCP synthesis (1201.5 g cf. 1635 g) and therefore in this particular situation the supply of ERDP is limiting and the amount of MCP leaving the rumen will be 1201.5 g/day.

As mentioned in Chapter 6 (page 70), only 0.75 of the MCP is actually true protein (the rest is nucleic acids etc.) and only 0.85 of the microbial true protein is absorbed into the blood stream to become metabolisable protein. The MP supply from the microbial protein is therefore 0.64 of the MCP.

$$MP_{\text{(from microbes)}} = 1201.5 \times 0.64 = 769 \text{ g/day}$$

10.2.3 *MP supplied by DUP (Table 20.22, pages 220 to 223)*

The dairy cow obtains her metabolisable protein from two sources, with the majority normally coming from microbial crude protein. The other source is the dietary protein that escapes microbial degradation and is digested in the small intestine. As discussed in Chapter 6 (page 67) the undegradable protein (UDP) is composed of two fractions, the Digestible Undegradable Protein (DUP) which can be digested in the small intestine, and ADIN which is largely indigestible. The amount of ADIN in a feed is constant, but the amount of DUP varies with the animal production level (APL) (see Figure 6.8). At low APL, protein remains in the rumen for a long time and most of it is degraded by the microbes and very little escapes to become DUP.

As production increases retention times of CP in the rumen fall and the feed is exposed to microbial degradation for less time and so the amount of DUP increases. However, only 0.90 of the DUP that enters the small intestine is absorbed. Table 10.1 shows the absorbed DUP content, or MP contribution, of a range of feeds at different Animal Production Levels (APL). As APL increases the amount of DUP in a feed increases so that for wheat grain it rises from 5.8 g/kg DM at an APL of 1.0 to 14.8 when APL = 4.0 and for soyabean meal it increases from 68.1 to 212.2 g/kg DM.

The calculation of MP supply from DUP is simply a matter of consulting Table 10.1 (see Table 20.22, pages 220 to 223 for more feeds), as the following example shows. Consider the cow in the previous section that was given 75 kg of fresh grass. Her APL was 3.0 and intake was 15.0 kg DM and the feed was Grass 65 to 70D as in Table 10.1.

$$\begin{aligned} \text{DUP content at APL} = 3.0 &= 34.4 \text{ g/kg DM} \\ \text{DUP supply} &= 34.4 \times 15.0 \\ &= 516 \text{ g} \end{aligned}$$

This is the same as the MP supplied from by-pass protein so

$$MP_{\text{(bypass protein)}} = 516 \text{ g}$$

10.2.4 *Total MP supply*

The total MP supplied by the diet is:

$$\begin{aligned} MP_{\text{(from microbes)}} + MP_{\text{(bypass protein)}} &= 769 + 516 \text{ g} \\ &= 1285 \text{ g} \end{aligned}$$

10.3 MP required by the animal

The calculation of an animal's metabolisable protein requirements is very similar to the method used for calculating the requirements for energy. In fact it is simpler as ration quality is not considered to influence requirements and hence the ration does not need to be specified before requirements can be calculated. All of the following tables and graphs include a recommended 5% safety margin.

10.3.1 *Maintenance (Table 20.11, page 210)*

Protein requirements for maintenance are defined in the same way as energy requirements as the amount of protein needed to keep the body functioning whilst the cow is doing nothing at all. The requirement is for net protein (NP) which needs to be converted to metabolisable protein (MP) by taking into account the efficiency of converting MP to NP for maintenance (1.00) and adding the safety margin (5%). The MP requirement for maintenance for cows of different liveweights is shown in Figure 10.1.

Figure 10.1   Metabolisable protein requirements for maintenance (AFRC, 1992)

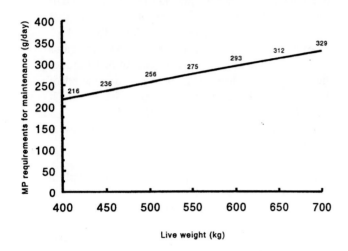

10.3.2   Lactation (Table 20.12, page 210)

Metabolisable protein requirements for milk production are related to milk protein content, but not to ration quality nor to the other milk constituents. Not all the protein reported in the milk is actual protein as some urea diffuses into the milk and this accounts for about 5% of the total nitrogen. The MP requirements for milk production are corrected for the urea in the milk, for the density of milk (1.032 g/ml) and for the efficiency of converting MP into NP for milk production. The requirements, shown in Figure 10.2, vary with milk yield and with the protein in the milk. A cow producing 30 litres of milk with an average composition (3.2% total protein/litre) requires about 1400 g MP/day; at all but the lowest milk yields the MP requirement for lactation is the major component of the total requirement.

Figure 10.2   Metabolism protein requirements for lactation (AFRC, 1992)

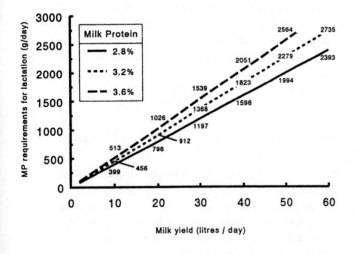

10.3.3   Pregnancy (Table 20.13 page 211)

The protein requirements for pregnancy increase with gestation in a way similar to that for energy

(Chapter 9, page 102) and are minimal (< 20g/day) for the first half of pregnancy (Figure 10.3); they only become a significant requirement in the last 10 weeks. The requirements shown in Figure 10.3 are for a 40 kg calf and require linear scaling to take into account other calf weights (Table 9.2).

Figure 10.3   Metabolisable protein requirements for pregnancy (40 kg calf) (adapted from AFRC, 1992)

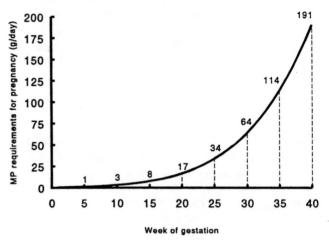

10.3.4   Weight change (Table 20.14, page 211)

The protein composition of weight change varies with its composition. Weight gain contains more lean and less fat in animals that are growing fast, in males compared to females, and in animals of late maturing breeds. But in mature dairy cattle it can be assumed to be of constant composition over the range of weight changes seen in practice. The amino acid composition of mobilised protein is not ideal for milk production nor for supporting the foetus, so mobilised protein is of less value than that required to lay down that weight gain in the first place (Figure 10.4).

Figure 10.4   Metabolisable protein allowances for weight change

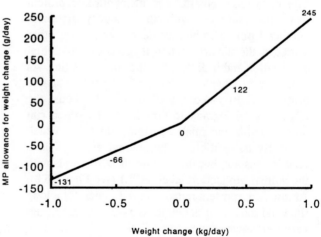

10.3.5 Activity

The amount of exercise carried out by the average dairy cow in the UK does not require much MP, and requirements for activity are generally ignored.

10.4 Examples

All the feed analysis data required have been taken from Table 10.1, but they can also be found in Table 20.22, pages 220 to 223. Examples 1 and 2 are laid out in full detail so that it is possible to see exactly how each calculation is carried out and where each number came from. The third example is shown in a more compact from and it is recommended that this style be used when calculating rations on farm.

Example 1

A 550 kg dry cow, 35 weeks pregnant to a Holstein bull, has a total energy requirement of 99 MJ ME and a maintenance requirement of 66 MJ. She is being fed on a diet of 55 kg poor grass (55 to 60D) which has the analysis shown in Table 10.1. How much MP will this supply and will it meet her requirements?

MP supply
APL $= 99/66 = 1.50$
DM intake $= 55 \times (20/100) = 11$ kg DM

ERDP $= 50.2$ g/kg DM (Table 10.1 with APL = 1.5)
Total ERDP $= 11 \times 50.2 = 552.2$ g/day

FME $= 6.9$ MJ/kg DM (Table 10.1)
Total FME $= 11 \times 6.9 = 75.9$

Y (g MCP/ MJ FME)$= 9.5$

If energy supply is limiting microbial activity then:
MCP $=$ Y x FME
$\qquad = 9.5 \times 75.9$
$\qquad = 721.05$ g

If protein supply is limiting microbial activity then:
MCP $=$ ERDP
$\qquad = 552.2$ g

Therefore rumen protein production will be limited by protein supply and MCP = 552.2 g
MP $_{(microbes)}$ $=$ MCP x 0.64
$\qquad = 552.2 \times 0.64$
$\qquad = 353.4$ g MP/day

MP from DUP:
DUP $= 35.4$ g/kg DM (Table 10.1 with APL = 1.5)
Total DUP $= 11.0 \times 35.4 = 389.4$ g
MP from DUP $= 389.4$ g MP/day

Total MP supply $= 353.4 + 389.4$
$\qquad\qquad\qquad = 742.8$ g MP/day

MP requirements
Maintenance
550 kg cow $=$ 275 g MP/day (Figure 10.1)

Pregnancy
35 weeks $= 114$ g MP/day   (Figure 10.3)
Correction for Holstein $= 43/40.0 \times 114$ (Table 9.2)
$\qquad\qquad\qquad\qquad = 122.6$

Total requirement $= 275 + 122.6 = 397.6$ g MP/day

The ration will meet this cows MP requirements with a surplus of 345 g MP/day (743 – 398). This is a considerable surplus and it is probable that the absorbed amino acids will be deaminated and used as energy sources to complement the ME supply.

Example 2

A farmer has been told that a ration of 45 kg of maize silage (30% DM) plus 2.5 kg of soyabean meal (88% DM) will supply sufficient energy for his 550 kg cows giving 25 l milk a day (3.2% protein) provided they lose 500 g/day. He wants to know if such a ration will be satisfactory for protein. The total energy require-ments are 180 MJ ME of which 60 MJ are required for maintenance.

MP supply
DM intake (Table 10.1)
Maize silage $45 \times (30/100)$ $= 13.5$ kg DM
Soyabean meal $2.5 \times (88/100)$ $=$ 2.2 kg DM
Total $= 15.7$ kg DM

APL $= 180/60 = 3.0$

ERDP
Maize silage $= 65.2$ g ERDP/kg DM (Table 10.1 with APL = 3.0)
ERDP (maize)$= 65.2 \times 13.5$ kg DM $= 880.2$ g/day
Soyabean meal $= 264.4$ g ERDP/kg DM (Table 10.1 with APL = 3.0)
ERDP (soya) $= 264.4 \times 2.2 = 581.7$ g/day
Total ERDP $= 1461.9$ g/day

FME
Maize silage $= 9.0$ MJ/kg DM (Table 10.1)
FME (maize) $= 9.0 \times 13.5 = 121.5$ MJ
Soyabean meal $= 12.8$ MJ/kg DM (Table 10.1)
FME (soya) $= 12.8 \times 2.2 = 28.2$ MJ
Total FME $= 149.7$ MJ

Y (g MCP/ MJ FME) $= 10.9$ (Table 10.1)

If energy supply is limiting microbial activity then:

MCP $=$ Y x FME
$\qquad = 10.9 \times 149.7$
$\qquad = 1631.3$ g

If protein supply is limiting microbial activity then:

$$MCP = ERDP$$
$$= 1461.9 \text{ g}$$

Therefore rumen protein production will be limited by protein supply and MCP = 1461.9 g

$$MP_{(microbes)} = MCP \times 0.64$$
$$= 1461.9 \text{ g} \times 0.64$$
$$= 935.6 \text{ g MP/day}$$

MP from DUP:
Maize silage = 12.3 g DUP/kg DM (Table 10.1 with APL = 3.0)
DUP (maize) = 12.3 x 13.5 = 166.1 g/day
Soyabean meal = 189.8 g DUP/kg DM (Table 10.1 with APL = 3.0)
DUP (soya) = 189.8 x 2.2 = 417.6 g/day
Total DUP = 583.7 g/day
MP from DUP = 583.7 g MP/day

Total MP supply = 935.6 + 583.7 = 1519.3 g MP/day

MP requirements
Maintenance
550 kg cow = 275 g MP/day (Figure 10.1)

Milk production
25 litres, 3.2% protein = 1140 g MP/day (Figure 10.2)
(Interpolated: 1140 = {912 + 1368} /2)

Weight loss
500g/day = –66 g MP/day (Figure 10.4)

Total requirement = (275 + 1140 - 66) = 1349 g MP/day

The ration will therefore supply sufficient MP for this level of milk production with a surplus of 170 g MP/day.

Example 3
A 600 kg dairy cow is giving 33 l/day of milk at 3.2% protein and is losing 500 g/day. Will the ration outlined below supply sufficient protein? Her total energy requirements are 224 MJ/day of which 64 MJ are required for maintenance.

Diet (kg fresh weight per day)

Grass silage 70D	50	kg
Wheat grain	4	kg
Soyabean meal	1	kg
Rapeseed meal	1	kg

MP supply
Calculate the APL   224 / 64 = 3.5
Look up the Y value = 11.2 (Table 10.1)

Look up the DM, FME, ERDP and DUP content of the feed at APL = 3.5 (Table 10.1).

	DM (%)	FME (MJ/kg DM)	ERDP (g/kg DM)	DUP (g/kg DM)
Grass silage	25	8.6	115.6	25.8
Wheat grain	87	12.9	99.2	13.9
Soyabean meal	88	12.8	250.4	202.4
Rapeseed meal	90	11.2	260.2	79.1

Calculate the DMI, FME, ERDP and DUP supplied by each ingredient and hence the total in the ration.

	DMI (kg)	FME (MJ)	ERDP (g)	DUP (g)
Grass silage	12.50	107.5	1445	322.5
Wheat grain	3.48	44.9	341.3	47.8
Soyabean meal	0.88	11.3	225.4	182.2
Rapeseed meal	0.90	10.1	231.6	70.4
Total	**17.8**	**174**	**2243**	**623**

It is worth assessing the total DMI at this stage to check that the cow can eat all of what is offered. As a rule of thumb intake of DM is 3% of body weight so this 600 kg can eat 18 kg DM. As intake is 17.8 kg, I am happy that she could eat all of this ration so on we go!

If energy supply is limiting microbial activity then:

$$MCP = 11.2 \times 174 = 1949 \text{ g}$$

If protein supply is limiting microbial activity then:

$$MCP = 2243 \text{ g}$$

Therefore rumen protein production will be limited by energy supply and MCP = 1949 g.

$$MP_{(microbes)} = 1949 \times 0.64$$
$$= 1247 \text{ g}$$

MP supply = 1247 + 623 = 1870 g/day

MP requirements
Maintenance
600 kg cow = 293 g MP/day (Figure 10.1)

Milk production
33 litres, 3.2% protein = 1505 g MP/day (Figure 10.2)

Weight loss
500 g/day = –66 g (Figure 10.4)

Total requirement = 1732 g MP / day

The ration therefore supplies sufficient MP, with a surplus of 138 g MP/day (1870 – 1732).

10.5   Manual exercises

These exercises require you to use Tables 20.11 to 20.14, pages 210 to 211. The answers obtained in these exercises differ slightly from the results obtained from the computer as the energy requirements have been altered slightly so that the APL value is on the tables. The solutions to these exercises can be found in Chapter 19 (pages 186 to 189).

Exercise 1
How much MP will the following ration supply to an animal that has an APL of 4.0?

Good silage 70D	40	kg
Wheat grain	4	kg
Sugar beet feed - molassed	3	kg
Soyabean meal	2	kg

Exercise 2
What are the MP requirements of the following animal?

650 kg body weight
20 litres of milk at 3.2% protein
Losing 0.5 kg weight a day
20 weeks pregnant to a Limousin bull

Exercise 3
Will a 550 kg cow giving 22 litres of milk at 4.25% fat and 3.2% protein receive adequate protein if she is eating 65 kg of good silage of 70D (ME = 11.7, GE = 19.5)?

Exercise 4
A farmer has his cows out at grass in mid-summer. He has been advised that any cow giving more than 18 litres of milk at 4.0% fat and 3.35% protein will require supplementing with compound feed to meet her protein requirements, but he is uncertain what sort of cake to use. The cows are 600 kg in weight, not pregnant and not changing weight and he reckons they can eat 75 kg fresh weight of the grass which has a D value of 67 (assume ME = 10.7, GE = 17.8). What do you advise?

10.6   Computer exercises

The computer exercises in Chapter 19 (page 189 to 191) briefly cover the relative importance of the different metabolic requirements and then look at some typical rations and the problems and misconceptions that commonly occur in practice.

APPENDIX

Calculation of ERDP and DUP supplied by a feed from the protein degradation characteristics

Although the tables of ERDP and DUP supply given (Table 10.1 and Table 20.22) make it unnecessary to have to calculate the amounts of ERDP and DUP from the feed degradation characteristics, in some instances this information will be available. As mentioned in Chapter 6, the MP system quantifies the protein in a feed by their CP content, ADIN content and the a, b and c values. If feed is analysed in the laboratory this should be the format of the results reported, as ERDP and DUP contents can only be calculated when animal details are available.

The amount of protein degraded in the rumen is calculated from the outflow rate (r) and the a, b and c parameters. Outflow rate is related to the Animal Production Level (APL) and can be obtained from Table 10.2 below.

Table 10.2 Rumen outflow rate (r) at different Animal Production Levels (APL)

APL	r
0.75	0.010
1.0	0.019
1.5	0.037
2.0	0.052
2.5	0.066
3.0	0.077
3.5	0.087
4.0	0.096
4.5	0.104
5.0	0.110
5.5	0.116
6.0	0.121

The amount of ERDP and DUP supplied by a feed when it is given to a specific animal can be determined using the following steps. To facilitate the understanding of each step an example will be used of feeding a soyabean meal with a CP of 550 g/kg DM,

ADIN = 0.9 g/kg DM, a = 0.15, b = 0.80, c = 0.1, to a cow with a total ME requirement of 150 MJ and a maintenance requirement of 60 MJ.

1. Calculate the Animal Production Level (APL)

   $APL = ME_{total}/ME_{maint}$

   $= 150 / 60$

   $= 2.5$

2. Determine the rumen outflow rate (r) from Table 10.2 above.

   $r = 0.066$

3. Calculate the amount of quickly degraded protein (QDP, g/kg DM).

   $QDP = a \times CP$

   $= 0.15 \times 550$

   $= 82.5$ g/kg DM

4. Calculate amount of slowly degraded protein (SDP, g/kg DM).

   $SDP = CP \times (b \times c)/(c + r)$

   $= 550 \times (0.80 \times 0.1)/(0.1+0.066)$

   $= 265.1$ g/kg DM

5. Calculate effective rumen degradable protein (ERDP, g/kg DM).

   $ERDP = (0.8 \times QDP) + SDP$

   $= (0.8 \times 82.5) + 265.1$

   $= 331.1$ g/kg DM

6. Calculate amount of digestible undegradable protein (DUP, g/kg DM).

   $DUP = 0.9 \times \{CP - QDP - SDP - (6.25 \times ADIN)\}$

   $= 0.9 \times \{550 - 82.5 - 265.1 - (6.25 \times 0.9)\}$

   $= 177.1$ g/kg DM

7. The amount of ERDP and DUP in the feed when given to the cow specified above is therefore:

   $ERDP = 331$ g/kg DM

   $DUP = 177$ g/kg DM

CHAPTER 11

CALCULATING MINERAL REQUIREMENTS

11.1 Introduction

11.2 Maintenance
  11.2.1 Calcium
  11.2.2 Magnesium
  11.2.3 Phosphorus

11.3 Lactation

11.4 Pregnancy

11.5 Weight change

11.6 Calculating supply of minerals

11.7 Examples

11.8 Manual exercises

11.9 Computer exercises

11.1 Introduction

This chapter considers the major minerals - calcium, magnesium and phosphorus. The other minerals covered in Chapter 7 are not discussed in this chapter, either because they rarely cause any clinical problems, or because their interactions with other minerals and other factors influencing their absorption are such that the calculation of ration supply is rarely worthwhile. In other situations our understanding of animal requirements and supply are insufficient to allow precise requirements to be determined. In many situations the animal's requirements for major minerals are met by a ration that contains sufficient energy and protein and it is the exception rather than the rule that minerals will be deficient.

Requirements for the major minerals, and recommended dietary allowances have been a topic of considerable debate over the past few decades, primarily due to difficulties in determining animal requirements and the efficiency with which the minerals are absorbed by the animal. In 1980 the ARC published a set of requirements which were then considered by an expert committee (ARC, 1980). This committee rejected most of the recommendations and reverted back to the earlier ARC recommendations (IDWP, 1983). These recommendations were considerably higher for some minerals, notably phosphorus. A second expert group (AFRC, 1991) was set up to reappraise the requirements for calcium and phosphorus and this

group reported in 1991. As a result of all these changes, magnesium allowances are based on work done in the 1960s and are relatively simplistic, whereas the requirements for calcium and phosphorus are more complex and take into account feed intake and ration quality.

The current situation is that requirements for phosphorus in particular are high and are not met in many rations that appear to perform satisfactorily on-farm. Given the high price of phosphorus supplementation many advisors are happy to formulate rations that are marginally deficient in phosphorus.

The basic requirements of an animal are those for maintenance and for the different productive processes such as milk production, growth and pregnancy. These can be likened to the requirements for net energy and net protein, described in Chapters 9 and 10. However, the minerals are not completely absorbed from the intestines and therefore more has to be supplied in the ration. The amount of a mineral required in the ration is known as the mineral allowance and is dependent on the requirement and the efficiency of absorption.

Efficiency of absorption can vary from 0.7 for phosphorus in high quality diets to as little as 0.17 for magnesium, thus dietary allowances are always greater than the requirements of the animal.

The rest of this chapter will refer to dietary allowances and the relevant safety margins will be used in all the figures and the associated tables in Chapter 20.

11.2 Maintenance

Requirements for maintenance are made up of the unavoidable losses into the intestines and the skin-related losses in hair and scurf (dandruff). Losses into the intestines are related to the amount the animal eats and the skin–related losses are dependent on the animal's skin area and hence its body weight. Although intake is closely related to body weight (Chapter 8), allowances for calcium and phosphorus are better predicted from absolute DM intake per day, as voluntary intake also varies according to level of production.

11.2.1 Calcium (Table 20.15, page 212)

Figure 11.1 shows the allowances for calcium for maintenance in dairy cows of differing weights and feed intakes. It can be seen that the major influence on the allowance is intake. A high-yielding cow eating 26 kg DM/day requires almost twice as much calcium as a dry cow consuming 10 kg DM/day (31 g Ca compared to 16 g Ca/day). In contrast, allowances only increase by about 2 g/day for a 50% increase in body weight.

Figure 11.1 Calcium allowances for maintenance AFRC, 1991)

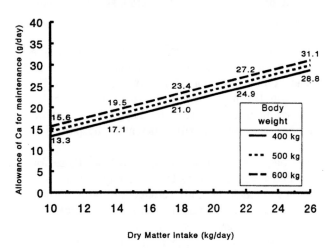

11.2.2 Magnesium (Table 20.16, page 212)

Figure 11.2 shows the allowances for magnesium for maintenance. These are considered to be related only to the animal's live weight, rather than to feed intake, and increase from 7 g/day for a small 400 kg Jersey to 13 g/day for a large Holstein cow.

Figure 11.2 Magnesium   allowances   for maintenance (IDWP, 1983)

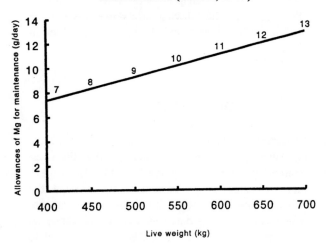

11.2.3 Phosphorus (Table 20.17, page 213)

Bovine saliva contains large amounts of phosphorus. The amount of phosphorus required for maintenance is therefore closely related to the amount of saliva produced, which in turn is related to the amount the animal eats. The amount of saliva produced is also dependent on the type of feed, with poor-quality forages and straws requiring more chewing and rumination and hence more saliva and phosphorus than concentrate feed sources. Dry feeds also require more saliva than wet feeds. As well as requiring more saliva and hence phosphorus, the efficiency of absorption of phosphorus is lower for poorer forages, especially when dry, which further increases the requirement for dietary phosphorus and hence dietary allowance.

Figure 11.3 shows the phosphorus allowances of dairy cows at different feed intakes. Two sets of allowances are specified according to the overall ration quality (q). One set is for animals on high-quality diets with a q over 0.7 which are assumed to be primarily concentrates which result in efficient absorption and low saliva production. Diets with a q of less than 0.7 are considered to be forages and the increased saliva flow and reduced efficiency of absorption of phosphorus are both reflected in increased allowances, such that they are almost twice those recommended for high quality diets. However, it is worth noting that most of the original work was carried out with hays given to sheep (AFRC, 1991), and it is possible that these were of a lower quality and promoted more saliva production than the silage-based rations normally given to dairy cows. It follows that the recommended allowances for phosphorus may be in excess of requirements for high-quality, low dry matter silage and therefore the slight deficiencies of phosphorus seen in many rations may not be of major importance.

Figure 11.3 Phosphorus allowances for maintenance (AFRC, 1991)

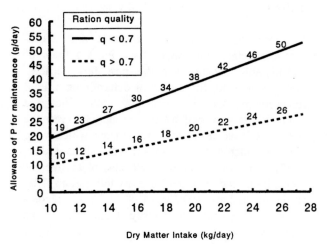

11.3 Lactation (Table 20.18, page 213)

Allowances for the major minerals for lactation are shown in Figure 11.4 for milk of a standard composition. In most instances it is not necessary to correct for the actual milk composition but Channel Island breeds, with high milk fat, may require more calcium. It can be seen that phosphorus allowances again vary according to ration quality, but compared to maintenance the difference is not so large.

Figure 11.4 Calcium, magnesium and phosphorus allowances for lactation (AFRC, 1991 and IDWP, 1983)

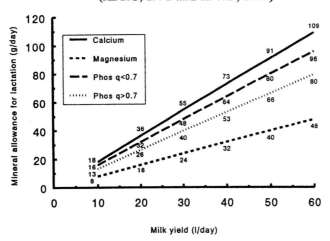

11.4 Pregnancy (Table 20.19, page 214)

Mineral allowances for pregnancy increase in a similar pattern to requirements for energy and protein in that they are minimal in the first half of gestation and only become important in the last 10 weeks (Figure 11.5). Again the efficiency of absorption of phosphorus is affected by ration quality but only the values for diets with q less than 0.7 are shown, as low-yielding cows and dry cows will generally be on poorer quality diets than those given to higher-yielding cows.

11.5 Weight change (Table 20.20, page 214)

The amount of calcium and phosphorus required for growth depends on what tissues are being laid down, with bone requiring far more calcium and phosphorus that either lean or fat tissue. Allowances are therefore considered to be influenced by the maturity of the animal, with immature animals having relatively higher requirements for calcium and phosphorus than mature animals.

In practice, most dairy cows can be considered as being of a mature body size and therefore mineral allowances per kilogram of weight change are considered as fixed (Figure 11.6). However, if rations are formulated for heifers using a computer, the stage of maturity should be taken into account. Magnesium requirements, by contrast, are considered to be independent of stage of maturity.

Figure 11.5 Calcium, magnesium and phosphorus allowances for pregnancy (AFRC, 1991 and IDWP, 1983)

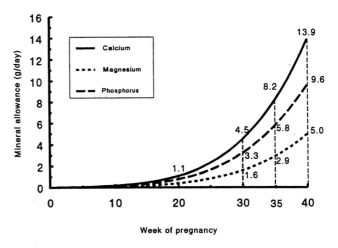

Figure 11.6 Calcium, magnesium and phosphorus allowances for weight change in dairy cows assuming that during weight loss q>0.7 and during weight gain q<0.7 (AFRC, 1991 and IDWP, 1983)

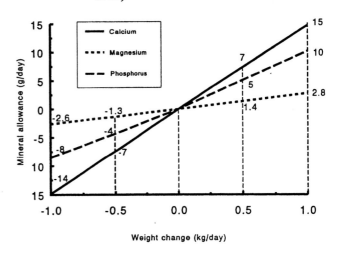

11.6 Calculating supply of minerals (Table 20.21, pages 215 to 219)

Calculating the supply of minerals is relatively simple. Using Table 20.21 the mineral composition of each feed in the ration can be determined and then multiplied by the relevant dry matter intake for that food. Summing the supply from each food gives the total.

11.7   Examples

Example 1

What are the mineral requirements of a 600 kg dry cow on a diet 40 kg of poor grass (25% DM, q = 0.6) when she is 35 weeks pregnant?

First calculate the dry matter intake (DMI), as this is needed for calcium and phosphorus maintenance requirements.

DMI = 40 x (25/100)
    = 10 kg

Maintenance
Calcium (Figure 11.1)
10 kg DMI and 600 kg body weight = 15.6 g

Magnesium (Figure 11.2)
600 kg body weight = 11 g

Phosphorus (Figure 11.3)
q = 0.6, 10 kg DMI = 19 g

Pregnancy (35 weeks pregnant) (Figure 11.5)
Calcium = 8.2 g
Magnesium = 2.9 g
Phosphorus = 5.8 g

Totals
Calcium (15.6 + 8.2) = 23.8 g
Magnesium (11 + 2.9) = 13.9 g
Phosphorus (19 + 5.8) = 24.8 g

Example 2

What are the mineral requirements of a 600 kg cow producing 20 litres of milk and eating 18 kg DM of a diet with a q of 0.68?

Maintenance
Calcium (Figure 11.1)
600 kg cow, 18 kg DMI = 23.4 g

Magnesium (Figure 11.2)
600 kg cow = 11 g

Phosphorus (Figure 11.3)
q = 0.68, 18 kg DMI = 34 g

Lactation (20 litres milk) (Figure 11.4)
Calcium = 36 g
Magnesium = 16 g
Phosphorus (q <0.7) = 32 g

Totals
Calcium (23.4 + 36) = 59.4 g
Magnesium (11 + 16) = 27 g
Phosphorus (34 + 32) = 66 g

Example 3

What are the mineral requirements of a 600 kg cow giving 40 litres of milk eating 22 kg DM of a ration with q = 0.67 and losing 1 kg/day?

Will a ration of the following feeds meet her mineral requirements?

	Fresh weight	DM	Ca	Mg	P
	kg	%		g/kg DM	
Average silage	30	27	6.8	1.6	3.1
Maize silage	20	30	3.9	2.4	1.8
Wheat grain	3.0	87	0.6	1.1	3.4
Fishmeal white	0.7	92	56.2	2.3	38.1
Maize gluten feed	5.0	89	2.8	4.3	10.0

Animal requirements

Maintenance
Calcium (Figure 11.1)
600 kg eating 22 kg DM = 27.2 g

Magnesium (Figure 11.2)
600 kg cow = 11 g

Phosphorus (Figure 11.3)
22 kg DM, q < 0.7 = 42 g

Lactation (40 litres) (Figure 11.4)
Calcium = 73 g
Magnesium = 32 g
Phosphorus = 64 g

Weight change (1 kg loss) (Figure 11.6)
Calcium = -14 g
Magnesium = -2.6 g
Phosphorus = -8 g

Totals
Calcium   (27.2 + 73 - 14)   = 86.2 g
Magnesium   (11 + 32 - 2.6)   = 40.4 g
Phosphorus   (42 + 64 - 8)   = 98 g

Ration supply

To determine the ration supply calculate the dry matter intake of each feed (DMI) and hence the amount of each mineral supplied.

	DMI	Ca	P	Mg
	kg	g	g	g
Average silage	8.1	55.1	25.1	13.0
Maize silage	6.0	23.4	10.8	14.4
Wheat grain	2.6	1.6	8.8	2.9
Fishmeal white	0.64	36.0	24.4	1.5
Maize gluten feed	4.5	12.6	45.0	19.4
Totals		**128.7**	**114.1**	**51.2**

	Ca (g)	P (g)	Mg (g)
Supply	129	114	51
Requirements	86	98	40
Balance	**43**	**16**	**11**

Therefore the ration will meet requirements.

11.8   Exercises

These exercises require you to use Tables 20.15 to 20.20 (pages 212 to 214) and the feed analyses in Table 20.21 in Chapter 20 that start on page 215. The solutions to these exercises can be found in Chapter 19, pages 191 to 192.

Exercise 1
What are the mineral requirements of a 600 kg cow giving 30 litres of milk and losing 0.5 kg a day when given 60 kg of a total mixed ration that has the following analysis: DM 33.3 %, ME 11.2 MJ/kg DM, GE 18.7 MJ/kg DM?

1   Calculate dry matter intake and ration q
2   Determine maintenance requirements
3   Determine lactation requirements (Table 20.18, page 213)
4   Determine requirements for weight change (Table 20.20, page 214)
5   Determine totals

Exercise 2
A 38 week pregnant dry cow (550 kg, no weight change) is being fed on a diet of poor grass (63D) *ad libitum*. If she consumes 43.5 kg fresh weight will this meet her mineral requirements?   See Table 20.21, page 216, for analysis of the silage.

Exercise 3
A 650 kg cow giving 36 litres of milk (not pregnant, losing 0.5 kg/day) is being given the following ingredients in a complete diet. Will the diet meet her mineral requirements?

Grass silage average	25 kg
Maize silage	25 kg
Wheat grain	4 kg
Soyabean meal	2 kg
Rapeseed meal	2 kg

11.9   Computer exercises

The computer exercises on mineral requirements (Chapter 19, pages 192 to 193) look at the relative importance of the different mineral requirements for the various nutritional commitments, the effect of different feeding systems, the mineral supplementation of maize silage-based diets and the mineral status of dry cow rations.

PART 4

PRACTICAL DAIRY COW FEEDING

CHAPTER 12

DESIGNING DIETS AND FEEDING SYSTEMS

12.1 Introduction

12.2 Designing diets
    12.2.1 Setting targets for animal performance
    12.2.2 Home–produced feeds
    12.2.3 Supplementary feeds

12.3 Assessing feed intake on the farm

12.4 Manipulating feed intake on the farm

12.5 Supplementary concentrates
    12.5.1 Feeding to yield
    12.5.2 Flat rate feeding of concentrates
    12.5.3 Complete diets or total mixed rations (TMR)

12.6 Achieving sufficient energy intake
    12.6.1 Changes in weight and in condition score
    12.6.2 Optimal levels of supplementary energy

12.7 The ideal diet

12.1   Introduction

The principal objective in feeding dairy cows is to make money, which means producing milk of acceptable quality and in the optimal quantity for the market at as low a cost as possible. Feeds are the largest single variable cost in milk production (Chapter 1), so it is vital that the diets given to the herd are the right ones and are capable of producing the desired output. This involves setting targets for performance and then designing diets capable of supplying the nutrients required to meet the targets. So the nutritional objectives to support the money–making activity are to design diets which are cost–effective, to know how to assess and manipulate feed consumption, to be able to make the rumen work at its optimal rate and thereby to avoid digestive upsets and to supply the correct amount and form of energy and protein so that nutrients are not wasted.

12.2   Designing diets

There are three stages in designing diets. First, deciding what level of animal performance is required from the herd. Second, assessing what home–produced feeds are available on the farm and third, deciding what feeds should be purchased. The process of designing diets from scratch may appear at first sight to be purely an academic exercise, but there are occasions when the diet has to be re–assessed completely. For example, pastures may have suffered from drought in summer, output may have been depressed and production may be under target as a result; or the herd may be over–quota and production may have to be held back for a period. Alternatively, the current diet may be failing to meet the desired level of performance, or it may be considered to be too expensive and a radical re–appraisal of the feeding strategy is desired.

12.2.1 Setting   targets   for   animal performance

Deciding the target level of animal performance involves:

i) taking a careful look at the quota position on the farm and evaluating possible changes in milk production which may be desirable in the coming months;

ii) assessing the grouping of animals in the herd, their calving pattern, stage of lactation, condition score, proportion of heifers in milk and likely level of output by each group;

iii) taking a view as to the overall level of performance, then

iv) making a decision as to how many different diets can be offered to different groups within the herd, given that each group will have different nutrient requirements.

There are two schools of thought on the grouping of animals in a herd. One school believes that dividing animals adds precision to feeding, reduces wastage, reduces problems of over-fat or over-thin cows and increases the ability to observe cows on heat. The other school believes that grouping causes instability, increases bullying, increases the complexity of rationing and increases the time taken to feed and milk the herd.

It is possible to avoid grouping the herd by feeding a significant part of the diet to each individual in the parlour during milking. An alternative is to offer one diet to all animals, thereby allowing the individual animal to eat according to its potential yield, stage of lactation and condition score. Trough space must be adequate so that bullying is minimal, and the diet must be capable of supporting the likely yield of the better animals. The single diet approach is simpler than giving different diets to different groups, but its major drawback is that lower-yielding cows can be overfed and become fat. Producing over-fat cows is wasteful, costly, and can be difficult to rectify during the dry period, especially if the animals are at pasture.

A single diet for all animals works best with a tight calving pattern with most animals at the same stage of lactation. The diet may be changed at intervals during the feeding period in response to changes in the requirements of the herd for nutrients, to changes in feed supplies and to the quota situation.

Feeding systems (feeding to yield, flat rate feeding or complete diet feeding – see Section 12.5) usually evolve to suit the farm layout, the machinery available and the desires of the people who have to do the work. There is no clear advantage to one particular system, though simplicity should always be an important consideration when assessing target levels of animal performance and when deciding how to deliver diets to the animals to meet targets.

Once the target level of animal performance has been set, the next priority is to decide whether the quality and quantity of the home-produced feeds are likely to be adequate, or whether there is likely to be a requirement for large amounts of purchased bulk feeds (e.g. brewers' grains) and dry concentrates. To decide the level of concentrate input, it is useful to have some idea of the **potential** annual milk yield which might be sustainable from forage alone. Experiments in which spring-calving cows were given grazed herbage and grass silage as the sole feeds, with no concentrate whatsoever showed that whole-lactation milk yields of 5000 litres were achievable by cows and 4000 litres by heifers. The quality of the silage was in excess of 11.0 MJ ME/kg DM. Clearly, if the quality of the silage is lower than 11.0 MJ ME/kg DM, then the level of output from forage is likely to be reduced. Furthermore, the substitution of forage by supplementary concentrates means that 5000 litres of milk from forage is rarely achieved in practice. A realistic target for a herd yielding 6000 to 7000 litres annually is 4000 litres of milk from forage.

12.2.2   Home–produced feeds

The main home–produced feeds are the forages (grass to be grazed, silage, and hay), roots such as potatoes and fodder beet and by–products such as straw. These feeds are very important and the quantities available must be assessed as carefully as possible.

Grass to be grazed may be less productive because of soil compaction as a result of damage by feet or wheels, weed ingress or soil nutrient imbalance. Each field should be checked for plant density, and soil nutrient status, and a view taken of its future productive potential. The best time of year to do the field check is midsummer so that a decision on

reseeding can be taken straight away and fields can be renovated or reseeded immediately, provided there is sufficient moisture in the soil for seed germination.

Field productivity can be recorded as cow grazing days per hectare during the grazing season plus the yield of grass harvested as silage or hay. Cow grazing days is the number of cows in the field each time the field is grazed, multiplied by the number of days they remain in the field, summed for the whole year.

Historical records of cow grazing days and yield of conserved grass per field can give a guide to the number of hectares of grass needed each season for the herd and its followers. Marked reductions in either cow grazing days or in the yield of conserved forage for a particular field indicate that it may be due for reseeding. Specialist silage crops (see Chapter 2) act as a buffer to grass by providing additional forages, which should be available throughout the year as buffer feeds to grazed pasture and as silages for the winter period to be fed with conserved grass.

Silage, hay and straw stocks should be checked before the winter feeding period commences, by calculating the amount in each stack, silo and big bale. First the volume of the stack, silo or bale is measured, then density is assessed by using Tables 12.1 and 12.2. The bulk (i.e. fresh weight) densities shown in Table 12.1 relate to a tower silo 10 metres in diameter filled to 18 metres height of settled silage. The values for bunker or clamp silos relate to a settled height of 2.5 metres. Bulk density depends both on dry matter content and on height of settled silage. For towers, average density should be reduced by 30 kg/m^3 for every metre reduction in settled height below 18 metres. For bunkers and clamps, density should be reduced by 40 kg/m^3 for every 0.5 metres reduction in height below 2.5 metres.

The total fresh weight of each feed is then calculated by multiplying the volume by the appropriate density. Dividing the total weight by the number of days during which the feed is to be used gives an average amount of fresh weight which can be offered daily. The objective is that home–produced conserved feeds should never be in short supply, otherwise major changes may have to be made to the diet, production may suffer and feed costs may escalate substantially, especially if other farmers in the area have also run out of silage.

The values in Tables 12.1 and 12.2 are only approximations so that a general picture can be obtained as to the likely amounts of home–produced feeds available, and should be reassessed once feeding has started. The next step is to assess the likely amount of actual dry matter available since dry matter is what really matters, not water.

Table 12.1 Typical fresh weight (and dry matter) density (kg/m³) of silage in tower and bunker or clamp silos, and in big bales

Dry matter content	Bunker/clamp		Big bale	Tower	
(g/kg)	Grass	Maize/Whole-crop	Grass	Grass	Maize/Whole-crop
150	800 (120)	-	-	-	-
200	725 (145)	700 (140)	430 (85)	-	-
250	680 (170)	650 (160)	400 (100)	-	-
300	650 (195)	620 (185)	380 (115)	830 (250)	790 (240)
350	630 (220)	600 (210)	350 (123)	800 (280)	760 (270)
400	610 (245)	590 (235)	330 (130)	770 (300)	730 (290)
450	600 (270)	580 (260)	300 (135)	750 (340)	720 (320)
500	590 (295)	570 (285)	275 (140)	730 (360)	700 (350)
550	580 (320)	560 (300)	240 (130)	710 (390)	680 (370)
600	570 (340)	550 (330)	210 (125)	690 (410)	660 (400)

Table 12.2 Typical density of hay and straw bales (kg fresh weight/m³)

	Type of bale		
	Large square	Large round	Small
Hay	155	125	145
Straw	120	100	80

Forages should be analyzed for dry matter content at monthly intervals during the feed–out period. If the silage is losing effluent, its dry matter content is likely to increase during the storage period. But if the silage is exposed to air or rain before being offered to the animals, then dry matter content is likely to decrease as the storage period progresses. Assessing dry matter in advance of the feeding period can only be done by core–sampling silos or bales. The dry matter of cored samples may be overestimated because the squeezing effect of the corer can lead to loss of liquid, especially from wetter material.

Having reached an assessment of the total dry matter available from home–produced feeds, it is important to take a view on the likely need for supplements, both during the grazing season (assuming there may well be a drought, or an extended winter period due to wet, cold weather) and during the winter period itself. The needs of the young stock must not be forgotten at this stage.

12.2.3 Supplements

The need for supplements depends not only on the quantities of forage feeds available, but also on their qualities. Large amounts of silage and hay may be made if harvests are delayed by cold, wet weather, but quality is reduced because the crops were over-mature at harvest. So part of the decision making process in designing diets is to assess whether or not the forages are likely to be eaten in the required amounts. If not, there will be an excess at the end of the winter. If the target level of performance is

relatively high – more than 6500 litres average total lactation yield per head – then it is unlikely that forages will comprise more than 65% of the total dry matter eaten during the entire period, however high their quality.

If the energy content of a forage is low (less than 10.5 MJ ME/kg DM), then extra energy will be required in the purchased supplements. If the protein content of a forage feed is low (less than 120 g crude protein/kg DM), as in maize and fermented whole–crop cereal silages, then high–protein supplements will be needed.

The storage facilities on the farm and the equipment for mixing and delivering feeds should be scrutinised because the extent to which feeds can be stored and mixed will determine what type of supplement can be purchased. Straights (raw material feeds) can be cheaper to purchase, but they need to be stored separately so that they can be used at different rates according to their particular composition. If there is little storage space, or no facilities on the farm to weigh out individual feeds, then balanced compounded supplements are likely to be of greater value than straights, even though they are likely to be more expensive to buy.

The most difficult decision in deciding the need for supplements is to judge how much total feed and how much of a particular forage is likely to be eaten. But an idea of total and forage intake must be gained, or the diet may be designed to meet target performance but not eaten by the animal.

12.3 Assessing feed intake on the farm

The importance of knowing what the animal is eating, or is likely to eat, has already been stressed (Chapter 8). Feed budgeting and designing diets are but two good reasons for knowing how much is likely to be eaten. A third important reason is diagnostic, when there may be health problems to solve which are related to the diet of the herd. Without knowing how much is being eaten it is considerably more difficult to diagnose the possible cause of the disease.

The first task in assessing feed intake on the farm is to draw up a simple balance sheet (Table 12.3). The amount of dry matter eaten of each feed must be estimated, even if the bulky feeds are not being weighed out to the animals (see example below).

The amount of concentrate being used daily per head is usually known, so the total fresh weight, corrected for dry matter (x 0.88), gives the dry matter eaten per head. The next step is to estimate the intake of purchased moist bulk feeds and forages. Purchased bulk feeds are bought by the truck load, so the quantity purchased and the time taken to use a load, less about 20% loss for wastage, divided by the number of animals being given the feed, corrected for dry matter content, is the average amount of dry matter being eaten per day.

Bulk density can be used (see Section 12.1 above) to assess the amount of silage being eaten. The volume of silage removed from the silo must be assessed, if necessary by placing chalk marks on the walls of the silo at regular intervals, and measuring the volume removed over a short period of time such as a week. The volume can then be converted to a weight by using Table 12.1: volume (m^3) x bulk density (kg/m^3) = fresh weight (kg). Correcting for the dry matter of the silage (or hay) and dividing by the number of days and by the number of animals in the group gives the dry matter eaten per animal per day. Shear–grab blocks and loads of silage removed by tractor–mounted front–loaders may be weighed by using a device which records the pressure of the tractor's hydraulic lifting system and then converts the pressure reading into a weight. Alternatively, silage can be weighed in a forage box or mixer wagon fitted with load cells.

The balance sheet (Table 12.3) can also be used to calculate total intake of gross energy (GE) and metabolisable energy (ME). These totals can be used to assess the ration quality and the adequacy of energy supply to the animals.

The next step is to ask if the diet is sensible. Are the animals capable of eating the diet? Is it providing enough energy to support the actual milk output? Are the animals gaining or losing weight on the diet? Starting from the premise that amount of dry matter eaten is related to body weight, milk yield and diet quality (Chapter 8, pages 98 to 99), check if the diet as assessed is likely to be eaten, and if so, whether it is providing too much or too little energy to the animal. If the indication is that the diet is being eaten and is also providing an excess of ME over requirements, then the animals should look as if they are gaining weight. If not, then start again with the diet assessment or look for reasons for modifying intake (Chapter 8, page 98).

From the above example (cow = 600 kg, milk yield = 20 litres, diet q (ME/GE) = 191/320 = 0.60) and from Table 8.1 (page 98) the predicted daily intake of DM is 17.0 kg. Therefore the intake (16.9 kg DM/day) is slightly underestimated, but still likely to be eaten in the amounts assessed as long as the presentation and feeding facilities are adequate.

From Tables 20.5 and 20.6 (pages 206 to 207), total ME required for maintenance = 59.1, milk production = (5.19 x 20 litres = 103.8) = 163 MJ. Therefore the cows are being overfed by 28 MJ and should be gaining in weight at about 0.8 kg/day (Table 20.8, page 208).

12.4 Manipulating feed intake on the farm

Ensuring high feed intake is the most important aspect of feeding the dairy cow, but feed intake can be manipulated considerably by the way the diet, or components of the diet, are presented to the animal. For example, dusty pelleted compounds, and very hard pellets, are not eaten as well as whole pellets. Compounders go to great lengths to ensure that their pellets are not too hard, but well–formed and unlikely to collapse when moved from factory to farm, or from farm store to animal. The intake of self–feed silage can be restricted by up to 20% by using an electric wire rather than a solid barrier. Intake of self–fed silage can be restricted further by not moving the barrier far enough each day in an attempt to eliminate wastage.

Table 12.3 **Example of a simple diet balance sheet for assessing feed intake on the farm (Cows giving 20 litres of milk of 3.35% protein and 4.0% fat, estimated liveweight = 600 kg)**

Feeds	Fresh weight (kg)	DM (kg)	GE (MJ/kg DM)	GE (MJ)	ME (MJ/kg DM)	ME (MJ)
Concentrate	6	5.3	18.8	100	12.5	66
Ensiled brewers' grains	10	2.8	19.0	53	11.5	32
Grass silage	35	8.8	19.0	167	10.6	93
TOTAL	51	16.9		320		191

Live weight can be estimated from the weight of barren cows sold off the farm.

Frequent feeding, although more laborious than once daily feeding, can increase intake by stimulating the animals to come to the feed trough. Complete diets are normally eaten in greater amounts than separate feeds. Restricted trough space can restrict intake, as the result of increased bullying, especially if heifers are grouped together with cows.

Length of chop of forages and straw affects intake. Generally, the shorter the length of chopping, the higher the intake, particularly when silage is self-fed, because the animal can pull the material out of the silo with greater ease than with longer material.

12.5 Supplementary concentrates

Dairy cows need supplementary concentrates during lactation. They can be given to animals in different ways. Traditionally, concentrates were given according to milk yield: the more milk the cow gives, the more concentrates she receives. In the 1970s, flat rate feeding of concentrates was developed and more recently complete diets, or total mixed rations have gained considerable popularity on larger units.

12.5.1 Feeding to yield

Feeding to yield is the traditional way of manipulating feed and nutrient intake. It is still a very common way of feeding cows. Forages and bulky feeds are offered outside the milking parlour, often with a midday feed of a concentrate like sugar beet pulp or maize gluten feed. Concentrates are then offered according to yield in the parlour, and sometimes also through out-of-parlour electronically controlled hoppers where the individual animal is identified as she approaches the feeder and is automatically given several small meals of concentrates through the day.

The system was developed as a way of matching nutrient supply to requirements. The depression in feed intake in the first weeks of lactation was recognised (see Chapter 8, page 97), and so a relatively high level of concentrate was provided as soon as possible after calving – concentrate was offered virtually *ad libitum* for the first few weeks after calving. This was called "challenge" or "lead" feeding – the cow was challenged to yield as much milk as possible as soon as possible in the lactation. Thereafter, concentrates were supplied at a fixed rate per litre of milk – either 0.25, 0.3 or 0.4 kg/litre depending on the yield of the cow and the perceived milk production supported by the rest of the diet.

One of the major problems with challenge or lead-feeding is that peak yield is reached after only 5 to 7 weeks post-calving. High levels of milk production soon after calving when feed intake is depressed can easily result in metabolic disorders such as fatty liver, ketosis and milk fever, reflecting the distortion of the cow's metabolism at this crucial stage of the lactation. Another major problem with feeding to yield is that reduced yield post-peak produces a reduced allowance of concentrates, which in turn reduces yield, especially if the quality of the rest of diet is poor. So the cow is placed on a downward treadmill and the decline in milk yield can be unacceptably rapid.

Feeding concentrates to yield also limits feed intake since most, if not all, the concentrates are given in the parlour in two daily feeds. The consequences of twice daily feeding of large quantities of concentrates are discussed in Chapter 4 (page 45). Essentially, the rumen is not working at its maximum rate, especially as far as digestion of fibre is concerned. Total feed intake is lower than it could be, and output is limited as a result.

12.5.2 Flat rate feeding of concentrates

The successful operation of flat rate feeding rests on the fact that it is the total quantity of concentrates that determines total milk output, not on the pattern of its distribution through the lactation. With a constant supplementation of *ad libitum* silage, milk production tends to follow the pattern of intake as the lactation progresses. So with flat rate feeding peak milk output is lower and later than when animals are offered greater quantities of concentrate early in lactation. The extent to which peak output may be limited depends on the actual level of concentrates and the quality of the silage.

Flat rate feeding of concentrates, in which the total amount of concentrate is set for the whole herd for the year and then divided equally between the animals to give a constant daily amount, can result in reduced feed intake if, for any reason, the amount of silage is restricted – either by inadequate amounts being offered to the animals, or as the result of poor preservation quality. On the other hand, if the forage is of high quality, more than 11.5 MJ ME/kg DM, then the difference between the ME content of the silage and that of a compound or a mix of straights is small, so feeding the correct amount of concentrate is less important than if the silage is of lower energy value.

A criticism of flat rate feeding is that cows of high potential milk yield are underfed early in lactation. This is true up to a point, but in addition to intake following the pattern of yield during the lactation, higher-yielding cows tend to eat more total feed – about 1 kg DM for every 10 litres extra milk above the average.

Some farmers have adopted a compromise between feeding to yield and true flat rate feeding, by having two or three "steps" during the lactation. Thus the first step is a relatively high flat rate of, say, 9 kg concentrates per cow for the first 100 days. There is then a sudden drop in the flat rate to 6 kg for the second 100 days of lactation followed by a further drop to 3 kg for the final 100 days or so.

12.5.3   *Complete diets or total mixed rations*

Complete diets, or total mixed rations (TMR), comprise a mixture of all the separate ingredients of the diet. Usually the mixing is done in a purpose–built mixer wagon, but on some units feeds are layered into a self–unloading forage box and the rather crude mixing occurs at the point of their discharge into the feed trough.

Changes to the mixture may be made in two different ways in response to changes in the size of the group being fed, in their rate of intake or in feed supplies. With "true" TMR the proportions of the feeds in the mix are kept constant, so a change in the total amount offered is made by increasing or decreasing the quantity of each fed in the mix *pro rata* so that the composition of the TMR stays the same.

On many units where so-called TMR are in operation, the concentrate pre-mix is kept constant per head but the quantity of silage is varied to ensure that enough total mix is on offer, yet wastage is not excessive. This form of TMR is less accurate than the true TMR approach, because changes in the proportions of concentrate to silage can result in the mix unwittingly being made unbalanced for one or more key nutrient.

The great advantage of TMR is that in most cases the feeds are weighed in the mixer wagon. Feed intake is known, and the effect on intake of changes in the mix can be seen. Nutrient intake can be checked against output to see if the diet is balanced, and adjustments can be made to improve the balance of the diet and efficiency of feed use.

Another important advantage of TMR is that feed intake is usually higher than with other feeding systems – by as much as 30%. This response in feed intake is attributed to greater synchronisation in the release of rapidly–digestible energy and nitrogen in the rumen, increased rumen microbial growth and accelerated fibre digestion, as discussed in Chapters 5 (page 55) and 6 (page 76).

The disadvantages of TMR are that the mixer wagon is an expensive specialised item of equipment, storage space is required for the individual feed ingredients and purchased feeds and blends are often sold in relatively large loads which means that cash flow problems may occur if all the feeds are bought at a similar time of the year. The main nutritional disadvantage is that individual cows can become too fat if they eat large amounts of the TMR and do not milk as well as they should.

12.6   Achieving sufficient energy intake

For most cows in early lactation, feed dry matter intake is the major limiting factor to milk production. As a result, weight loss can be rapid and considerable as the animal "milks off her back". Later in lactation weight gain can be equally significant with cows becoming too fat by the time they calve down again, especially if their condition has been ignored during the dry period (see Chapter 15, page 146).

Regular, careful monitoring of condition score, coupled with an appropriate system of delivering supplementary feeds so that energy intake can be manipulated are very important practical nutritional objectives in achieving the desired outcome of acceptable profits from milk production.

12.6.1   *Changes in weight and in condition score*

The typical pattern of the changes in feed intake, milk yield and body weight through the lactation is shown in Figure 12.1. The depressed feed intake in the first weeks of lactation coincides with a sudden and large increase in energy requirements for milk production. Even on the highest quality diets, cows in early lactation lose weight. So it is essential that cows and heifers calve with reserves of body tissue to mobilise during the first two months of lactation. Target condition scores for cows are shown in Figure 12.1.

Much of the fat stored in the body of the dairy cow is in the abdomen, surrounding the intestines and the kidneys, and this fat is mobilised as the cow loses weight in early lactation. The target is for a decrease of one condition score in cows giving average yields and 1.5 condition scores in high-yielding cows between calving and peak yield, with a subsequent increase in weight so that the original condition score is reached by the time the cow calves again (Figure 12.2). The UK condition scoring system is described in detail in Chapter 17 (page 159).

Table 12.4   Changes in body tissues associated with a change of one condition score in milking cows (Wright and Russel, 1984)

Fat (kg)	84.1
Protein (kg)	7.35
Total (kg)	114.8
Energy (MJ)	3478
Diet energy equivalent (MJ ME)	4576

The weight and energy changes associated with a change of one condition score are considerable, as shown in Table 12.4. Although most of the change in weight is as fat, there is also some loss of protein. The energy equivalent of the total change in weight can be translated into a dietary equivalent, assuming that the mobilised energy is used to meet requirements for milk production.

Figure 12.1 Typical changes in feed intake, milk yield and liveweight during lactation for a mature cow

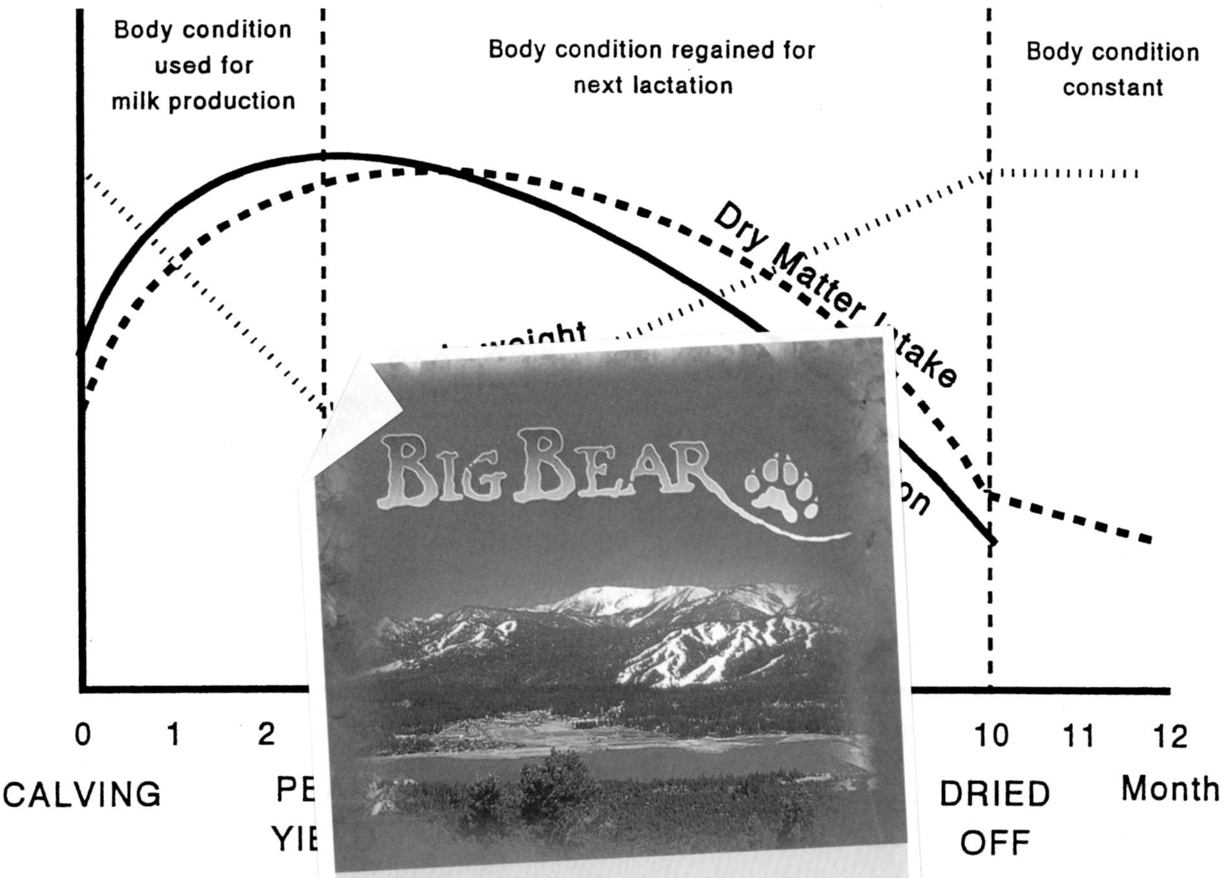

Body condition
used for
milk production

Body condition regained for
next lactation

Body condition
constant

Dry Matter Intake

0   1   2   10   11   12

CALVING   PE   DRIED   Month
                 YIE   OFF

Figure 12.2   Target conditi scores for milking   *12.6.2   O*   *vels of supplementary*
cows   *energy*

mic) compromise has to be
struck between givin   he cow a diet of forages
ly adequate energy for high
milk yiel   a diet consisting entirely of
ng energy and risking
etabolic problems. Upper
hapter 5 (page 59) for the
nd oil in the diet to reduce
rumen. Exceeding these
guarantee disaster. High-
very high levels of high-
ded care is taken to ensure
on offer all the time.

rate at calving is about 5
. This level should be
ate of 1 kg/day until the
Out-of-parlour feeders
luce the risk of digestive
at this critical period of
he cow to take frequent

mplete diet in groups
-calved cow should be
placed first in a group of medium yielders for 14
days post–calving and then moved into the highest
yielding group, as described in Chapter 15.

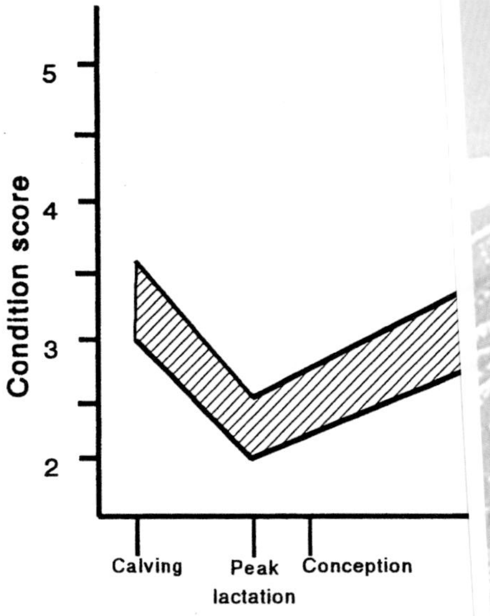

It is quite possible for a high-y
100 kg of live weight betweer
lactation. The weight lost must
the cow will become anoestrus
heat) and will be difficult, if not
back in calf. The timing of weig
important. If the cow loses wei
period of time, conception rates will suffer. Energy
deficiency and weight loss in the first third of
pregnancy may result in increased early embryonic
death.

Condition score

5

4

3

2

Calving   Peak   Conception
          lactation

Table 12.5 Ideal diets for dairy cows

	Stage of lactation			
	Early	Mid	Late	Dry
Milk yield (litres/day)	35	25	15	-
Dry matter (g/kg)	550	500	400	-
pH	5.5	5.0	4.5	-
ME (MJ/kg DM)	11.5 to 12	11 to 11.5	10.5 to 11	9.0
Crude protein (%)	18	17	16	15
NDF (%)	35	40	45	55
Oil (%)	<6	<5	-	-
Sugar (%)	4 to 6	3 to 5	-	-
Starch (%)	14 to 18	10 to 14	-	-

12.7   The ideal diet

It is possible to state in general terms the ideal specification for diets for cows, without identifying individual ingredients which depend on the farm concerned, the relative values of different feeds (Chapter 3), and their actual costs. Assuming a similar type of animal receives the diet throughout lactation, the specifications in Table 12.5 should meet requirements for ME and MP. Supplementary minerals and vitamins will also be required, but are not considered here (see Chapter 11).

CHAPTER 13

MANIPULATING THE COMPOSITION OF MILK

13.1 The importance of manipulating milk composition

13.2 Milk protein
  13.2.1 Raising the concentration of milk protein
  13.3.2 Lowering milk protein

13.3 Milk fat
  13.3.1 Raising the concentration of milk fat
  13.3.2 Lowering milk fat

13.4 Producing milk with minimal milk solids

13.5 Conclusions

13.1 The importance of manipulating milk composition

The milk price received by most producers is influenced significantly by its content of fat and protein. In November 1994 more than a dozen dairies in the UK were paying on a simple milk composition basis. On average, 56% of the average milk price was for protein content (4.20 pence per % per litre) and 44% was for milk fat content (2.63 pence per % per litre). As long as the consumer prefers semi–skimmed and skimmed milk, and there is a surplus of butter, payment for protein is likely to be higher than for fat. Farmers have a quota ceiling on the volume of milk they can produce, which is adjusted for its fat content. There is, however, currently no limit, within the overall volume of milk quota, for protein production. Therefore one way of increasing milk income is by raising the content of protein in milk, preferably without increasing milk fat or the volume of milk produced. Furthermore, where quota is a major constraint it is desirable to be able to reduce milk volume and content of milk fat whilst maintaining or lifting milk protein.

A smaller part of the dairy sector, usually near big cities, is being offered contracts to produce milk of a fixed composition with no premia if it is exceeded. These producers of "flat milk" do not want to incur any additional expenditure to achieve improved milk composition, but they must ensure that the cows produce large volumes of milk and that they do not impair herd health or fertility.

Over the next decade we can expect more emphasis on "designer" milks, with farmers wanting to be able to raise or lower yields and to change composition in a wide range of different combinations,

all of which must be done in a manner that is reversible over a period of weeks and which has no long–term adverse effects on animal health, fertility or welfare. Limited research work has been done on manipulating milk composition to suit the market place, and unfortunately the best researched effect, raising the concentration of milk fat, is the least wanted!

Raising milk protein content is clearly desirable, but the determination of the mechanisms controlling the on-farm production of milk protein is proving elusive. Without this information the response to dietary modifications is likely to continue to be varied and unpredictable.

Given that the major milk compositional change of importance is raising milk protein content, it is worth looking at the economics of such increases. Table 13.1 shows the increase in milk income achieved if milk protein is raised at varying milk yields. Achieving an increase in milk protein of more than 0.1% is difficult and with many strategies costing about 10p/cow/day, care must be taken to ensure that the cost of treatment is less than, and preferably less than half, the predicted benefits. When the total costs of the extra feed needed for the improved milk protein, and quota limits, are taken into account, many approaches currently advocated may not prove to be cost–effective.

Table 13.1 Increase in milk income (pence) from increasing milk protein composition at different milk yields. The milk protein price is 4.2 pence/% per litre

Milk yield	Increase in milk protein (% units/l)						
litres/day	0.05	0.075	0.10	0.125	0.15	0.175	0.20
10	2.1	3.2	4.2	5.3	6.3	7.4	8.4
15	3.2	4.7	6.3	7.9	9.5	11.0	12.6
20	4.2	6.3	8.4	10.5	12.6	14.7	16.8
25	5.3	7.9	10.5	13.1	15.8	18.4	21.0
30	6.3	9.5	12.6	15.8	18.9	22.1	25.2
35	7.4	11.0	14.7	18.4	22.1	25.7	29.4
40	8.4	12.6	16.8	21.0	25.2	29.4	33.6
45	9.5	14.2	18.9	23.6	28.4	33.1	37.8
50	10.5	15.8	21.0	26.3	31.5	36.8	42.0

Figure 13.1 shows the changes in the composition of milk with amount of concentrate eaten daily. The magnitude of the change is typical of that seen with many dietary modifications. Changes in milk fat

content are far more responsive than protein, with the former changing by about one percentage point. Milk protein content, on the other hand, only changes by about half a percentage point.

Figure 13.1 Effect of increasing concentrate intake on milk composition (adapted from Poole *et al.*, 1992)

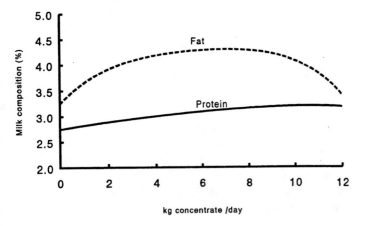

13.2   Milk protein

Changes in the concentration of milk protein can be brought about by dietary manipulations but compared with those possible in fat concentration (Section 13.3), the scope is far smaller and the response less predictable. There are various possible reasons for this poor state of affairs. Firstly, the natural variation in milk protein concentration is much smaller than that for fat. Secondly, the important dietary and physiological factors controlling the content of milk protein are less well identified.

Thirdly, milk protein concentration has only become a major factor affecting the unit price of milk within the last decade, so the subject has attracted less research interest than milk fat content. Finally, the cow has a relatively high ratio of milk protein to fat compared to other species, and at high yields her protein metabolism is already working very hard (5 to 7 times maintenance). Thus further improvements of a worthwhile size are likely to be difficult to achieve.

Despite these difficulties, some dietary variables have been clearly identified as affecting milk protein concentration and others merit closer study. In most situations it should be possible to achieve an annual herd average milk protein composition of 3.4% for Holstein/Friesian cows.

13.2.1   Raising the concentration of milk protein

Principles. Milk is comprised of water (88%), lactose (4.6%), fat (3.5 to 4.5%) and protein (3.0 to 3.8%). All four components must be available in the udder for milk production to occur. The diet contains water, energy and protein and whilst water supply has a major effect on milk volume, energy rather than protein supply seems to be the major influence on milk protein production.

The two main sources of energy in a dairy cow ration are the fibre components and sugars and starch (Chapter 3). In very simple terms, fibre stimulates milk fat whereas sugars and starch stimulate milk protein. In the rumen fibre is broken down by the microbes with the production of acetate and butyrate which are absorbed and are used to synthesise milk fat. Starch stimulates the production of propionate in the rumen which is a precursor for glucose and non–essential amino acids. If these sources of energy are partitioned to the udder, milk production will increase, but alternatively they can be partitioned towards the production of body fat. Cows in early lactation and with a high genetic potential are more likely to partition their energy to the udder whereas stale milkers and cows with low genetic potential will use the energy to gain body weight.

In practice, when starch is included in the diet it generally replaces energy from grass silage and so increases the amount of energy which is readily available for fermentation by the rumen microbes (FME). The enhanced supply of FME increases the amount of microbial protein synthesised which, in turn, increases protein supply to the small intestine and the supply of amino acids to the blood stream. A small but variable amount of dietary starch escapes degradation by the rumen microbes and passes into the small intestine (by-pass starch). The small intestine has a high energy demand which it meets by metabolising nutrients absorbed from the gut contents. With a low-starch diet there is little glucose in the small intestine and amino acids are deaminated and used as an energy source. By-pass starch is thought to supply glucose to the small intestine and therefore spares the use of amino acids in the intestinal wall, thus increasing the supply of amino acids to the liver and to the general circulation.

Milk protein has a specific amino acid profile and so conventional wisdom predicts that certain essential amino acids limit production and hence supplementation with essential amino acids is likely to increase milk protein production, with methionine and lysine being the best candidates. However, research carried out in the UK to date has failed to identify any limiting amino acids for milk production.

Energy supply. Increased amounts of concentrate in the diet are associated with elevations in milk protein (Figure 13.1). Milk yield also increases, and thus there can be a substantial rise in milk protein yield (Table 13.2). On average, the animals in the experiment shown in Table 13.2 gave increases in milk protein content of about 0.06 % units per extra 10 MJ ME intake per day.

The effect of increasing energy intake appears to be independent of the type of feed given, so an increased energy supply from forage is equally likely to lift milk protein and milk yield as that from concentrates. To raise milk protein with forages, they should be of high quality, highly palatable and presented to the animals in a way which maximises their intake. Supplementary molasses has also been shown to raise milk protein, presumably by increasing energy consumption.

Table 13.2 Response to increasing quantity of concentrates offered with silage *ad libitum* (Gordon, 1984)

	Concentrates (kg/day)				
	3.8	5.3	6.7	8.1	9.4
Silage DM/Total DM	0.73	0.65	0.58	0.53	0.49
ME intake (MJ/day)	189	196	215	232	237
Milk composition (g/kg)					
Fat	40.0	40.1	39.9	40.3	40.7
Protein	30.8	31.5	31.5	32.9	33.5
Yield (kg/day)					
Milk	20.2	21.2	22.6	23.5	24.3
Fat	0.81	0.85	0.90	0.95	0.99
Protein	0.62	0.67	0.71	0.77	0.81

Figure 13.2 Effect of different types of concentrate on milk yield and milk protein content (adapted from Poole *et al.*, 1992)

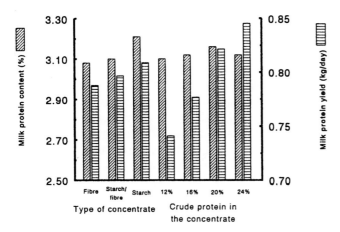

Starch in the diet. Increased starch intakes generally increase milk protein production. For example a study in which 6 kg of concentrates of differing compositions were given to cows, the high–starch

concentrate resulted in a higher milk yield and milk protein content than the high–fibre concentrate (Figure 13.2).

Similarly, substituting grass silage (generally low in sugar and starch) with either 33 or 75% of the total forage DM intake by other forages (higher in sugar or starch), was reflected in increases in both milk yield and milk protein content (Figure 13.3), but total feed intakes were also higher for the mixed forage diets and so total energy intake was increased as a result.

Figure 13.3 Effect of different forage mixes on daily milk protein composition and yield (adapted from Browne *et al.*, 1995)

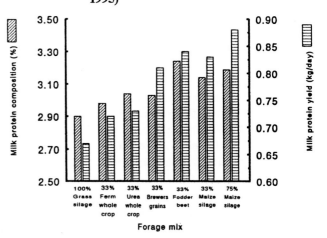

Protein supply. Increased protein intake increases milk protein production (Figure 13.2), but does not appear to have a major effect on milk protein content. Increased protein intake usually results in higher dry matter and energy intakes. Once these changes in intake are taken into account, changes in protein supply have little effect on milk protein composition. Fishmeal in particular is noted for its effect on increasing milk protein, but again this is thought to be due to elevations in dry matter and energy intakes.

Condition score. Fat cows, with condition scores over 3.5, have lower appetites, mobilise more body fat in the early stages of lactation and produce milk with a lower protein content. Cows should be calved at a condition score between 2.5 and 3.0 to ensure high voluntary intake and hence maximum energy consumption to promote high milk protein content (see Chapter 16 for further details).

Selective breeding. Selective breeding has the potential to alter milk composition. However, if AI bulls are selected for increased yield of milk protein, there is likely to be a proportional increase in milk production and in milk fat - both of which are undesirable in a quota-limited situation. If bulls are selected for increased milk protein percentage rather than yield of protein, milk volume and the total value of the milk falls. It is also worth remembering that altering the genetic make-up of a herd is a long-term process which may not be desirable in today's volatile milk market.

Protected amino acids. Recent work, principally in France, has shown large milk protein responses (0.2 to 0.3 % units) from the feeding of protected amino acids such as methionine, as shown in Table 13.3. However, most scientific trials in the UK have failed to obtain a consistent lift in milk protein from such supplements. French diets are typically based on maize silage and are generally formulated to a lower overall crude protein content (160 g CP/kg DM) than UK diets (170 to 185 g CP/kg DM). It is likely that the excess protein intake by cows in the UK prevents dietary amino acid imbalances.

Workers at Reading University have recently shown that infusions of specific amino acids have the potential to raise milk protein by 0.5% over a range of yields. Whilst such results are very exciting the work is still in the initial stages and it will take 3 to 4 years to determine if a commercial feed supplement can be developed with the same potential.

Table 13.3 Effect of supplementing different basal diets with 12 g/day of protected methionine (Rider, 1994)

Basal diet	Milk yield (litres/day)	Milk protein (%)	
		Control	Supplemented
Grass silage	30	3.14	3.27
Grass silage + fodder beet	30	3.59	3.73
Maize/grass silage	28	3.34	3.53
Maize/grass silage + sugar beet pulp	27	3.23	3.37
Maize silage	25	3.05	3.21

The response to protected methionine seems to be relatively rapid, with initial benefits seen within 7 days and full effects within 21 to 28 days. It would therefore seem sensible to use a "try–it–and–see" approach to determine its effectiveness in any diet. Supplementation with protected amino acids will only work if the overall CP, ERDP and DUP aspects of the ration are adequate; protected amino acids are really fine tuning. This type of supplementation may, however, become important in the UK if tighter constraints on the pollution of water with nitrogen from cow slurry have the effect of reducing the excessive use of CP towards the levels recommended by the feeding standards.

Dry cow management. Feeding a small amount (1 to 2 kg) of high–protein (24%) compound feed containing a high proportion of digestible undegradable protein (DUP) has been shown to increase milk protein production (Table 13.4). In the four trials reported, milk production was increased in two without a change in composition, whilst in the other two milk protein content rather than milk yield was increased. The financial benefit depends on the exact response obtained as increased milk yield requires additional quota. In all the trials fertility was improved by supplementation. The exact mechanism behind the response is uncertain but the extent of the response to supplementary protein appears to be greater in animals which are milking well at the time of drying off, or those which have a short dry period, suggesting that replenishment of protein reserves may be important.

Within current quota constraints, a response in milk composition rather than yield is more desirable (Table 13.4), but the effects on fertility (Chapter 15, page 150) are likely to make the use of high DUP dry cow compounds desirable in all situations.

Table 13.4 Effect of DUP supplementation in the dry period on milk production and protein content

Trial	Milk yield response	Milk protein response
1	no effect	increased 0.3 % points
2	milk yield up 2.4 kg/day	increased 0.05 % points
3	milk yield up 3.6 kg/day	minimal change in milk protein
4	no effect	increased 0.25 % points.

A supplement that supplies 250 to 300 g DUP/day should have the desired effect, as long as the basal ration is altered to ensure that energy intake remains at about 90 to 100 MJ ME/day. The response is not restricted to specific protein sources but whatever is used must supply considerable amounts of DUP to be of use.

Dry cows have considerably lower intakes than high-yielding cows (10 kg DM cf. 18 to 20 kg DM). This reduces outflow from the rumen and hence increases the degradability of feed protein. The best feeds therefore have a low and flat degradability (a low "a" and "c" fraction). The feed which fits this profile best is fishmeal, but unfortunately it is high in calcium and so should be avoided as one is trying to minimise calcium intakes to reduce the incidence of milk fever (Chapter 7, pages 82 to 83). Dark distillers' grains and dark samples of maize gluten have low degradabilities but much of the DUP is indigestible and does not contribute towards the MP intake. The best feeds would seem to be prairie meal (maize gluten meal) and protected soyabean meal.

Table 13.5 Methods of increasing milk protein

Method	Likely response in milk protein content	Comments
Extra energy	0.06 % units per 10 MJ ME	Best if energy comes from starch and fibre, but not fat.
Better forage	0.1 % units per MJ ME	Increased energy intake.
Multiple forages	0.1 to 0.15 % units	Increased dry matter and energy intake, often comprising starch and/or sugars
Starch rather than fibre-based compound	0.1 % unit	Ensure starch over 30% in compound and NDF over 35% of total diet DM
Give more concentrates	0.1 % unit per 2 kg compound	Increased energy intake but rarely cost-effective
Protected amino acids	0.1 to 0.2 % units	Only when basal diet is low in crude protein (< 16%)
Fishmeal (0.5 kg/day)	0.1 % unit	Increased dry matter and energy intake
Maize silage	0.1 % unit	Increased dry matter, energy (> 20% starch) and starch intake
Caustic wheat	0.1 to 0.2 % unit	Increased starch intake, buffered rumen pH
High DUP compounds fed in dry period	0.2 to 0.3% units	Ensure ration still balanced for energy and overall CP less than 160 g/kg DM.
Feed more protein	None	Increased milk yield.

The original work used a low CP forage (straw) and therefore could use a high inclusion of supplementary protein to give a ration containing a excess of DUP of 490 g with an overall CP of only 153 g/kg. Overall CP content should be kept below 160 g CP/kg DM, as an increased incidence of "downer cows" is likely in animals given a dry cow diet containing more than this level of crude protein. Therefore the crude protein of the forage should be as low as possible to allow sufficient supplementary feed to be given without increasing the overall protein content of the diet to too high a level. On diets based on fresh grass the amount of supplementary protein that can be given is limited, and it is difficult to achieve an excess of DUP of more than 350 g/day. When animals are calving indoors on diets based on silage a low–protein forage such as maize silage, fermented whole–crop wheat or straw is desirable to allow sufficient supplementation to achieve the excess UDP.

A suitable supplement would be 2 kg/day of a feed containing 1.0 kg rolled wheat, 0.9 kg protected soyabean meal and 0.1 kg of a high-magnesium, low-calcium dry cow mineral.

The various ways of increasing milk protein are summarised in Table 13.5.

13.2.2 Lowering milk protein
Producers who supply milk solely to the liquid market are unlikely to be paid for high milk protein composition because, at the moment, premia for protein cannot be recouped from the end consumer. However, reducing milk protein is not a simple matter.

Whilst relatively low concentrations of milk protein have been reported on many occasions, the most frequent situation leading to depressed concentrations of protein in milk is that of low energy intake, which is likely to depress milk yield and fertility.

The best policy at the moment for producers of milk for the liquid market is to maximise milk yield and animal fertility, and to allow the concentration of milk protein to change naturally.

Fat supplements. Dietary fat supplements usually, though not always, reduce the concentration of milk protein. The cause is not understood but it is presumed that it is extra-ruminal as the effect is found with protected as well as unprotected fats. However, no form of fat supplement so far developed has reliably prevented the depression in the concentration of milk protein. The size of the depression varies but is usually up to about 0.3 % units (3 g/kg).

High milk yield. High milk yields tend to be associated with a depression in milk protein concentration. This is partially because the high–yielding animal is in energy deficit and partially due to a possible dilution effect of the high volume of milk on milk protein (see Table 14.1).

13.3 Milk fat

The scope for altering milk fat concentration is much larger than is possible for milk protein. In previous decades milk fat was the main constituent of interest, with farmers being rewarded for high concentrations. As a result there are several well researched methods of increasing milk fat but few for depressing milk fat without causing serious side–effects.

13.3.1 Raising the concentration of milk fat
Fibre content of the diet. The fibre content of the diet has a major influence on the concentration of milk fat, with high-fibre diets promoting higher milk fat contents than diets of lower fibre content.

Quantifying the response is, however, difficult. For diets containing more than 60% concentrates or less than 250 g ADF/kg DM, dietary ADF is closely related to milk fat concentration (Figure 13.4). The "chewability" of the forage is important in maintaining milk fat, and it can be reduced by offering forage chopped to lengths of less than about 0.7 cm. Very young forage such as spring pasture also tends to reduce fat concentration, but evidence regarding the effects of the maturity of preserved forages such as grass silage or hay on milk fat content is inconclusive.

Figure 13.4 The effect of dietary fibre intake (ADF) on milk fat content (from Sutton and Morant, 1989)

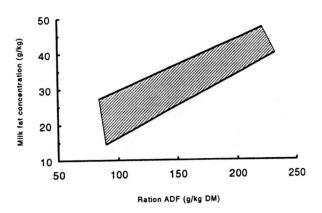

Meal frequency. Offering concentrate feeds little and often will reduce a depression in milk fat induced by large meals of concentrates eaten twice a day, but frequent feeding of concentrates will not otherwise raise the concentration of milk fat.

Fat supplements. The effects of dietary fats on milk fat synthesis are complex and so accurate prediction of the response to a particular supplement is difficult. In practice it is important to stay within certain reasonably well defined guidelines regarding both the amount and type of supplement to be fed. The inclusion of fats at up to about 6% to 8% of the total diet DM generally increases milk yields but the response in concentration of milk fat varies widely. Generally, moderate levels of saturated fats increase milk fat by a small amount, whereas similar amounts of unsaturated fats and large amounts of most sources of fat cause milk fat concentration to fall (Table 13.6). Yield of milk fat usually remains unchanged or increases.

The effects of fat supplements on milk fat concentration are due partly to their effect on rumen

fermentation. This has led to various attempts to reduce the effect of fat supplements by using whole or crushed whole oil seeds, fats protected from rumen processes by formaldehyde-treated protein, selected fatty acids (fat prills) and calcium soaps of fatty acids (see Chapter 5, page 62). These different techniques are effective to variable degrees in either maintaining the concentration of milk fat or even increasing it above "normal" levels, though occasional reductions in milk fat content have also been reported.

Table 13.6 Responses of milk yield and composition to various forms of lipid supplements (Sutton and Morant, 1989)

Supplement	(% of diet DM)	Milk yield kg/day	Milk composition Fat g/kg	Protein g/kg
Hydrogenated tallow	2.7%	+2.3	-3.7	-1.6
Soyabean oil	2.7%	+2.2	-8.6	-3.4
Dairy fat prills	3.4%	+1.5	+1.0	-0.9
Free triglycerides	3.4%	+1.8	-2.7	-2.4
Protected triglycerides	4.7%	+1.7	-4.0	-2.4
Protected tallow	12%	-0.7	+7.1	-3.3
Protected tallow				
weeks 1-6	19%	+2.3	+5.8	-1.0
weeks 7-13	20%	+1.9	+4.8	-3.6
Protected tallow	18%	-2.0	+7.3	-3.1

13.3.2 Lowering milk fat

With milk quota based on milk yield and milk fat content and the reducing financial incentive for milk fat (see Section 13.1 above), there is considerable interest in decreasing the concentration of fat in milk. To maximise returns from a fixed quota allocation the reduction in the concentration of milk fat should be coupled with a lowered milk yield and raised milk protein content, which is very difficult to achieve. The move away from fat production is relatively new and few experiments have been performed to investigate how to depress milk fat production. Whilst farmers have been able to achieve low milk fat on farm it has often been at the expense of the animals' health and fertility and therefore has not been cost-effective.

Low fibre. Just as high dietary fibre promotes high concentration of milk fat, low fibre can depress the fat content of milk (Figure 13.4). If the NDF content of the diet is reduced to less than 300 g/kg DM the production of acetate in the rumen is likely to be reduced, with a consequent reduction in milk fat content. However, cows given diets low in fibre are prone to dietary acidosis and to indigestion, which can depress feed intake and milk yield, and adversely affect health and fertility. Unfortunately all the steps recommended to counter acidosis (see Chapter 5, Section 5.9.1) are likely to increase milk fat production. The precise balance between inducing ruminal acidosis and depressing milk fat differs from farm to farm, depending on the other nutritional factors such as protein degradability, fat intake and trace element status.

High starch and sugar. A high intake of starch and sugar is likely to promote the production of propionate in the rumen and to depress that of acetate and butyrate, with a consequent reduction in the production of milk fat. Increasing the content of starch and sugar in the ration usually reduces the overall content of fibre in the diet, so it is difficult to determine which is the cause of the low milk fat. Figure 13.5 shows the effect of changing from a high-fibre concentrate to one high in starch; milk fat was depressed from just over 4.0% to 3.92% and as milk yield was virtually unchanged, total milk fat production was also reduced.

High milk yield. High yields are usually associated with depressed milk fat content (see Table 15.1). This is partially due to the increased starch and reduced fibre content of the ration but may also be a "dilution" effect of the high volume of milk. Unfortunately all too often milk protein is also depressed and generally to a greater extent.

Protein content of the ration. In a series of experiments carried out at Reading (Poole *et al.*, 1992), increasing the protein content of the concentrate from 12% to 24% was reflected in a reduction in milk fat content from 4.12% to 3.89% (Figure 13.5), but because silage intake and milk yield were also increased, there was an increase in total daily yield of milk fat. These results emphasise the importance of considering milk compositional changes together with changes in yield rather than in isolation.

Figure 13.5 **Effect of different types of supplementary energy sources and crude protein content in concentrates on milk fat content and yield (adapted from Poole *et al.*, 1992)**

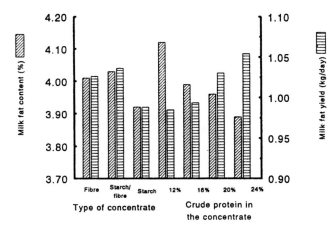

The various ways of changing the content of fat in milk are summarised in Table 13.7.

Table 13.7 Methods of altering the fat content of milk

Method	Comments
Raising milk fat	
Dietary fibre content	Fibre content needs quantifying (e.g. NDF) but physical form and "chewability" important.
Fibrous concentrates	Can depress milk protein and possibly feed intake.
More frequent and smaller meals of concentrates	Only effective at high intakes of concentrates.
Fat supplements	Response very variable; depends on basal diet, type and amount of fat.
Reducing milk fat	
High starch, low fibre rations	Can cause acidosis and indigestion and may raise yields.
High yields	Often produces a greater depression in milk protein.
Increase protein content of ration	Depresses milk fat content but diet increases yields and hence total fat production.

13.4 Producing milk with minimal milk solids

As mentioned in Section 13.1, a small proportion of farmers have been offered contracts for producing milk of the minimal legal quality at a fixed price with no premia for increased composition. If farmers are to move closer to the market place and produce for specific markets, these contracts are likely to become more common and the question of how to produce this type of milk efficiently will become more important. Whilst these producers do not want to take any actions that result in the production of milk of high protein or high fat, they may not wish to pursue low milk quality actively. Again, little research has been done on this approach to milk production, but the logical choice would seem to be to aim for high milk yields. This will have several benefits. Firstly high-yielding cows tend to have lower milk quality than lower-yielding animals and a depressed milk fat content due to the high feeding of concentrates will allow more milk to be produced within a given quota constraint. High-yielding cows use proportionately less of their energy and protein intake to support maintenance and this reduces feed inputs per litre of milk.

13.5 Conclusions

Research carried out to date has concentrated on the manipulation of the composition of milk produced by the cow by altering her diet. However, in a world where animal welfare is paramount and interference with "natural" processes seems to be an anathema to most of the population, should we manipulate the cow to such an extent?

Should we not be trying to manipulate the milk after it has been produced? Can we not find ways of converting the milk the cow naturally produces into what the consumer wants? We already have the technology to remove fat (skimmed milk) and water (condensed milk) and this would give low fat high protein milk. Such processes are routinely used in other countries and consumers do not seem to come to any harm. Perhaps we should be looking at manipulating milk quality in the factory and concentrating on animal welfare and hygiene at the cowside.

Letting the cow produce milk of natural composition and manipulating composition at the milk processing factory is likely to generate large surpluses of milk fat, but it might be possible to find alternative uses for this fat in the pharmaceutical, cosmetic or other industries.

CHAPTER 14

FEEDING THE HIGH-YIELDING COW

14.1 Why aim for high yields?

14.2 Possible disadvantages of high yields
   14.2.1   Effect of yield on margins

14.3 How to achieve high yields

14.4 How to formulate diets for high-yielding cows
   14.4.1   Nutrient requirements
   14.4.2   Maximising intakes
   14.4.3   Formulating diets

14.5 How to manage high-yielding cows

14.6 Bovine somatotrophin (BST)
   14.6.1   Side–effects of BST
   14.6.2   Feeding the BST-treated cow

14.1   Why aim for high yields?

There is considerable interest in increasing the milk yield of the dairy cow. The average milk yield per cow per year is rising slowly (50 litres/year), but the UK national average still remains at 5,500 litres. The principal reason for increasing milk yield is the greater proportion of total nutrient intake which is available above maintenance for milk production (Figure 14.1). Therefore, the higher the level of production the more efficient the cow is at converting consumed nutrients into milk. This increase in efficiency is due solely to the dilution of the maintenance requirement, as the efficiency with which ME is converted to milk (i.e. k_l) does not alter substantially.

Increased milk yield per cow will either result in fewer cows being needed for a given total herd yield, or a greater output of milk from the same number of cows. If the number of cows in the herd is reduced, the fixed costs of milk production may also fall, as fewer buildings and less labour may be required per litre of milk produced. Fewer cows produce less slurry, which can be a great benefit to the farm and the farmer if there is a risk of pollution of nearby water courses.

14.2   Possible disadvantages of high yields

In the UK most dairy farmers are paid for milk fat and protein as well as for the volume of milk produced, but they are constrained by quotas for both volume and fat. Where quota is the main constraint the objective is to produce milk with a high con-

centration of protein so that the value of each litre produced within the quota is maximised. If the content of milk protein is low the value of milk per litre is reduced, but the total volume that can be produced within the quota constraint does not change. It follows therefore that for those farmers who are paid on the basis of milk protein, the production of milk of low protein content reduces income within the constraint of quota.

Figure 14.1   Effect of increasing milk yield (litres/day) on the proportion of nutrient intake available for milk production

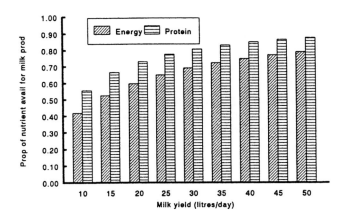

On many farms as the milk yield increases the milk quality falls. This is partially because of the change in the genetic make-up of the herd in that selection for increased yields usually depresses milk quality (see chapter 13, page 131). However in many instances the ration and farm management are not adequate for the quality of cows being kept and this depresses milk quality. Achieving high milk composition for an entire herd can be done but it requires excellent management to ensure the highest yielders are fed to their full potential.

14.2.1   Effect of yield on margins
Traditionally it has been accepted that farmers should maximise the margin per cow. The number of cows in the herd was the major constraint on the expansion of the business, and increasing cow numbers was the least cost-effective method of expansion for most dairy farmers. Increased milk yield was associated with increased margin over purchased feeds (Figure 14.2), which gave the impetus to increased output per cow.

Figure 14.2 Effect of milk output per cow on margin over purchased feed per cow (£/year) and per litre (pence/litre). Data from Genus costed farms 1992/93 for the top 10% of herds in each yield band

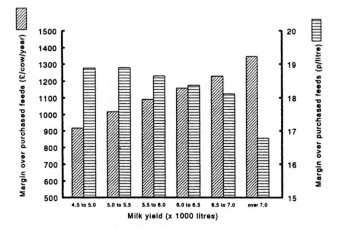

higher than average yields is likely to be reflected in little change in milk composition as the yield of milk is increased.

In conclusion, where the objective is to maximise margin per litre of quota, high milk yields may not always be an appropriate objective. This conclusion may be altered by tighter controls on environmental pollution from large dairy herds and the need for better animal welfare during winter housing of cows. If milk yields are to be increased this must be done in conjunction with raising the genetic merit of the herd and improving the nutrition of the higher-yielding cow, otherwise the combination of declining milk value and increased use of concentrates is likely to reduce, rather than increase, profitability.

14.3 How to achieve high yields

The pattern of production of milk of higher-yielding cows is similar to that of lower-yielding cows. Higher-yielding animals take slightly longer to reach peak production than lower-yielding cows (Figure 14.3), but the decline in milk production is at a similar rate so that after 300 days of lactation they may still be giving in excess of 25 litres of milk. This has led some research workers to suggest that 305–day lactations and 365–day calving intervals are not suited to high-yielding cows, and that conception should be delayed until well after peak yield when the cow is under less nutritional stress.

Figure 14.3 Milk production curves for cows with different total lactation yields

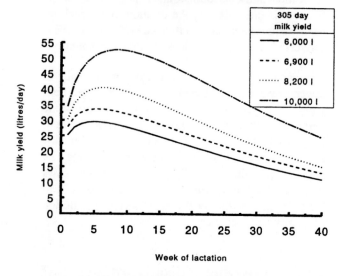

However, in a situation where the availability of milk quota is a major limitation to output on many dairy farms, the purchase or leasing of quota, rather than cow numbers in the herd or area of land for the herd, is the limiting factor to increasing profit margins. Thus the objective becomes one of maximising margin per litre of milk production. In this situation the relationship between annual milk yield and margin is reversed, with high yields being penalised and lower yields giving the greater margins.

The major limitation to output will vary from farm to farm; if little quota has been acquired over the past few years then quota will be limiting and hence margin per litre should be maximised. Where an active quota-acquisition policy has been followed the limitation may be cow numbers, in which case margin per cow should be maximised. Land may be the major limiting factor in which case margin per hectare should be maximised. Careful study is required to determine what is the limiting factor for a specific farm and to ensure the cows are managed to maximise the whole-farm margin.

The reasons for the decline in margins per litre (Figure 14.2) as milk yield is increased are twofold. Firstly, the proportion of milk from forage declines with increasing milk yield from about 70% at 4,500 to 5,000 litres/cow to about 40% for cows yielding over 7,000 litres. Secondly, the value of milk tends to decrease as yield increases, reflecting a decline in milk protein content.

If the cost of concentrate feeds falls and the true cost of conserving winter forages increases, the decline in margin per litre may be reduced. Also, an improvement in the nutritional status of herds with

There is some evidence that high-yielding cows can remain in milk for a very long time. For example a Scottish cow that gave 13,500 litres in her fourth lactation was milked for 923 days in her fifth (and final) lactation during which time she gave 26,833 litres of milk, an average of 29 litres/day over almost three years. Whilst delayed conception may be cost–effective for high-yielding herds (over 9,000 litres), this strategy should only be adopted after careful consideration of the costs and benefits and should not be used as an excuse for inadequate fertility management.

If insemination is to be delayed, then cows should still be block-calved, otherwise the birth of heifers from the best cows will occur throughout the year making heifer rearing and the management of the milking herd more complex.

14.4 How to formulate diets for high-yielding cows

In this and subsequent sections high milk yields will be taken to mean at least 10,000 litres/year. In many cases it may be preferable to aim for slightly lower yields in the range of 8,000 to 9,000 litres/year, and diets for these outputs are also considered where relevant.

It is not possible to use the normal approach of balancing nutrient requirements for a given yield (Chapter 18), as often we do not want to specify or limit milk production. It is also difficult to predict how much milk a high-yielding dairy cow is likely to give. For example a recent world record holder for milk production gave 89 kg milk when given a diet that was only predicted to be adequate for 41 kg of milk. The efficiency of energy use had probably changed relatively little so this cow must have eaten 2.2 times more feed than was predicted initially. Furthermore, the lower milk quality of many high-yielding cows complicates the calculation of nutrient requirements as it will reduce the requirements for each litre of milk and considerably reduce the overall requirements.

Diet formulation for the high-yielding cow therefore revolves around two factors: achieving the correct nutrient density in the diet and maximising feed intake.

14.4.1 Nutrient requirements
Surveys in the USA of herds which averaged over 13,000 kg milk/year revealed the following points. Firstly, there is no magic forage in diets for high-yielding cows. A whole range of forages were used, including grass and maize silage, lucerne hay, haylage and grass hay. Secondly, there was no common supplement although some animal protein was used in most rations. The one common thing about the feeds offered were that they were all of high quality. Whilst the ingredients used in diets for high-yielding cows differed widely when the rations were analysed, a common pattern emerged (Table 14.1).

Table 14.1 Analysis of diets given to very high-yielding dairy cows (over 13,000 kg milk/year) in the USA

	Herd A	Herd B	Herd C
Crude protein (g/kg DM)	180	185	180
Degradability (g RDP/g CP)	0.60	0.62	0.63
Sugars and starch (g/kg DM)	380	350	390
Fibre (g NDF/kg DM)	320	310	360
Fat (g/kg DM)	50	70	45
DMI required to meet observed output (kg/day)	–	29	24

The three diets shown in Table 14.1 are very similar in their gross chemical composition. Total fibre content of the diet is relatively low compared to typical UK diets, at less than 360 g NDF/kg DM. Diets for high-yielding cows need to be low in fibre (NDF) as excessive amounts can restrict total feed intake. American workers (Ruiz *et al.*, 1992) found that reducing the total content of NDF in the diet from 390 to 310 g NDF/kg DM increased voluntary intake of DM by 9%, with an increase in milk yield and milk protein content. However, care must be taken to ensure that the diet contains adequate fibre to maintain normal rumen function, to promote rumination and to stimulate the flow of saliva. An important characteristic of fibre in this respect is its "chewability". Therefore some long fibre should be included in the ration to promote rumination. A rough rule-of-thumb is that more than 90% of the cows that are lying down at any one time should be chewing the cud.

The total content of sugar and starch in diets for high-yielding cows is high at 35 to 40% of the DM. This is partially an inevitable consequence of the reduction in NDF content, but is also required to supply both FME to the rumen microbes and a source of by-pass starch to the small intestine. American research (Batajoo *et al.*, 1994) has shown that increasing the content of sugar and starch from 240 to 420 g/kg DM was associated with an increase in dry matter intake. Digestibility of NDF was lowest for the diet which contained 420 g total sugar and starch/kg total diet DM, which suggests there may be little benefit to be gained from increasing sugar and starch above about 350 g/kg DM. The content of sugar in the ration seems to be important, both to make the ration sweet to stimulate intake and for its supply of readily available FME to the rumen microbial population.

The protein content of these rations is only 180 to 185 g CP/kg DM which is considerably lower than that used in many diets for higher-yielding cows in the UK. An excessive intake of protein can increase the load of amino acids and ammonia on the liver and has been linked to reduced cow fertility. Therefore, if milk production can be maintained, diets containing less than 200 g crude protein/kg DM are to be preferred.

Table 14.2 Required energy density (MJ/kg DMI) for different milk yields and different dry matter intakes. Assumed body weight of 650 kg, 500 g weight loss per day, milk fat of 3.8% and milk protein of 3.0%

Milk yield (litres/day)	30	35	40	45	50	55	60
Total ME required (MJ/day)	205	232	259	286	313	341	370
Intake (kg DM/day)							
18	11.4	12.9	14.4	15.9	17.4	18.9	20.6
20	10.3	11.6	13.0	14.3	15.7	17.1	18.5
22	9.3	10.5	11.8	13.0	14.2	15.5	16.8
24	8.5	9.7	10.8	11.9	13.0	14.2	15.4
26	7.9	8.9	10.0	11.0	12.0	13.1	14.2
28	7.3	8.3	9.3	10.2	11.2	12.2	13.2

Despite the need for high energy intakes the oil content of these diets is relatively low. There is little or no fat supplementation and the total content of fat is between 45 and 70 g/kg DM.

14.4.2 Maximising feed intake

The remarkable thing about the diets shown in Table 14.1 are the reported intakes: for a 600 kg cow the intake is more than 4% of body weight. It is the relatively high intake, more than anything else, that allows the nutrient requirements for high yields to be met. This can be seen by examining Table 14.2 which shows the energy densities required to achieve different milk yields with different total dry matter intakes.

If we assume the ME of good quality silage to be about 11.0 MJ/kg DM, that of concentrates to be 13.0 MJ/kg DM, and that a diet should contain no more than 50% concentrates, then a mixture of these two feeds can supply the energy requirements up to the first diagonal line. To the right of this the energy density required cannot be met by a 50:50 mix of forage and concentrates.

To increase the energy density of the diet further, we need to add an energy–dense feed. Fat, with about 35 MJ/kg, is the most energy-dense source available. If we limit the total content of fat in the diet to 10% of DM we can satisfy rations up to the next diagonal line in the table; any ration density to the right of this line is impossible.

The values in the table clearly demonstrate the importance of achieving high voluntary DM intakes in high-yielding dairy cows. The urge to eat large quantities of food is in fact likely to be there in the high-yielding cow but we must do our best not to foil her desires!

How some cows manage to eat 4 to 5% of their body weight a day whilst others only consume about 3% of body weight as dry matter is not well understood. American workers (Dado *et al.*, 1993) studying high-yielding cows showed that milk production was correlated positively with intake of both DM and water. High-yielding cows ate the same number of meals and at the same rate as their low-yielding counterparts, but the higher-yielding cows ate for a longer total amount of time per day and hence consumed bigger meals. However, the high-yielding cows spent less time ruminating and chewing per unit of dry matter ingested suggesting that they chewed more efficiently.

How to maximise feed intake. The most important aspect of maximising voluntary feed intake is to look after the rumen. Firstly, do not insult the rumen. Secondly, feed the rumen correctly. The major insults the rumen suffers are high intakes of starch and fat, large meals of these nutrients, and acid over-load. Starch and fat must therefore be included in the diet with care, to ensure that they do not adversely affect the balance and growth of the rumen microbial population. The best way to do this is to ensure that starch and fat (i.e. the concentrated feed ingredients of the diet) are eaten in several small meals each day, or mixed together intimately with forage in a complete diet.

The rumen has to buffer both the acids in silage and the VFA produced by the microbes. Reducing the acid load in silage and feeding alkali feeds (e.g. soda grain) will help to maintain the pH of the rumen at approximately 6.5.

Whilst looking after the rumen is the most important consideration in achieving high feed intake, we must remember the cow herself. The diet should be presented in a way that will encourage the cow to eat as much as possible. The feeding area should be away from draughts and rain, and should preferably be sited adjacent to the living area such that the cows have maximal access to the feed trough throughout the day.

The diet should be offered *ad libitum*, which implies a certain amount of wastage. About 10% of the total amount of feed offered to high-yielding cows should be refused and removed from the feed trough frequently. This material need not be totally wasted as it can be "diluted" and offered to lower-yielding groups of cows where maximising voluntary intake is not so important.

If there is a stampede of cows when new feed is put in the trough the diet is not being offered *ad libitum*. No more than half the cows should show an interest in the feed as the feed trough is filled or refilled. Feed troughs should be cleaned out several times a week, but never by the cow. Trough space should be adequate, both in terms of the volume of feed it contains and the length of feed space allocated per cow.

Cows are gregarious animals and voluntary intake will be maximised if all the group can feed at once. Similarly, intake will be maximised if sufficient feed is within reach and the cow does not have to strain against awkward feed barriers. Feeding areas should be quiet and peaceful; the cow is most vulnerable to attack (from predators and other cows) when she is feeding and so a secure environment will ensure long uninterrupted feeding sessions.

Milk contains about 85% of its weight as water. Reduced water intake can quickly restrict milk production. Cows should have access to water immediately after milking, especially if they receive dry feeds in the parlour. The water trough and piped water supply should be adequate to meet requirements, so that the tank is still full when the last cow to be milked arrives to take a drink. Voluntary intake is maximised if the water is clean and fresh. When troughs are first installed a large drainage bung should be fitted so that washing out is easy and can be performed regularly.

Recent work in Wales (Phillips *et al.*, 1994) suggests that diets for high-yielding cows should contain in excess of 3 g sodium/kg DM. Applying sodium fertiliser (32 kg/ha) to grassland increased the content of sugar in fresh grass and decreased non–protein nitrogen, but no change in the content of digestible organic matter in the DM was observed.

Water intake and outflow of digesta from the rumen were raised following the application of sodium fertiliser to the pasture. Herbage intake, degradability of dry matter and rumen pH were elevated, resulting in an increased fat content in milk.

14.4.3   Formulating diets

When formulating diets for high-yielding cows all the ingredients must "work" – there is no room for "rubbish" or fillers. All ingredients must be included for a specific purpose – if there is no nutritionally sound reason for including a feed in a particular diet it should be left out! Some producers go so far as to say that all feeds must be analysed before they are used to ensure that their quality is satisfactory.

Certainly any feed that contributes more than 2 kg of the dry matter intake should be analysed for its primary nutrient. For example wheat should be analysed for starch, soya and rapeseed meal for protein content and straw for fibre (NDF) content. "Straights" – raw material feeds – are often used rather than compounds or blends to obtain better control of diet composition and quality. Some producers use very complex mixes with several sources of protein and several sources of energy in a bid to minimise the effects of variation between batches of raw materials. Maize silage is a common factor in many diets for high-yielding cows, but it should contain at least 30% starch in the total DM.

Table 14.3 shows a possible blueprint for the composition of diets for very high and high-yielding cows. Diets should be formulated to meet specific targets for the concentrations of essential nutrients, rather than to a specific content of energy alone.

Table 14.3 Blueprints for diets for very high and high-yielding cows

Nutrient	Very high yield > 10,000 litres/year	High yield 8,000 to 9,000 litres/year
Crude protein (g/kg DM)	175 to 190	170 to 185
Starch (g/kg DM)	250 to 300	200 to 250
Sugars (g/kg DM)	100	80
NDF (g/kg DM)	300 to 320	320 to 360 (70% from forage)
QDP	50% of ERDP	50% of ERDP
Fat (g/kg DM)	50 to 70	40 to 60
Energy (MJ ME/kg DM)	12.5	12.0

Once formulated, the actual yield achieved by cows of high genetic merit depends entirely on how successful the diet and management are in stimulating a high level of intake.

In most high-yielding herds, the aim is to breed cows of high genetic merit and to allow them to perform to the best of their abilities. The cows are given a very high quality diet and as long as they do not get fat they remain on the same diet for as long as possible. Cows that put on too much weight in mid-lactation are moved on to a lower plane of nutrition; either their genetic ability is limited or they are too late in their lactation to partition sufficient nutrients to milk production.

A possible diet is shown in Table 14.4. Grass silage has been included as it is made on most farms, if only to facilitate pasture management in the summer. If it has received adequate nitrogen fertiliser in the spring it is usually a good, low–cost source of ERDP. Maize silage has been used for its starch (300 g/kg DM) and because maize starch may bypass the rumen and supply glucose directly to the small intestine. The above two forages are the main sources of fibre, but they are usually chopped short, to less than 2 cm average particle length, so the "chewability" of the fibre is limited.

Table 14.4 A possible diet for high-yielding dairy cows

Ingredient	Amount (kg/day)		Analysis (g/kg)	
	Fresh	Dry	of total diet	
Grass silage	20.0	5.4	Dry Matter	448
Maize silage	20.0	6.1	Protein	178
Good hay	1.0	0.9	Starch	235
Caustic wheat	3.5	2.7	Sugar	95
Wheat grain	3.5	3.0	ADF	159
Molasses	2.0	1.5	M/D	12.5
Soyabean meal	2.5	2.2	Oil	44
Rapeseed meal	3.0	2.7	NDF	305
Fat prills	0.50	0.5		
Minerals	0.20	0.2		
TOTAL	56.2	25.2		

Good hay is provided, possibly in racks, to supply a highly chewable long forage that will stimulate cudding and saliva flow. The main energy sources are caustic wheat and ground wheat. The amount of caustic wheat (soda grain) included is a compromise; a large amount will supply significant amounts of sodium bicarbonate which will buffer the rumen and supply slowly released starch, but the high content of sodium can put an excessive load on the kidneys and increase urine production substantially as the sodium is cleared from the body.

Ground wheat must be included with care, as part of a complete diet or on a little–and–often basis to avoid acidosis. Molasses is included to enhance palatability (cows like sugar) and to raise the total sugar content to 95 g/kg DM. Fat prills are included as a high–density energy supplement, but at a low level so that the overall fat content of the diet is maintained at less than 50 g/kg DM.

The main protein sources in the diet are soyabean meal and rapeseed meal. Rapeseed meal is used as a source of ERDP in the diet. Soyabean meal is used as a source of by-pass protein and is well balanced for the essential amino acids to support high levels of milk production. Fishmeal could be added as a protein source but this would increase the cost of the diet. Minerals are added to supply phosphorus in particular.

The overall fibre (NDF) content is about 30%, so particular care must be taken over the chewability of the diet, the control of other rumen "insults" and to monitor the cows and their faeces to ensure that they are receiving enough long fibre to stimulate sufficient rumination (see Chapter 5, page 57).

The overall crude protein content of the diet is 178 g/kg DM. When formulated for 55 litres of milk/day

the ration predicted is deficient in ERDP and supplies a surplus of only 143 g MP/day. The deficit in ERDP is principally due to the large amount of FME supplied by the diet, but it is likely that a proportion of the starch will not be degraded in the rumen and hence FME supply will be closer to microbial requirements.

The total content of starch and sugar in the diet is relatively high, so care must be taken that acidosis does not develop. The total content of oil is relatively low at 44 g/kg DM, which reduces the risk of possible adverse effects of unprotected fat on rumen function.

14.5 How to manage high-yielding cows

In the survey carried out in the USA into high-yielding herds (Section 14.4.1.), the management of the cows was also investigated. Herd size, housing, milking routine and management all varied considerably between the herds. Some cows were loose housed, others tied and fed individually, some milked twice a day and others three times a day. Some cows were fed on a total mixed ration whilst others were given forage and concentrates in separate meals However, when the latter was done it was on a little-and-often system. For example, one farmer gave the cows 17 separate meals during the day!

Farmers were also asked what they felt was important in managing very high-yielding cows. Their responses are summarised in Table 14.5. The importance of managing the cow correctly after calving was highlighted by the survey and this topic is considered in more detail in Chapter 15.

Table 14.5 How American farmers consider they achieve high yields

Use only high–quality forage.
Use feeds of known analyses or test them regularly.
No sudden changes – ensure continuity.
Maximise dry matter intake, especially after calving.
Avoid problems after calving – for some producers this extended to watching the cows carefully after calving and ensuring that they ate.
Monitor rumen activity closely post–calving and take action if necessary.
Detect sub–clinical milk fever and fatty liver early and take action. Both reduce the cow's appetite and digestive ability.
Look after cow comfort.
Pay attention to detail.

To summarise the management of high-yielding cows the following is a blueprint:

The dry cow:

- Traditionally the cow's diet changes radically at calving from one based on poor forages to a high-quality high-concentrate ration and this reduces performance. The rumen should be prepared during the last two weeks of the dry period for the next lactation (see Chapter 15, page 149) by feeding 4 kg concentrates plus a limited amount of the milking-cow forage to supply about 100 to 110 MJ ME/day. The concentrates feeding should be increased in two steps. Firstly feed 2 kg/day two weeks before calving and then 4 kg/day one week before.

- If the dry period was short (less than 50 days) or the cow was yielding well (more than 25 l/day) at drying off a high-DUP cake may be used to promote milk protein production (see page 150).

- Ensure that more than 40% of the diet given in the week before calving consists of concentrates but restrict forage intake to meet target conditions score of 3.0 to 3.5 at calving.

- Calve down at a target condition score of 3.0 to 3.5. High yielders will lose slightly more weight in the first 100 days of lactation so should carry sufficient fat to allow 70 to 85 kg of liveweight to be lost in this period.

The freshly–calved cow:

- Once the calf has been removed from the cow place the cow in a medium-yielding group for 10 days so that she receives about 5 to 6 kg concentrates in a total intake of 18 to 20 kg DM.

- After 10 days give the cow a diet of high energy density (at or above 12.5 MJ ME/kg DM), but limit the fat intake to less than 6% of the total DM of the diet and use protected fat if supplementary fat is needed. Starch and sugar are likely to be high (over 30% of total diet DM) and fibre will be relatively low (approx. 30% of total diet DM), so pay attention to the chewability of the diet. Intake should be about 23 kg DM/day for a cow yielding 45 litres of milk per day, and higher for greater yields.

- Offer hay or good straw in mangers to help saliva flow etc. and/or keep the cows well bedded on clean, palatable straw.

- Feed the diet truly *ad libitum*, reckoning to remove about 5 to 10% of the daily amount offered. If animals are eating more than predicted, increase the overall mix rather than simply adjusting the forage part of the diet.

- Keep the cows on this diet until they start to get fat or regain a condition score of 3.0 and then move them to a group of lower- yielding cows on a poorer diet. If animals remain at a condition score of less than 3.0, keep them in the group of high yielders; some cows may never be moved!

- Lower-yielding cows should be moved from the group given the high–energy diet sooner than higher yielders, otherwise they will put on too much weight. Similarly if higher-yielding cows are moved too soon they are likely to suffer excessive weight loss.

14.6 Bovine somatotrophin (BST)

Bovine growth hormone, or bovine somatotrophin (BST) is a naturally occurring hormone produced in the pituitary gland that stimulates milk production in lactating cattle. Higher-yielding animals tend to have higher concentrations of BST in the blood than lower-yielding cows. Attempts to increase milk production by including supplementary BST in the diet have failed, but biotechnology has allowed a synthetic form of BST (differing in only a few amino acids from the natural hormone) to be synthesised in bacteria. This "recombinant" BST can be extracted and administered to the cow by injection.

The use of BST is currently illegal in Europe, but it is licensed for use in the USA. The licensed preparation is recommended to be used from the ninth week after calving and injected every 14 days at a cost of about £4.00 per injection or 29 p/day. Given a variable cost of producing a litre of milk of about 8 p/litre (Table 1.1, page 1) and a sale value of 25 p/litre the gross margin per litre is 17 p/litre and therefore the response must be in excess of 1.7 litres/day to be cost–effective. In routine use, American farmers have obtained increases in milk yield of up to 4.5 litres/day from BST – a potential return of more than 2.5:1 on the investment of using BST.

The response to BST reflects a change in the partitioning of nutrients by the animal, with more being diverted to milk production and less to other processes. The increase in output is similar to that observed from intense selective breeding, but it occurs in one season rather than over 10 to 15 years. The response to BST is only likely to be as good as the management of the herd. If the intention is to maximise the response, then excellent management and feeding are required.

The response observed in trials has not been consistent (Figure 14.4). Although the average increase was 13.5% in annual milk yield, about a third of herds experienced an increase of less than 10%. Much of this variation was ascribed to the pre–treatment milk yield and suggests that the response is related not only to the standard of management of the herd, but also to the point in the lactation when the administration of BST commences.

Figure 14.4 Yield responses in different BST trials (Hallberg 1992)

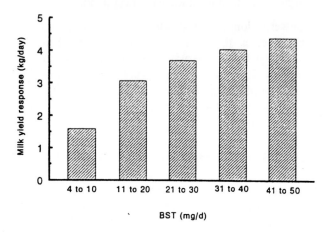

The use of BST does not increase the efficiency of milk synthesis, but it does improve the overall efficiency of energy use as the increased milk yield dilutes the effect of the maintenance requirement. If a farm has a fixed output constraint, such as a quota restriction on milk sales, then the increased milk yield per cow from BST may allow a reduction in the size of the herd and in the number of followers required. This may increase the efficiency of the whole farm, if other enterprises can be expanded.

The initial response to BST is an increase in milk yield. It takes 6 to 8 weeks for feed intake to rise in response to the higher milk output (Figure 14.5). During this period milk production is increased without an corresponding increase in nutrient intake and therefore the cow is in a greater energy deficit and draws on body reserves to a greater extent than normal.

Figure 14.5 Response in milk yield and in feed intake from a single injection of BST (Hallberg, 1992)

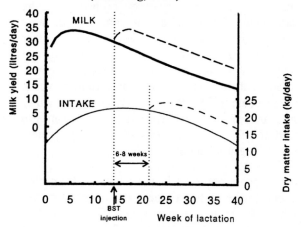

Animals with adequate body reserves are therefore more likely to be able to respond to treatment with BST than cows in low body condition. In the short

term BST can be used to promote the partitioning of nutrients towards milk production rather than to body weight gain, but care should be taken to ensure that the increased energy deficit does not occur at the time of service or during the proceeding weeks.

14.6.1 Side–effects of BST

It is widely accepted that the incidence of some diseases is increased in cattle treated with BST, but there is also much debate as to whether the increases are due to the increased yield of milk alone, or whether the increase is specific to treated animals.

Fertility. Some BST trials have indicated a reduction in fertility following administration of BST (Table 14.6), but at the dose rates currently licensed in the USA, it is likely that such a reduction is due to the greater metabolic demand on the animal of the increased milk yield and the resultant increased energy deficit.

Table 14.6 Effects of BST on the fertility of dairy cows (from Hallberg, 1989)

	Number of trials				
Effect	Conception rate	Days open	Services per conception	Conception rate at first service	Days to first service
No significant effect	11	8	3	1	2
Increased	0	9	7	1	2
Decreased	8	1	1	0	0

Mastitis. The overall incidence of mastitis increased by about 30 to 40% in treated cows compared to untreated cows. This increase, however, masked the fact that a change in the incidence of mastitis was only observed in about a third of all herds. When observed, the increases in the incidence of mastitis were great. The size of the increase in mastitis was not linked to the pre-treatment incidence, suggesting that this was not linked to the standard of management of the animals. Moreover, the increased incidence of mastitis was greater than that associated with the increase in milk yield, and it would seem that there was some specific effect of BST on the incidence of mastitis.

14.6.2 Feeding the BST-treated cow

Once the cow's voluntary intake has increased in line with the increased milk yield (Figure 14.5) the feeding of the BST-treated cow is no different from feeding the normal high-yielding cow. A high quality ration composed of high quality ingredients should be offered *ad libitum* to promote maximal intakes. In the period when intake is lagging behind production the energy deficit can be minimised by feeding a ration with a high energy density to maximise energy intake. Supplementary fat will often be required but care should be taken to minimise the insult on the rumen and protected fats should be used.

CHAPTER 15

FEEDING THE COW BEFORE AND AFTER CALVING

15.1 Introduction

15.2 Target condition score for dry cows
    15.2.1 Fat dry cows
    15.2.2 What is the ideal condition score at calving?
    15.2.3 When to change condition score
    15.2.4 How fast can body condition be changed?
    15.2.5 How to manage fat cows at calving

15.3 Preventing milk fever

15.4 Preparing the rumen

15.5 Feeding the dry cow
    15.5.1 Intake
    15.5.2 Energy requirements
    15.5.3 Protein

15.6 Blueprint for managing dry cows

15.1 Introduction

Thinking about nutrition once a cow has calved is similar to starting to dig a well once you are thirsty; the nutrition of the cow should comprise a series of planned actions throughout the year with the aim of maintaining the cow in optimal condition score at all times. Management problems and their solutions, or at least their alleviation, by correct nutrition at and around calving are considered in this chapter. The range of problems requiring extra attention at this crucial stage of the productive cycle include:

Long dry periods. Restrictions on output, such as milk quota, sometimes force producers to dry cows off early in order to reduce their liability for super-levy charges. These cows may have dry periods of three to four months or even longer. The high quality of forages available on most dairy farms means that a prolonged dry period is almost bound to lead to over-fatness at calving.

Fat dry cows and down-calvers. Cows calving in summer are dry during the spring, when the growth of grass is at its most rapid. By contrast, cows calving in the autumn are dry when grass growth is often limited in mid-summer and of lower quality. Unless dry cow management is changed, cows calving in summer can easily become over-fat by the time they calve.

To avoid over-fat cows, they should be stocked very tightly (8 to 12 cows/hectare) and the grass sward height kept below 7 cm. If appetite is severely restricted by this tight stocking policy, straw can be provided as a supplement. A separate group of down-calvers (within 10 days of calving) should be maintained. These animals should be given restricted amounts of a diet based on silage and a concentrate low in calcium (see Section 15.5). Thought should be given to housing animals at this stage to spread the introduction of the components of the winter, milking environment and hence reduce any risk of laminitis associated with the rapid introduction of the concentrate part of the diet.

Under-fed high-yielding cows. In wet years the availability of autumn grass is often adequate to feed all the stock, and many farmers are tempted to leave freshly-calved animals out at pasture. However, autumn grass is of lower feed value than spring grass, partly as a result of lower levels of sugar in autumn grass compared to the spring, but also as a result of lower intake of grazed pasture. Autumn grass is therefore unlikely to be able to support high yields of milk and performance is often disappointing as a result. In such circumstances it is vital to house animals to ensure they receive high-quality forages which are capable of meeting the nutritional requirements for high milk yields.

Silage requirements. Housing cows at the time of calving in summer effectively prolongs the winter feeding period and may increase silage requirements by as much as 20%. Not only must sufficient land be allocated for conservation as silage, but adequate provision must be made for the storage of the extra forage. In the light of environmental protection legislation, the cost of constructing new silos is high, and this potential additional expense must be taken into account as a consequence of summer calving.

15.2 Target condition scores for dry cows

Given the effect of the growing unborn calf on the cow's weight the best way to assess whether cows are gaining or loosing body weight is using condition scores (see Chapter 17, page 159). The major problem seen with dry cows is one of over-fatness.

15.2.1 Fat dry cows

Several problems can occur when cows are over-fat at calving. Firstly, there is an increase in calving difficulties. Holstein/Friesian cows in particular store large amounts of fat in the pelvic area and animals with high condition scores – more than 3.5 on a scale of 1 (thin) to 5 (obese) – have sufficient intra-pelvic fat to reduce the size of the pelvic canal. The reduced size of the birth canal hampers the passage of calves, even those of normal size. Very fat cows also seem to be slow to calve. This is possibly due to fatty infiltration of muscles and the resistance of the intra-pelvic fat to the passage of the calf out of the cow. On some farms this can lead to increased peri-parturient calf mortality which can easily be confused with iodine deficiency (Chapter 7, page 91).

Secondly, over-fatness at calving also has a major effect on the subsequent lactation. Work at Nottingham University (Garnsworthy and Topps, 1982) involved setting up three groups of cows that were thin (condition score (CS) 1.5 to 2.0), medium condition (CS 2.5 to 3.0) or fat (CS 3.5 to 4.0) at calving, and then observing their milk production, feed intake and condition score over the subsequent lactation. · The effect of condition score at calving on milk production is shown in Figure 15.1.

Figure 15.1 Effect of condition score at calving on milk production in the first part of lactation (Garnsworthy and Topps, 1982)

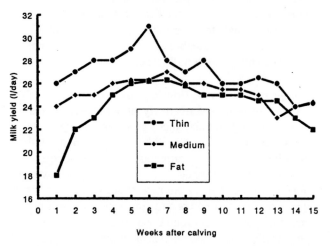

Fat cows had a much lower milk production in the first 7 weeks of lactation, and, although the differences diminished subsequently, the thinner cows out-yielded the fatter animals throughout the study period. Why then was milk yield depressed in the fat cows? A possible answer can be seen by looking at the effect of condition score at calving on feed intake in the early part of lactation (Figure 15.2).

Figure 15.2 Effect of condition score at calving on dry matter intake in the first part of lactation (Garnsworthy and Topps, 1982)

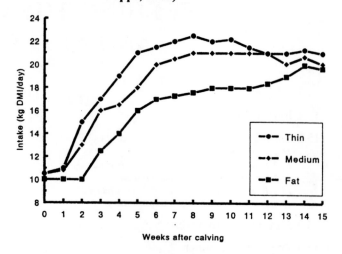

The fat cows ate considerably less than the thin animals with the difference between the extreme groups being more than 4 kg DM per day over the first 10 weeks of lactation. Given the importance of high feed intakes at this time, it is not surprising that the lower voluntary intakes were reflected in lower milk yields. A possible explanation for the reason that fat cows eat less can be seen from the changes in condition score in the first part of the lactation (Figure 15.3). Over the complete 15-week experimental period the condition score of the three groups converged to an average of about 2.5. The fat animals lost a large amount of body condition (about 1.25 units of condition score) whereas the thin animals actually gained weight whilst yielding more milk than the fat cows. The possible reason for this anomaly will be discussed in a later section when we consider what can be done with fat cows.

Figure 15.3 Effect of condition score at calving on condition score in the first part of lactation (Garnsworthy and Topps, 1982)

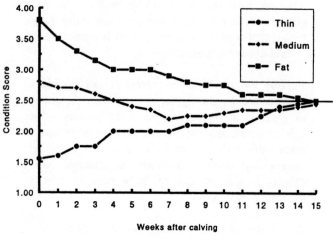

Similar work at the Institute for Animal Health, Compton (Treacher *et al.*, 1986), using a hay and concentrate diet, produced similar results. Fat animals (CS 4.0 at calving) lost more weight and gave less milk than thinner animals (CS 2.5 at calving). The fat animals lost more weight than thin cows in the first eight weeks of lactation (48 kg and 27 kg respectively). Fertility was slightly impaired; an average of 98 days calving to conception in the fat group compared to 89 days in the thinner group. Additionally the fat group suffered significantly more disease than the thin group.

15.2.2 What is the ideal condition score at calving?

A suitable target condition score 15 weeks post-calving is 2.0 to 2.5 (Figure 15.3). Given this target, what condition score should be the aim at calving? Traditionally it was considered desirable for cows to be fatter at calving to allow for body condition loss during early lactation. However, as shown above fat animals eat less and may yield less, which suggests that thinner cows are preferable to fat cows. It must be emphasised that both the experiments quoted above were carried out with high-quality diets. With poorer-quality rations thinner animals gave reduced milk yields than fatter animals. Given that high-quality diets are not always available, it would seem sensible to aim for a condition score at calving in the range of 2.5 to 3.0.

15.2.3 When to change condition score

Dairy cows gain weight and use body reserves with differing efficiencies at different times (Table 15.1). Thus it takes less energy to put on weight whilst milking than to gain the same weight when dry, and the energy available to the cow for milk production from mobilised body weight is less than the same weight lost during pregnancy (Table 15.1). It follows that it is more efficient to put weight on during the final stages of lactation than during the dry period. Therefore one should aim to dry the cow off at a condition score of 2.5 to 3.0 and to keep her at that condition score until she calves. In many instances, especially on stepped feeding systems with good silage offered *ad libitum*, cows are too fat at drying off and need to lose weight during the dry period.

Table 15.1 Energy value of weight changes in lactating and dry cows (calculated according to AFRC, 1990 assuming a ration M/D of 11 MJ ME /kg DM)

	Energy value of weight change (MJ ME/kg)	
	Weight gain	Weight loss
Lactating (Energy used for milk production)	36.7	22.0
Dry (Energy used to support foetus)	42.3	24.8

15.2.4 How fast can body condition be changed?

Scottish workers (Wright and Russel, 1984) investigated the relationship between weight change and change in condition score in cows. For the British Friesian one point change in condition score was equivalent to about 115 kg of body weight. To change weight at a kilogram a day requires as extreme a diet as most people would dare feed and more rapid changes are rarely achieved on farms. Therefore to change one condition score takes about three months to achieve, even with relatively extreme diets.

In conclusion, to achieve a target condition score of 2.5 to 3.0 at calving not only requires attention to feeding during the dry period but necessitates that condition score is monitored regularly throughout the production cycle. If body condition is grossly incorrect at any stage of production it takes a considerable length of time to correct.

15.2.5 How to manage fat cows at calving

Bearing in mind that fatter cows at calving eat less in early lactation, an appropriate feeding strategy should be developed if the majority of cows in the group or herd are over-fat when they calve otherwise feed intake and milk yield will be depressed early in lactation.

A possible feeding strategy can be derived from the results of a study in which the effects of body condition at calving and the content of UDP in the diet were studied with cows during the first 20 weeks of lactation (Jones and Garnsworthy, 1988). Four groups of 6 cows were fed from 12 weeks before calving to achieve average condition scores at calving of 3.15 (fat) and 2.15 (thin) (Table 15.2). For the first 20 weeks of lactation all cows were given 8 kg/day of a concentrate (14.0 MJ ME, 200 g CP) that contained either high UDP (70 g/kg DM) or low UDP (49 g/kg DM) together with 3 kg/day of sugar beet pulp and grass silage *ad libitum*.

Table 15.2 Effect of feeding a high (70 g/kg DM) or a low UDP (49 g/kg DM) concentrate to cows that were fat or thin at calving on feed intake and body condition (Jones and Garnsworthy, 1988)

Condition at calving	Fat	Fat	Thin	Thin
UDP in concentrate	High	Low	High	Low
Feed intake kg DM/day	18.1	16.9	17.5	18.2
Condition score				
at calving	3.17	3.13	2.21	2.08
week 10	2.25	2.50	2.21	1.83
week 20	2.46	2.83	2.16	1.96
Proportion of calving weight lost (0 to 20 weeks)	0.09	0.02	0.01	0.04

There was no significant effect of treatment on milk yield or on milk composition, but feed intake and the changes in condition score were considerably different (Table 15.2).

Increasing the supply of UDP to cows that are fat at calving resulted in a greater negative energy balance and a small increase in mobilisation of body fat reserves. At the concentration of energy and protein used in the experiment, the thin cows did not respond to the increased supply of UDP.

The high-yielding cow is frequently unable to meet all her nutritional requirements from dietary sources and therefore requires to mobilise body reserves. However the cow can only store about 20 kg of mobilisable protein in her body, whereas she can store between 100 and 200 kg of fat. Thus the animal is able to mobilise considerably more energy than protein during a period of weight loss. The result is that the amount of milk production sustained by the mobilised reserves is limited by their protein content. It can be calculated that a kilogram of weight loss will supply sufficient energy for about 6.7 litres of milk but will only supply enough protein for about 3.7 litres. The rational for feeding a high-protein diet therefore is that it supplies the extra protein needed to produce the extra three litres of milk (3.7 to 6.7). However, as the energy for this milk production comes from body reserves there will be a shortage of energy in the rumen and the microbes cannot utilise any additional ERDP. Thus undegradable protein (DUP) must be used to supplement the ration.

If this strategy is to be used in practice two points must be borne in mind:

- If high-protein supplements are to be used then there is a greater likelihood that all the mobilised energy will be used and will not accumulate in the liver as fatty deposits which can prevent further energy mobilisation. If the animal does not have sufficient body reserves to mobilise it is unlikely to respond to supplementary protein, but excessive weight loss might occur.

- Fat deposition in the liver may lead to ketosis if excessive, due to reduced efficiency of liver metabolism. This has two implications in practice. Firstly if over-fat animals are being deliberately underfed to reduce weight then a high DUP diet will ensure that weight loss occurs and that the mobilised fat does not collect in the liver. Secondly high-yielding animals that are susceptible to ketosis and are dependent on body reserves for some of their energy requirements must be given a diet high in DUP to minimise the risk of fatty liver.

15.3   Preventing milk fever

Milk fever, discussed in detail in Chapter 7, is primarily a problem of a delay in adjusting from a relatively low demand for calcium to a high demand. The disease is most commonly seen in animals in their third lactation and onwards and usually occurs between 12 hours before and 72 hours after calving. Some breeds, notably the Channel Island breeds, may suffer from milk fever when there are high concentrations of oestrogen in the blood, particularly at oestrus.

The concentration of calcium in the blood is under close homeostatic control and if the homeostatic mechanisms fail to adjust to the change in demand rapidly enough, hypocalcaemia and milk fever can occur. In late pregnancy the calcium requirement of a Friesian cow is about 42 g/day. This doubles to 82 g/day when she is giving 20 litres of milk. With careful management and the use of the following measures coupled with sensible milking management of the freshly-calved cow, the incidence of milk fever should be reduced to within acceptable levels (less than 9% of the herd per annum).

The prevention of milk fever must be a major objective when designing rations for cows at and around calving. The control procedures discussed in Chapter 7 are:

1. Modifying homeostatic mechanisms to increase the efficiency and extent of absorption of calcium post-calving by:

   a) *Using diets low in calcium during the dry period*. If cows are given low-calcium diets during the dry period the efficiency of absorption of calcium is raised leading to adequate absorption post-calving. Unfortunately with UK feeds it is very difficult to formulate diets to provide less than 50 g calcium a day at *ad libitum* intake. An alternative is to limit intake so that the animals are in energy balance – this usually limits calcium intake to a level where the cow is in balance or slightly in deficit. It should also be noted that it is important to change to high-calcium diets (>100 Ca g/day) 1 to 2 days before calving to prevent milk fever immediately after calving.

   b) *High-magnesium diets in the dry period*. Magnesium is involved in the mobilisation of calcium, and so diets low in magnesium reduce calcium mobilisation. Unfortunately autumn pastures are usually low in magnesium but high in calcium. The use of a low calcium/ high magnesium dry cow mineral can prove very effective in this situation.

c) *Supplementary vitamin D*. Vitamin D is involved in the homeostatic mechanisms controlling calcium mobilisation. Increased levels of vitamin D increase the efficiency of absorption of calcium. Injection of vitamin D therefore increases efficiency of calcium absorption. It is necessary to inject the vitamin D several days before calving as it takes some time to alter homeostatic mechanisms. If, however, the cow does not calve soon after injection, then the raised level of blood calcium triggers the homeostatic control of calcium mobilisation and reduces absorption. The doses of many preparations of vitamin D are much greater than daily requirements which has lead to concern about the risk of calcification of blood vessels and soft tissues. The doses of the modern analogues of vitamin D are considerably lower and thus the risk of calcification is reduced.

d) *Acids and acid salts*. The use of mineral acids or acid salts in diets for dry cows increases the efficiency of calcium absorption. Magnesium sulphate, ammonium sulphate, calcium chloride and aluminium sulphate have all been used with varying degrees of success. Silage, with or without the addition of mineral acids, has been shown to be beneficial which suggests that the feeding of silage pre-calving may help to limit the incidence of milk fever.

e) *Culling old cows and recurrent cases of milk fever*. As cows get older the amount of mobilisable calcium in the bones declines and hence body reserves fall. Milk fever cases tend to recur so that culling persistent offenders may be beneficial.

2. Reducing the amount of calcium required in early lactation and hence reducing the relative change in calcium requirement at calving.

This is actually the most commonly practised method for controlling milk fever. Cows are only partially milked out during the first few days of lactation. As milk production is limited by back pressure in the udder this reduces milk synthesis and hence the demand for calcium. The old technique of inflating the udder worked on this principle, but increased the risk of mastitis.

3. Supplying large amounts of dietary calcium.

a) *Oral drenching with a preparation high in calcium, magnesium and phosphorus*. These preparations are usually given at calving and may be too late for early cases of milk fever. However, their use may tip the balance for borderline cases. Drenching freshly calved cows can be dangerous due to the strong maternal instincts of the cow around calving.

b) *Sub-cutaneous infusion of minerals*. Infusion allows large quantities of calcium (4 to 12 g) to be placed in the blood stream quickly. This is the treatment method of choice but the practicalities, and ethics, of recommending it as a routine preventive measure limit its use for this purpose.

15.4 Preparing the rumen

The rumen is a dynamic ecosystem which needs time to adjust to the changes in level and composition of the diet that occur at calving. Such adaptation involves both a change in the microbial flora and a change in structure of the rumen wall. On low-energy, high-fibre dry cow diets the rumen papillae of the cow are small and reduced in size. On introduction to high-energy diets the size of the rumen papillae increases, but they do not return to the same size as at the end of the previous lactation until 3 to 4 weeks after calving. The papillae achieve their maximum size 6 to 8 weeks after calving (Mayer *et al.*, 1986).

The size of the rumen papillae affects their functional capacity, with large papillae absorbing volatile fatty acids five times faster than small papillae. The effect of these changes is that the freshly calved cow, with small rumen papillae, has a relatively low rate of absorption of VFA and hence higher concentrations of VFA within the rumen, lowered rumen pH and reduced buffering capacity.

Introduction to high-energy diets, low in fibre and high in soluble carbohydrates, two weeks prior to calving resulted in maximal papillae size being reached three weeks after calving as opposed to 6 to 8 weeks, higher feed intake at calving and maximal intake at 3 to 4 weeks after calving. However, care must be taken to limit the intake of high-energy feeds in the dry period to avoid excessive weight gain and to avoid the complications of the fat cow syndrome.

A low-calcium compound containing around 6 g Ca/kg (compared to 12 g in normal compounds) is used to achieve a low calcium intake. Silage is used to ensure an acidic diet to increase calcium absorption. Intake should be restricted and ample trough space must be supplied to prevent bullying and ensure consistent intakes.

15.5 Feeding the dry cow

There are several considerations to be borne in mind when feeding dairy cows and these can be subdivided into intake, energy, protein and specifically DUP requirements.

15.5.1 Intake

The intake of dry cows is low compared to lactating cows and declines as birth approaches, only to increase considerably once lactation starts (Figure 15.4). These changes are partially due to the sudden changes in nutrient requirements but, given the sudden change occurring at calving, must also be due to the effect of the bulk of calf and uterus on the rumen volume. In the last 2 to 3 weeks of pregnancy dry cows have a low intake of about 10 to 12 kg DM/day, which is less than 2% of body weight. As a result of these low intakes moderate nutrient densities (10 MJ ME/kg DM) are required to ensure adequate energy intake.

Figure 15.4 Dry matter intake of cows and heifers around calving (adapted from Saun *et al.*, 1993 and Zamet, *et al.*, 1979)

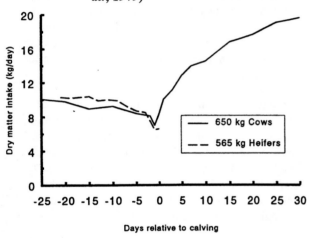

15.5.2 Energy requirements

The energy requirements of the modern dairy cow increase about twofold over the calving period from about 100 MJ pre-calving to 200 MJ when producing 25 litres milk daily after the first week of lactation (Table 15.3). However, when probable intakes are taken into account (Figure 15.4), the energy density required in the diet DM to supply the required amounts of ME does not alter considerably and a diet of 10 to 11 MJ/kg DM is adequate throughout this period with the exception of the last three weeks of pregnancy when a higher energy density is needed in the diet (Table 15.3). Concentrates should be offered at 2 kg/day in the final two weeks before calving (Section 15.6)..

15.5.3 Protein

Supplementary DUP in diets for dry cows can increase milk production in the subsequent lactation (Chapter 13, page 132). However, of the four UK trials reported to date, milk yield was increased in two experiments and milk protein content, rather than yield of milk, was increased in the other two

trials. In the original American work (Saun *et al.*, 1993) milk yields of heifers given supplementary DUP in the dry period did not differ over the first six weeks of lactation from those of unsupplemented animals, but milk protein content and protein yield were higher (Figure 15.5). The differences in protein content and in yield of milk protein were greatest in the first five weeks of lactation and by week six there was no significant difference between supplemented and unsupplemented animals.

Table 15.3 Approximate energy requirement, intake and required energy density for a cow around calving

	ME required (MJ/day)	DMI (kg/day)	M/D (MJ/kg DM)
38 weeks pregnant	95	10	9.5
39 weeks pregnant	100	10	10.0
40 weeks pregnant	105	9	11.7
20 litres milk (week 3 of lactation)	170	17	10.0
25 litres milk (week 4 of lactation)	200	18	11.1

Figure 15.5 Yield of milk protein and percentage composition of heifers fed a diet high or low in DUP in the dry period (Saun *et al.*, 1993)

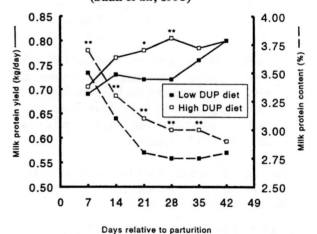

Over the whole lactation there was no difference in milk yield or in the production of milk fat or milk protein. Heifers given supplementary DUP required only 1.2 serves per conception, with 113 days from calving to conception, whereas the low DUP group took 2.1 services per conception and had an interval of 125 days from calving to conception. The small numbers of animals meant these differences were not statistically significant, but they indicate major differences in fertility associated with the inclusion of additional DUP in the dry cow diet.

Within quota constraints a response that gives an increase in milk quality rather than in yield is more desirable, but the effects on fertility are likely to make the use of compounds high in DUP desirable for dry cows in all situations. The response does not appear to be restricted to specific sources of protein, but whatever feed source is used it must supply considerable amounts of DUP to be of use. Dry cows have considerably lower intakes than high-yielding cows and this will reduce outflow from the rumen and hence increase degradability of any feed. The best feeds therefore will have a low and flat degradability (a low "a" and a low "c" fraction – see Chapter 6).

The feed with the best degradability for this purpose is fishmeal but unfortunately it is also very high in calcium and so should be avoided as the intake of calcium by the dry cow should be low to reduce the incidence of milk fever. Dark distillers grains and dark samples of maize gluten have low protein degradabilities but much of the undegradable protein fraction is also indigestible and does not contribute towards the supply of metabolisable protein to the animal. The best feeds are either prairie meal (maize gluten meal) or protected soyabean meal.

The original work used a low-protein forage and therefore could use a high inclusion of supplementary protein to give a ration containing a excess of DUP of 490 g with an overall CP of only 153 g/kg DM. However, overall CP content should if possible be kept below 160 g CP/kg DM as there has been one report of increased downer cows in animals given a dry cow diet containing this amount of protein. Therefore the crude protein of the forage needs to be as low as possible to allow sufficient supplementation. On grass-based diets (120 g CP/kg) this restricts the amount of supplementary protein that can be fed and it will be difficult to get a DUP excess of more than 350g. When animals are calving indoors on silage a low-protein forage such as maize silage will have to be used to allow sufficient supplementation to get more than 300g excess DUP. A suitable supplement would be a 2 kg/day of a concentrate containing 1.0 kg rolled wheat, 0.9 kg protected soyabean meal and 0.1 kg of a high-magnesium, low-calcium dry cow mineral.

15.6 Blueprint for managing dry cows

The recommendations made in the previous sections of this chapter can be drawn together to form a "blueprint" for the management of the dairy cow before and after calving.

The two weeks before and the two weeks after calving can be seen as the most important of the productive cycle. Good management in this period ensures a good, productive lactation and subsequent conception; poor management can mar the lactation and hamper conception.

Cows should be dried off 70 to 60 days before the next calving date at a condition score of 2.5 to 3.0. The condition score is that at which we wish the cow to calve down. To achieve this it is necessary to manage the cows in the last third of the previous lactation to ensure that the correct condition score is achieved. A gap of 60 to 70 days is recommended between lactations to ensure there is sufficient time for the udder tissue to regenerate sufficiently to support the next lactation.

In copper-deficient areas (Chapter 7, page 89) it may be necessary to inject supplementary copper either at drying off or when the cow calves down.

In the first part of the dry period (all but the last 14 days) the dry cow can be fed on cheap feeds such as grass, silage and straw to maintain her condition. Care must be taken to ensure the cows do not get fat during this period. In summer grazing situations this can mean stocking the cows at 8 to 12 cows/hectare and maintaining the sward below 7 cm.

Fourteen to 10 days before calving the cows should be put on a diet similar to that for the medium-yielding cows in the milking herd. The diet should be formulated to support 20 litres of milk per day when 15 kg DM is being eaten. If compound feeds are being used in the milking ration they should be replaced with a low-calcium pre-calving nut, incorporating a high-DUP supplement such as 900 g of protected soyabean meal. If compound feeds are not being used, 1 kg/day of rolled wheat and 900 g/day of protected soyabean meal can be used together with a 100 g/day low-calcium, high-magnesium mineral.

Cows should be offered about 10 kg dry matter of the diet to supply about 100 MJ ME/day. This will be about 90% of appetite when the cows start on the diet, so ample trough space should be supplied to avoid bullying. As the cows approach calving intakes fall and 10 kg DM/day will be all they can eat. Crude protein content should be kept below 160 g/kg DM to minimise the risk of "downer cows" after calving. A typical diet is shown in Table 15.4.

Table 15.4 Suggested diet for the last 14 days of the dry period

Ingredient	Amount (kg)	Daily intake	
Average grass silage	15.0	Dry matter	10.0 kg
Maize silage	14.0	ME	103 MJ
Rolled wheat	1.0	MP	848 g
Protected soyabean meal	0.9	MP surplus	339 g
Dry cow minerals	0.1		
		Analysis (g/kg DM)	
		CP	149
		NDF	410
		Starch and sugars	190

A diet based solely on grass silage would have too high a crude protein content, so a mixture of grass and maize silages has been used to lower the forage protein content. This allows 900 g of protected soya-bean meal to be included in the ration whilst still maintaining the crude protein content below 150 g/kg DM. The maize silage, in conjunction with the wheat, also increases the starch and sugar content and depresses the fibre (NDF) such that they are similar to those found in milking rations which will help prepare the rumen and its microbial contents.

This ration assumes that the dry cows will be housed. In nutritional terms this may be preferable to keeping the animals at grass but in summer it may be necessary to allow the cows access to a small "loafing area" of grass at a stocking rate of over 20 cows/hectare.

At calving ensure that the birth is not unduly prolonged by dystokia and that the cow is eating again within 6 to 8 hours after calving. Minimising dystokia involves correct nutrition, careful selection of bulls and careful observation and stockmanship. If an animal giving birth does not make any progress in a 60-minute period then assistance should be offered. Great care should be taken to spot early signs of milk fever, as this disease can severely constrain feed intake. Paradoxically the early signs of milk fever are hyper-excitability with muscle tremors and twitching. If these symptoms are observed the animal should be treated with subcutaneous fluids.

The freshly-calved cow should be managed in an active manner. Do not leave the cow with a bit of silage and the odd bit of cake for a few days to "settle down" – these are vital days in establishing the subsequent intake and hence lactation curve. The milking diet (see below) should be offered little and often with palatability enhancers such as molasses.

As soon as the cow has calved she should be placed on the diet described below (Table 15.5) for medium

yield (20 litres milk/day) for 10 to 14 days to acclimatise the rumen. The medium yield ration is chosen for two reasons. Firstly, merely by scaling up the intake of each of the feeds, changing the minerals and increasing the protein intake slightly a suitable ration can be devised. The ration differs minimally from that offered pre-calving and so the cow is more likely to eat large amounts as the microbes will be adapted to it already. Secondly, voluntary intake is often low at calving (10 to 14 kg DM/day – Figure 15.4) and offering such a diet prevents overfeeding of concentrates when separate compound feeding is used, which will minimise the risk of acidosis developing.

Table 15.5 Suggested diet for the first 14 days of the lactation

Ingredient	Amount (kg)	Daily intake	
Average grass silage	21.0	Dry matter	14.6 kg
Maize silage	19.0	ME	164 MJ
Rolled wheat	1.5	MP	1245 g
Soyabean meal	0.50	MP surplus	79 g
Rapeseed meal	1.5		
Dairy minerals	0.1		
		Analysis (g /kg DM)	
		CP	157
		NDF	408
		Starch and sugars	191

Rapeseed meal has been introduced to supply ERDP and the amount of DUP has been reduced by using a smaller amount of untreated soya. These small changes result in an increase in the content of crude protein content of the diet, but the contents of fibre, sugar and starch remain virtually constant.

Only after the cows have been on the medium-yield ration for 10 to 14 days should they be moved on to the high yield diet. Ideally this should be done in stages but in most situations management constraints require that this final change is abrupt.

CHAPTER 16

NUTRITION, FERTILITY AND LAMENESS

16.1 Introduction

16.2 Nutrition and fertility
16.2.1 *Energy*
16.2.2 *Protein*
16.2.3 *Other nutritional factors affecting fertility*
16.2.4. *Milk composition and fertility*

16.3 Nutrition and lameness
16.3.1 *Energy*
16.3.2 *Protein*
16.3.3 *Silage*
16.3.4 *Concentrates*

16.1   Introduction

Deficiencies or excesses of nutrients such as energy and minerals can cause clinical problems (see Chapters 5 and 7), but health problems can also occur in a more indirect manner. The effects of energy and protein nutrition on fertility and lameness are discussed in this chapter. Whilst there are links between nutrition and these disease problems, they are by no means clear and it is important to remember that both diseases can be significantly influenced by other aspects of animal management on the farm.

16.2   Nutrition and fertility

The most likely nutritional factor to influence fertility is the energy balance of the animal early in lactation, particularly at the time of service. Although deficiencies of specific minerals and vitamins have been shown to be important these have been considered in Chapter 7 and so will not be discussed here.

16.2.1 Energy
The energy status of the cow is generally considered to be the major nutritional factor that influences fertility, with low energy status impairing fertility. Energy status can be assessed via the metabolic profile (Chapter 17, page 165) using blood glucose or beta-hydroxy butyrate as an indicator of energy status. Miettinen (1984) collected blood samples for 2 months after calving from eight herds of cattle each containing 20 to 30 cows, which were tested for glucose and urea. The intervals from calving to conception and from calving to first insemination were significantly shorter in the group with the higher concentrations of blood urea and glucose, and the conception rate to the first service was also higher for these animals. They concluded that serum glucose concentrations below 2.9 mmol/litre impaired fertility.

The concentration of blood metabolites can change quickly and may give a false impression of the long-term energy status over the several weeks in which the cow is likely to conceive. A better indicator of long term energy status is the condition score of the animals and this has been used by research workers to assess the impact of nutritional status on fertility.

Condition score. Haresign (1980) reviewed the interactions between body condition, milk yield and reproduction in cattle and proposed that cows have a critical condition at mating, below which conception rates are reduced if the animals are still in negative energy balance. If cows are above this critical condition at mating, because they calve with a high condition score, or do not lose very much condition before service, energy balance has little or no effect on conception rates. Support for the critical condition concept is provided by the data of Leaver, (1983) which showed that cows served with both low condition scores (under 2) and low milk protein content (under 30 g/kg, a sign of negative energy balance) had significantly reduced conception rates.

A survey of 65 commercial dairy herds (Mulvaney, 1977) showed that conception rate to first service was not affected by condition score at first insemination within the range 1.0 to 3.0. Cows with extremely low or very high condition scores (0.5 or 3.5 to 4.0) showed reduced fertility. However, the very thin animals were likely to have had disease problems or to have been poorly managed, whilst those served at scores of 3.5 or above may have gained condition because they were served later in lactation.

A survey of 2000 high-yielding dairy cows (yield over 7,000 l/annum) was conducted by ADAS and Nottingham University (Bourchier *et al.*, 1987) to study the relationships between condition score, milk yield and fertility. Neither condition score at calving nor condition score at first service significantly affected conception rates until condition scores dropped below 1.5 (Table 16.1). Milk yield had no significant effect on conception rate over the range of yields reported and this appears to be the same at even higher yields.

Table 16.1 Effects of condition score at calving or first service and milk yield during the first 12 weeks of lactation on conception rate to first service (Bourchier et al., 1987)

	Condition score at calving					
	<1.5	1.5	2	2.5	3	3.5+
Conception to first service (%)	47	56	57	57	56	56

	Condition score at first service				
	<1.5	1.5	2	2.5	3+
Conception to first service (%)	47	56	54	51	58

	Milk yield in first 12 weeks of lactation (litres/day)		
	<30	30 to 36	>36
Conception to first service (%)	55	53	52

Traditionally it has been suggested that the worst problems occur in high-yielding cows that are in low condition at service. However, if the interactive effects of condition score at service and milk yield from this survey are examined (Table 16.2), it can be seen that within the lowest condition score group, it was the lower yielders that had the poor conception rates and not the higher-yielding cows.

Table 16.2 The interactive effects of condition score at service and milk yield in the first 12 weeks of lactation on conception rate to first service (Garnsworthy and Bourchier, unpublished)

	Condition score at service				
	<1.5	1.5	2.0	2.5	3.0+
Milk yield (l/day)	Conception rate (%)				
< 30	42	65	56	54	46
30 to 36	44	53	54	51	74
> 36	61	49	55	48	55

It can be concluded that there is little relationship between actual body condition and fertility over the normal range seen on dairy farms. However, animals in either extreme of body condition can suffer impaired fertility, but this may not be due to their condition score but rather to an underlying problem that affects both body condition and fertility at the same time.

Changes in condition score. As has been seen in the above section, the actual condition score does not have a great effect on fertility except at the extremes. However the **change** in condition score during the breeding period, and hence the energy status of the cow has a greater effect, as can be seen in Table 16.3.

Table 16.3 Effect of change in condition score from calving to time of service on conception rates to first service (%) (from Anon, 1984)

Change in body condition	Number of cows	Conception to first service (%)	
		Year 1	Year 2
Decreasing	369	47	30
No change	663	57	60
Increasing	318	59	71

Animals that lost weight between calving and conception had considerably lower conception rates, particularly in the second year, whilst animals that gained condition during the same period had the best conception rates. Looking in more detail at changes in condition score (Table 16.4) it can be seen that conception rates only started to decline if the condition loss was excessive ($\geq$ 1.0 condition score). In practice, most good management systems aim to restrict weight loss to less than one condition score unit between calving and first service and in such situations fertility will not be significantly impaired. Managing cows to be in a positive energy balance at conception is the optimum but is sometimes difficult to achieve in higher-yielding animals.

Table 16.4 Relationship between change in condition score between calving and first service and conception rate. (Ferguson, 1994)

Change in condition score (calving to first service)	Conception to first service (%)
more than + 1.0	62
0.0	50
0.0 to -0.5	65
-0.5 to -1.0	53
-1.0	38
more than - 1.0	17

Looking at the three factors of loss in condition score, condition score at calving and milk yield (Table 16.5) it can be seen that conception rates were only low in high-yielding cows that lost a lot of condition (44%), or that were thin at serving, having lost a lot of condition since calving. Both groups of animals were likely to have been mismanaged after calving and this therefore suggests that careful management and regulation of weight loss will minimise the effects of energy status on fertility.

Energy deficiency. The energy status of the cow can, in severe circumstances, influence fertility. Negative energy balance delays the onset of normal ovarian activity which limits the number of oestrus cycles before breeding and may account for the observed decrease in fertility (Butler and Smith, 1989). Cows with a low energy status also have lower progesterone concentrations during the second and third luteal phases which may impair embryo implantation in the uterine wall and survival in the early stages of pregnancy (Butler and Smith, 1989) such that cows come into oestrus but do not hold to services. Ultrasonic scanning (Lucy *et al.*, 1991) has shown that the number of immature follicles (less than 9 mm diameter) in the ovaries decreased with increasing energy balance but the number of mature ones (over 10 mm) increased. This suggests that the final development of the follicle is inhibited by the negative energy balance.

Table 16.5 Effect of milk yield and loss in condition score from calving to service on conception to first service (Garnsworthy and Bourchier, unpublished)

Loss in condition score from calving to first service			
	>1.5	1.0	0.5	<0
Conception to first service (%)			
Milk yield (l/day)	*All cows*		
<30	51	63	53	59
30 to 36	49	53	53	68
>36	44	55	54	63
Milk yield (l/day)	*Cows with condition score less than 1.5 at first service*		
<30	30	53	30	-
30 to 36	29	46	67	-
>36	61	66	-	-

16.2.2 Protein

The effect of concentration of dietary protein on fertility is also confusing. However, given the complexity of protein digestion in the cow (Chapter 6) this is not surprising. It is probable that as our understanding of protein digestion improves we will be able to minimise the effect of protein on fertility.

Table 16.6 Effect of concentration of crude protein in the diet on dairy cow fertility (Anon 1984)

Crude protein content of diet (g CP/kg DM)	127	163	193
Calving to conception (days)	69	96	106
Calving to oestrus (days)	36	45	27
Services per pregnancy	1.47	1.87	2.47

Crude protein. A wide range of trials have shown that high concentrations of dietary protein reduce cow fertility, but there are considerable differences in the concentration of protein above which fertility is impaired. For example, American work using diets based on maize silage (Table 16.6) showed that the number of services per conception increased as the concentration of dietary protein increased from 127 to 193 g CP/kg DM. Interestingly, the trial showed that the interval from calving to first oestrus decreased with increasing concentration of dietary protein and this may have been due to a higher dry matter intake. However, other workers (Carroll *et*

al., 1988) reported that there was no significant difference in fertility when cows were fed on diets containing either 130 g CP or 200 g CP/ kg DM.

In another trial (Howard *et al.*, 1987) cows were given a diet containing either 150 or 200 g CP/kg DM crude protein diet from 10 days after parturition to 149 days after parturition. Milk yields were higher for the high crude protein diet but average daily dry matter intake was unchanged. Although blood urea was consistently higher in the high crude protein group the days to first oestrus (80 days), days to conception (140 days) and pregnancy rate (85%) were unaffected by diet. In contrast, German workers (Roever *et al.*, 1982) found that for diets containing 130, 146 and 175 g CP/ kg DM, the number of inseminations per conception increased (1.64, 1.72 and 1.93) as did days to conception (87.8, 88.2 and 97.3 days).

In practice rations should be formulated to contain no more than 180 to 190 g CP/kg DM. Such diets should be adequate for even the highest milk yields. The contrasting effects of concentration of CP in the diet suggest that more research is needed on this aspect of dairy cow nutrition. An obvious step would be to sub-divide increases in CP into those for ERDP and those for DUP.

ERDP. Recent German work looked at two rations based on maize silage both containing 190 g CP /kg DM but in one diet a third of the protein supplement was treated with formaldehyde to reduce its degradability in the rumen. This high level of crude protein in the diet was reflected in reduced fertility, but the reduction was less when rumen degradability was lower. The results suggest that excessive amounts of rumen degraded protein are possibly the cause of the depressed fertility. Other workers (Ferguson *et al.*, 1988) reported lower conception rates in cows with concentrations of serum urea nitrogen more than 200 mg/litre, suggesting that the diffusion of excess ammonia out of the rumen may be the problem. Miettinen (1984) found that concentrations of serum urea of 2.5 to 6.3 mmol/litre were required to help ensure optimal fertility.

Raised concentrations of blood urea may reduce fertility by raising concentrations of urea in the uterus which impairs conception and survival of the embryo (Plym Forshell, 1994). Alternatively, the additional metabolic load of converting absorbed ammonia into urea in the liver and excreting it via the kidneys increases the energy demands on the animal which may reduce fertility. Interpreting this in the light of the metabolisable protein system would indicate that an excess of ERDP (relative to FME) in the rumen would predispose the animal to impaired fertility as the protein cannot be utilised fully by the microbes (they lack sufficient energy).

The ammonia from the degraded protein passes into the blood stream from which it must be excreted. In practice, therefore, it would seem desirable to formulate diets to have a minimal excess of ERDP.

16.2.3 Other nutritional factors affecting fertility

Rapeseed meal. In recent years there has been concern in some farming circles over the use of rapeseed meal in dairy cow rations and many farmers are reluctant to use high inclusions of this feed. The origin of such concern probably stems from the time when the use of "double-zero" varieties was not mandatory in Europe and samples high in erucic acid and in glucosinolates were incorporated in compound feeds which affected palatability and possibly also fertility. However, work in the mid 1980s (Vincent *et al.*, 1985) with concentrates containing 250 g to 320 g rapeseed meal/kg feed compared to concentrates containing 210 g soyabean meal/kg found that rapeseed meal had no significant effect on ovarian cyclic activity or on behavioural oestrus.

Carotene. Vitamin A is required in the maintenance of the various membranes in the body (Chapter 7, page 93) and in breeding animals deficiencies of this vitamin can result in lowered fertility. Vitamin A does not exist in plants but must be synthesised in the gut from carotinoids. Carotene can be denatured in grass silages particularly if these silages have over-heated or over-oxidised. Similarly, carotene can be low in sun-bleached hays and therefore some diets can be deficient. In a trial in Israel (Ascarelli *et al.*, 1985) supplementation with carotene resulted in improved conception rates in younger cows (in their second and third lactations) during the first part of the experiment (cows calving in September to December). However, during the second part of the experiment (cows calving in January to April), there was no significant benefit from supplementation, suggesting that carotene is not always a limiting factor.

Brassicas and red clover. Extended periods of feeding brassica forages (the cabbage family which includes kale) and red clover, can reduce fertility. For both feeds there is evidence of an adverse effect on embryo survival in sheep. Possible modes of action are small increases in maternal temperature, asynchrony of the embryo with its uterine environment, a disturbance in the amino acid composition of the uterine fluid or a reduction in the availability of glucose. As a result of these problems it is recommended that the brassicas and red clover do not form more than 10% of the total DM intake of breeding cows.

16.2.4 Milk production and fertility

The concentration of protein in the milk is an indication of the cow's energy status (see Chapter 13, page 130) and should, therefore, be related to fertility. Figure 16.1 shows the relationship between content of protein in the milk and the interval between calving and conception. It is probable that low contents of protein in the milk and poor fertility are manifestations of an inadequate intake of energy. Taking action to improve milk quality will also raise fertility. Leaver (1983) showed that cows with low milk protein content (under 30 g/kg) also had reduced conception rates.

Figure 16.1 Relationship between milk protein and fertility (from Anon, 1984)

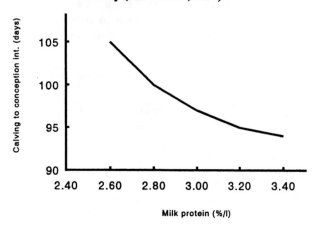

16.3   Nutrition and lameness

Lameness in dairy cattle is a major cause of financial loss and ranks only after mastitis and reproductive losses in importance. The cause of solar ulcer and white line disease (the main diseases associated with lameness in cows) is multifactorial, involving husbandry, management, genetics, infectious agents and nutrition. A great deal of attention has been paid in recent years to the possible importance of subclinical laminitis, caused by nutritional factors, in solar ulcer and white line disease. It is important to examine the link between nutritional factors and specific lesions rather than generalised "foot lameness" which may include diseases as different as solar ulcer and foul-in-the-foot. There are a number of other miscellaneous conditions which cause lameness, such as the joint changes associated with rickets and copper deficiency, and muscle wastage associated with vitamin E and/or selenium deficiency, but these will not be discussed in this chapter.

The relationship between nutrition and the development of major hoof lesions is still far from clear. The difficulty in practice is how much importance to place on nutrition, but generally nutrition is only a minor factor. This does not mean that nutritional factors can be ignored when investigating herds with a high incidence of lameness.

Diets and feeding regimes should always be examined to assess the degree of risk of abnormal conditions in the rumen which might predispose to lameness. Attention to nutritional factors alone will rarely have an impact on a major lameness problem caused by solar ulcer or white line disease.

16.3.1 Energy

Excessive intake of energy, especially starch, has been associated with increased lameness particularly laminitis, solar ulcer and white line disease. The hypothesis linking diet to lameness is via the development of clinical and subclinical aseptic laminitis. Maclean (1971) reported that lesions such as solar ulcer were a common sequel to attacks of acute laminitis. The vascular damage caused by laminitis to the horn-forming tissues of the hoof (corium) and the resultant changes in horn quality (such as the reduction in the level of sulphur-containing amino acids in the horns), are thought to increase the susceptibility of the hoof to the development of further lesions. Sub-clinical laminitis is thought to occur in many dairy herds, causing long-term damage to the hoof but the cause of the laminitis is uncertain. Cows which have suffered attacks of acute clinical laminitis may be more likely to develop other lesions subsequently, such as solar ulcer and white line disease, but whether this happens after sub-clinical cases is uncertain.

Excessive starch in the diet is thought to modify the pattern of fermentation in the rumen which leads to an increase in some toxic factor in the blood. This factor damages the small blood vessels in the horn-forming tissues in the feet, which become hot and inflamed and horn synthesis is disrupted. Mortensen *et al.* (1986) described mild laminitic symptoms in calves which had been infused inter-arterially with endotoxin (a toxic factor) and in calves given lethal amounts of grain in the diet. However, there has been no experimental work reported in which sub-clinical laminitis has been reproduced by giving milking cows specific diets. Laminitis has also been associated with metritis, mastitis and occasionally acetonaemia. Mouldy feed has also been suggested as a possible triggering factor.

16.3.2 Protein

Diets high in protein have been suggested as possible causes of laminitis. Bazeley and Pinsent (1984) related laminitis in heifers to the feeding of a 25% protein supplement. The use of large amounts of oil seed cakes and ground-nut cake has also been implicated. However specifically designed experiments (e.g. Manson and Leaver, 1988) have shown no difference in the incidence of clinical lameness between groups of cows fed rations containing 160 g CP/kg DM and 190 g CP/kg DM although the duration of lameness cases increased with the higher levels of protein in the diet.

16.3.3 Silage

Low rumen pH is one of the features of an unhealthy rumen. Whether this is a causal factor in lameness problems is uncertain. David (1989) failed to find any association between silage pH and herds with a high incidence of solar ulcer.

Bazeley and Pinsent (1984) reported a high percentage of ammonia nitrogen (over 15%) in the silage in herds having a high incidence of laminitis in heifers although no detailed figures were given. Ammonia nitrogen in silage is usually expressed as a percentage of total nitrogen and levels exceeding 10% are regarded as indicative of poor silage fermentation which is associated with poor nutritive value and reduced palatability. Low silage intakes are likely to be associated with an increased proportion of concentrates in the diet and their relative meal sizes, thus predisposing the animal to rumen instability.

In a survey of herds in the north and west of England Clarkson *et al.* (unpublished) found a lower incidence of lameness in herds where the dry matter content of the silage was relatively high. This effect may be a reflection of a higher content of fibre in the drier silages than in wetter silages, which promoted more rumination, more saliva production and less risk of sub-clinical acidosis in the animals.

16.3.4 Concentrates

Much of the recent concern about lameness and nutrition has centred on low ratios of forage DM to concentrate DM, but the picture is not clear. Livesey and Fleming (1984) demonstrated a higher incidence of sole ulcer in heifers fed a 40:60 (forage: concentrate) ration compared to 50:50 and Peterse *et al.* (1984) reported a high level of sole ulcer in heifers fed 50:50 ratio compared to 80:20. However Manson and Leaver (1988) failed to demonstrate any significant difference in the incidence of clinical lameness in cows fed ratios of 56:44 (low concentrate) compared to 42:58 (high concentrate) although there were differences in locomotion score. Similarly Smit *et al.* (1986) found no significant differences in the incidence of solar ulcers between two groups of cows given 4 kg and 12 kg of concentrate daily. Furthermore, David (1989), investigating herds with a high incidence of sole ulcers, found a range of forage:concentrate dry matter ratios from 32:67 to 50:50 and Bee (1986) described a high incidence of both sole ulcer and white line disease in cattle fed a very low flat rate of concentrate (approximately 80:20 forage to concentrate dry matter ratio). There does not seem to be any particular forage to concentrate ratio that is a trigger factor in herds with lameness problems. However, given the inadequacies of the forage: concentrate ratio in describing modern diets (Chapter 5 - page 57) this is not surprising.

Given that concentrate feeding influences lameness by altering the rumen environment, the pattern of feeding of the concentrate part of diet should also be important. However, Peterse (1986) found no difference between the lameness lesion scores of cows fed a flat rate of 10 kg of concentrate from 3 days after calving and the cows that were built up to 10 kg by two weeks after calving. Similarly, Smit *et al.* (1986) showed no correlation between the incidence of solar ulcer or haemorrhagic lesion scores and rate of increase in concentrate feeding. Furthermore, David (1989) noted no consistency in the rate or frequency of concentrate feeds in herds with a lameness problem and Bazeley and Pinsent

(1984) found no association between laminitis in heifers and whether peak concentrate feed was being achieved within 8 days of calving. Such findings suggest that pattern of feeding is of minor importance and that it is the overall impact of the feeding regime on rumen health that is likely to influence the incidence of laminitis and lameness. It follows that the steps outlined in earlier chapters to maintain a healthy rumen, such as monitoring intake of NDF, protein, fat, sugar and starch, as well as length of fibre, chewability and feeding pattern, can all contribute to minimising the effects of nutrition on lameness.

CHAPTER 17

ASSESSING NUTRITIONAL STATUS

17.1 Introduction

17.2 Condition score

17.3 Milk yield

17.4 Milk composition

17.5 Blood metabolic profiles
    17.5.1   When to sample
    17.5.2   Energy status
    17.5.3   Protein status
    17.5.4   Mineral status

17.6 Milk metabolic profiles

17.7 Fertility records

17.8 Faeces

17.1   Introduction

Diet formulation is not an exact science. Our ability to characterise and measure the nutrient content of feeds is relatively poor, our understanding of the use of nutrients in the animal is imperfect and, because of the practical constraints on the farm, the proposed ration may not be that which the cow is actually offered. Given these limitations, it is of vital importance that actual animal performance is checked against predictions and targets so that an attempt can be made to diagnose reasons for the differences observed and modifications made to the diet where necessary. For dairy cows there is a range of different ways of assessing nutritional status of the animals on the farm.

The first and the most important act when assessing performance on the farm is to inspect the condition of the animals themselves. Having done so, the next step is to assess the level of output and compositional quality of the milk. Blood metabolic profiles, if available, should be considered along with information on condition score, output of milk and its quality. Records of fertility and the state of the dung can also help to indicate the general nutritional status of the herd. In the rest of this chapter, each component part of the assessment of nutritional status is considered in turn.

17.2   Condition score

The definitive method of assessing the fatness or thinness of a cow is to use ultra-sonic scanning.

Scanning is more difficult in cows than in other types of farm livestock, mainly because the deposits of fatty tissue are not easy to view accurately, which makes calibration of the equipment a complicated process. An alternative approach, a simple visual assessment of whether the cow appears thin, fat or somewhere in between is now accepted as being crude, but adequate for routine on-farm use.

The main problem with condition scoring is to make the assessment as consistent as possible between different operators and over time. Fatness is assessed on a numerical score by comparing the living animal with a series of descriptions and pictures which describe the fat cover in certain key areas such as the tail head, over the lumbar processes and over the ribs. Unfortunately several different systems have evolved in different parts of the world. The Australians and some Americans use a score from one (very thin) to eight (obese) whereas other Americans and British workers use a score from 1 (very thin) to 5 (obese), with experienced scorers using half-scores where necessary. Condition scoring was initially designed to be carried out on restrained animals but it has since been developed to allow scoring to be based on visual assessment of loose housed animals.

The five-point score is based on an assessment of two areas; the lumbar area and the tail head (sacral) area. The former is of more use at scores of less than 3 whereas the latter becomes more important in fatter animals. The appearance of different areas of the animal at different condition scores is described in Table 17.1.

Ideally, animals should be condition scored as often as possible (e.g. every two weeks) and their score compared to the desired target for that stage of lactation (Figure 12.2, page 127). Animals not at their desired condition score should have their diet re-formulated if possible. Changing the condition score of an animal is a relatively slow process; one condition score unit is equivalent to about 115 kg of body weight and a weight change of more than 1 kg a day is hard to achieve. Thus it can take more than three months to produce a change of one unit of condition score. It is therefore important to regard condition scoring as a continual process so that extremes of fatness and thinness can be avoided, and so that current condition score and feeding are reviewed together to achieve future targets.

Table 17.1 Body condition scoring in dairy cattle (adapted from Edmonson *et al.*, 1989)

	1	2	3	4	5
General	Emaciated Frame protruding	Moderate condition Frame obvious	Good condition Frame and covering well balanced	Fat Covering more obvious than frame	Obese Severe over-conditioning
Lumbar area Vertebral spinous processes	Sharp ends Little flesh	Easily discernible	Smooth ridge Individual processes not visible	Not discernible Covering almost flat	Buried in fat
Transverse processes	Half length visible	Third of length visible	Quarter of length visible	Not discernible Smooth, rounded edge	Buried in fat
Transition between transverse processes and para-lumbar fossa	Prominent shelf, gaunt	Overhanging shelf	Slight shelf	None	Bulging
Palpation	Transverse processes and vertebral bodies feel sharp	Transverse processes feel sharp	Need to apply pressure to feel transverse processes Smooth	No bones palpable	No bones palpable
Tail head Sacral vertebrae	Individual vertebrae distinct	Individual vertebra not visible	Smooth covering	Smooth covering	Smooth covering
Hook bones (Tuber coxae) P in bones (Tuber ischii) Between hook and pin bones	Extremely sharp No tissue cover Severe depression	Prominent Very sunken	Smooth Depression Little fat deposition	Rounded by fat Slight depression	Surrounded by fat Flat
Between hook bones	Severely depressed No flesh	Very depressed	Moderate depression	Flat	Rounded
Tailhead	Deep V-shaped cavity under tail	U-shaped cavity under tail	Shallow cavity under tail	Slight depression	Folds of fatty tissue under tailhead.
Palpation	No fatty tissues Skin drawn tight over pelvis	Some fatty tissue	Can feel pelvis with slight pressure; fatty tissue over whole area	Bones difficult to feel	Bones difficult to feel

Condition score is most easily lost in the early stages of lactation when demands for nutrient are high and concentrate feeding is being used to meet requirements. Losing body condition in late lactation and during the dry period is difficult, because on most farms the forages available are of relatively high quality and can support maintenance and some milk production. Weight loss should be minimised during the period when animals are being served, since conception rate can be markedly improved if heifers are on a rising plane of nutrition (equivalent to 0.7 kg daily liveweight gain) for the 6-week period either side of conception. Similarly, cows are more likely to conceive if they are not losing weight at the time they are served. Deficiencies in energy supply during the first third of pregnancy can result in reduced implantation rates and increased levels of early embryonic loss.

The regular monitoring of condition score is a subjective procedure, and is only accurate to about 0.5 units at best. Therefore condition scoring is unsuitable for monitoring the **rate** of loss in live-weight because by the time it is realised that condition score is not changing at the correct rate, it is too late in the production cycle to do anything about it.

For cows with a high glucose requirement (early lactation or late pregnancy) beta-hydroxy-butyrate is a good indicator of the degree of energy deficit of the cow (see Section 17.2.4). The relationship between energy deficit and the concentration of beta-hydroxy-butyrate in the blood plasma of housed beef suckler sows is shown in Figure 17.1.

Figure 17.1. Relationship between plasma beta-hydroxy-butyrate and energy status in housed suckler cows during late pregnancy (adapted from Russel, 1986)

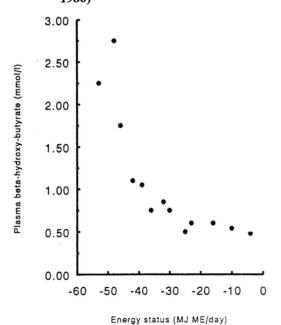

Although the relationship shown in Figure 17.1 has not been used in dairy cattle work with suckler cows and sheep suggests that it can be used to assess the energy deficit and hence the rate of daily weight loss, assuming the energy values for weight loss in Chapter 9 (page 103).

Gains in condition score are very difficult to achieve in early lactation, especially at high levels of milk output. As milk yield falls, weight gain becomes possible and the aim should be to dry the cow off in the condition in which she should calve. Weight gain in the dry period is very common, especially with summer-calving cows dried off on to spring pasture.

17.3   Milk yield

The typical pattern of milk production through the course of the lactation is shown in Figure 12.1 (page 127). The curve shows a peak in yield between 8 and 12 weeks from calving, and a decline thereafter. Examination of lactation curves in relation to month of calving can reveal major effects of diet on milk output. For example, cows calving in late summer at pasture often show relatively lower peak yields, and a steeper decline post-peak, than cows which calved in late autumn and received full winter diets from the outset of lactation. Differences like these illustrate the need to pay relatively more attention to the nutrition of the animals which calve prior to the main winter period.

Similarly, examination of the pattern of milk yield at the time of turn-out to spring grazing can be very revealing. If milk yield increased after turn-out to pasture, then the diet on offer in late winter was inadequate to support the potential yield of the herd. If, on the other hand, milk yield decreased after turn-out, then there was a need to buffer feed at that time of the year to maintain nutrient intake, possibly because adverse spring weather conditions reduced herbage intake from grazed pasture.

The typical rate of decline in milk yield post-peak is 2.5% per week. Animals showing a greater rate of decline than this are most likely to be in severe energy deficit, particularly if the relatively steep decline is associated with a low content of protein in milk. A similar effect is often evident when animals are deficient in their supply of metabolisable protein, so it is important that the correct nutritional diagnosis is made. A steep decline in yield post-peak is usually accompanied by only a short period of less than a week when the animals are actually at peak production. In extreme situations clinical symptoms of metabolic disorders are evident, and metabolic profiles (Section 17.2.4) can assist in identifying whether the problem is a shortage of energy, of protein, or of both energy and protein, i.e. low feed intake.

A feature of heifer lactations and those of cows on total mixed rations is a flat lactation curve in which peak milk yield may not be exceptional, but the decline thereafter is very small. A similar pattern is often observed in herds which are given a flat rate of concentrates throughout lactation. In all these situations, total lactation yield can be relatively high, but because peak production may not exceed 35 litres per cow per day, the risk of excessive weight loss and of metabolic disorders in early lactation, and of low conception to first service is much reduced. A problem with flat lactations is that when the animal is dried off it may still be yielding more than 20 litres a day.

17.4   Milk composition

Examination of the regular reports of milk composition received by the farmer can reveal trends in nutrition which can readily be altered if necessary. For example, a chronically low milk fat content may be linked to digestive disorders such as acidosis, displaced abomasa, high incidence of calving difficulty because of over-fat animals at calving, and downer cows. The general problem is one of inadequate long fibre in the diet. A small amount of long straw or unchopped big bale silage can rectify the problem. Low contents of milk protein are indicative of inadequate energy supply to the animal (Chapter 13, page 130). Low milk lactose contents indicate a chronic infection in the udder, such as mastitis, which may be responsible for the herd under-achieving targets for output.

The typical composition of milk from Holstein/Friesian and Channel Island dairy cattle is shown in Table 17.2. Major deviations from typical values indicate that close assessment of the nutrition and health of the herd is warranted.

Table 17.2   Typical composition of milk from Holstein/Friesian and Channel Island dairy cows

	Holstein/Friesian	Channel Island
Fat (g/kg)	40	50
Total protein (g/kg)	32	37
Lactose (g/kg)	46	46

The typical seasonal trend in the content of milk fat is a peak in late winter and a trough in mid-summer. Part of this trend is a reflection of the difference between summer grazing (relatively short fibre, limited buffer feeding) and the diets used in late winter which tend to be based on a relatively high content of silage in the diet and high-energy (high-

fat) concentrate supplements. Part of the seasonal trend in milk fat content is due to the stage of the lactation of the animals themselves. When the majority of the herd is in late lactation, the fat content of the milk produced on the farm is likely to be higher than normal.

Traditionally, milk protein reaches a low point in late winter, reflecting under-feeding of the herd, and shows a rapid rise once the herd is fully at pasture day and night as a reflection of the higher feed intake and the higher energy content of grazed spring herbage. With the increased popularity of total mixed rations, this trend has become somewhat less pronounced, and on some farms operating the total mixed ration system, relatively high milk protein contents are maintained throughout the year. As with milk fat, the protein content of animals in early lactation is typically lower than those in late lactation.

Milk composition changes with the stage of lactation (Figure 17.2). As yield increases over the first few months of lactation the protein and fat content fall and then increase as yield declines. Lactose shows opposite changes, increasing in early lactation and then declining once peak yield has been achieved.

Figure 17.2   Effect of stage of lactation on the composition of milk (adapted from Waite *et al.*, 1956)

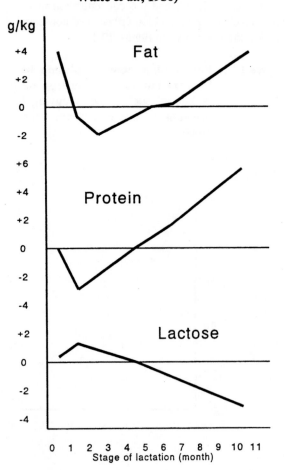

17.5   Blood metabolic profiles

All nutrients have to pass from the digestive tract to the target organs, such as the udder, through the blood stream. If the target tissues require more of a metabolite than is being absorbed from the digestive tract (or synthesised in other organs) then the concentration in blood falls. Alternatively, if more is being absorbed from the digestive tract into the blood than can be utilised or excreted then concentrations in blood rise.

Measuring the concentration of blood metabolites should give an indication of the balance between supply and demand. The metabolic profile was first proposed for dairy cattle in the 1960s when routine laboratory analyses of blood metabolites became possible (Payne *et al.*, 1970). A wide range of blood components and metabolites was determined in the original profile, but over the years this has been refined to three or four measurements to assess the energy, protein and possibly the mineral status of the animal. In problem herds it may also be used for specific trace elements such as copper. When considering metabolic profiles for farm use several factors must be considered; when to sample, what to measure and how to interpret the results.

17.5.1   When to sample

It is imperative to realise that the blood metabolic profile only measures the balance of nutrient flow between inputs and outputs. Nothing can remain out of balance for long and the cow quickly responds by altering her outputs (milk yield, milk constituents, weight change) until they are in line with inputs and the normal balance of the blood is re-established.

It follows that animals must be sampled **before** a change in production occurs, rather than after. If a group of animals are under-performing - failing to reach a target peak milk yield for example, it is pointless sampling that group as they have reduced their milk output already in order to bring yield in line with their dietary inputs. The group that should be sampled are the animals that calved 3 to 4 weeks later and are still trying to reach their peak yields; this group will not have balanced output and input and hence meaningful information will be found in the metabolic profile. Similarly the animals sampled should be "typical" of that group. It is tempting to include sick animals or exceptionally high yielders in the sample - both types of animal would be expected to be out of balance and the profile results will normally just confirm this!

The use of the blood metabolic profile has fallen into disrepute in some countries. There were two main reasons for this, and if they are corrected the test can still be a useful method of on-farm assessment of a ration. Firstly, as mentioned already, animals were being sampled at the incorrect times once production had changed. The animals had already adjusted to imbalanced dietary inputs and had brought their outputs into balance. Thus blood metabolites were normal. Secondly, too much was being expected of the metabolic profile. The control of blood metabolites is complex and results should be interpreted in the light of other information about the animals and their diets, and against a good set of normal values for similar animals are the same stage of lactation.

Early work showed that a random sample of six animals from a group gives a useful picture of the status of the entire group. However the animals sampled must be a truly random selection from the "normal" animals in the group - animals with average yields and no clinically detectable disease or production problems.

Sampling can be determined either according to the animals' stage of production or the time of year. If sampling occurs after a change in diet, it should be remembered that it takes seven to ten days for a cow's rumen to adapt to a new diet and therefore sampling should not occur too soon after the change. Suitable times for sampling include mid-summer; grass quality is starting to decline at this time, and is often insufficient to support high milk yields. Sampling animals allows the production potential of the grass to be determined and the level of supplementation to be determined.

When cows are still out at grass in early autumn, and given a partial winter ration, diet formulation is very difficult as the intake and value of the grass cannot readily be determined. A metabolic profile at this stage allows assumptions of feed intake to be checked and corrective action taken if necessary.

The testing of groups of animals seven to ten days after changing to full winter rations allows the total ration to be assessed and corrective action taken before major problems arise. The introduction of a new feed, such as maize silage, or changing from first to second-cut silage alters the diet considerably. A metabolic profile seven to ten days after a major change in the diet allows the effectiveness of the change to be determined.

High-yielding animals should be sampled three to six weeks post-calving, the time when they are reaching peak yield. These animals should be in negative energy balance, but the point of interest is the extent of the imbalance. Too severe an imbalance and the cows will fail to reach peak yield which will reduce total lactational yield. Too small a deficit indicates a dietary imbalance or over-feeding (for genetic merit) which may result in over-fat cows later in lactation.

In the last two weeks of lactation, protein-related analyses can be dropped in favour of those for calcium and magnesium. Concentration of magnesium should not be low as this impairs calcium mobilisation at calving. Concentration of calcium should be normal or low, indicating that the animal is actively absorbing calcium from the diet and will be capable of mobilising sufficient calcium when she calves.

The ideal blood components are stable in blood samples, easy to measure, vary little in cows in nutritional balance but change widely when imbalances are present. Unfortunately these metabolites do not exist. The following sections consider what blood components can be measured and their relative advantages and disadvantages.

17.5.2   Energy status

Glucose is the most obvious candidate for assessing the energy status of an animal, but it is the least useful. Glucose concentrations are under tight homeostatic control and so rarely change except in extreme circumstances - by which time the problem can be diagnosed clinically. Concentration of glucose does show considerable diurnal variation and concentrations are also elevated by adrenaline which is released in times of stress. Therefore a raised blood concentration of glucose may merely indicate that the animal was difficult to catch! Low blood concentrations of glucose can be interpreted at face value but normal or raised concentrations are more difficult to interpret. Swedish workers have shown that conception rate to first service is significantly higher in animals with a normal plasma glucose content at service (Figure 17.3).

Figure 17.3   Relationship between plasma glucose concentration and conception rate to first service in dairy cows (Plym Forshell, 1994)

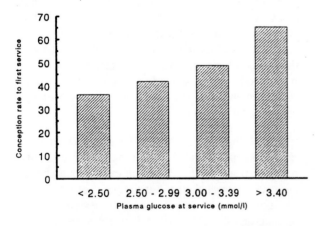

Ketone bodies are produced when glucose requirement outstrips glucose production, intermediate products of energy metabolism are depleted and mobilised energy reserves accumulate. Aceto-acetate is the major ketone body in dairy cows but is unstable in blood samples. Beta-hydroxy-butyrate (βHB)

is more stable in blood and is commonly used, but concentrations of βHB change after a feed so samples should be taken 2 to 3 hours after a major concentrate feed. Raised concentrations of βHB indicate a deficit of energy in the animal (Figure 17.1), but care must be taken to compare results with standards derived from animals at a similar stage of production, since the concentration of βHB rises in early lactation. Low concentrations of βHB indicates that the animal is not mobilising many body reserves which may be regarded as a problem at certain stages of production.

In times of dietary energy deficit, energy reserves (fat deposits) are mobilised and the extent of mobilisation can be assessed by measuring the concentration of non-esterified fatty acids (NEFA) in blood. NEFA are not as easy to measure as glucose or beta-hydroxybutyrate; they show some prandial (meal to meal) and stress-related variation and can decay in stored samples. Raised concentrations of NEFA or free fatty acids (FFA) are indicative of mobilisation of body reserves and should be interpreted in a similar fashion as βHB.

17.5.3   Protein status

The concentration of urea in blood is an indication of the status of the rumen with regard to degradable protein (ERDP) supply. It should be remembered that energy and protein metabolism in the rumen are closely interlinked, thus changes in the concentration of urea in the blood can indicate both an energy and a protein problem. Low blood urea suggests an inadequate supply of nitrogen to the rumen in relation to the amount of energy available, either due to a high FME intake or a low ERDP supply. Such rations will have a low Y (g ERDP/MJ FME) value.

High concentration of urea in the blood is indicative of a high rumen ammonia concentration, with excess ammonia passing into the blood stream and being converted into urea in the liver. Given the high Y value of most grass silages, the concentration of urea in blood is often raised in animals not supplemented with adequate FME. Very high concentration of urea in the blood may be associated with fertility problems.

Albumin is synthesised in the liver and its concentration in blood gives an indication of longer-term protein status. A low albumin and an adequate or low concentration of urea suggests the ration is deficient in both ERDP and DUP. High concentration of urea and low contents of albumin is indicative of an overall shortage of MP due to insufficient supply of DUP and an excess of ERDP that cannot be converted to microbial protein due to a lack of FME. Depressed levels of albumin in the blood can also indicate liver damage (such as liver fluke) or chronic infection (abscesses).

Figure 17.4   Diagrammatic interpretation of energy and protein status by the blood metabolic profile

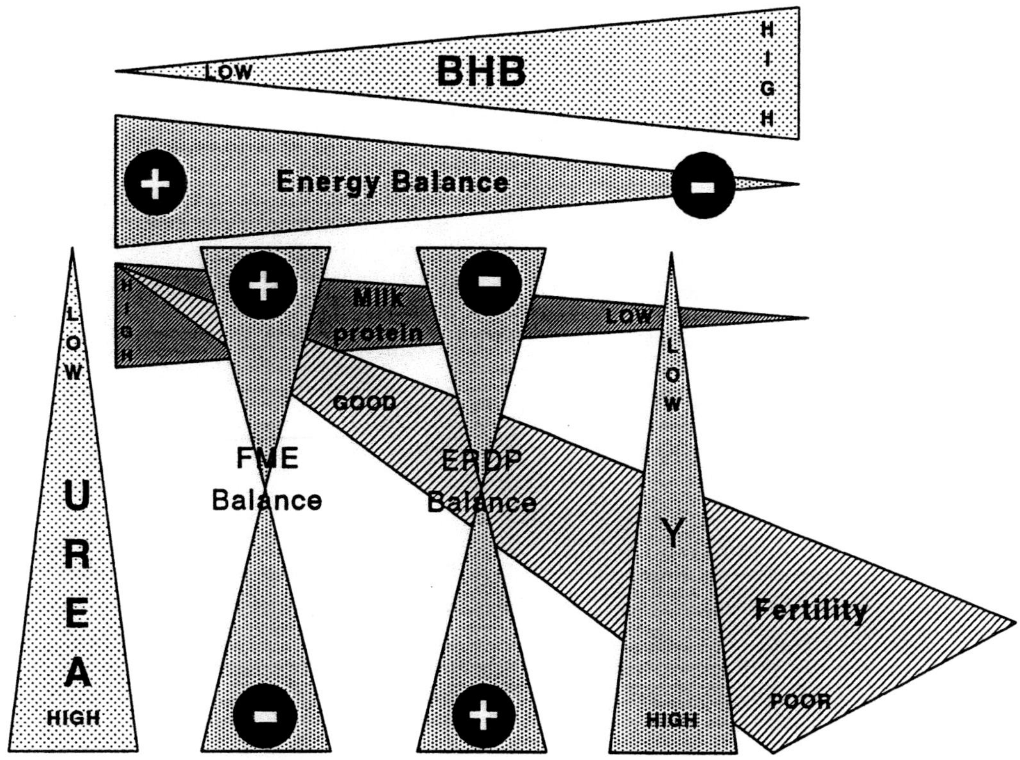

Concentrations of globulin in the blood change very little in response to dietary changes but are raised in infectious diseases and therefore may be used to differentiate nutritional problems from those associated with infections.

Figure 17.4 is a diagrammatic summary of the interpretation of a blood metabolic profile with regard to energy and protein status. High concentrations of βHB indicate a declining energy balance with mobilisation of body reserves. As the energy balance becomes increasingly negative then output of milk protein and reproductive performance are likely to decline. As the concentration of urea in the blood increases a fall in FME and a rise in ERDP in the rumen, associated with a rising Y ratio for the diet, can result in reduced fertility.

17.5.4   Mineral status
As mentioned in Chapter 7 (page 80), the concentration of calcium in the blood is closely controlled and therefore the concentration of calcium in blood is a poor predictor of calcium status. Parathyroid hormone (PTH) is a good indicator of the risk of milk fever, with high concentrations in the dry cows indicating a lower risk of milk fever. However, PTH is not easily measured on a routine basis.

The homeostatic control of magnesium by the animal is poor, therefore a low content of magnesium in blood is a good indicator of staggers (hypomagnesaemia) and of predisposition to milk fever.

Other minerals and trace elements are assessed rarely as part of the routine blood metabolic profile, but if samples are taken for assessment of phosphorus, they must be taken from the tail vein rather than the jugular vein as phosphate losses into the saliva can reduce concentrations of blood from the jugular vein by 20%. Concentrations of trace elements in blood must be interpreted with great care (see Chapter 7), as many do not reflect the true body status and others are very difficult to measure.

Provided that sampling is planned and carried out correctly, metabolic profiles can be very valuable in the nutritional management of a herd. Blood profiles should only be used in conjunction with a full management programme; used in isolation they can give confusing or meaningless results.

17.6   Milk metabolic profiles

Work in Sweden (Plym Forshell, 1994) has assessed the use of milk analyses to determine the metabolic status of the dairy cow. Assessing milk rather than blood has two advantages. Firstly, milk is easier to collect and, on many farms, individual cow samples are collected and analysed on a routine basis. Secondly, because milk is secreted throughout the day there is less variation in its composition during the day than is the case with blood. For the measurement of energy status, acetone seems to be the best indicator as it is the most abundant ketone body in milk, is stable for up to seven days in preserved milk, and shows little diurnal or daily variation. Table 17.3 shows the distribution of milk acetone at different sampling times after calving. Increases in milk acetone are also linked with reduced fertility.

Table 17.3 Distribution (per cent) of acetone concentration in milk samples at different intervals after calving and fertility performance. Values above 0.4 mmol/l are considered to be raised above the normal range (from Plym Forshell, 1994)

	Milk acetone (mmol/l)			
	≤ 0.40	0.41 to 1.00	1.01 to 2.00	≥2.01
Milk test after calving				
1	91.1	6.0	2.1	0.8
2	95.3	3.1	1.1	0.5
3	98.9	0.7	0.3	0.1
Days from calving to first service	81.2	85.1	85.6	89.6
Days from calving to conception	103.5	110.4	112.3	116.5
Ovarian cysts (% cows)	0.98	1.75	2.93	4.11

Table 17.4 Possible nutritional interpretation of milk acetone and urea concentrations at different stages of lactation (Plym Forshell, 1994)

	Milk urea (mmol/l)		
	Low	Moderate	High
Early lactation (Days 1 to 50)			
Acetone			
	<3.5	3.5 to 6.0	>6.0
Normal (< 0.7 mmol/l)	Low ERDP	All OK	Excess ERDP
Moderate (0.7 to 1.4 mmol/l)	Low ERDP + FME	Low FME	Low FME Excess ERDP
High (> 1.4 mmol/l)	Low ERDP + FME + poss low DUP	Low FME + poss low DUP	Low FME + poss low DUP Excess ERDP
Mid-lactation (Days 51 to 110)			
	<3.5	3.5 to 5.5	>5.5
	Low ERDP	All OK	Excess ERDP + poss low FME
Late lactation			
	<3.0	3.0 to 6.5	>6.5
	Low ERDP	All OK	Excess ERDP + poss low FME

There was also a significant relationship between the concentration of acetone in the milk and milk yield. Cows with concentrations of acetone in milk greater than 1.4 mmol/litre in weeks two to five of lactation yielded 10 to 20% less milk than contemporary animals with milk acetone contents less than 0.4 mmol/l.

Concentration of urea in the milk can be used to assess the protein metabolism of the cow in a similar manner to assessment of urea in the blood, and is a good indicator of the balance between FME and ERDP supply.

A possible nutritional interpretation of a milk metabolic profile of acetone and urea is outlined in Table 17.4.

17.7 Fertility records

Unless good records are kept, fertility analysis is usually too historic for routine ration assessment. However if submission rates and/or conception rates are monitored over time and dietary changes are super-imposed on these charts then it may be possible to associate periods of poor fertility with nutritional problems.

17.8 Faeces

The dung-pat is what the cow has not digested and therefore it should be able to tell us something about the diet she has consumed. The shape of the dung-pat is influenced by the amount and type of indigestible fibre in the diet. A highly fibrous diet produces a tall, pyramid shaped dung-pat (Figure 175), for example as are often produced by dry cows given a diet high in straw. Rumen retention time is relatively high on high-fibre diets, hence feed intake tends to be lower than for diets which contain lower amounts of indigestible fibre.

A diet deficient in fibre is associated with the production of flat dung-pats with little or no structure (Figure 17.5). This type is seen in cows grazing spring grass. Milk production is high but the low intake of fibre is associated with depressed saliva flow and a low ratio of acetate to propionate in the rumen and a depressed concentration of fat in milk. The correct balance is shown in the middle diagram in Figure 17.5. The dung-pat forms a gently curved mound and the last drop leaves a small depression in the top of the pat, into which a flower could be placed! Cows housed on concrete should sound as if they are giving a slow handclap when producing this type of dung-pat, which is indicative of the correct fibre intake and an acceptable rate of passage of digesta through the alimentary tract.

Figure 17.5 Profiles of dung-pats

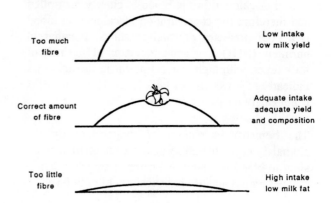

Too much fibre — Low intake low milk yield

Correct amount of fibre — Adequate intake adequate yield and composition

Too little fibre — High intake low milk fat

CHAPTER 18

PRACTICAL DIET FORMULATION

18.1 Introduction

18.2 What are the animals' nutritional requirements?

18.3 Determining the diet to be offered

18.4 Dry matter intake

18.5 Metabolisable energy supply and requirements

18.6 Protein supply and requirements

18.7 Mineral supply and requirements

18.8 Additional nutritional considerations

18.9 Comparison with computer-formulated nutrient supply and requirements

18.10 On-farm calculation of animal requirements

18.11 Case studies
    18.11.1 Case study 1 - low milk fat
    18.11.2 Case study 2 - low milk protein
    18.11.3 Case study 3 - gaining weight, not achieving yield

18.12 Manual exercises

18.13 Computer exercises

18.1 Introduction

The formulation of a ration for a dairy cow using a simple calculator and the tables given in Chapter 20 (pages 204 to 223) is outlined in this chapter. To aid the work the same example will be used throughout: a group of Friesian/Holstein cows in mid-lactation giving 28 litres of milk a day given a ration based on grass silage and three supplementary feeds. The supplements have been chosen to illustrate their different nutritional properties.

The imprecision and uncertainties in assessing feeds and animal requirements mean that formulating rations is, and will remain, an art as well as a science. It is therefore essential that the animals are inspected and assessed (Chapter 17). Formulating rations without visiting the farm or according to fixed "blueprints" will invariably omit factors and result in a poorer ration.

Ration formulation is complex. It is tempting to rely totally on tables or computers to assess animal needs and the adequacy of the ration and to treat a visit to the farm merely as an information-gathering exercise. It is important, however, that some assessment of the requirements of the animals and of their diet is made on-farm. Manual (back of envelope) calculations of the requirements of the animals is possible and whilst it will lack the precision of a computer-based assessment, it is often sufficient to help shape the identification of problems on-farm and is considered in Section 18.9.

18.2 What are the animals' nutritional requirements?

The first stage in any ration formulation exercise is to determine, as precisely as possible, the details of the group of animals for which the ration is being formulated. This should be the average of a group of at least ten cows. The nutritional predictions considered in earlier chapters are for the average performance of a group of animals rather than an individual. When investigating a nutrition problem on-farm it is important to remember that the cows will have adapted to any nutritional deficiencies by modifying their output of milk or liveweight change. Therefore, using actual performance data fails to identify any shortfalls in the ration. It is therefore important to formulate the ration to the desired performance rather than what is actually being achieved. The information required to ensure the accurate prediction of the performance of a diet are:

Liveweight. The weight of the cow is a major factor in determining voluntary dry matter intake and hence nutrient requirements. The degree of fatness of the animal should be assessed as fat deposits are reflected in increased body weight. The volume of the gut probably has a greater effect on intake than actual body weight, but, unfortunately, the relationship between gut volume and weight has changed since the predictive equations were derived. Such complications result in many advisors using a fixed weight for different types of cattle with 650 kg commonly being the assumed weight of Holstein cows and 600 kg for Friesians.

Great care must be taken not to overestimate body weight as overestimation raises predicted voluntary intake. This lowers the required density of nutrients in the total diet, making it easier to formulate to meet requirements. The liveweight of the animals in this example is 600 kg.

Milk yield. Daily yields of milk of individual cows vary considerably. The average yield for a group over a period of at least a week should be used as the yield for formulation purposes. In many cases farmers ration to achieve a level of milk production to match their quota. The target milk yield in this example is 28 litres/day.

Milk composition. The composition of milk, the requirements of the cow for both energy and protein and the content of fat and protein (to a lesser extent) in milk can vary from farm to farm and from week to week. Most farmers are paid according to the content of fat and protein of the milk, and hence these parameters are readily available for formulation purposes. The lactose concentration in the milk is not widely reported, but, although it influences requirements of energy to synthesise milk, it rarely alters from 4.6%. This is used as a standard value. If the average herd milk composition is being used (as obtained from the milk recording sheets) it should be remembered that composition changes with stage of lactation (Figure 17.2). High-yielding cows tend to have a lower level of milk solids in milk than low-yielding cows. This is important for the rationing of high-yielding cows as a small reduction in level of milk solids can have a significant effect on total requirements for energy. Where possible, composition of milk should be considered only for the group in question, rather than the whole herd. The composition of milk cited in the example is 4.1% fat, 3.3% protein and 4.6% lactose.

Weight change. If a cow is losing or gaining weight this affects her nutrient requirements. In very high-yielding animals some weight loss early in lactation is inevitable because the cow cannot consume sufficient to meet her requirements. The amount of nutrients required to support growth or available as the result of mobilisation of tissues depends on the amount of tissue involved and the composition of that tissue.

The assessment of how much body tissue is involved in gain or loss is difficult at farm level for several reasons. Firstly, most farmers are unable to weigh their cows. Secondly, the weight of a cow changes during the day when she is milked (10 to 20 kg each milking), drinks (up to 20 kg at a time), eats, urinates or defecates. With these changes in weight the daily weight of the dairy cow varies more than any expected weight change caused by diet or physiological change.

A further complication is the development of the calf and uterus during pregnancy and changes in the water content in the body. Therefore it is not possible to measure the amount of tissue being laid down or mobilised in the short term (10 to 20 days) on the farm. Most nutritionists therefore work within the "expected" changes in weight as outlined in Table 18.1. In general, cows lose weight in the first third of lactation, maintain (or slightly gain) weight in the second period and then re-gain the lost weight in the last third of lactation. Therefore there is no net weight change over the complete lactation.

The cows in the example cited are expected to lose 0.5 kg/day.

Stage of pregnancy. The requirements for energy and protein to support the growth of the foetus increase exponentially during pregnancy. Nutrient requirements are also dependent on the birth weight of the calf and thus the breed of bull. The cows cited in the example are 5 weeks pregnant and in calf to a Holstein bull, so the expected calf weight is at term 40 kg.

Table 18.1 Expected daily weight change (kg/day) of milking cows with different potential lactation yields

Period of lactation	High yield >7,000 litres/year	Moderate yield 5,000 to 7,000 litres/year	Low yield <5,000 litres/year
0 to 100 days	-0.7	-0.5	-0.3
101 to 200 days	0	0	0
201 to 305 days	0.7	0.5	0.3
Dry period	0	0	0

Stage of lactation. The stage of lactation affects the voluntary feed intake of the cow (Figure 8.6, page 99). By knowing the stage of lactation, the nutritionist can estimate the expected weight change (Table 18.1) and the daily milk yield (Figure 14.3, page 136). The cows in this example are in the 15th week.

Feed intake. As mentioned in Chapters 4 and 8, the voluntary feed intake of a cow is difficult to predict and is influenced by a wide range of factors that cannot be quantified easily on-farm (Table 8.1, page 98). It is important, therefore, that both the cows and the feeding system are assessed to determine how the predicted intake may need to be modified. The cows in the example are given maize gluten in the parlour and wheat and soyabean meal sprinkled on top of grass silage in the trough.

Activity level. As mentioned in Chapter 1 (page 3) activities such as walking, standing up and lying down require energy. An allowance for these activities is included within the requirements of energy for maintenance. The allowance varies with the degree of activity, for instance the allowance is greater for animals grazing extensive pasture than for those on lowland pastures (Chapter 9, page 103).

Condition score. Although the condition score of the animal is not taken into account in any of the predictions made in earlier chapters, it is likely to influence how rations are formulated. Fat cows tend to have a lower intake than thin cows (Figure 4.1, page 42) and the amount of condition the cow carries influences the target weight changes used in diet formulation. A strategy of using diets high in DUP might allow the cow to utilise her body reserves for milk production. The cows cited in the example are in condition score 2.0.

The cow details required in the example cited below are summarised in Table 18.2.

Table 18.2 An example of the animal parameters required to determine nutrient requirements

Parameter	Example	Comment
Body weight	600 kg	At condition score 2.5
Milk yield	28 l	Target to meet quota constraints
Milk composition		
Fat	4.1%	Required target for
Protein	3.3%	composition of
Lactose	4.6%	milk produced
Weight change	-0.5 kg/day	Desired weight loss at the stage of lactation
Stage of pregnancy	5 weeks	
Stage of lactation	15 weeks	Affects voluntary intake
Dry matter intake correction	1.0	Effect of method of presentation of the diet
Activity level	Low	Housed cattle
Condition score	2.0	Group average

18.3 Determining the diet to be offered

After the animal data have been collected, the next stage in ration formulation is to determine what feeds are being used, what other feeds are available and what additional feeds the farmer might consider buying in. In all but a few situations a formulated ration is already being used or firm commitments have been made to use certain feeds (usually forages). Therefore formulation of a new ration is often a process of assessing a basic ration and making the necessary alterations and additions that will be acceptable to the farmer and result in a high-quality diet to achieve the farmer's production target. Designing diets from scratch and the pros and cons of different systems of feeding are discussed in Chapter 12 (pages 124 to 126).

Forages. Forages, either fresh or conserved, form the basis of the ration and various supplements are required to match the requirements of animals to the nutrients supplied in the diet. The quality of the forages should be assessed by analysis in a laboratory and by inspection on the farm. The quantity available and being consumed at the time of inspection should also be assessed, using the methods described in Chapter 12 (page 123). The cows in this example are being offered 40 kg grass silage fresh weight a day (dry matter content 27%) with a ME content of 10.4 MJ/kg DM and a crude protein content of 150 g/kg DM.

Supplements. The supplements being used in the existing ration, or planned to be used, should be assessed. This again should be both a visual inspection as well as an assessment based on laborat-

ory analyses. Where compound feeds are being used, every effort should be made to obtain either a detailed compositional analysis of the feed or a declaration of the ingredients and their level of inclusion in the feed. Whilst this may be regarded as commercially-sensitive information by the feed compounder, most are willing to make the data available to *bona fide* clients upon request. If this information is not available, formulation of the ration may become grossly inaccurate. Where straights are being used in diets, many nutritionists use standard textbook figures (Table 20.21). Individual batches of feeds can vary from the figures cited in the textbooks, and where a feed contributes more than 2 kg of DM to the ration it is advisable to have it analysed for its principle nutrient.

As well as determining the nutritive composition of the feeds offered, the amount the farmer intends to feed and any constraints on these amounts should be noted. In this example the farmer intends to feed 4 kg of rolled wheat grain and 1 kg soyabean meal on the top of the grass silage, with maize gluten feed in the parlour at 3 kg a day for 28 litres milk.

Additional feeds. In many instances, additional feeds may be required to optimise the quality of the ration. By discussion with the farmer it should be possible to identify what the farmer can (and wants) to feed and what is not practical. For example, can liquid feeds such as molasses be handled? How many straights can be stored? Can such feeds be weighed accurately?

The feeds, their basic chemical composition and method of presentation used in the example are summarised in Table 18.3.

Table 18.3 Basic nutritive data

	Intake (kg fresh weight/day)	DM (%)	ME (MJ/kg DM)	CP (g/kg DM)	Presen-tation
Grass silage (average)	40	27	10.4	151	In troughs
Soyabean meal	1	88	13.4	507	On silage
Wheat grain	4	87	13.6	123	On silage
Maize gluten feed	3	89	12.7	232	In parlour

18.4 Dry matter intake

To predict the voluntary intake of a milking cow we need to know the liveweight of the animal, milk yield and quality of the ration. The quality of the ration (q) is not known, so this needs to be calculated by determining the total ME and GE (Table 20.21) supplied by the feeds shown in Table 18.3. The calculations are illustrated in Table 18.4.

Table 18.4 Calculating dietary ME and GE supplied by a ration and the calculation of q (ME/GE)

	Intake kg	DM %	DMI kg	ME MJ/kg DM	GE MJ/kg DM	ME intake MJ/day	GE intake MJ/day
Grass silage (average)	40.0	27	10.6	10.4	19.5	110.2	206.7
Soyabean meal	1.0	88	0.88	13.4	19.7	11.8	17.3
Wheat grain	4.0	87	3.48	13.6	18.2	47.3	63.3
Maize gluten feed	3.0	89	2.67	12.7	19.0	33.9	50.7
TOTAL	48.0		17.6			203.2	338.0

$$q = 203.2/338.0 = 0.60$$

Given the ration quality (0.6), and consulting Table 20.1 and interpolating between the two milk yields given, gives an initial predicted intake of 17.8 kg DM/day. The cows are in the fifteenth week of lactation, hence the correction factor for intake is 1.00 (Table 20.2) and the method of feeding is such that it will not influence voluntary intake (Table 20.3). The final prediction of voluntary intake is therefore 17.8 kg DM/day. This compares well with the expected intake of 17.6 kg/day (Table 18.4), so it is likely the animal will consume all of this ration presented. Further calculations are therefore worthwhile.

If the intake of feed *ad libitum* is not known then an estimate has to be made. The estimate is used to calculate the quality of the ration and hence the predicted voluntary intake. This can then be used to re-estimate the intake of the *ad libitum* feed from the observed intake. If the first two estimates of the intake of the feed offered *ad libitum* are within 5%, then, for the purpose of manual calculations, the second estimate can be used with little loss in accuracy.

18.5 Metabolisable energy supply and requirements

As mentioned in Chapter 5, the calculation of ME requirements is initially carried out in a factorial manner, considering requirements for maintenance, lactation, pregnancy and weight change individually using Tables 20.5 to 20.9 and then correcting the total requirement for the level of production (Table 20.10).

Table 18.5 Calculating ME requirements

		ME (MJ)	Source
Maintenance	600 kg	61.9	Table 20.5, page 206
Lactation	28 l at 4.1% fat and 3.3% protein	146.0	Table 20.6, page 207
Pregnancy	5 weeks	0.3	Table 20.7, page 208
Weight change	-0.5 kg/day	-11.0	Table 20.8, page 208
Activity	Low	0	Table 20.9, page 209
TOTAL		197.2 MJ ME/day	
$APL = ME_{total}/ME_{maint} = 197.2/61.9 = 3.19$			Chapter 9, page 104
$C_L = 1.04$			Table 20.10, page 209
ME requirements = 197.2 x 1.04 = 205			Chapter 9, page 104

The calculation of ME requirements are shown in Table 18.5. The total energy requirement of the cow of 205 MJ ME is almost the same as the supply of 203.2 MJ ME from the ration.

18.6 Protein supply and requirements

Protein supply. Protein supply is determined by the content of crude protein and the degradability of the protein of the feed at the given level of animal production (APL). As we already know the APL (3.19 - Table 18.5), we can use Table 20.22 to determine the amount of ERDP and DUP supplied per kg of DM, and by using the predicted dry matter intake for each feed calculated in Table 18.3 we can determine the amount of ERDP and DUP supplied by the ration (Table 18.6). The amount of microbial protein (MCP) produced in the rumen is dependent on the amount of protein (ERDP) available for synthesis, the amount of available fermentable energy (FME) and the rate of outflow of microbial biomass from the rumen. The amount of FME in each feed can be determined from Table 20.22 and hence the total supply of FME can be calculated (Table 18.6). The value for Y at an APL of 3.19 is 11.0 (Table 20.22).

The next stage is to determine how much microbial protein (MCP) will be produced in the rumen. Protein synthesis will be limited by either the supply of energy or protein to the microbes. If energy is limiting:

$$
\begin{aligned}
MCP_{energy\ limiting} &= Y \times FME \\
&= 11.0 \times 164.9 = 1814\ g \\
&\text{(Chapter 10, page 109)}
\end{aligned}
$$

If protein is limiting then the MCP synthesised will be:

$$
\begin{aligned}
MCP_{protein\ limiting} &= ERDP \\
&= 1942.8\ g \\
&\text{(Chapter 10, page 109)}
\end{aligned}
$$

Table 18.6 Calculating ERDP, DUP and FME supply

	DMI	ERDP	ERDP supply	DUP	DUP supply	FME	FME supply
	kg	g/kg DM	g/day	g/kg DM	g/day	MJ/kg DM	MJ/day
Grass silage 65D	10.6	93.6	992.2	18.5	196.1	7.6	80.6
Soyabean meal	0.88	259.4	228.3	194.3	174.0	12.8	11.2
Wheat grain	3.48	99.9	347.7	13.2	45.9	13.1	45.6
Maize gluten feed	2.67	140.3	374.6	29.4	75.5	10.3	27.5
TOTAL			1942.8		491.5		164.9

Microbial protein synthesis in the rumen is therefore limited by available fermentable energy (FME). 1814 g MCP will pass out of the rumen daily. Only 0.64 of the MCP is true protein that is absorbed in the small intestine (Chapter 10, page 109) and hence the total MP supplied by the ration is:

(1814 x 0.64) + 491.5 = 1652 g (Chapter 10, page 109)

This ration is deficient in FME as there is 1943 g ERDP which could have been fixed as MCP but there was only sufficient FME to fix 1814 g. This is typical of rations based on grass silage because they are low in FME (only 0.74 of ME in this case) and high in ERDP.

Protein requirements. The MP requirement of the animals is calculated according to the requirements for maintenance, lactation, pregnancy and weight change (Table 18.7).

Table 18.7 Calculation of metabolisable protein requirements for cows (g/day)

		MP (g/day)	Source
Maintenance	600 kg	293	Table 20.11, page 210
Lactation	28 l at 3.3% protein	1316	Table 20.12, page 210
Pregnancy	5 weeks	1	Table 20.13, page 211
Weight change	-0.5 kg/day	-66	Table 20.14, page 211
TOTAL		1544	

The requirement of MP by the cow of 1544 g/day compares to a supply of MP from the ration of 1652 g/day. Therefore there is a surplus of 108 g MP/day or 7% of requirements.

18.7 Mineral supply and requirements

As mentioned previously it is only worth calculating the supply and requirements of calcium, magnesium and phosphorus on a regular basis; the requirements for the trace elements are influenced by so many other factors that it is very difficult to calculate requirements.

Mineral supply. These are calculated from the dry matter intake of each feed together with their mineral composition (Table 20.21). The mineral content of each feed and the amounts supplied in the ration are shown in Table 18.8.

Mineral requirements. Mineral requirements are calculated as the sum of the requirements for maintenance, milk production, pregnancy and weight change (Table 18.9). To determine the maintenance requirements of calcium we need to know the dry matter intake (17.8 kg) and for phosphorus we also need to know the ration quality (q = 0.6).

18.8 Additional nutritional considerations

Given the limitations and inadequacies of the ME and MP systems at identifying optimal formulations (see Chapter 5, page 59, and Chapter 6, page 74, respectively), many advisors also look at the total fibre (NDF) in the diet, content of fat, combined contents of sugar and starch and content of crude protein, each expressed as a percentage of the total dry matter intake (Table 18.10). The feed analyses have been obtained from Table 20.21.

Table 18.8 Calculating mineral supply

	DMI kg	Ca g/kg DM	Ca supply g/day	P g/kg DM	P supply g/day	Mg g/kg DM	Mg supply g/day
Grass silage (average)	10.6	6.8	72.1	3.1	32.9	1.6	17.0
Soyabean meal	0.88	4.5	4.0	7.6	6.7	2.9	2.6
Wheat grain	3.48	0.6	2.1	3.4	11.8	1.1	3.8
Maize gluten feed	2.67	2.8	7.5	10.0	26.7	4.3	11.5
TOTAL			85.7		78.1		34.9

Table 18.9 Calculating mineral requirements

		Ca (g/day)	P (g/day)	Mg (g/day)	Source
Maintenance	600 g, DMI	23.1	33.9	11.1	Tables 20.15, 20.16 and
	17.8 kg, q = 0.6				20.17, pages 212, 212 and 213
Lactation	28 l milk	51.0	44.8	22.5	Table 20.18, page 213
Pregnancy	5 weeks	0.1	0.0	0.0	Table 20.19, pages 215 to 219
Weight change	-0.5 kg/day	-7.4	-5.1	-1.4	Table 20.20, pages 219 to 223
Total requirements		66.8	73.6	32.2	
Supply		85.7	78.1	34.9	Table 18.8
Balance		18.9	4.5	2.7	

The diet is therefore adequate in all three major minerals.

Table 18.10 Calculating fibre (NDF), fat, starch, sugar and crude protein in the ration

	DMI kg	NDF g/kg DM	NDF supply g/day	Fat g/kg DM	Fat supply g/day	Starch g/kg DM	Starch supply g/day	Sugar g/kg DM	Sugar supply g/day	CP g/kg DM	CP supply g/day
Grass silage (average)	10.6	546	5788	35	371	7	76	17	180	151	1601
Soyabean meal	0.88	154	136	16	14	11	10	107	94	507	446
Wheat grain	3.48	166	578	19	66	660	2297	58	202	123	428
Maize gluten feed	2.67	390	1041	34	91	151	403	21	56	232	619
TOTAL	17.8		7543		542		2786		532		3094
As per cent of DMI			42%		3.0%		15.6%		3.0%		17.4%

The ration content of the different energy fractions and crude protein content can be compared to the figures given in Table 5.6 (page 59). The NDF content of 42% is sufficient to support a healthy rumen and high concentrations of milk fat. However, if the silage is precision-chopped none of the feeds will be supplying a source of long fibre so the cows should be observed for cudding and dung-pat consistency. The fat content is low at 3.0% so should not interfere with rumen function. Similarly the combined sugar and starch content (18.6%) is within acceptable bounds (12 to 22%) so that the rumen should not suffer from acidosis but milk protein should be high. The crude protein content is 17.4% which is high enough to maintain intakes but not so high as to increase the demands on the liver.

18.9   Comparison with computer-formulated nutrient supply and requirements

The above ration can also be formulated using the computer program distributed with this book (see Chapter 19 for further details) and can be found as number 17 in the stored rations under the title of "Chapter 18 - running example". Table 18.11 summarises the computer formulated ration. Various comparisons are worthy of note. The total energy requirements are the same. The requirements for each nutritional commitment seem much higher in the computer version but this is because each commit-

ment has been corrected for C_L individually so that the total makes mathematical sense.

The supply of ERDP and DUP estimated by the computer differs considerably; this is because we had to estimate the ERDP and DUP supply at APL = 3.28 from the values given in Table 20.22. The MP requirements differ by only 2 g. The mineral requirements estimated manually and by the computer differ slightly. Similarly the amount of fibre (NDF), fat, crude protein and sugars and starches are very similar. However despite the differences between the two sets of figures the nutritional conclusions are very similar. It is probable that in most cases the size of any error incurred by manual calculations using the tables in this book will be smaller than that likely to result in a clinical lack of performance.

The requirement for NDF is the amount needed to make up 40% of the total DMI. The requirement for ERDP is that needed to allow all the FME to be utilised and the requirement for FME is that needed to allow the microbes to fix all of the ERDP. It follows that either FME or ERDP will be in deficit and the other in surplus; it is the size of the surplus/deficit that matters. Trial work at ADAS Bridgets suggests that imbalances of ERDP and FME less than 10% of requirements are not important as they do not affect the cow's performance.

Some of the additions and subtractions in the table may seem wrong but the computer is working to a far greater degree of accuracy than is shown.

Table 18.11 Results from ration formulated by the computer program

Requirements	Energy MJ ME	Protein g MP	Ca g	P g	Mg g
Maintenance	64	293	23	34	11
Lactation	151	1313	48	45	22
Pregnancy	0	1	0	0	0
Liveweight change	-11	-66	-7	-5	-1
Totals	204	1542	64	73	32

Ration assessment	Fresh weight (kg)	DMI kg	ME MJ	FME MJ	NDF g	ERDP g	DUP g	Ca g	P g	Mg g
Average silage	40	10.6	110	86	5788	1070	218	72	33	17
Maize gluten feed	3	2.7	34	31	1041	418	93	7	27	11
Wheat grain	4	3.5	47	45	578	334	45	2	12	4
Soyabean meal ext.	1	0.88	12	11	136	235	173	4	7	3
Totals	48	17.6	203	173	7542	2066	522	85	78	35
Requirements		17.8	204	187	7052	1905	328	64	73	32
Balance		-0.2	-1	-15	490	161	194	22	5	3

Protein balance		Additional nutrients	
MP supply	= 1740g	NDF	43% of DM
MP requirements	= 1542g	Fat	3 % of DM
Surplus	= 198g/day	Starch	16 % of DM
		Sugar	3 % of DM
		Crude protein	17.6 % of DM

18.10 On-farm calculation of animal requirements

As mentioned previously the ability to be able to calculate a cow's requirements on-farm is important to allow early targeting of farm problems. Poor performance can be due to a wide range of factors such as management, disease, genetics and nutrition and it is important to try and determine what is the likely cause of the poor performance whilst on the farm. This allows one to concentrate on the major area of poor performance in greater detail increasing the likelihood of resolving the problem. To be of maximum benefit it should be possible to carry out such estimations manually using only a scrap of paper and mental arithmetic. Whilst this reduces the sophistication of the assessments it is surprising how often these help identify the problems.

Dry matter intake. The probable dry matter intake can be assessed according to the animal's weight and milk yield. The simplest equation is 3% of live weight which gives an intake of 18 kg for a 600 kg cow. It should be remembered that this is the weight of the cow when she is barren and at condition score 2.5 which may not be the same as the actual weight of animals that are sold off the farm. Milk yield also has a major influence on intake; the predicted intake of a milking cow is 2.5% of body weight plus 10% of milk yield. Therefore for the 600 kg cow giving 28 litres of milk the intake is 15 + 2.8 = 17.8 kg DM and this declines by one kilogram for every 10 litres less milk. When the two calculations give different answers the lower value should be taken as this is the major limitation on intake.

The effects of ration quality (q) and presentation are generally too complex to determine precisely but if animals are on poor quality forages intake should be reduced and careful examination of the method of feeding should be used to further modify the intake. Similarly the effect of stage of lactation is also too complex to apply on farm but a downward adjustment should be made for fresh calvers. When a final figure has been derived this can be compared to the expected intake of feed as calculated in Chapter 8 (page 96).

Table 18.12 Simplified estimates of energy requirements of high- and medium-yielding Friesian/Holstein cows

Main-tenance	say	70 MJ ME for 600 kg cow	
		Less for smaller animals	8 MJ/100 kg
		More on poor quality rations	3 MJ per 0.1 fall in q
Milk production	say	5 MJ ME / litre of milk	
		Less if butter fat under 4%	0.7 MJ/% unit
		More if protein over 3.2%	0.8 MJ/% unit
Weight change	say	30 MJ ME/kg weight change	

Energy. The predicted energy requirements of a cow are dependent on her liveweight, productive state (milk yield, stage of pregnancy, weight change), the nutritional composition of such products and the quality of the ration. Whilst a full consideration is complex (see section 18.5 above) for high- and medium-yielding Friesian/Holstein cows several simplifications can be made as shown in Table 18.12. For such animals ration quality is usually good, milk composition can be taken as constant and the requirements of pregnancy can be ignored.

For a 600 kg cow giving 28 litre of milk and loosing 0.5 kg a day the total requirements will be

$$70 + (28 \times 5) - (0.5 \times 30) = 70 + 140 - 15 = 195 \text{ MJ ME}$$

This figure should be corrected for the level of production (C_L) and for this animal it is about 4% which adds about 8 MJ ME to give a total of 203 MJ, which compares very well with the estimate made in Section 18.5.

Once the intake and energy requirements have been estimated it is possible to estimate the required energy density. For the example used in this chapter the intake is 17.8 kg DM/day and the energy requirement about 203 MJ/day and therefore each kilogram of intake needs to contain, on average, 203/17.8 MJ ME. Such divisions are usually too difficult to perform in the head but it can be deduced that the answer will be between 11.3 and 11.5 MJ ME/kg DM. This can either be compared with the average energy density of the ration or, more simply, with the energy contents of the principle ingredients in the ration. For example to achieve an average energy density of 11.3 with a ration based on grass silage of 10.4 ME will require considerable supplementation with a cake of 12.5 ME and there will be little call for low energy feeds such as straw or poor hay.

Protein. The metabolisable protein system is too complex to perform calculations by mental arithmetic. However it should be possible to estimate the requirement for crude protein which is usually a good indicator. Suggested crude protein targets are given in Table 18.13.

Table 18.13 Suggested crude protein requirements of dairy cows

Milk production (litres/day)	Estimated crude protein requirement (% of DMI)
40	19
30	18
20	17
10	16
Dry	15

The estimated protein requirements can be compared to the ration ingredients in the same was as the energy density. For example a cow giving 30 litres milk a day requires considerable protein supplementation if she is given a ration based on maize silage (90 g CP/kg DM) and grass silage (140 g CP/kg DM). In certain feeds such as grass silage the majority of the crude protein is quickly degradable (QDP) and the amount of protein supplied should be downgraded. Reducing the protein content of high-protein silages (over 14% CP) by 1.0 to 1.5 % CP in manual calculations has been suggested as a crude way of improving the estimate of the crude protein balance.

The numerical assessment of minerals, fat, fibre and sugars and starches is usually beyond most people's powers of mental arithmetic but it can be assessed subjectively by considering the ingredients in the ration and by observing the cow and her dung

18.11   Case studies

The reader is now in a position to apply the information presented in this and previous chapters. This section contains three case studies on manipulating milk composition and yield. The basic problems are laid out here and possible solutions are presented in Chapter 19 (pages 199 to 201). The rations are also stored on the enclosed floppy disc. As with many nutritional problems there is no one "correct" solution and this is reflected in the answers given. For each case study a farm scenario has been given and it is important that the solution should fit within the scenario; a small farmer may not be able to cope with many straight feeds and a complete diet feeder may not to want to pay an extra cost for compound feeds. For each case study it is recommended that you assess the basic ration and work out both the reason for the problem and the reason why it has occurred before going on to propose a solution.

When assessing problem rations it is best to assess the original ration against the desired performance to identify the problem. By the time the farmer notices the under-performance the cows have adjusted to the ration fed and actual performance will often match actual intakes.

Suggested approach
- Assess the case history and see if the feeding system can be linked to the nutritional problem on history alone.

- Set up or retrieve the original ration on the computer and identify the dietary problem.

- Determine the nutritional pathway by which the problem has arisen. This will equip you better to determine suitable solutions.

- Formulate an alternative ration that also overcomes the nutritional deficiencies. In some cases it may be advisable to formulate several solutions and then consider which one will best fit the system on the farm.

18.11.1 Case study 1 - low milk fat
Case history
Mr Jones has a small council farm in Somerset of 18 hectares (45 acres) and milks 50 cows through a 3:6 abreast milking parlour with simple in-parlour feeding and easy-feed silage from ring feeders. He complains that although his cows are milking well the milk fat is down on last year and is well below the 4.0% minimum that his buyer is requesting and unless he can raise it he will be penalised in the near future. Assess his diet and determine what is the nutritional problem. What do you recommend he alters?

Animal Description
Weight	650 kg
Weight change	-0.5 kg
Milk Yield	30 litres
Current condition score	2.5
Activity level	Low
Time post calving	10 weeks
DMI Correction	1.0
Stage of pregnancy	0 weeks

Milk quality	**Actual**	**Desired**
Fat (%)	3.5	4.0
Protein (%)	3.2	3.2

Ration
Poor silage	*ad libitum*
Compound 18% CP	14.0 kg

18.11.2 Case study 2 - low milk protein
Case history
Mr Ffloyd has a mixed farm of 140 hectares (345 acres) in Pembrokeshire and milks 100 cows through a 10:10 herringbone milking parlour with in-parlour feeding. He complains that although his cows are milking well the milk quality is down on last year. Initially he was feeding silage and cake with some straw being taken from the cubicles and he thought that the poor milk protein was due to his poor quality silage limiting intake so he added molasses (1 kg) to increase the palatability. This did not solve the problem so he started feeding 0.5 kg of soya as a mid-day feed by sprinkling it on top of the silage in round feeders but the problem remained. Assess his diet, what is the nutritional problem and what do you recommend he alters?

Animal Description
Weight	650 kg
Weight change	-0.3 kg
Milk Yield	30 litres
Current condition score	2.5
Activity level	Low
Time post calving	15 weeks
DMI Correction	1.0
Stage of pregnancy	6 weeks

Milk quality	**Actual**	**Desired**
Fat (%)	4.0	4.0
Protein (%)	2.9	3.2

Ration
Poor grass silage	*ad libitum*
Spring barley straw	0.5 kg
Compound 18% CP	8.0 kg
Molasses Cane	1.0 kg
Soyabean meal	0.5 kg

18.11.3 Case study 3 - gaining weight, not achieving yield
Case history
Mr Smith farms 423 hectares (1045 acres) in Dorset and milks 180 cows through a 20:20 low level herringbone milking parlour. He feeds no concentrates in parlour but uses a mixer wagon to make a complete diet which is offered outside in troughs. He complains that although the milk quality is better than last year his cows are not achieving their potential yield and do not seem to have lost the weight they usually do by this stage of lactation. Last year he grew maize for the first time and fed about 10 kg/day/cow through the winter together with *ad libitum* grass silage and the animals performed well. He found that maize suited his thin chalky soils better than grass as it was more drought tolerant, so this year he grew enough to feed 35 kg/cow/day and kept the rest of the ration the same. Assess his diet, what are the nutritional problems and what do you recommend he alters?

Desired Animal Description
Weight	600 kg
Target weight change	-0.5 kg
Target Milk Yield	35 litres.
Current condition score	2.5
Activity level	Minimal
Time post calving	15 weeks
DMI Correction	1.2
Stage of pregnancy	6 weeks

Milk quality	**Actual**	**Desired**
Fat (%)	4.0	4.0
Protein (%)	3.2	3.2

Ration made up in mixer wagon to give
Average Grass Silage	*ad libitum*
Maize silage	last year 10 kg
	this year 35 kg
Sp barley straw	0.5
Molasses cane	1.2
Caustic wheat	3
Sugar beet feed	2
Rapeseed meal	2
Soyabean meal	0.7
Minerals	0.1

18.12   Manual exercises

These exercises bring together many of the ideas and calculations used in the previous chapters and take the assessments further to consider such supplementary analyses as crude protein, oil, fibre (NDF), sugars and starch content. The results obtained in the manual exercises differ slightly from that obtained with the computer "Ration formulation exercises - Manual I" as the calculations throughout the computer assessment are carried out with far greater precision. The solutions to these exercises can be found in Chapter 19 (pages 194 to 197).

Exercise 1

Will the ration outlined below satisfy the requirements of a 650 kg cow giving 30 litres of milk (4.0% fat and 3.2% protein) losing 0.5 kg a day in week 14 of her lactation and not pregnant? The silage is offered in ring feeders, the wheat as a midday feed and the compound feed in the parlour.

Ration

Average clamp silage (ME = 10.4)	41.0 kg
Compound 20% CP	6.5 kg
Wheat grain	2.0 kg

Suggested approach:

Carry out the calculations in the following order:

1. Work out ration DMI.

2. Work out ME and GE supplied by ration and hence ration q.

3. Work out predicted dry matter intake and compare.

4. Work out animal ME requirements and compare.

5. Work out supply of ERDP and DUP and hence MP supply.

6. Work out MP requirements and compare.

7. Work out minerals supply and requirements and compare.

8. Work out ration fibre (NDF), fat and CP contents.

9. Work out sugar and starch content.

Exercise 2

A group of high-yielding cows are being given a mixture of grass and maize silage and a 24% compound feed in the parlour as outlined below. The ration has been formulated for 650 kg cows yielding 40 litres of milk a day (4% fat and 3.2% protein), losing 0.7 kg a day and in week 8 of lactation.

Ration

Average grass silage	21 kg
Maize silage	26 kg
Compound 24% CP	10 kg

Assess the ration and suggest any alterations that you feel may be necessary.

18.13   Computer exercises

Exercise 1

A farmer has made equal amounts of grass silage (average quality) and maize silage for the winter and wants to feed a 20% CP compound in the parlour and up to 15 kg brewers grains. Devise a suitable ration for 28 litres of milk assuming the cows weigh 600 kg are in week 12 of lactation, not pregnant and losing 0.25 kg weight a day.

Exercise 2

A farmer has his cows out on silage aftermath in mid-August which are assumed to have a nutritive composition of 10.7 MJ ME and 121 g CP/kg DM. Most of the cows have passed their peak yield and are expected to be giving about 24 litres milk a day. They are given 4 kg of an 18% CP compound in the milking parlour and there are no other facilities for feeding other feeds. The farmer reports that the cows are waiting to come in for milking and that there is some ungrazed grass left at the end of each grazing session. The cows are only yielding 20 litres of milk and analysis of the grass by NIRs shows that it is 9.8 MJ ME and 106 g CP/kg DM (poor grass). Assess the ration and make any changes that you feel are required. Assume the cows are 600 kg weight, not losing or gaining weight, in week 25 of the lactation and 17 weeks pregnant.

PART 5

EXERCISES

CHAPTER 19

EXERCISES

19.1 Computer program

19.2 Predicting feed intake - Chapter 8
    19.2.1 Manual exercises
    19.2.2 Computer exercises

19.3 Energy - Chapter 9
    19.3.1 Manual exercises
    19.3.2 Computer exercises

19.4 Protein - Chapter 10
    19.4.1 Manual exercises
    19.4.2 Computer exercises

19.5 Minerals - Chapter 11
    19.5.1 Manual exercises
    19.5.2 Computer exercises

19.6 Diet formulation - Chapter 18
    19.6.1 Manual exercises
    19.6.2 Computer exercises

19.7 Case studies
    19.7.1 Case study 1 - low milk fat
    19.7.2 Case study 2 - low milk protein
    19.7.3 Case study 3 - gaining weight, not achieving yield

19.1   Computer program

Computer requirements

The program distributed with this book is a condensed version of a commercial ration formulation program. To run the program you will require an IBM-compatible computer running DOS version 2.11 or later. A 286 machine or later (generally any machine that is less than 5 to 7 years old) is required. The program also requires a hard disc with at least 2.0 Mbyte of space free. The following instructions assume that the hard disc is called C, the floppy disc is called A and that there is no directory called DAIRY on the machine before installation.

Installation of computer program

To install the program on your computer, insert the floppy disc in drive A. At the DOS prompt (C:>) type A:INSTALL. Installation will create a directory called DAIRY below the root directory (don't worry if you don't know what this means!). The installation program will copy a compressed file into this directory, expand it and delete the compressed version. Finally a file called DAIRY.BAT will be copied into the root directory so that the programs can be run from any directory on the computer. The program on the disc enclosed with the book has "share-ware" status. Anyone can distribute copies to anyone else provided the program is only used for private educational use and not for commercial purposes, and that all the files on the disc are copied to the new user. If you wish to use the program for commercial purposes you will need to buy a full version which has more features (see below).

How to obtain the larger disc size for older computers

Some older machines do not have 3½" floppy disc drives but only have the older 5¼" drives. As long as these machines have a 80286 processor or better the programs will still run. If you require the larger disc size please return the disc to Dr A. T. Chamberlain, PO Box 208, Fareham, Hants, PO17 5DX, UK requesting that it is exchanged.

Obtaining a full version of the computer program

The full version of the computer program is available commercially and an order form can be found on the floppy disc enclosed with the book. To print it type **PRINT A:ORDERFRM.PRN** when at the DOS prompt and with the DAIRY floppy disc in the disc drive. The full version of the program allows users to enter feeds of known analyses, save rations, make mixes and alter prices, etc.

Program instructions

The following are instructions for using the dairy cow program - it is suggested that you read through them and carry out the ration formulation actions in **bold** type. Finally read the "short-cut" comments at the end of this section and experiment with them so that you are comfortable with the program for use in the later exercises.

This program is loaded by typing **DAIRY**. After the program has been loaded the screen will display the title banner page. Pressing the **RETURN** key (the large key marked ↵ or 'Enter') displays the program status screen giving brief details about the program. Whilst the user is reading this screen the program loads the feed database which contains 23 feeds that are required for the exercises. When prompted press **any key** to continue. The next screen allows the user to define details about the animal to be fed (Figure 19.1). Use the **arrow keys** to move the diamond-shaped cursor from one highlighted field to another; as you do this the box at the bottom of the screen displays information relevant to that field. The other questions concern basic information relating to the cow such as weight, daily milk yield, stage of lactation, etc.

Figure 19.1   Screen display of animal requirements screen

```
TEACHING VERSION DISTRIBUTED WITH BOOK    ANIMAL              16-09-95
                                     REQUIREMENTS
              ◆Dairy cow ration
ANIMAL DESCRIPTION
Weight              :   650   kg   Live Weight Change   :  -.5 kg/day
Milk Yield          :   30    l/day Current condition score:  2.5
Activity level      :   Low        Weeks post calving   :  16
DMI Correction      :   1          Weeks pregnant       :  6
Production month    :   0

                 Energy    Protein              Ca      P      Mg
                 MJ ME     g MP                 g       g      g
Maintenance        68        311               25      37     12
Lactation         159       1365               51      48     24
Pregnancy           0          0                0       0      0
L.W. Change       -11        -66               -7      -5     -1
Activity            0          0                0       0      0
                 _____

Totals            216       1611               69      80     35
```
```
Ration title - to identify stored ration

                                    ← → ↑ ↓  ‖ END - RETURN
```

Set the animal description to be as follows:

Ration title:	**Title to identify any print-outs**
Cow weight:	**650 kg**
Milk yield:	**30 litres**
Liveweight change:	**-0.5 kg**
Condition score:	**2.5**
Weeks post calving:	**16 weeks**
Weeks pregnant:	**6 weeks**
Activity level:	**Low**
Dry matter intake correction:	**1**
Production month:	**0 (no month considered)**

Press **RETURN** when all entries have been made. All inputs are checked to ensure they are within reasonable bounds and the user is then asked if the entries are correct. Press **Y** or **RETURN** to continue or **N** to amend them. The subsequent screen is the main menu to which you are returned after all activities. In case of difficulties pressing the **RETURN** key will usually return you to this menu. Options may be selected either by number or by positioning the highlighted bar (by using the arrow keys) over the required option and pressing the **RETURN** key. The menu options are as follows:

1.   Retrieve rations on the hard disc
     Allows you to retrieve rations for use in the examples and exercises given later in this section.

2.   Select [Add] feeds (up to a maximum of 12)
     Allows you to select from a range of feeds. To select a feed either enter the feed number or position the highlighted bar over the required feed and press **RETURN**. After selecting a feed you will be prompted for the amount to be fed in wet weight (enter **99** to feed a food to appetite) and then returned to the feed selection screen. To finish feed selection press **F** or **RETURN** at this stage.

     Select the following feeds:
     Average silage   *ad libitum* (enter **99**)
     Maize Gluten Feed **4 kg**

3.   Alter feeds
     Allows the user to alter feed amounts or delete feeds from a ration. Select the number of feed to alter, then respond **A** to alter or **D** to delete feed. If you respond **A** then you will be prompted for the new feed amount, if you respond **D** then you will be asked to confirm your decision. There is a quicker way to make alterations - see below.

4.   Display ration on screen
     Displays amount of each feed consumed and nutritional value of each ingredient. The total nutritional value of the ration and the animal's requirements are displayed together with the balance of supplied nutrients minus require-ments. The ration ingredients are sorted so

forages are at the top of the list of feeds. Pressing **S** brings up a supplementary screen with financial details and additional ration analyses; pressing **F** brings up a full analysis of the ration. Press **M** to return to the main screen and **RETURN** from any other screen to return to the main menu.

Look at the formulated ration:
How much silage will the cow eat - is this realistic?
Have we met her requirements for energy and protein?

5. View requirements or alter animal and ration identity details
The two options available are :
View nutritional requirements (**V**). Displays animal description and predicted dry matter intake, energy, protein and major mineral requirements.
Alter animal description (**A**). Allows alteration of information given at the beginning of the program.

6 Print ration
Either the main screen or both main and supplementary screens can be printed out together with the animal details. Up to three comment lines can be entered which are then appended to the bottom of the print-out.

7 Alter animal default values
Allows alteration of calf weight, milk composition and pricing.

8 Make a mix
Calls up a second menu that allows the user to specify, alter, inspect, name and print out a mix of feeds that can subsequential be included in the diet. Not available in the educational version distributed with this book.

9. Quit program
Finish using the ration formulation program. You will be asked to confirm your selection.

Short-cuts
The following features have been incorporated into the DAIRY program to make it easy and quicker to use:

At the bottom of the formulated ration screen is the command line. In addition to the **S**, **F** and **M** keys mentioned above it has the following facilities.

Entering the feed number (shown against each feed), a space, then the new amount changes the specified feed to this amount.
e.g. **1 20** changes feed 1 to 20 kg.

Entering the feed number, space, then **D** deletes that feed.

Pressing **E** transfers you to the feed database to select additional feeds.

Pressing **P** transfers you to the printing options.

Pressing **I** when viewing a ration will display the Intermediate protein calculation screen which shows the amounts of ME and FME and four protein fractions supplied by each feed.

Pressing **F7** when viewing a formulated ration will change the balance line from actual differences to percentage differences and back again.

Pressing **F8** when viewing the feed data-base turns the display of the basic feed analyses of dry matter (DM), energy (ME) and protein (CP) on and off.

19.2 Predicting feed intake - Chapter 8

19.2.1 *Manual exercises*
Exercise 1
A 625 kg cow is being fed on a ration with a q of 0.65. If she is giving 30 litres of milk in the third week of lactation how much will she eat? If she peaks at 45 litres milk/day in Week 10 of lactation, how much will she be eating then? If the ration is made up of compound in the parlour and silage offered behind an electric fence off the clamp-face how will this alter the predicted intake?

Solution
From Table 20.1 (page 204) a 625 kg cow giving 30 litres milk a day on a ration of q over 0.60, the basic prediction of dry matter intake is 18.6 kg DM. As she is in the third week of lactation the correction factor shown in Table 20.2 (page 205) is 0.84 giving a final predicted intake of:

$$18.6 \times 0.84 = 15.6 \text{ kg DM / day}$$

When the same cow is giving 45 litres of milk on the same ration quality predicted intake will be 18.8 kg DM (Table 20.1). In Week 10 the correction factor for stage of lactation is 0.98 (Table 20.2) to give a final predicted intake of

$$18.8 \times 0.98 = 18.4 \text{ kg DM / day}$$

If the silage is offered behind an electric fence this will depress intake by about 10 to 20% of the initial prediction (see Table 20.3, page 205). The exact amount of silage consumed should be assessed by estimating how fast the silage is being removed from the clamp.

Exercise 2

A barren, late lactation cow weighing 575 kg is giving 15 litres of milk in the 35th week of her lactation. She is given a silage with a q of 0.55 and no supplementary feeds. How much is she predicted to be able to eat? How much is she predicted to eat the week before she is dried off (Week 43) when she is giving 10 litres of milk? How will silage quality affect these predictions?

Solution

From Table 20.1 (page 204) a 575 kg cow giving 15 litres of milk on a ration of q = 0.55 will consume 15.7 kg DM. At this stage of lactation there is no correction factor (Table 20.2, page 205) so the final prediction is 15.7 kg. At drying off she is predicted to consume 14.7 kg and again there is no correction for stage of lactation.

The only feed on offer is silage and so we are expecting the cow to eat 14.7 to 15.7 kg of silage DM. At 25% dry matter this is about 59 to 63 kg fresh weight. As discussed in Chapter 4 (page 46), to achieve such high intakes the silage would need to be dry (DM > 30%), have a moderate pH, low lactic and total acids, no detectable butyric acid, low ammonia nitrogen (< 5% of total nitrogen) and high residual sugars. With typical 25% DM silage, intakes will most likely be less than 14 kg of silage DM.

Exercise 3

A dry cow in Week 34 of pregnancy is on a straw-based diet with a q of 0.4. If she weighed 625 kg in condition score 2.5, how much will she eat? How much will she eat 4 weeks later after the farmer has started feeding a ration with a q of 0.5. How would you expect her voluntary intake to change if she was carrying twins rather than one calf?

Solution

From Table 20.4 (page 205) a 625 kg cow on a ration with q = 0.4 will be predicted to eat 8.4 kg of dry matter.

On a ration of q = 0.5 she will be predicted to eat 11.6 kg dry matter.

If the cow was carrying twins this would increase the size of the uterus and in the latter stages of pregnancy this would significantly reduce rumen volume and hence, especially on lower quality feeds, voluntary intakes would be depressed. Her energy requirements would increase but work with pregnant sheep suggests that this would not increase her voluntary intake on the type of diet offered.

Exercise 4

A 700 kg cow giving 35 litres of milk in the 5th week of lactation is being fed the diet given below. The compound is given in the parlour twice a day and silage is offered in troughs with sugar beet feed (dry molassed) sprinkled over the top as a midday feed.

	Intake (kg fresh weight/day)	DM (%)	ME (MJ/kg DM)	GE (MJ/kg DM)
Grass silage	36	26	10.9	19.0
Sugar beet feed	3	86	12.5	17.1
Compound feed	9	87	12.5	18.4

Will she eat the ration offered and if not how can the farmer change what he is doing to ensure she does?

Solution

1. Calculate the dry matter intake of each feed (Table 20.21, pages 215 to 219).

	Intake (kg fresh weight/day)	DM (%)	DMI (kg)
Grass silage	36	26	36 x (26/100) = 9.36
Sugar beet feed	3	86	3 x (86/100) = 2.58
Compound feed	9	87	9 x (87/100) = 7.83

2. Calculate the total ME and GE in the ration (Table 20.21, pages 215 to 219) and hence q.

	DMI	ME Intake (MJ)	GE Intake (MJ)
Grass silage	9.36	102.0	177.8
Sugar beet feed	2.58	32.3	44.1
Compound feed	7.83	97.9	144.1
TOTALS	**19.8**	**232.2**	**366.0**

q = ME/GE = 232.2/366.0 = 0.63

At q ≥ 0.60 the predicted intake is 21.0 kg DM/day (Table 20.1, page 204).

The cow is in the fifth week of lactation and so the correction factor is 0.91 (Table 20.2, page 205) which gives a final predicted intake of:

21.0 x 0.91 = 19.1 kg DM

The final predicted voluntary intake is lower than that required to consume the ration offered (19.1 cf. 19.8 kg DM) and so the cow will probably not eat all of the ration offered.

Feeding 9 kg of compound feed in the parlour twice a day will give a meal of 4.5 kg at each milking. This is a large amount of feed to be consumed in a short period of time and, if the compound feed is high in starch, may lead to ruminal acidosis and indigestion. Intake might be increased by feeding a part of this compound feed (say 3 kg) in the troughs in the middle of the day.

19.2.2 Computer exercises

The objective of the computer exercises is to allow the user to see how voluntary intake is affected by various factors in practical situations and to assess the relative importance of the differing factors considered in Chapters 4 and 8. These and subsequent computer exercises assume familiarity with the computer program distributed with the book and readers are advised to work their way through Section 19.1 above before carrying out these exercises.

Start up the computer program by typing **DAIRY** at the DOS prompt (C:\> or similar); with all but the newest, fastest machines there will be pause whilst the program loads. Press **RETURN** to move on from the introductory banner screen and then press **RETURN** again to move on from the next screen. The next screen should be the ANIMAL REQUIRE-MENTS screen and should be similar to the display in Figure 19.1 with today's date in the top right hand corner.

The various "boxes" in inverse video are the data entry boxes that are used to define the animal to be rationed. The small diamond cursor in the top box can be moved to other boxes by using the arrow keys on the right of the keyboard. The middle part of the screen gives the energy, protein and mineral requirements of the cow (these will be considered later) and the box at the bottom of the screen further information about the animal details being entered. Press the **DOWN** arrow key. The diamond cursor moves down to the box alongside the word "Weight" on the screen and the bottom box states that this is the weight at condition score 2.5 and barren and that the valid range is from 300 to 800 kilograms.

Press **RETURN** and the bottom box is replaced by different text. The right hand block of text shows the predicted dry matter intake (DMI) (17.6 kg in this case) and the method used to calculate the intake. The "97% of 2.5% BW + .1 Y" shows that the basic method of calculation was based on body weight (BW) and milk yield (Y) and was corrected by 97% to take into account the week of lactation. We will use this screen to investigate the relative importance of the different factors discussed in Chapter 8.

Body weight

Press **N** (for No) to return to the data entry screen. Move the diamond cursor down to the "Weight" box and enter **500** kg for a small cow. Move the cursor right and down two boxes to the "Weeks post calving" and enter **20** to eliminate the effect of stage of lactation. Press **RETURN** to see what the intake of this cow will be. The intake has fallen to 15.0 kg (bottom right corner) and is calculated according to 3% of the body weight. Note the intake and then press **N** to return to data entry and change the body

weight to 600 kg. Press **RETURN** again to see the predicted intake for a cow of this body weight (18.0 kg) and then change the weight to **700** kg (Press **N** then change the weight) and look at the predicted intake again. Note that the intake has only risen to 20.5 kg and is now limited by body weight and milk yield.

Milk yield

Change the weight to 600 kg and then determine the predicted intake at milk yields of 10, 20, 30 and 40 l/day. The results are as shown in Table 19.1

Table 19.1 Predicted effect of increasing milk yield on dry matter intake in a 600 kg cow

Milk yield (l/day)	DMI (kg)	Limiting factor
10	16.0	2.5% BW + .1 Y
20	17.0	2.5% BW + .1 Y
30	18.0	3% BW
40	18.0	3% BW

Initially voluntary intake increases in proportion with milk yield, but above 30 litres it remains constant as gut volume restricts the capacity of the animal to eat more feed.

Stage of lactation

Set the animal weight to 600 kg, the yield to 35 litres and the weeks post calving to 2 weeks. Press **RETURN**, note the intake and then increase it to 4, 6, 8, 10, 12, 14 and 16 weeks post calving. The results are shown in Table 19.2.

Table 19.2 Predicted effect of stage of lactation on dry matter intake

Weeks	DMI (kg)	Reason
2	14.0	77% of 3% BW
4	15.8	87% of 3% BW
6	16.7	92% of 3% BW
8	17.3	96% of 3% BW
10	17.6	97% of 3% BW
12	17.9	99% of 3% BW
14	18.0	100% of 3% BW
16	18.0	100% of 3% BW

Note that the depression of intake does not disappear until 14 weeks post-calving but the major depression is in the first 6 weeks; after this the reduction is relatively small . In practice milk yield also changes with stage of lactation. With cows reaching their peak yield 4 to 6 weeks after calving, intakes may severely limit performance at this stage of lactation.

Quality of the ration

So far we have been working with a constant ration quality (q = 0.6). Answer **Y** to the question at the bottom of the screen to proceed to the main menu. Select Option 1 by pressing **1**, press **R** to retrieve a ration and then select the first ration entitled "DMI

Exercises - Ration quality" and press **RETURN**. This is a ration for a 600 kg cow giving 20 litres of milk, 25 weeks post-calving and 15 weeks pregnant fed a ration of *ad libitum* poor silage, a 18% CP compound feed and 0.5 kg of straw. Select Option **4** to display the ration. On the current ration the pre-dicted intake is 17.0 kg DMI/day. Press **F** to look at the full ration analysis and work out the ration "q" from the ME and GE figures given in the first column. The q of the initial ration is 0.56 (10.3/18.5). Press **M** to return to the main screen and increase the straw to 3 kg by typing **2 3** and pressing **RETURN**. Note that the intake has dropped by 0.3 kg to 16.7 kg. This is because the addition of a poor quality feed such as straw has reduced to overall quality of the ration.

Look at the "Full" ration screen again and re-calculate q (10.0/18.5 = 0.54). The small reduction in quality has increased retention time of the diet in the rumen and depressed intake. Return to the main screen (**M**) and make a note of the requirements for ME (176), FME (139), ERDP (1485) and DUP (270). Then remove the straw by entering **2 0** and pressing **RETURN**. The ME requirements have fallen to 174 MJ, the FME risen to 154 MJ, the ERDP risen to 1537 g and DUP fallen to 230g.

The reasons for all these changes in requirements have been outlined in Chapters 5 and 6 and will be considered in more detail in the next two sections, but they help to demonstrate the complex inter-actions between intake, energy and protein require-ments that are captured in the current feeding standards.

Subjective assessment

As mentioned in Chapters 4 and 8 a wide range of factors will influence feed intake but cannot be captured in the basic prediction equations. Some of these factors are outlined in Table 8.1 (page 98) and it can be seen that the subjective correction can vary from 0.8 to 1.3. To look at the importance of such alterations retrieve the ration entitled "DMI Exer-cises - Subjective assessment" (Option **1**, **R**, select ration 2, press **RETURN**). This is a ration for 30 litres of milk based on *ad libitum* average silage, compound feed (18% CP) and sugar beet feed. Display the ration (Option **4**). With an intake of 18.0 kg the ration is balanced for energy and contains an excess of DUP and hence MP and costs £2.32/day. To look at the importance of factors that modify the intake let us assume that this ration is being fed as a complete diet and that intake is increased by a factor of 1.2 (Table 8.1, page 98). Press **RETURN** to return to the main menu, select option **5** then press **A** to make alterations. The DMI correction value in the left hand column is set at 1 which means intake is not altered. Change this to **1.2** to reflect the likely changes if a complete diet feeder was used. Return

to the main menu and view the ration (Option **4**). Intake has risen to 21.6 kg and there is a surplus of 35 MJ of ME. Even if all the compound is taken out there is still an energy surplus suggesting that a much cheaper ration could be formulated.

Now look at what the effect of an electric fence at the silage face would be if it reduced intake by 10%, i.e. to 0.9. Return to the main menu, select Option **5** then **A** and alter DMI correction to **0.9**. Re-display the ration. Intake has fallen to 16.2 kg DM/day and there is a serious energy deficit.

It can be seen that the practical impact of altering feed intake is considerable and this has various implications. Firstly, it reinforces the need to ensure that intake is correctly assessed at the farm level, and secondly, it shows the considerable benefits that can be gained by encouraging cows to eat as much as possible.

19.3   Energy - Chapter 9

19.3.1   Manual exercises
Exercise 1
What are the energy requirements of a 600 kg cow, not pregnant, giving 25 litres of milk containing 4.0% fat and 3.2% protein when fed on a ration with a q of 0.6?

Solution
Maintenance (Table 20.5, page 206)
600 kg cow at q = 0.6
61.9 MJ ME/day

Lactation (Table 20.6, page 207)
4.0% fat and 3.2% protein at q = 0.6
5.11 MJ ME / litre
25 litres x 5.11 = 127.75

Calculate C_L (Table 20.10, page 209)
APL =   (61.9 + 127.75) / 61.9
     = 3.06
C_L = 1.037

Calculate total requirements
(61.9 + 127.75) x 1.037 = 197 MJ ME/day

Exercise 2
What are the energy requirements of a 650 kg cow giving 43 litres of milk containing 3.75% BF and 3.3% protein and losing 0.75 kg/day when given a ration with a q of 0.7?

Solution
Maintenance (Table 20.5, page 206)
650 kg cow at q = 0.7
62.5 MJ ME/day

Lactation (Table 20.6, page 207)
3.75% fat and 3.3% protein at q = 0.7
4.72 MJ ME / litre
43 litres x 4.72 = 203.0 MJ ME / day

Weight change (Table 20.8, page 208)
-0.75 kg/day at q = 0.7 and cow milking
-15.6 MJ ME / day

Calculate C_L (Table 20.10, page 209)
APL $\quad$ = (62.5 + 203.0 - 15.6) / 62.5
$\quad\quad$ = 4.0
C_L = 1.054

Calculate total requirements
(62.5 + 203.0 - 15.6) x 1.054 = 263 MJ ME/day

Exercise 3

What will the energy requirements be of a 600 kg dairy cow be the week after she is dried off if she is 35 weeks pregnant to a Charolais bull, losing 0.5 kg a day and fed on a straw based ration with q = 0.4?

Solution

Maintenance (Table 20.5, page 206)
600 kg cow at q = 0.4
68.7 MJ ME/day

Pregnancy (Table 20.7, page 208), 35 weeks pregnant
22.1 MJ ME
Correction for Charolais (Table 20.7)
42.5 / 40 = 1.06
22.1 x 1.06 = 23.4 MJ ME / day

Weight change (Table 20.8, page 208)
-0.50 kg/day at q = 0.4 and cow dry and pregnant
-12.4 MJ ME / day

Calculate C_L (Table 20.10, page 209)
APL $\quad$ = (68.7 + 23.4 - 12.4) / 68.7
$\quad\quad$ = 1.16
C_L $\quad$ = 1.003

Calculate total requirements
(68.7 + 23.4 - 12.4) x 1.003
= 79.9 MJ ME/day

Exercise 4

Consider a 640 kg Friesian dairy cow on silage with the following analysis:

Dry matter: $\quad$ 25%
q: $\quad\quad\quad\quad$ 0.6
Energy content: 11.5 MJ / kg DM

Calculate her energy requirements for maintenance. Calculate the required dry matter intake of silage to supply this amount of energy and hence the amount of silage to feed daily to meet her maintenance requirements.

Now calculate her lactation requirements assuming that the cow is giving 15 litres of milk a day with the following analysis:

Fat: $\quad$ 4.0%
Protein: $\quad$ 3.2%

Calculate the total ME requirements per day and hence the required silage intake. Is this a realistic figure?

Solution

Maintenance (Table 20.5, page 206)
640 kg. Ration q = 0.6
64.8 MJ ME/day

Calculate intake
Silage DM $\quad\quad$ = 25%, ME = 11.5
DMI required $\quad$ = 64.8 / 11.5
$\quad\quad\quad\quad\quad\quad$ = 5.6 kg DMI /day
Fresh weight: 5.6 / (25/100) = 22.4 kg

Lactation (Table 20.6, page 207)
Fat 4.0%, Protein 3.2%. Ration q = 0.6
5.11 MJ ME/litre
15 x 5.11 = 76.7 MJ ME / day

Calculate C_L (Table 20.10, page 209)
APL $\quad$ = (64.8 + 76.7) / 64.8
$\quad\quad$ = 2.18
C_L $\quad$ = 1.022

Calculate total requirements
(64.8 + 76.7) x 1.022 = 145 MJ ME/day

Calculate intake
Silage DM = 25%, ME = 11.5
DMI required $\quad$ = 145 / 11.5
$\quad\quad\quad\quad\quad\quad$ = 12.6 kg DM/day

Fresh weight: 12.6 / (25/100) = 50.4 kg

The required dry matter intake of 12.6 kg is well within the predicted intake of 17.5 kg (Table 20.1, page 204), but whether in practice the cow would eat this amount of silage on its own would depend very much on the fermentation quality which can only be assessed by visiting the farm and inspecting the silage.

Exercise 5

A 650 kg Holstein cow giving 28 litres of milk (Fat = 3.75%, Protein = 3.4%) and 10 weeks pregnant (in calf to a Holstein bull) and losing 0.5 kg/day is being fed on the following ration.

	Amount (kg fresh weight/day)	DM (%)	ME (MJ/kg DM)	GE (MJ/kg DM)
Grass silage good	36.0	27	10.8	19.8
Caustic wheat	3.0	77	12.6	18.8
Soyabean meal Ext.	1.0	88	13.4	20.0
Compound 18% CP	6.0	87	13.5	21.5

Will this ration meet her energy requirements?

Solution
Ration assessment:

Determine the total DM, ME and GE intakes from the figures given above.

	Amount	DMI	ME intake	GE intake
	(kg)	(MJ)	(MJ)	(MJ)
Grass silage good	36.0	9.72	105.0	192.5
Caustic wheat	3.0	2.31	29.1	43.4
Soyabean meal Ext.	1.0	0.88	11.8	17.6
Compound 18% CP	6.0	5.22	70.5	112.2
TOTALS		18.1	216.4	365.7

Calculate q. q = ME / GE
                 = 216.4 / 365.7
                 = 0.59

The calculated dry matter intake (DMI) of 18.1 kg is within the predicted value from Table 20.1 (page 204) so further calculations are warranted. If the calculated DMI is greater than that predicted, the amounts of each feed offered has to be reconsidered.

Calculate the energy requirements:

Maintenance (Table 20.5, page 206)
650 kg cow at q = 0.59
65.8 MJ ME/day

Lactation (Table 20.6, page 207)
28l milk, q = 0.59, fat = 3.75%, protein = 3.4%
5.05 MJ ME / litre
5.05 x 28 = 141.4 MJ ME

Pregnancy (Table 20.7, page 208)
10 weeks pregnant
0.7 MJ ME
Correction for Holstein
43.4 / 40 = 1.085
0.7 x 1.085 = 0.76 MJ ME / day

Weight change (Table 20.8, page 208)
-0.50 kg/day at q = 0.59 and cow milking
-11.06 MJ ME / day

Calculate C_L (Table 20.10, page 209)
APL = (65.8 + 141.4 + 0.76 - 11.06) / 65.8
    = 2.99
C_L = 1.036

Calculate total requirements
(65.8 + 141.4 + 0.76 - 11.06) x 1.036 = 204 MJ ME/day

The requirements of 204 MJ compare to a supply of 216 MJ to give a surplus of 12 MJ ME/day which represents an over-supply of 6%.

19.3.2 Computer exercises
The objectives of these computer exercises are to show the relative importance of the different metabolic commitments and to look at some of the inter-actions between feeds and requirements. The figures calculated on the computer for the requirements for each metabolic activity (such as maintenance and lactation) differ from those obtained in manual exercises even when the precise value of q has been taken into account. This is because the computer corrects each requirement for the level of production (C_L) so that the numbers on the screen add up to the total shown.

Load the DAIRY program by typing **DAIRY** at the DOS prompt and then press **RETURN** three times to go to the Animal Requirements screen (Figure 19.1) at which you can enter the animal details. The initial screen shows the requirements for a 600 kg cow losing 0.5 kg/day and giving 30 litres of milk on a ration of medium quality (q=0.6). The total ME requirements are 212 MJ ME/day and the predicted intake 17.6 kg DM/day. These two figures can be used to calculate the average energy density required. This is often referred to as the "M/D" (short for ME MJ/ kg DMI) and is shown in the bottom left hand part of the screen. For this animal the M/D is 12 MJ/kg DM. This information can be used in conjunction with a knowledge of the energy content of feeds (Table 20.21, pages 215 to 219) for an initial assessment of the ration. In this instance the average energy density needs to be 12 which implies that a high quality forage will be required (11.0 MJ ME/kg DM or better) and it will need to be supplemented with a high energy concentrate (ME 12.5 or better). Poor quality feeds such as straw (ME 6.5) have no place in such a ration as they will depress the average energy content too much.

Body weight
The ME requirements for maintenance for a 600 kg cow are shown on the computer as 64 MJ. Change the weight to 400, 500 and 700 kg and look at the change in ME requirements. The requirements increase by about 7.5 MJ for each 100 kg increase in body weight. In terms of the total requirements (about 200 MJ) this is a very small increase and when formulating rations for milking cows the correct estimate of requirements for maintenance are very much secondary to estimating requirements for milk production. However, reducing the body weight has a major effect on predicted dry matter intake and hence the required M/D. For example, if the body weight is 500 kg rather than 600 kg the M/D increases to 14 MJ/kg DMI which will only be attainable if considerable amounts of fat (35 MJ/kg DM) are used in the ration.

Estimating the body weight is therefore more important for assessing the dry matter intake than the ME and other nutrient requirements. In practice, care must be taken not to over-estimate body weight as this artificially depresses the M/D required and hence makes ration formulation cheaper.

Milk yield

Look at the ME requirements of a 600 kg cow for milk yields between 10 and 50 litres of milk. Table 19.3 shows the energy requirements and the lactation requirements as percentage of the total.

Table 19.3 ME requirements for milk production and as a percentage of total requirements

Milk yield (litres)	ME req. for lactation (MJ)	Percentage of total (%)
10	51	50
20	104	66
30	159	75
40	215	80
50	272	83

Note that the energy required per litre increases from 5.10 MJ ME when the cow is giving 10 litres of milk to 5.44 MJ ME when she yields 50 litres of milk. This is because the level of production (APL) increases from 1.6 to 5.0 and this increases C_L (correction for level of production - Chapter 9, page 102) from 1.01 to 1.07. In practice, it is unlikely that the cow giving 50 litres of milk requires 272 MJ ME for lactation as in most circumstances the fat and protein concentrations in the milk decline and hence energy requirements fall.

Weight change

Look at the energy value of weight change when the cow is gaining or losing weight and milking (30 litres/day) or dry (Table 19.4).

Table 19.4 ME value of weight change (MJ ME/kg) in milking and dry cows

	Milking	Dry
Gaining	39	49
Losing	-23	-24

These differing values reflect the differences in the efficiency of the use of energy in dry and milking cows and differing uses to which such energy is put as considered in Chapter 9 (page 102). Look at the effect that losing 0.5 kg a day has on the total energy requirements and M/D for a cow 600 kg yielding 30 milk. This reduces ME requirements from 224 to 212 MJ which reduces the M/D from 13 to 12 MJ/kg DM. Whilst the reduction in energy requirements is small (12 MJ) it makes the ration much easier to formulate.

Pregnancy

Look at the requirements for pregnancy from Weeks 5 to 40. In Week 5 the requirements are so small (less than 0.5 MJ ME) they do not show on the computer screen; by Week 10 they are 1 MJ and thereafter they approximately double every five

weeks. To maintain an annual calving interval, conception should take place about 12 weeks into the lactation. Hopefully by this stage the cow has reached or is past her peak yield and it is possible to formulate rations for a positive energy balance and a slight weight gain which will increase pregnancy rates. In most situations the late lactation cow is on sufficiently good feeds that the 5 to 15 MJ ME required can be met without supplementation. It is only in the dry period that the ME requirement for pregnancy becomes a practical issue and this is particularly the case in the last couple of weeks when the increasing requirement (Chapter 9, page 102) and declining intake (Chapter 15, page 150) mean that a good quality ration (ME over 10 MJ/kg DM) must be offered.

Effect of different feeds on energy requirements

Retrieve the ration called "ME Exercises - Ration quality" from the hard disc (main menu Option 1, **R** to retrieve ration number 3). This is a typical winter ration for a 600 kg cow giving 25 litres of milk in the 15 week of lactation and not pregnant or losing weight. The ration contains a slight excess of ME (1 MJ) but this would be within the practical limits of assessing feed quantities and quality. Look at the animal requirements (Main menu Option **5** then **V** to view). Note the ME requirements for each metabolic activity and add 2 kg of straw and then remove the straw and add 1 kg of fat prills. The results are shown in Table 19.5.

Table 19.5 Energy requirements for same animal on three different diets

	ME$_{maint}$	ME$_{lact}$	ME$_{total}$	Ration q
Basic ration	64	132	196	0.60
+ 2 kg straw	65	133	198	0.59
+ 1 kg fat prills	63	129	192	0.64

Adding the straw increases the requirements and adding the fat reduces them. The reason for this can be found in the changes in the ration q value. The changes in q alter the efficiency with which ME is converted to NE required for metabolic commitments (Chapter 5, page 53) and hence the ME requirements change (Chapter 9, page 101). As ration quality falls, the energy requirements increase, the intake usually falls and the energy density of the ration declines, which all combine to make the effects of poor quality (ME content) feeds greater than first thought.

Ration formulation computer exercises

Computer exercise 1

If the ration given below is offered as a complete diet will it be adequate for a 630 kg cow giving 36 litres of milk 8 weeks into her lactation if she is losing 600 g/day weight and is not pregnant?

Ration

Average silage	*ad libitum* (enter 99 for feed amount)
Maize silage	20 kg
Sp Barley Straw	2 kg
Soyabean meal	2 kg
Rapeseed meal	2 kg
Minerals	0.1 kg

Why has the farmer incorporated straw into the ration?

If the straw was omitted and replaced by caustic wheat how much would need to be fed to balance the energy supply?

Would there be any problems with the final ration? What sort of milk quality would you expect?

Solution
The formulated ration has been stored as "ME Exercises - Exercise 1". The ration is being offered as a complete diet, so the intake is estimated to be 1.2 times higher than predicted (Table 20.3, page 205). The suggested ration is deficient in energy by 16 MJ ME. This is 6% of the requirement and equivalent to about 3 litres of milk so would probably show on farm as a decline in performance.

The straw has been included in the ration as a source of fibre (NDF) to support rumen function and maintain milk fat content. However there is too much in the ration. The NDF content is 46.7% (Supplementary screen - press S) and the incorporation of a low energy density feed such as straw is part of the reason the ration is energy deficient. Rations high in fibre and low in energy are likely to promote the production of high fat, low protein milk.

If the straw is omitted (**3 0**) silage intake increases to 45.7 kg and the energy deficit is reduced to 8 MJ. Fibre intake (NDF) falls but is still 44.7% of the dry matter intake. Inclusion of 3.3 kg of caustic wheat eliminates the energy deficit and the fibre content falls to 41.7% of DMI.

The inclusion of the caustic wheat has reduced the NDF content to 41.7% and raised the combined sugars and starch to 16.7% as well as eliminating the energy deficit. Such a ration is more likely to promote milk protein production but milk fat is likely to remain high as fibre content is still high at 41.7%. The inclusion of 3.3 kg of caustic wheat will introduce a considerable amount of sodium (as sodium bicarbonate) to the ration. A special low sodium mineral should be used and plans made to cope with the increased urine production as the cow clears the sodium from the body.

Computer exercise 2
A farmer groups his cows according to milk yield. The late lactation cows (600 kg) are giving, on average, 10 litres milk a day, are 40 weeks into the lactation and 32 weeks pregnant. He reckons the cows should be gaining 0.25 kg/day to ensure they dry off in condition score 3.0. He is feeding them *ad libitum* silage and 2 kg of a 18% CP compound in the milking parlour. He estimates (from block cuttings) that the cows eat 50 kg silage a day. He has been advised to incorporate straw in the ration to help the energy balance. Would you support this and if so how much straw would you recommend? Would there be any problems with this diet?

Solution
The formulated ration has been saved as "ME Exercises - Exercise 2". The ration contains an excess of 17 MJ ME. At this stage of the lactation the surplus energy is likely to be directed towards body reserves and such animals are likely to be putting on 0.7 kg/day rather than 0.25 kg/day. This is a common problem on farms; cows are offered *ad libitum* silage and the farmer feeds a small amount of concentrates to entice the cows into the parlour. Such animals will be too fat when they are dried off and hence too fat when they calve down again with consequent problems in the subsequent lactation (Chapter 15 - page 146).

Incorporating straw in the diet reduces the energy content and hence puts the ration in balance. Add 2 kg of straw to the ration and set the silage intake to *ad libitum* (enter **99**) and the energy balance is now zero. However 2 kg of straw is a large amount; placing it on top of the silage or in separate racks will not ensure it is all eaten. The cows will have to be "forced" to eat it. Care must be taken to reduce the amount of silage offered to 40 kg a day so that it is all consumed by mid-evening.

19.4 Protein - Chapter 10

19.4.1 Manual exercises
Exercise 1
How much MP will the following ration supply to an animal that has an APL of 4.0?

Grass silage 70D	40 kg
Wheat grain	4 kg
Sugar beet feed - molassed	3 kg
Soyabean meal	2 kg

Solution
1. Determine Y from the APL from Table 10.1 (page 108) or Table 20.22 (pages 220 to 223)
   Y = 11.5

2. Look up the amounts of DM, FME, ERDP and DUP in each kg of feed DM from Table 20.22 (pages 220 to 223).

	DM (%)	FME (MJ)	ERDP (g/kg DM)	DUP (g/kg DM)
Grass silage 70D	25	8.6	114.7	26.7
Wheat grain	87	12.9	98.2	14.8
Sugar beet feed - molassed	86	12.4	52.2	31.4
Soyabean meal	88	12.7	239.5	212.2

3. Calculate the amounts of DM, FME, ERDP and DUP contributed by each feed and hence the totals.

	DM (kg)	FME (MJ)	ERDP (g)	DUP (g)
Grass silage 70D	10.0	86.0	1147.0	267.0
Wheat grain	3.48	44.9	337.8	50.9
Sugar beet feed - molassed	2.58	32.0	134.7	81.0
Soyabean meal	1.76	22.4	421.5	373.1
TOTALS	**17.8**	**185.3**	**2041.0**	**772.0**

4. Determine MCP output from rumen.

If energy supply is limiting microbial activity then

$$MCP_{energy} = Y \times FME$$
$$MCP_{energy} = 11.5 \times 185.3$$
$$= 2131 \text{ g protein}$$

If protein supply is limiting microbial activity then

$$MCP_{protein} = ERDP$$
$$= 2041 \text{ g protein}$$

$$MCP_{energy} > MCP_{protein}$$

Therefore protein (ERDP) supply will limit rumen microbial protein production.

MCP = 2041 g protein

The difference between the two figures is small due to the use of high FME supplements such as wheat and sugar beet feed and the rumen will be in balance and intake should therefore be optimal.

5. Determine MP supplied by the ration.

$$MP = (0.64 \times MCP) + DUP$$
$$= 0.64 \times 2041 + 782.8$$
$$= 2089 \text{ g protein}$$

Exercise 2
What are the MP requirements of the following animal:

650 kg body weight
20 litres of milk at 3.2% protein
losing 0.5 kg weight a day
20 weeks pregnant to a Limousin bull

1. Maintenance requirements (Table 20.11, page 210)

650 kg cow = 312 g

2. Lactation requirements (Table 20.12, page 210)

20 litres of milk at 3.2% protein = 912 g

3. Weight changes (Table 20.14, page 211)

losing 0.5 kg weight a day = -66 g

4. Pregnancy (Table 20.13, page 211)
20 weeks pregnant to a Limousin bull

Basic requirements = 17 g
Correction factor = 37.6 / 40
= 0.94
Corrected requirements = 17 x 0.94
= 16

5. Total requirements

312 + 912 - 66 + 16 = 1174 g MP / day

Note that even at this low milk yield (20 litres) protein requirements for lactation are the dominant component accounting for 78% of the total.

Exercise 3
Will a 550 kg cow giving 22 litres of milk at 4.25% Fat and 3.2% Protein receive adequate protein if she is eating 65 kg of good silage of 70D (assume ME = 11.7, GE = 19.5)?

Solution
1. Firstly we need to calculate Y and hence we need to know the APL. To get the APL we must consider the animals energy requirements and so we need to calculate q.

$$q = ME / GE$$
$$= 11.7 / 19.5$$
$$= 0.60$$

ME_{maint} = 58.2 MJ /day (Table 20.5, page 206)

ME_{lact} = 22 x 5.27 (Table 20.6, page 207)
= 115.9

APL = ME_{total} / ME_{maint}
= (58.2 + 115.9) / 58.2
= 3.0

Y = 10.9 (Table 20.22, pages 220 to 223)

2. Now determine amounts of DM, FME, ERDP and DUP in the silage (Table 20.22, pages 220 to 223).

	DM (%)	FME MJ/kg DM	ERDP g/kg DM	DUP g/kg DM
Grass silage 70D	25	8.6	116.7	24.8

3. Determine amounts in the ration.

	DMI (kg)	FME (MJ)	ERDP (g)	DUP (g)
Grass silage 70D	16.25	139.7	1896.4	403.0
TOTALS		**139.7**	**1896.4**	**403.0**

4. Determine MCP output from rumen.

If energy supply is limiting microbial activity then

MCP_{energy} = Y x FME
MCP_{energy} = 10.9 x 139.7
        = 1522.7 g protein

If protein supply is limiting microbial activity then

$MCP_{protein}$ = ERDP
        = 1896.4 g protein

$MCP_{energy} < MCP_{protein}$

Therefore energy (FME) supply will limit rumen microbial protein production.

MCP = 1522.7 g protein

The balance in the rumen will be in excess for ERDP by 373.7 g which can also be thought of as a shortfall of FME of 34.3 MJ. Such an imbalance is typical of a grass silage based diet where much of the metabolisable energy has been converted to non-fermentable forms when the silage was preserved in the silo.

5. Determine MP supplied by the ration.

MP = (0.64 x MCP) + DUP
   = (0.64 x 1522.7) + 403.0
   = 1377.5 g

6. Determine maintenance MP requirement (Table 20.11, page 210)

550 kg cow   = 275 g

7. Lactation requirement (Table 20.12, page 210).

22 litres of milk at 3.2% protein = 1003 g

8. Total requirements.

275 + 1003 = 1278 g MP / day

The ration contains 1377.5 g MP and the cow requires 1278 g MP so the ration is in surplus for MP by 99.5 g/day or 7.8%.

Exercise 4

A farmer has his cows out at grass in mid-summer. He has been advised that any cow giving more than 18 litres of milk at 4.0% fat and 3.35% protein will require supplementing with compound feed to meet their protein requirements but is uncertain what sort of compound to use. The cows are 600 kg in weight, not pregnant and not changing weight and he reckons they can eat 75 kg fresh weight of the grass which has a D value of 67 (assume ME = 10.7, GE = 17.8).

Solution

1. Firstly we need to calculate Y and hence we need to know the APL. To get the APL we must consider the animals energy requirements and so we need the calculate q.

q = ME / GE
  = 10.7 / 17.8
  = 0.60

ME_{maint} = 61.9 MJ/day (Table 20.5, page 206)

ME_{lact} = 18 x 5.16 (Table 20.6, page 207)
      = 92.9

APL = ME_{total} / ME_{maint}
    = (61.9 + 92.9) / 61.9
    = 2.50

Y = 10.5 (Table 20.22, pages 220 to 223)

2. Now determine amounts of DM, FME, ERDP and DUP in the grass (Table 20.22, pages 220 to 223).

	DM (%)	FME (MJ/kg DM)	ERDP (g/kg DM)	DUP (g/kg DM)
Grass D 67	20	10.0	83.2	31.6

3. Determine amounts in the ration.

	DMI (kg)	FME (MJ)	ERDP (g)	DUP (g)
Grass D 67	15.0	150.0	1248.0	474.0
TOTALS		**150.0**	**1248.0**	**474.0**

4. Determine MCP output from rumen.

If energy supply is limiting microbial activity then

MCP_{energy} = Y x FME
MCP_{energy} = 10.5 x 150.0
        = 1575.0 g

If protein supply is limiting microbial activity then

$MCP_{protein}$ = ERDP
        = 1248.0 g

$MCP_{protein} < MCP_{energy}$ therefore protein (ERDP) supply will limit rumen microbial protein production.

MCP = 1248.0 g

The balance in the rumen is in deficit for ERDP by 327 g which can also be thought of as a surplus of FME of 31.1 MJ. Such an imbalance is typical of a diet based on fresh grass as compared with grass silage. Much of the metabolisable energy in fresh grass is in a fermentable form and the protein has not been partially degraded by bacteria as it is in the case of silage.

5. Determine MP supplied by the ration.

MP = (0.64 x MCP) + DUP
   = (0.64 x 1248.0) + 474.0
   = 1272.7 g MP

6. Determine maintenance requirement (Table 20.11, page 210).

   600 kg cow =293 g

7. Lactation requirement (Table 20.12, page 210).

   18 litres of milk at 3.35% protein = 859 g

8. Total requirements.

   293 + 859 = 1152 g MP / day

The ration contains 1272.7 g MP and the cow requires 1152 g MP so the ration is in surplus for MP by 121 g/day. The ration therefore does not need supplementing with protein. The ration supplies 160.5 MJ ME against a requirement of 154.8 MJ (61.9 + 92.9). In rough terms then the ration contains sufficient protein for a further 2.5 litres of milk (121/47.7) but only sufficient energy for a further 1.1 (5.7/5.16) litres. Any supplementation must supply more energy than protein and a source of ERDP is to be preferred to DUP as this will help use up the surplus FME.

19.4.2 Computer exercises

The computer exercises consider cover the relative importance of the different metabolic requirements and look at some typical rations and the problems and misconceptions that commonly occur in practice.

Exercise 1

What are the MP requirements of the following cow?

Weight	650 kg
Milk yield	25 litres at 4% fat, 3.2% protein
Weight change	-0.5 kg / day
Stage of lactation	25 weeks
Pregnancy	15 weeks

Can you calculate the ERDP and DUP requirement from this information?

Solution

The requirements can be determined by entering the animal description into the DAIRY program (see Section 19.1) or by retrieving ration number six entitled "MP Exercises - Exercise 1". The requirements and their relative importance are shown in Table 19.6.

Table 19.6 MP requirements of cow in Exercise 1

Maintenance	Lactation	Pregnancy	Weight change	Total
311 g	1137 g	8 g	-66 g	1390 g
22%	82%	0.6%	-5%	100%

Note that, as for energy, the MP requirements for lactation dominate even at 25 litres /day. It is not possible to calculate the ERDP and DUP requirements because we have no knowledge of the ration being offered and hence the amount of FME in the ration. From the information supplied it would be possible to determine the APL and hence the rate of rumen outflow and the yield of MCP per MJ of FME (Y). However we need to know what feeds are being offered to determine the amounts of ERDP, DUP and FME supplied by the different feeds. Only with a knowledge of the FME and ERDP supply to the rumen can the MCP supply and the amount of DUP required be determined.

Exercise 2

Consider the above cow on a diet of 50 kg average grass silage and 5 kg of an 18% CP compound. Does this ration supply sufficient MP to meet her requirements? What is limiting rumen production of MCP?

Solution

This ration is stored as ration number seven entitled "MP Exercises - Exercise 2". The ration does not meet the predicted intake (17.6 kg cf 18.8 kg DM) but the intake of 13.3 kg DM of silage is probably a realistic assessment and hence the intake assessments are likely to be acceptable. The ration meets the animals MP requirement (MP supply = 1550 g; MP requirement 1390 g; Surplus = 160 g) and the surplus is 12% of the predicted requirements. The overall ration crude protein content (supplementary screen - press **S**) is 16.5% which is probably sufficient for 25 litres of milk.

As shown at the bottom of the main ration screen in bold type the rumen function is limited by the supply of FME in the ration. If the surplus of 254 g ERDP could all be utilised to synthesise MCP it would halve the requirement for DUP. However the ration can only be supplemented with additional FME if more ME is added or feeds with a low FME:ME ratio are replaced with feeds with a higher ratio. Feeding more ME and hence FME is not desirable as this would increase ME supply and result in a surplus. Press **I** to look at the Intermediate calculations screen and look at the top half of the screen. The third column of numbers is the FME content of each feed expressed as a percentage of the ME content. It is the low percentage figure for the silage (78%) that is restricting the amount of FME available in the rumen. This is often seen with fermented feeds. Press **M** to return to the main screen.

The total supply of FME is 13% less than that required by the rumen microbes to utilise all the ERDP. Imbalances of ERDP and FME of greater than 10% may reduce rumen function which will restrict microbial activity and may limit voluntary intake.

Exercise 3

In June a farmer is expecting to get maintenance plus 25 litres off good grass. If the cows weigh 600 kg, are not changing weight and are in Week 20 of lactation and 10 weeks pregnant will such a ration be sufficient?

Solution

The formulated ration is stored as ration eight entitled "MP exercises - Exercise 3". The ration supplies sufficient energy and there is a surplus of 158 g MP a day which is 11% of the requirements. There is a large deficit of ERDP (25%) and a surplus of FME (34%). This contrasts with the previous exercise and is due to the difference in the forage. Although the energy (ME) contents of the grass and silage are similar, the silage has been modified in the ensiling process. The microbial action in the silo converts sugars (FME) to lactic and volatile fatty acids (non-FME sources) and acts on the protein to increase its degradability. The result is a feed low in FME and high in ERDP. The surplus of FME in this ration is probably not important. In terms of chemical analyses it is due to the high sugar content of the ration (17.4% sugars on Supplementary screen). If the intake of sugar was due to infrequent large meals of sugar-rich feeds this might cause indigestion and ruminal acidosis (as seen when feeding high-starch supplementary feeds), but as the sugars are being consumed all day and the ration is rich in fibre it is probable that the rumen health will not be affected.

The supplementary screen (Press S) shows that the crude protein content of the ration is only 13.9% against a suggested minimum for this milk yield of 15%. The ration may therefore benefit from supplementing with a high CP compound in the parlour. Given the shortage of ERDP in the ration there is no need to use feeds of a low degradability (and high price) as a high degradability and a supply of ERDP will be more effective.

Exercise 4

This exercise demonstrates the interactions between the supply and requirements of FME, ERDP and DUP. Retrieve ration number nine entitled "MP exercises - Exercise 4". This is a typical ration for 30 litres milk based on 45 kg average grass silage (ME 10.4) and straights plus a mineral. The ration is balanced for energy supply and has a surplus of MP (312 g) and a crude protein content of 17.3%. Note down the requirements for ME, FME, ERDP and DUP (Table 19.7). Now increase the amount of wheat to 5.0 kg.

The additional wheat has not altered the ration quality (q) sufficiently to alter the ME requirements but the additional ERDP supplied in the ration has increased the requirement of FME by 8 MJ. One kg

of wheat supplies 11 MJ FME and this increases the requirement for ERDP by 123 g. In the basic ration there was slightly more ERDP available in the rumen than there was FME to allow the microbes to convert it to MCP. Adding the wheat altered the balance of ERDP and FME in the rumen and increased supply of FME relative to ERDP. The rumen microbes can therefore synthesis more MCP and hence the amount of DUP required falls.

Table 19.7 ME, FME, ERDP and DUP requirements

	Requirements			
	ME (MJ)	FME (MJ)	ERDP (g)	DUP (g)
Basic ration	215	192	2029	316
1 kg additional wheat	215	200	2153	237
1.2 kg additional rapeseed	215	215	2162	231

Now return the wheat to 4 kg and increase the rapeseed meal to 2.2 kg. Again, the ME requirements have not altered because q has not changed much. At this level of animal production rapeseed meal is imbalanced for ruminally available energy and protein. The feed supplies more protein (ERDP) than energy (FME) to the microbes such that there will be an excess of ERDP when the amount of rapeseed meal is increased. To allow all of the ERDP in the ration to be converted into MCP the rumen microbes would require 220 MJ FME. However, by definition (Chapter 6, page 69) the FME content of a feed cannot be greater than the ME content and therefore it is considered that the requirements for FME cannot exceed the ME requirements and so the computer screen shows an FME requirement of 215 MJ ME.

Exercise 5

Look at ration number 10 saved as "MP Exercises - Exercise 5". This is a ration for a 630 kg cow giving 30 litres of milk in Week 8 of lactation and losing 0.5 kg weight a day. The cow is being fed on a mixture of grass and maize silage supplemented with wheat, maize gluten and rapeseed meal. Assess the ration - how can the deficiencies be corrected?

Solution

When assessing a formulated ration on the computer screen the various nutritional factors should be considered in the order of limiting factors outlined in Chapter 1, page 3). The voluntary intake must be assessed first followed by ME, MP, NDF then ERDP and DUP followed by the major minerals and finally the chemical analyses on the supplementary screen. The overall intake and that of each ration ingredient seem plausible (but a farm inspection would be needed to make sure) but there is a significant energy deficit of 10 MJ ME which needs correcting.

Given the high energy density of the ration (M/D 11.4 on Supplementary screen) and the low fat content (3.2%) supplementing with fats would effectively resolve the ME deficit. Adding 0.4 kg of fat prills eliminates the energy deficit, raises the fat content to an acceptable 5.3% and the ration is now balanced for energy and protein.

On closer inspection of the original ration, there is also a significant deficit of FME (-27 MJ) and a corresponding surplus of ERDP (304 g/day). The MP surplus (86 g/day) is quite small (5% of requirements) and animal performance could be increased by better use of the surplus ERDP. Increasing the amount of wheat in the ration would increase the supply of FME. Increasing the amount of wheat to 3.0 kg increases the supply of FME as well as ME. The energy deficit is reduced to 2 MJ ME and the MP surplus (132 g/day) has increased slightly. The combined sugars and starch content of the ration has increased to 19.7% and this will probably promote better milk protein contents.

19.5   Minerals - Chapter 11

19.5.1   Manual exercises
These exercises will require you to use the mineral requirement Tables 20.15 to 20.20 (pages 212 to 214) and the feed analyses in Table 20.21 in Chapter 20 that start on page 215.

Exercise 1
What are the mineral requirements of a 600 kg cow giving 30 litres of milk and losing 0.5 kg a day when given 60 kg of a total mixed ration that has the following analysis: DM 33.3%, ME 11.2 MJ/kg DM and GE 18.7 MJ/kg DM?

1. Calculate dry matter intake and ration q.

    DMI = 60 x (33.3/100)
         = 20.0 kg

    q   = 11.2 / 18.7
         = 0.60

2. Determine maintenance requirements.

    Ca = 25.3 g   (Table 20.15, page 212)
    Mg = 11.1 g   (Table 20.16, page 212)
    P   = 38.1 g   (Table 20.17, page 213)

3. Determine lactation requirements (Table 20.18, page 213).

    Ca = 54.6 g
    Mg = 24.1 g
    P   = 48.0 g

4. Determine requirements for weight change (Table 20.20, page 214).

    Ca = -7.4 g
    Mg = -1.3 g
    P   = -5.1 g

5. Determine totals.

    Ca = 25.3 + 54.6 - 7.4 = 73 g/day
    Mg = 11.1 + 24.1 - 1.3 = 34 g/day
    P   = 38.1 + 48.0 - 5.1 = 81 g/day

Exercise 2
A 38 week pregnant dry cow (550 kg, no weight change) is being fed on a diet of poor grass (63D) *ad libitum* (see Table 20.21, page 216, for analysis). If she consumes 43.5 kg fresh weight will this meet her mineral requirements?

Solution
1. Calculate dry matter intake and ration q.

    DMI = 43.5 x (23/100)
         = 10.0 kg

    q   = 9.8/18.4 (Table 20.21, pages 215 to 219)
         = 0.53   Therefore q < 0.7

2. Determine maintenance requirements.

    Ca = 15.0 g   (Table 20.15, page 212)
    Mg = 10.2 g   (Table 20.16, page 212)
    P   = 19.0 g   (Table 20.17, page 213)

3. Determine pregnancy requirements (Table 20.19, page 214).

    Ca = 11.4 g
    Mg =   4.1 g
    P   =   8.0 g

4. Determine totals.

    Ca = 15.0 + 11.4 = 26.4 g/day
    Mg = 10.2 + 4.1 = 14.3 g/day
    P   = 19.0 + 8.0 = 27.0 g/day

5. Calculate ration supply (Table 20.21, page 216).

	DMI	Ca	Mg	P
Poor grass (63D)	10.0 kg	4.4 g/kg DM	1.4 g/kg DM	2.5 g/kg DM
TOTALS		44.0 g	14.0 g	25.0 g

6. Compare requirements with supply.

	Ca	Mg	P
Supply (g/day)	44.0	14.0	25.0
Requirements (g/day)	26.4	14.3	27.0
Balance (± g/day)	+17.6	-0.3	-2.0

This is a typical mineral status for a dry cow which often leads to milk fever. The ration contains an excess of calcium which will reduce the efficiency of calcium absorption (see Chapter 7, page 80). The marginal status for magnesium will slowly deplete the cows status and further reduce her ability to mobilise calcium after calving. The small phosphorus deficiency is probably not worth taking action over as the grass is wet and will not require the saliva flow that a dry feed would.

Exercise 3

A 650 kg cow giving 36 litres of milk (not pregnant, losing 0.5 kg/day) is being given the following ingredients in a complete diet - will the diet meet her mineral requirements?

Grass silage average	25 kg
Maize silage	25 kg
Wheat grain	4 kg
Soyabean meal	2 kg
Rapeseed meal	2 kg

Solution

1. Calculate dry matter intake and ration q (Table 20.21, page 216).

	Fresh weight (kg)	DM (%)	ME (MJ/kg DM)	GE (MJ/kg DM)
Grass silage average	25	27	10.4	19.5
Maize silage	25	30	11.5	18.5
Wheat grain	4	87	13.6	18.2
Soyabean meal ext	2	88	13.4	19.7
Rapeseed meal	2	90	12.0	19.5

	DMI (kg)	ME (MJ)	GE (MJ)
Grass silage average	6.75	70.2	131.6
Maize silage	7.50	86.3	138.8
Wheat grain	3.48	47.3	63.3
Soyabean meal ext	1.76	23.6	34.7
Rapeseed meal	1.80	21.6	35.1
TOTAL	**21.29**	**249.0**	**403.5**

$$q = 249.0 / 403.5 = 0.62$$

2. Determine maintenance requirements.

Ca	=	27.0 g	(Table 20.15, page 212)
Mg	=	12.0 g	(Table 20.16, page 212)
P	=	40.5 g	(Table 20.17, page 213)

3. Determine lactation requirements (Table 20.18, page 213).

Ca	=	65.6 g
Mg	=	28.9 g
P	=	57.6 g

4. Determine contributions from weight loss (Table 20.20, page 214).

Ca	=	-7.4 g
Mg	=	-1.3 g
P	=	-5.1 g

5. Determine totals.

Ca	=	27.0 + 65.6 - 7.4	=	85.2 g/day
Mg	=	12.0 + 28.9 - 1.3	=	39.6 g/day
P	=	40.5 + 57.6 - 5.1	=	93.0 g/day

6. Calculate ration supply (Table 20.21, page 216).

	DMI (kg)	Ca (g/kg DM)	Mg (g/kg DM)	P (g/kg DM)
Grass silage average	6.75	6.8	1.6	3.1
Maize silage	7.50	3.9	2.4	1.8
Wheat grain	3.48	0.6	1.1	3.4
Soyabean meal ext	1.76	4.5	2.9	7.6
Rapeseed meal	1.80	7.8	4.5	12.0

	Ca (g)	Mg (g)	P (g)
Grass silage average	45.9	10.8	20.9
Maize silage	29.3	18.0	13.5
Wheat grain	2.1	3.8	11.8
Soyabean meal ext	7.9	5.1	13.4
Rapeseed meal	14.0	8.1	21.6
TOTALS	**99.2**	**45.8**	**81.2**

7. Compare requirements with supply.

	Ca (g)	Mg (g)	P (g)
Supply	99.2	45.8	81.2
Requirements	85.2	39.6	93.0
Balance	14.0	6.5	-11.8

The calcium and magnesium balances are satisfactory but there is a considerable deficiency of phosphorus. This is a result of the maize silage in the diet which is low in phosphorus. Diets including maize silage invariably need supplementing with a high phosphorus mineral.

19.5.2   Computer exercises

Exercise 1

What are the mineral requirements of a 630 kg cow giving 25 litres of milk losing 0.5 kg a day if she is in Week 25 of the lactation and 17 weeks pregnant? If the cow is on a complete diet rather than a conventional feeding system will this change her requirements, and if so why?

Solution

This ration is not stored on the computer but will need to be created. The requirements for the cow on a conventional feeding system are shown in Table 19.8. In order to ensure that the calculated requirements are the same as Table 19.1 it is best to quit the program and restart it to ensure that previously entered rations do not affect the calculations. By changing the cow to a complete diet feeding system the intake is likely to be increased by a factor of about 1.2. The maintenance requirements for calcium and phosphorus are both based on dry matter intake and hence these will increase (Table 19.8). The increase in the phosphorus allowance is greater than that for calcium as the former requirements are dependent solely on intake (Chapter 11, page 116) whereas calcium is dependent on body weight and intake.

Table 19.8 Requirements (g/day) for calcium, phosphorus and magnesium for a cow on a conventional diet and a complete diet feeding system

	Main-tenance	Lacta-tion	Preg-nancy	Weight change	TOTAL
Conventional feeding					
Calcium	24	43	1	-7	60
Phosphorus	35	40	0	-5	70
Magnesium	12	20	0	-1	31
Complete diet					
Calcium	27	43	1	-7	64
Phosphorus	42	40	0	-5	77
Magnesium	12	20	0	-1	31

Exercise 2

The ration outlined below is typical of maize silage based diets fed in the east of England to promote milk protein and depress milk fat. What is the mineral balance if it is fed to a 630 kg cow giving 33 litres milk and losing 0.5 kg weight a day in Week 15 of lactation and 7 weeks pregnant? Would you recommend any mineral supplements?

Ration

Maize silage	*ad libitum* (enter **99** for feed amount)
Sp Barley Straw	0.5 kg
Wheat grain	2.0 kg
Soyabean meal	1.5 kg
Rapeseed meal	3.0 kg
Sugar beet feed	2.0 kg

Solution

The formulated ration is saved as ration number 11, "Mineral Exercises - Maize silage diet". The basic ration is balanced for intake, has a very slight energy deficit (-2 MJ which can be ignored), a shortage of fibre (33.8% NDF), a surplus of FME (19 MJ) and hence a deficit of ERDP (-212 g/day), a surplus of DUP (212 g/day) and MP (212 g/day). The ration contains an excess amount of calcium and magnesium but a considerable (17%) deficit in phosphorus. The ration is deficient in fibre (33.8% NDF) and high in starch and sugars (24.5%). The principal problem then is the deficiency of phosphorus. This is common to many diets based on maize silage and is a result of its low content of phosphorus. The ration has a relatively low dry matter (41%) and it is probable that saliva production is not as high as the feeding standards (AFRC, 1991) assume and therefore the deficiency is probably not as severe as it seems. A mineral supplement would be recommended. If a standard mineral is used, a high inclusion (250 g/day) is required to meet the phosphorus requirements and this reduces the intake of silage and makes the ration more deficient in energy (ME). Alternatively a specialist, and more expensive, high phosphorus mineral could be used when 120g/day would suffice. Another alternative would be to supplement with about 500 g of fishmeal a day which would supply the required phosphorus, improve the balance of ERDP and FME in the rumen and possibly have more effect on raising milk protein concentration and fertility performance.

Exercise 3

A farmer is feeding a ration of 37 kg poor grass plus 2.0 kg straw to his 600 kg dry cows. They are in Week 37 of pregnancy and are not gaining or losing weight. Assess the ration.

Solution

The ration is saved as ration number 12, "Mineral Exercises - Dry cow diet". The ration does not meet the predicted dry matter intake but this limitation of intake ensures that the energy status of the cow is nearly balanced and the animals do not gain weight. The intake of this ration would only be achievable if the stocking rate is high so that the animals actually eat 2 kg of straw. There is a surplus of 188g MP and a surplus of DUP. The deficit of ERDP (200 g/day) is due to the high sugar and hence FME content of the grass. The ration contains a large excess of calcium (75%) and a deficit of phosphorus and magnesium (10% and 10%). Such rations are typical of those given to dry cows in the autumn where farmers are trying to control body weight gain. The large surplus of calcium results in the mechanisms that control calcium being adjusted to a low efficiency of absorption (see Chapter 7, page 80). The low content of magnesium in the diet reduces the ability of the animal to mobilise calcium from the bone. This makes the cow prone to milk fever as she cannot adjust to meet the sudden increase in calcium requirements once milk production commences. Supplementation of such rations at grass is difficult but a low-calcium, high-magnesium mineral should be added possibly in combination with a small amount (2 kg/day) of a supplementary feed low in calcium which could be a high-protein, high-DUP compound as discussed in Chapter 15 (page 180).

19.6 Diet formulation - Chapter 18

19.6.1 Manual exercises

These exercises bring together many of the ideas and calculations used in the previous chapters and take the assessments further to consider such supplementary analyses as crude protein, oil, fibre (NDF), sugars and starch content. The results obtained in the manual exercises differ slightly from that obtained with the computer "Ration formulation exercises - Manual I" as the calculations throughout the computer assessment are carried out with far greater precision.

Exercise 1

Will the ration outlined below satisfy the requirements of a 650 kg cow giving 30 litres of milk (4.0% fat and 3.2% protein) losing 0.5 kg a day in Week 14 of her lactation and not pregnant? The silage is offered in ring feeders, the wheat as a midday feed and the concentrates in the parlour.

Ration

Average clamp silage (ME = 10.4) 41 kg
Compound 20% CP   6.5 kg
Wheat grain   2.0 kg

Suggested approach:

Carry out the calculations in the following order:

1. Work out ration DMI.
2. Work out ME and GE supplied by ration and hence ration q.
3. Work out predicted dry matter intake and compare.
4. Work out animal ME requirements and compare.
5. Work out supply of ERDP and DUP and hence MP supply.
6. Work out MP requirements and compare.
7. Work out minerals supply and requirements and compare.
8. Work out ration fibre (NDF), fat and CP contents.
9. Work out sugar and starch content.

Solution

1. Ration DMI.

   Determine dry matter intake of each ration ingredient (Table 20.21, pages 215 to 219).

	Fresh (kg)	DM (%)	DMI (kg)
Silage (ME = 10.4)	41.0	27	11.07
Compound 20% CP	6.5	87	5.66
Wheat grain	2.0	87	1.74
TOTAL			18.47

2. Work out ME and GE supplied by ration and hence ration q (Table 20.21, pages 215 to 219).

	DMI (kg)	ME (MJ/kg DM)	GE (MJ/kg DM)	ME (MJ)	GE (MJ)
Silage	11.07	10.4	19.5	115.1	215.9
Compound	5.66	13.5	18.4	76.4	104.1
Wheat grain	1.74	13.6	18.2	23.7	31.7
TOTAL				215.2	351.7

   $$q = 215.2 / 351.7$$
   $$= 0.61$$

3. Work out predicted dry matter intake and compare (Table 20.1, page 204).

   Ration q = 0.61, Weight = 650 kg, Milk yield = 30 litres

   Basic intake = 19.3 kg DM/day

Correction factors (Tables 20.2 and 20.3, page 205)
   Stage of lactation - Week 14 = 1.00
   Feeding methods: no correction

Predicted intake = 19.3 kg.

The ration supplies 18.47 kg DM and so the whole ration is likely to be eaten.

4. Work out animal ME requirements and compare.

   Maintenance (Table 20.5, page 206)
   650 kg body weight, q = 0.61
   ME_{maint} = 65.2 MJ

   Lactation (Table 20.6, page 207)
   q = 0.61, 4.0% fat, 3.2% protein
   ME_{lact} = 5.08 MJ / litre
   30 litres = 30 x 5.08 = 152.4 MJ

   Weight change (Table 20.8, page 208)
   -0.5 kg/day, milking cow, q = 0.61
   ME_{weight} = -10.9 MJ

   Correct for level of production (Table 20.10, page 209)
   APL = (65.2 + 152.4 - 10.9) / 65.2
       = 3.17
   C_L = 1.040

   Total requirements
   ME = (65.2 + 152.4 - 10.9) x 1.040
      = 215.0 MJ

   The ration supplies 215.2 MJ ME/day and so there is a very slight surplus of ME of 0.2 MJ/day.

5. Work out supply of ERDP and DUP and hence MP supply.

   Obtain the FME, ERDP and DUP content for the feeds at this APL (3.17). Use Table 20.22 (pages 220 to 223) and use the high energy 18% CP compound and the grass 65D silage.

	FME (MJ /kg DM)	ERDP (g/kg DM)	DUP (g/kg DM)
Silage	7.6	93.7	18.5
Compound 18% CP	10.3	123.6	56.8
Wheat grain	13.1	99.9	13.2

   Determine FME, ERDP and DUP supplied by each feed and hence the total supplies.

	DMI (kg)	FME (MJ)	ERDP (g)	DUP (g)
Silage	11.07	84.1	1037.3	204.8
Compound	5.66	58.3	699.6	321.5
Wheat grain	1.74	22.8	173.8	23.0
TOTAL		165.2	1910.7	549.3

   Y = 11.0 (Table 20.22, pages 220 to 223)

   $MCP_{protein}$ = ERDP = 1910.7

   MCP_{energy} = Y x FME = 11.0 x 165.2 = 1817.2

   Supply of FME is limiting the MCP production therefore MCP supply = 1817.2 g/day.

$$MP = (MCP \times 0.64) + DUP$$
$$= (1817.2 \times 0.64) + 549.3$$
$$= 1712.3 \text{ g/day}$$

This figure differs considerably from that shown on the computer and the main reason is that we have had to use an analysis for a 18% CP compound rather than a 20% CP compound. This is a limitation of the publically available database and in practice one should request the necessary analyses from the manufacturer of the compound.

6. Work out MP requirements and compare.

Maintenance (Table 20.11, page 210)
650 kg cow MP_{maint} = 312 g/day

Lactation (Table 20.12, page 210)
30 litres at 3.2% protein
MP_{lact} = 1368

Weight change (Table 20.14, page 211)
-0.5 kg/day
MP_{weight} = -66

Total MP requirements
312 + 1368 - 66 = 1614 g MP /day

The ration supplies 1712 g against a requirement of 1614 g leaving a surplus of 98 g/day (6.1%).

7. Work out mineral supply and requirements and compare (Table 20.21, pages 215 to 219).

Supply	DMI (kg)	Ca (g/kg)	Ca (g)	Mg (g/kg)	Mg (g)	P (g/kg)	P (g)
Silage	11.07	6.8	75.3	1.6	17.7	3.1	34.3
Compound	5.66	11.0	62.3	6.0	34.0	8.0	45.3
Wheat grain	1.74	0.6	1.0	1.1	1.9	3.4	5.9
TOTAL			**138.6**		**53.6**		**85.5**

Requirements (Table 21.15 to 21.20, pages 212 to 214), using the actual intake and not the predicted appetite.

		Ca	Mg	P q = 0.61
Maintenance	650 kg, DMI = 18.47	24.4	12.0	35.2
Lactation	30 litres	54.6	24.1	48.0
Weight loss	-0.5 kg/day	-7.4	-1.3	-5.1
REQUIREMENT		71.6	34.8	78.1
SUPPLY		138.6	53.6	85.5
BALANCE (± g/day)		**+67.0**	**+18.8**	**+7.4**

The ration contains an excess of all three major minerals.

8. Work out ration fibre (NDF), fat and CP content in percentage terms of the DMI (Table 20.21, pages 215 to 219).

	DMI (kg)	NDF (g/kg)	NDF (g)	Fat (g/kg)	Fat (g)	CP (g/kg)	CP (g)
Silage	11.07	546	6044	35	387	151	1672
Compound	5.66	180	1019	70	396	230	1302
Wheat grain	1.74	166	289	19	33	123	214
TOTALS	18.47		7352		816		3188
% of DMI			**39.8**		**4.4**		**17.3**

The fibre content is only marginally less than the recommended 40%, but as long as the rest of the diet is satisfactory this can be ignored as such a deficit is unlikely to impair rumen function on its own. The fat content is satisfactory at 4.4% and the protein within the acceptable range at 17.3%.

9. Work out sugar and starch content in percentage terms.

	DMI (kg)	Sugars (g/kg DM)	Sugars (g)	Starch (g/kg DM)	Starch (g)
Silage	11.07	17	188	7	77
Compound	5.66	150	849	250	1415
Wheat grain	1.74	58	101	660	1148
TOTAL	18.47		1138		2640
% of DMI			**6.2**		**14.3**

The combined starch and sugar content is 20.5% which should be sufficient to support the observed milk protein at this level of production.

Exercise 2
A group of high-yielding cows are being fed a mixture of grass and maize silage and a 24% compound in the parlour as outlined below. The ration has been formulated for 650 kg cows yielding 40 litres of milk a day (4% fat and 3.2% protein), losing 0.7 kg a day and in Week 8 of lactation.

Ration

Average grass silage	21 kg
Maize silage	26 kg
Compound 24% CP	10 kg

Assess the ration and suggest any alterations that you feel are necessary.

Solution
1. Ration DMI.

Determine dry matter intake of each ration ingredient (Table 20.21, pages 215 to 219).

	Fresh (kg)	DM (%)	DMI (kg)
Grass Silage (ME = 10.4)	21 kg	27	5.67
Maize silage	26 kg	30	7.8
Compound 24% CP	10 kg	88	8.8
TOTAL			**22.27**

2. Work out ME and GE supplied by ration and hence ration q (Table 20.21, pages 215 to 219).

	DMI (kg)	ME (MJ/kg DM)	GE (MJ/kg DM)	ME (MJ)	GE (MJ)
Grass Silage	5.67	10.4	19.5	59.0	110.6
Maize silage	7.8	11.5	18.5	89.7	144.3
Compound 24%	8.8	13.0	18.4	114.4	161.9
TOTAL				**263.1**	**416.8**

$$q = 263.1 / 416.8$$
$$= 0.63$$

3. Work out predicted dry matter intake and compare (Table 20.1, page 204).

Ration q = 0.63, Weight = 650 kg, Milk yield = 40 litres

Basic intake = 19.5 kg DM/day

Correction factors (Tables 20.2 and 20.3, page 205)
    Stage of lactation - Week 8: 0.96
    Feeding methods: no correction

Predicted intake = 18.7 kg.

The ration supplies 22.3 kg DM and so the cow is unlikely to be able to eat the ration offered.

The forage part of the ration is being offered via a mixer wagon and if the entire ration was to be offered in this way, there would be an increase in feed intake. The farmer should be persuaded to feed most, if not all, of the compound feed through the mixer wagon. If there is concern over enticing cows into the parlour 1 kg could be kept out so that 0.5 kg can be given at each milking.

If a complete diet is used, intake will be increased by a factor of about 1.2 (Table 20.3, page 205). This will increase the intake as follows:

18.7 x 1.2 = 22.5 kg

With such a modification in feeding method the predicted intake is sufficient to allow the cow to eat all of the diet.

4. Work out ME requirements and compare with supply.

Maintenance (Table 20.5, page 206)
650 kg body weight, q = 0.63
ME_{maint} = 64.6 MJ

Lactation (Table 20.6, page 207)
q = 0.63, 4.0% fat, 3.2% protein
ME_{lact} = 5.03 MJ / litre
40 litres = 40 x 5.03 = 201.2 MJ

Weight change (Table 20.8, page 208)
-0.7 kg/day, milking cow, q = 0.63
ME_{weight} = -15.2 MJ

Correct for level of production (Table 20.10, page 209)
APL = (64.6 + 201.2 - 15.2) / 64.6
    = 3.88
C_L = 1.052

Total requirements
ME = (64.6 + 201.2 - 15.2) x 1.052
    = 263.6 MJ

The ration supplies 263.1 MJ ME/day and so there is a very slight deficit of 0.2 MJ/day even at the increased intake; care must be taken to ensure that the cows eat the predicted intake or more.

5. Work out supply of ERDP and DUP and hence MP supply.

Obtain the FME, ERDP and DUP content for the feeds at this APL (3.88). Use Table 20.22 (pages 220 to 223) for FME, ERDP and DUP. Use the "Maize balancer" compound which is 24.5% CP of a fresh (bag declared) basis, the grass silage 65D and the maize silage.

	FME (MJ /kg DM)	ERDP (g/kg DM)	DUP (g/kg DM)
Grass Silage 65 D	7.6	92.3	19.7
Maize silage	9.0	64.4	12.9
Compound 24%	10.2	160.5	88.9

	DMI (kg)	FME (MJ)	ERDP (g)	DUP (g)
Grass Silage	5.67	43.1	523	112
Maize silage	7.8	70.2	502	101
Compound 24%	8.8	89.8	1412	782
TOTAL		203.1	2437	995

Y = 11.4   (Table 20.22, pages 220 to 223)

$MCP_{protein}$ = ERDP = 2437

MCP_{energy} = Y x FME = 11.4 x 203.1 = 2315

Supply of FME is limiting the MCP production therefore MCP supply = 2315 g/day.

MP = (MCP x 0.64) + DUP
    = (2315 x 0.64) + 995
    = 2477 g MP/day

This figure differs considerably from that shown on the computer and the main reason is that we have had to use an analysis for a maize balancer compound rather than a 24% CP compound. Again one should request the necessary analyses from the manufacturer of the compound.

6. Work out MP requirements and compare with supply.

Maintenance   (Table 20.11, page 210)
650 kg cow MP_{maint} = 312 g/day

Lactation   (Table 20.12, page 210)
40 litres at 3.2% protein MP_{lact} = 1823 g/day

Weight change (Table 20.14, page 211)
-0.7 kg/day MP_{weight} = -92 g/day

Total MP requirements
312 + 1823 - 92 = 2043 g MP /day

The ration supplies 2477 g against a requirement of 2043 g leaving a surplus of 434 d/day (21%) which is high and a lower CP compound could probably be used.

7. Work out minerals supply and requirements and compare (Table 20.21, pages 215 to 219).

Supply	DMI (kg)	Ca (g/kg)	Ca (g)	Mg (g/kg)	Mg (g)	P (g/kg)	P (g)
Grass Silage	5.67	6.8	38.6	1.6	9.1	3.1	17.6
Maize silage	7.8	3.9	30.4	2.4	18.7	1.8	14.0
Compound 24%	8.8	12.0	105.6	2.5	22.0	6.0	52.8
TOTAL			**174.6**		**49.8**		**84.4**

Requirements (Tables 21.15 to 21.20, pages 212 to 214)

		Ca (g/day)	Mg (g/day)	P q = 0.63 (g/day)
Maintenance	650 kg, DMI = 22.27	28.0	12.0	42.4
Lactation	40 litres	72.8	32.1	64.1
Weight loss	-0.7 kg/day	-10.4	-1.8	-7.2
REQUIREMENT		90.4	42.3	99.3
SUPPLY		174.6	49.8	84.4
BALANCE (± g/day)		**+84.2**	**+7.5**	**-14.9**

The ration contains an excess of calcium (almost twice the requirements), is satisfactory for magnesium and deficient in phosphorus. As mentioned previously (Mineral exercise, Section 19.5.1) maize silage diets are often deficient in phosphorus and require special mineral supplementation.

8. Work out ration fibre (NDF), fat and CP content in percentage terms (Table 20.21, pages 215 to 219).

	DMI (kg)	NDF (g/kg DM)	NDF (g)	Fat (g/kg DM)	Fat (g)	CP (g/kg DM)	CP (g)
Grass Silage	5.67	546	3096	35	198	151	856
Maize silage	7.8	390	3042	30	234	88	686
Compound 24%	8.8	170	1496	60	528	270	2376
TOTAL	22.27		7634		960		3918
% of DMI			34.3		4.3		17.6

The fibre content is considerably less than the recommended 40% and such a ration may not support adequate milk fat synthesis. Given that all the fibre has been chopped, rumen function might be impaired. If acidosis and indigestion is suspected some long fibre might be included in the ration. The fat content of the diet is satisfactory. The CP content of 17.6% would be considered inadequate by many nutritionists who would often recommend 18 to 19% CP for a cow giving 40 litres of milk. However the MP system predicts the ration has a considerable excess of protein (28% surplus). This is due, in part, to the well-balanced situation in the rumen.

9. Work out sugar and starch content as a percentage of total diet DM.

	DMI	Sugar (g/kg DM)	Sugar (g)	Starch (g/kg DM)	Starch (g)
Grass Silage	5.67	17	96	7	40
Maize silage	7.8	5	39	206	1607
Compound 24%	8.8	130	1144	220	1936
TOTAL	22.27		1279		3583
% of DMI			5.7		16.1

The combined starch and sugar content is 21.8% which is acceptable (page 56).

19.6.2 Computer exercises
Exercise 1
A farmer has made equal amounts of grass silage (average quality) and maize silage for the winter and wants to feed a 20% CP compound in the parlour and up to 15 kg brewers grains. Devise a suitable ration for 28 litres of milk assuming the cows weigh 600 kg are in Week 12 of lactation, not pregnant and losing 0.25 kg weight a day.

Solution
There will be more than one solution to the rationing problem, each of which would satisfy the nutrient requirements on the main and supplementary ration computer screens. To come up with the best ration additional constraints should be set to maximise the use of cheap feeds (usually the forages) and to minimise the use of the more expensive supplements.

Approach - assessment of feeds
The farmer has made equal amounts of grass and maize silage and he may want to feed them in equal proportions through the winter so a balance of 50:50 grass silage:maize silage would be best. This should be offered *ad libitum*. The farmer has said that he wants to feed up to 15 kg brewers' grains a day and, as this feed is usually bought in advance and does not keep well long-term, it would be best to start by looking at using the amount suggested. The compound feed is the most flexible ingredient in the ration. Farmers tend to buy relatively small loads of compound feeds, the amounts offered can be altered simply and, within reason, it is possible to change from one compound feed to another with few problems.

Assessing requirements
By entering the animal description into the computer program it can be seen that the voluntary intake is about 17.7 kg DM/day and the energy requirement about 207 MJ, giving a required energy density (M/D) of 12 MJ ME/kg DM. The ME content of the grass silage, maize silage and brewers grains are, however, all less than 12.0, so some supplementation with compound feed (ME = 13.5) will be required.

Ration formulation
In general, cows giving 25 to 30 litres milk are likely to eat about 12 kg forage DM supplemented by concentrates. Fifteen kg of brewers grains at 25% DM will be about 4 kg DM and so we are looking for another 8 kg forage DM which would be 4 kg DM of each silage. Assuming the DM content of the grass silage is 25%, 16 kg fresh weight equals 4 kg DM and, as maize silage is usually a little drier, approximately 15 kg fresh weight maize silage would be required. Enter the following ration:

Average grass silage   16 kg
Maize silage   15 kg
Brewers' grains   15 kg

The energy is 66 MJ in deficit, which would need to be supplied in 4.7 kg DM of supplement. The compound is 13.5 MJ ME/kg DM so 4.7 kg DM will supply about 63 MJ ME. This does not seem quite enough energy but the requirements of the animal will fall and DMI increase when supplements are added and ration quality improves. Add 5.5 kg of 20% CP compound to the ration.

By adding the compound feed, the energy requirement has been reduced so that there is a surplus of 4 MJ of ME and all the other nutrients are also satisfactory. This ration would be adequate but a little expensive at £1.85/cow/day. There is, however, quite a large excess of MP (498 g) and a lot of this protein is being supplied by the compound, an expensive source of protein. What happens if compound intake is reduced and the silage intake rises? Reduce the compound to 4.5 kg. This gives an intake deficit of 0.8 kg, so raise the intake of maize silage by 2 kg and that of grass by 1 kg. We now have a slight excess of intake, so it might be best to set the grass silage to *ad libitum* at this stage (enter **1 99**). The ME is now in balance, the surplus of MP has fallen to 408 g and the cost to £1.76 which is a saving of 9p/cow/day. Phosphorus is deficient due to the increased dependence on maize silage and 50 g of a high-phosphorus mineral could be used. All the analyses on the supplementary screen are satisfactory. The final ration is saved as "Dairy cow computer exercise I".

We have a choice of two rations, both of which are close enough to being balanced given the limitations of feed and animal assessment. We can either feed 5.5 kg of compound and slightly less forage at a cost of £1.85/cow/day or cut the compound back to 4.5 kg/day, feed slightly more forage and save 9p/cow/day. In practice what one may choose to do is, provided there is sufficient forage available, feed the low compound diet first and if animal performance is disappointing increase it to 5.5 kg and observe the response. If there is no response to 5.5 kg of compound the problem might lie elsewhere and more detailed investigations are required.

Exercise 2
A farmer has his cows out on silage aftermath in mid-August which are assumed to have a nutritive composition of 10.7 MJ ME and 121 g CP/kg DM. Most of the cows have passed their peak yield and are expected to be giving about 24 litres milk a day. They are given 4 kg of an 18% CP compound in the milking parlour and there are no other facilities for feeding other feeds. The farmer reports that the cows are waiting to come in for milking and that

there is some ungrazed grass left at the end of each grazing session. The cows are only yielding 20 litres of milk and analysis of the grass by NIRs shows that it is 9.8 MJ ME and 106 g CP/kg DM (poor grass). Assess the ration and make any changes that you feel are required. Assume the cows are 600 kg weight, not losing or gaining weight, in Week 25 of the lactation and 17 weeks pregnant.

Solution
When assessing a farm problem it pays to look at the history of the situation first, assess the original diet for any shortcomings and only then work out a new ration. The major problem is failure to reach the target milk yield of 24 litres; actual yield is 4 litres short suggesting a nutritional problem. Intake may be a problem but the farmer reports that the cows are leaving some grass which suggests they are getting enough to eat. The problem would seem to be the over-estimation of the nutritive value of the grass; the actual analysis was considerably lower than the original assumption. A lack of energy in mid-lactation would result in a failure to reach predicted yield.

Create the assumed ration on the computer to check that the animals would have performed satisfactorily if the grass had been of better quality. (The ration is called "Dairy cow computer exercise II" on the computer.) The assumed ration is generally adequate for 24 litres of milk. There is a deficiency of ERDP, due to the high sugars and hence surplus of FME from the grass, and a deficiency of phosphorus. The ration has a low dry matter (24.8%) and the deficiency in phosphorus is probably is of no consequence. The supplementary screen shows that the ration only contains 13.8% crude protein against a suggested requirement of 14.8%. Now alter the grass to poor quality grass. Delete the average grass first, then select the poor grass, set this to *ad libitum* (**99**), then return to the ration. The ration is now deficient in energy by 17 MJ ME/day which is sufficient for about 3.7 l milk. The ration has a greater deficiency in ERDP, the MP surplus is small (67g), there is a deficiency of phosphorus (14 g/day) and the crude protein content has dropped to 12.6%

The actual ration being eaten is therefore deficient in energy and protein. Increasing the amount of compound will supply both of these so try this simple solution first by slowly increasing the compound until energy is in balance. Nine and a half kg of compound is required to reduce the energy deficit to zero, which increases the cost from £1.06/day to £1.70/day. This would also pose problems at each milking as 4.75 kg is a large meal of compound which may upset the rumen. An alternative would be to alter the compound to a higher energy, higher protein type. Looking at the list of feeds, the compound 20% CP has more energy (13.5

cf. 12.5) and more protein (230 cf. 207). Try replacing the 18% CP compound with a 20% CP compound. Just under 7 kg of compound are required to balance the energy in the ration. This amount of compound gives a larger surplus of MP, a slight surplus of phosphorus and a higher CP content (14.9%). However the combined starch and sugar content is high at 24.9%. Of this 15.3% is sugars which will come primarily from the grass and so will be consumed throughout the day. Therefore the risk of carbohydrate overload and hence acidosis and indigestion is reduced.

19.7   Case studies - Chapter 18

In Chapter 18 (page 174) three case studies relating to milk composition and yield were presented. The following section presents some possible solutions. When assessing problem rations it is best to assess the original ration against the desired performance to identify the problem. By the time the farmer notices the under-performance the cows have adjusted to the ration fed and actual performance will often match actual intakes.

19.7.1   Case study 1 - low milk fat
Mr Jones has a very high stocking rate (2.7 cows/ hectare or 1.1 cows/acre). It is probable that he is very short of grass in the spring and therefore to maximise the yield of grass silage from a limited number of acres he has elected to delay harvest and go for forage bulk rather than quality.

Original ration. The original ration has been saved on disc as "Case Study 1 - Mr Jones - Basic ration". The energy (ME) is in balance, there is a large surplus of MP (670 g), all the mineral intakes are adequate and the ration CP is 18.8%. The major problem would appear to be the lack of fibre (NDF) in the ration (34.6%).

Nutritional pathology. A lack of fibre in the diet will restrict the production of acetic and butyric acid in the rumen (Chapter 5, page 57). These are precursors for about half of the milk fat (Chapter 5, page 62) and so milk fat content falls.

Alternative rations. The root of the problem is a lack of forage hectares and therefore possible solutions can be thought of as buying in alternative forages which are high in fibre (NDF). Such feeds can be identified from Table 20.21 (pages 215 to 219) but it can be seen that most of them are low in ME and would therefore place the animal in an energy deficit. If the energy density of the forage component is going to be decreased as fibre is brought in then the energy density of the supplements must be increased. The advantage of using a compound feed is that, in many instances, the farmer has frequent deliveries of small amounts of compound and it is relatively straightforward to change to a different compound within the range offered by the compounder.

A final consideration is how the proposed alternative ration will be fed on the farm. On many small farms with a simple feeding system there is little space to store additional feeds and few facilities for feeding them out. This often means that the new feed must come bagged or in small units and be palatable enough to be eaten on its own. In many cases this will rule out feeds that need to be ensiled (maize silage, whole crop, etc.) or feeds that are commonly only available in bulk loads such as maize gluten feed.

A possible solution is to increase the quality of the supplement so that reduced amounts can be fed and some appetite is freed up for a bought-in fibre source. Sugar beet feed is attractive in this instance as it is relatively high in fibre (294 g NDF/kg DM) and energy (12.5 MJ ME/kg DM), palatable and is commonly available in bags. A small amount of good hay could also be bought in and fed at the front of the cubicles or in hay racks if they are available. Changing the compound to a high energy (13.5 ME) 20% CP compound increases the energy density of the ration such that 3 kg sugar beet feed can be added as a source of fibre and the compound intake cut to 8.3 kg. Such a ration is balanced for energy and the fibre (NDF) has increased to 39.5%. The protein and mineral status of the ration are relatively unchanged.

If could be argued that sugar beet feed is not a good source of fibre as it is a pelleted feed and therefore will promote less cudding than a long-fibre source such as hay. However the energy density of the hay available (8.7 MJ ME) is considerably less than the silage or sugar beet feed so including it in the ration will worsen the energy balance. If a higher energy compound feed is to be used this will probably have a high fat inclusion which will depress the FME intake and increase fat intake. However when the ration contains 3 kg of sugar beet feed it has a slight surplus of FME.

19.7.2   Case study 2 - low milk protein
It is important to differentiate between poor nutritional quality (low ME) and poor fermentation quality as it is the fermentation quality that will make a silage unpalatable. The silage should be inspected on a visit to the farm and its dry matter, acidity, butyric acid content, extent of fermentation and the quality of ensiling assessed as discussed in Chapter 2 (page 26). This visual assessment should be backed up with a detailed analysis looking particularly at dry matter, pH, butyric acid content, VFA profile and ammonia and amino acid nitrogen

contents and any prediction of intake. Efforts should also be made to quantify the intake of the silage on-farm as a low palatability silage will have a low intake potential.

Original ration. The final original ration is saved on the computer disc as "Case study 2 - Mr Ffloyd - Basic ration"'. The intake of 19.3 kg is being met and the cows are predicted to eat 10.7 kg DM of silage which is acceptable as long as the fermentation quality is acceptable and the feed palatable. Energy supply is in severe deficit (20 MJ ME/day), but the protein (MP) and mineral supply are in excess. All the analyses on the supplementary screen are satisfactory but the energy density is low (10.6 MJ/kg DM) for a cow giving 30 litres of milk and fibre content is high (42.7% NDF).

Nutritional diagnosis. The main problem with this ration is the lack of energy. This is a common cause of low milk protein (Chapter 13, page 130) and is thought to be due to the cow using protein as an energy source and therefore reducing the supply of amino acids to the liver and udder.

Alternative rations. Looking at the original ration and the farm description it is likely that the farmer wants to carry on feeding a sizeable amount of concentrate in the parlour as this is often the only way of varying the diet for different yields. If farmers are feeding molasses they have often made a considerable investment in specialist equipment to handle this feed and so may be reluctant to drop it from their rations. Any additional feeds must be palatable as they can only be sprinkled on top of the silage. If feeds such as fishmeal and fat prills are required they will need to be incorporated in the compound.

As the nutritional problem is a lack of energy it is helpful to look at the energy density of each feed and determine if it has a role in the diet. The silage is low in energy (9.2 MJ ME/kg DM) but the farmer will have conserved a large amount and so it must be fed. The straw is also low in energy (6.8 MJ) and the only useful nutrient it is contributing towards the ration is fibre (NDF) which is in excess. The first thing to do would be to remove the straw. Unfortunately this does not improve the ration much as it is replaced by low energy silage and so the energy deficit only falls by 1 MJ. It will therefore be necessary to increase the energy density of the supplementary feeds. The 20% CP compound on the feed data-base is high in energy so this could be used to replace the 18% compound. Feeding 10 kg of the 20% compound will eliminate the energy deficiency. However the ration is now slightly high in crude protein (19.1%). Looking at the ration the role of the soyabean meal was to supply protein and in particular DUP. As we are now feeding a 20% CP compound the soyabean meal can be removed from the ration. The ration is now slightly deficient in

energy (-2 MJ) and fibre (38.4%) but if the farmer wanted to keep things simple such a ration might suffice. However the compound intake is high (10 kg/day); if this is fed as two meals in the parlour it will be a large meal of a starchy feed which might cause acidosis and indigestion and a mid-day feed would be preferable. The mid-day feed could be the 20% compound or it could be replaced with a palatable, high-energy high-fibre feed such as sugar beet feed. Adding 2 kg of sugar beet feed allows the compound to be reduced to 9 kg but as the intake of silage declines the fibre content is worsened (37.6%). Because of this the sugar content is increased and so the idea of feeding sugar beet feed in this ration should be dropped.

The revised ration contains an large surplus of MP (668 g) and this is because we used a 20% CP compound for its higher energy content. Most compounders also offer a high energy 18% CP and although it is not on the feed database it could be mimicked by adding fat to the ration. Return to feeding the 8 kg of 18% compound and add 0.5 kg of fat prills. This leaves the ration energy balance 6 MJ short and the fat needs increasing to 0.7 kg to get the energy in balance. This is an additional 8% (0.7/ 8.7) fat inclusion in a compound which probably already contains 4 to 5% fat and producing such a compound would probably not be possible in many mills. In addition the overall fat content of the ration has increased to 7.1% which may depress rumen activity. If we increase the intake of compound to 10 kg a day the amount of fat required falls to 0.4 kg. The overall fat content has fallen to 5.9% and the crude protein 16.9%.

We have now derived two possible rations; any further progress can only be made after detailed consideration of the different types of compound available from the mill. The underlying problem is one of poor quality silage being inadequate to support the milk yield - in future years attention must be given to make better forages to support high-yielding animals.

19.7.3 Case study 3 - gaining weight, not achieving yield

The main change between the two years is the switch in forages. Looking at the analyses (Table 20.21, pages 215 to 219) it can be seen that maize silage contains more energy (11.5 cf. 10.4 MJ ME/kg DM) and almost half the amount of protein (88 cf. 151 g CP/kg DM) than the grass silage. If the ration last year was balanced for energy and protein (and the animals **did** perform satisfactorily) it is probable that it is now deficient in protein and contains excess energy. Such rations will limit milk production as amino acid supply to the udder may be in short supply but the surplus energy can be used to lay down fat.

Original ration. The original ration to assess would be the one fed last year. This is stored on the computer as "Case study 3 - Mr Smith - Basic ration". It can be seen that the ration is balanced for energy, has a slight excess of FME (due to the maize silage, molasses and wheat), a surplus of DUP and MP and a slight (but probably acceptable) deficiency in phosphorus. The supplementary analyses shows that the crude protein is only 16.2% against a suggested 17%.

When the amount of maize silage is increased to 35 kg the grass silage intake drops to from 40.5 to 12.2 kg such that maize is accounting for more than 75% of the forage dry matter intake. Such changes have considerably altered the supply of energy and protein from forage. There is now an excess of energy (12 MJ/ME) and a deficiency of MP (47g) and the ration crude protein content has fallen to 14%.

Nutritional diagnosis. The deficiency of protein will restrict milk production as there will be insufficient amino acids for milk protein synthesis. If milk production falls there will be a surplus of ME and this will augment the surplus dietary ME intake. The energy cannot be used for milk production as protein is limiting and so it will be used to lay down body fat or reduce the rate of mobilisation and hence the animals will not loose weight as fast as budgeted.

Alternative rations. The two priorities in adjusting this ration are to reduce energy intake and increase protein intake. The root of the problem is the sudden increase in maize silage feeding without any other adjustments. Given that many of the straights will have been "bought forward" on contract and that maize silage can be used as a valuable buffer feed in the summer it may be useful to reduce the amount of maize silage. This requires that there is sufficient grass silage and that the maize clamp is narrow such that the silage will be stable in the summer heat. Let us assume that the farmer budgets that this year he can feed a maximum of 25 kg grass silage. Set the grass silage to 25 kg and the maize silage to *ad libitum*. This has reduced the energy surplus to 6 MJ and there is now a small surplus of DUP (95 g) although the ration is still only 15% CP. The ration is also slightly low in fibre and high in starch and sugars so reduce the wheat to 2 kg. This improves the fibre and starch situation but only reduces the energy to a surplus of 5 MJ as the intake of maize silage has increased. Increase the straw intake to 1 kg/day which reduces the energy surplus to 2 MJ. However the ration is still low in protein; the MP surplus is only 66 g (4%) and the CP content has fallen to 14.8%. The ration is deficient in ERDP and so a high degradability feed is required. Increase the amount of rapeseed meal to 3 kg. This increases the MP surplus to 260 g (14%) and the crude protein to 16.2%. Some nutritionists would be a little concerned about the domination of rapeseed meal as the main protein source and might increase the amount of soyabean meal to 1 kg to ensure a balanced supply of amino acids to the udder and increases the CP content to 16.7%. The slight phosphorus deficiency would probably be regarded as insignificant.

Part 6

TABLES

CHAPTER 20

TABLES OF REQUIREMENTS AND FEED ANALYSES

Dry matter intake

Table 20.1   Predicted dry matter intake of milking cows
Table 20.2   Dry matter intake correction for week of lactation
Table 20.3   Possible correction factors for dry matter intake on farm
Table 20.4   Predicted dry matter intake of dry cows

Energy

Table 20.5   Metabolisable energy requirements for maintenance
Table 20.6   Metabolisable energy requirements for milk
Table 20.7   Metabolisable energy requirements for pregnancy
Table 20.8   Metabolisable energy value of weight change
Table 20.9   Metabolisable energy requirements for activity
Table 20.10   Correction for level of production (APL)

Protein

Table 20.11   Protein (MP) requirements for maintenance
Table 20.12   Protein (MP) requirements for lactation
Table 20.13   Protein (MP) requirements for pregnancy
Table 20.14   Protein (MP) requirements for weight change

MINERALS

Maintenance

Table 20.15   Calcium allowances for maintenance
Table 20.16   Magnesium allowances for maintenance
Table 20.17   Phosphorus allowances for maintenance

Lactation

Table 20.18   Calcium, magnesium and phosphorus allowances for lactation

Pregnancy

Table 20.19   Calcium, magnesium and phosphorus allowances for pregnancy

Weight changes

Table 20.20   Calcium, magnesium and phosphorus allowances for weight changes

Feed analyses

Table 20.21   Principal nutrient composition of feeds
Table 20.22   Protein fraction composition of feeds

NOTE   The data used to generate Tables 20.21 and 20.22 have been taken from a range of sources. The major ones are AFRC (1993), MAFF (1992) and MAFF (1990), with data being selected as being most representative of feeds used in the industry. Where necessary some values have also been obtained from the scientific literature and commercial companies.

Table 20.1 Predicted dry matter intake of milking cows (kg DM/day) (ARC, 1980 and MAFF, 1975)

Milk yield (kg/day or l/day)

Ration q = 0.50

Weight (kg)	0	5	10	15	20
400	7.5	8.4	9.2	10.1	10.9
425	8.0	8.9	9.7	10.6	11.4
450	8.5	9.3	10.2	11.0	11.9
475	9.0	9.8	10.7	11.5	12.4
500	9.4	10.3	11.1	12.0	12.8
525	9.9	10.7	11.6	12.4	13.3
550	10.3	11.2	12.0	12.9	13.7
575	10.8	11.6	12.5	13.3	14.2
600	11.2	12.0	12.9	13.7	14.6
625	11.6	12.5	13.3	14.2	15.0
650	12.1	12.9	13.8	14.6	15.5
675	12.5	13.3	14.2	15.0	15.9
700	12.9	13.7	14.6	15.4	16.3
725	13.3	14.2	15.0	15.9	16.7
750	13.7	14.6	15.4	16.3	17.1

Ration q = 0.55

Weight (kg)	0	5	10	15	20	25
400	8.9	9.9	10.9	11.5	12.0	12.0
425	9.4	10.4	11.4	12.1	12.6	12.8
450	10.0	11.0	12.0	12.8	13.3	13.5
475	10.5	11.5	12.5	13.4	13.9	14.3
500	11.1	12.1	13.1	14.0	14.5	15.0
525	11.6	12.6	13.6	14.6	15.1	15.6
550	12.1	13.1	14.1	15.1	15.8	16.3
575	12.7	13.7	14.7	15.7	16.4	16.9
600	13.2	14.2	15.2	16.2	17.0	17.5
625	13.7	14.7	15.7	16.7	17.6	18.1
650	14.2	15.2	16.2	17.2	18.2	18.8
675	14.7	15.7	16.7	17.7	18.7	19.4
700	15.2	16.2	17.2	18.2	19.2	20.0
725	15.7	16.7	17.7	18.7	19.7	20.6
750	16.1	17.1	18.1	19.1	20.1	21.1

Ration q ≥ 0.60

Weight (kg)	0	5	10	15	20	25	30	35	40	45	50
400	10.0	10.5	11.0	11.5	12.0	12.0	12.0	12.0	12.0	12.0	12.0
425	10.6	11.1	11.6	12.1	12.6	12.8	12.8	12.8	12.8	12.8	12.8
450	11.3	11.8	12.3	12.8	13.3	13.5	13.5	13.5	13.5	13.5	13.5
475	11.9	12.4	12.9	13.4	13.9	14.3	14.3	14.3	14.3	14.3	14.3
500	12.5	13.0	13.5	14.0	14.5	15.0	15.0	15.0	15.0	15.0	15.0
525	13.1	13.6	14.1	14.6	15.1	15.6	15.8	15.8	15.8	15.8	15.8
550	13.8	14.3	14.8	15.3	15.8	16.3	16.5	16.5	16.5	16.5	16.5
575	14.4	14.9	15.4	15.9	16.4	16.9	17.3	17.3	17.3	17.3	17.3
600	15.0	15.5	16.0	16.5	17.0	17.5	18.0	18.0	18.0	18.0	18.0
625	15.6	16.1	16.6	17.1	17.6	18.1	18.6	18.8	18.8	18.8	18.8
650	16.3	16.8	17.3	17.8	18.3	18.8	19.3	19.5	19.5	19.5	19.5
675	16.9	17.4	17.9	18.4	18.9	19.4	19.9	20.3	20.3	20.3	20.3
700	17.5	18.0	18.5	19.0	19.5	20.0	20.5	21.0	21.0	21.0	21.0
725	18.1	18.6	19.1	19.6	20.1	20.6	21.1	21.6	21.8	21.8	21.8
750	18.8	19.3	19.8	20.3	20.8	21.3	21.8	22.3	22.5	22.5	22.5

Table 20.2   Dry matter intake correction for week of lactation (adapted from Vadiveloo and Holmes, 1979)

Week of lactation	DMI as percent of predicted	Correction factor
1	67	0.67
2	78	0.78
3	84	0.84
4	88	0.88
5	91	0.91
6	93	0.93
7	95	0.95
8	96	0.96
9	97	0.97
10	98	0.98
11	99	0.99
12	100	1.00
13	100	1.00
14	100	1.00
15	100	1.00
16	100	1.00

Table 20.3   Possible correction factors for dry matter intake on farm

Reason	Correction factor	Comments
Complete diet	1.2 - 1.3	Depends how good the basic ration was
Holstein	1.1 - 1.2	Larger frame and gut size
Out of parlour feeders	1.05 - 1.1	As for complete diet
Mixed forages	1.0 - 1.05	Depends on "fit" of blend of forages
Heifers grouped with cows	0.9 - 0.95	Intake of heifers reduced when housed with cows
Self feed silage	0.9 - 0.95	Depends on silo face width
Poorly preserved silage	0.9	Depends on proportion of diet
Electric fence at silage face	0.8 - 0.9	Greatest in short-necked animals
Week of lactation	0.67 - 1.00	See Table 20.2

Table 20.4   Predicted dry matter intake of dry cows (kg DM/day) (ARC, 1980)

	Ration q				
Weight (kg)	0.40	0.45	0.50	0.55	0.60
400	5.5	6.4	7.5	8.9	10.4
425	5.8	6.8	8.0	9.4	11.1
450	6.1	7.2	8.5	10.0	11.8
475	6.5	7.6	9.0	10.5	12.4
500	6.8	8.0	9.4	11.1	13.0
525	7.1	8.4	9.9	11.6	13.7
550	7.5	8.8	10.3	12.1	14.3
575	7.8	9.1	10.8	12.7	14.9
600	8.1	9.5	11.2	13.2	15.5
625	8.4	9.9	11.6	13.7	16.1
650	8.7	10.2	12.1	14.2	16.7
675	9.0	10.6	12.5	14.7	17.3
700	9.3	11.0	12.9	15.2	17.8
725	9.6	11.3	13.3	15.7	18.4
750	9.9	11.7	13.7	16.1	19.0

Table 20.5   Metabolisable energy requirements for maintenance (MJ/day) (AFRC, 1990)

Weight (kg)	Ration q								
	0.35	0.40	0.45	0.50	0.55	0.60	0.65	0.70	0.75
400	52.9	51.5	50.1	48.8	47.6	46.4	45.3	44.2	43.2
410	53.8	52.4	51.0	49.7	48.4	47.2	46.1	45.0	44.0
420	54.8	53.3	51.9	50.5	49.3	48.0	46.9	45.8	44.8
430	55.7	54.2	52.7	51.4	50.1	48.9	47.7	46.6	45.5
440	56.6	55.1	53.6	52.2	50.9	49.7	48.5	47.3	46.3
450	57.5	55.9	54.5	53.1	51.7	50.5	49.2	48.1	47.0
460	58.4	56.8	55.3	53.9	52.5	51.2	50.0	48.9	47.7
470	59.3	57.7	56.2	54.7	53.3	52.0	50.8	49.6	48.5
480	60.2	58.6	57.0	55.5	54.2	52.8	51.6	50.3	49.2
490	61.1	59.4	57.9	56.4	54.9	53.6	52.3	51.1	49.9
500	62.0	60.3	58.7	57.2	55.7	54.4	53.1	51.8	50.6
510	62.9	61.1	59.5	58.0	56.5	55.1	53.8	52.6	51.4
520	63.7	62.0	60.4	58.8	57.3	55.9	54.6	53.3	52.1
530	64.6	62.8	61.2	59.6	58.1	56.7	55.3	54.0	52.8
540	65.5	63.7	62.0	60.4	58.9	57.4	56.1	54.7	53.5
550	66.3	64.5	62.8	61.2	59.7	58.2	56.8	55.5	54.2
560	67.2	65.4	63.6	62.0	60.4	58.9	57.5	56.2	54.9
570	68.0	66.2	64.4	62.8	61.2	59.7	58.3	56.9	55.6
580	68.9	67.0	65.2	63.6	62.0	60.4	59.0	57.6	56.3
590	69.7	67.8	66.0	64.3	62.7	61.2	59.7	58.3	57.0
600	70.6	68.7	66.8	65.1	63.5	61.9	60.4	59.0	57.7
610	71.4	69.5	67.6	65.9	64.2	62.6	61.1	59.7	58.3
620	72.2	70.3	68.4	66.6	65.0	63.4	61.9	60.4	59.0
630	73.1	71.1	69.2	67.4	65.7	64.1	62.6	61.1	59.7
640	73.9	71.9	70.0	68.2	66.5	64.8	63.3	61.8	60.4
650	74.7	72.7	70.8	68.9	67.2	65.5	64.0	62.5	61.1
660	75.5	73.5	71.5	69.7	67.9	66.3	64.7	63.2	61.7
670	76.4	74.3	72.3	70.4	68.7	67.0	65.4	63.8	62.4
680	77.2	75.1	73.1	71.2	69.4	67.7	66.1	64.5	63.1
690	78.0	75.9	73.8	71.9	70.1	68.4	66.8	65.2	63.7
700	78.8	76.6	74.6	72.7	70.9	69.1	67.5	65.9	64.4
710	79.6	77.4	75.4	73.4	71.6	69.8	68.1	66.5	65.0
720	80.4	78.2	76.1	74.2	72.3	70.5	68.8	67.2	65.7
730	81.2	79.0	76.9	74.9	73.0	71.2	69.5	67.9	66.3
740	82.0	79.7	77.6	75.6	73.7	71.9	70.2	68.5	67.0
750	82.8	80.5	78.4	76.4	74.4	72.6	70.9	69.2	67.6

Table 20.6 **Metabolisable energy requirements for milk (MJ/l milk) (AFRC, 1990). Assumes lactose of** 4.6%

Ration q = 0.5	Milk protein (%/litre)								
Milk fat (%/l)	**2.80**	**2.90**	**3.00**	**3.10**	**3.20**	**3.30**	**3.40**	**3.50**	**3.60**
3.00	4.57	4.61	4.65	4.69	4.73	4.77	4.81	4.85	4.89
3.25	4.74	4.78	4.82	4.86	4.90	4.94	4.98	5.02	5.06
3.50	4.91	4.95	4.99	5.03	5.07	5.11	5.15	5.19	5.23
3.75	5.08	5.12	5.16	5.20	5.24	5.28	5.32	5.36	5.40
4.00	5.25	5.29	5.33	5.37	5.41	5.45	5.49	5.53	5.57
4.25	5.42	5.46	5.50	5.54	5.58	5.62	5.66	5.70	5.74
4.50	5.59	5.63	5.67	5.71	5.75	5.79	5.83	5.87	5.90
4.75	5.76	5.80	5.84	5.88	5.92	5.96	6.00	6.04	6.07
5.00	5.93	5.97	6.01	6.05	6.09	6.13	6.17	6.20	6.24

Ration q = 0. 6	Milk protein (%/litre)								
Milk fat (%/l)	**2.80**	**2.90**	**3.00**	**3.10**	**3.20**	**3.30**	**3.40**	**3.50**	**3.60**
3.00	4.32	4.36	4.39	4.43	4.47	4.51	4.54	4.58	4.62
3.25	4.48	4.52	4.55	4.59	4.63	4.67	4.70	4.74	4.78
3.50	4.64	4.68	4.71	4.75	4.79	4.83	4.86	4.90	4.94
3.75	4.80	4.84	4.87	4.91	4.95	4.99	5.02	5.06	5.10
4.00	4.96	5.00	5.03	5.07	5.11	5.15	5.18	5.22	5.26
4.25	5.12	5.16	5.19	5.23	5.27	5.31	5.34	5.38	5.42
4.50	5.28	5.32	5.35	5.39	5.43	5.47	5.50	5.54	5.58
4.75	5.44	5.48	5.51	5.55	5.59	5.63	5.66	5.70	5.74
5.00	5.60	5.64	5.67	5.71	5.75	5.79	5.82	5.86	5.90

Ration q = 0.7	Milk protein (%/litre)								
Milk fat (%/l)	**2.80**	**2.90**	**3.00**	**3.10**	**3.20**	**3.30**	**3.40**	**3.50**	**3.60**
3.00	4.09	4.13	4.16	4.20	4.23	4.27	4.30	4.34	4.37
3.25	4.24	4.28	4.31	4.35	4.38	4.42	4.46	4.49	4.53
3.50	4.40	4.43	4.47	4.50	4.54	4.57	4.61	4.64	4.68
3.75	4.55	4.58	4.62	4.65	4.69	4.72	4.76	4.79	4.83
4.00	4.70	4.73	4.77	4.80	4.84	4.87	4.91	4.95	4.98
4.25	4.85	4.89	4.92	4.96	4.99	5.03	5.06	5.10	5.13
4.50	5.00	5.04	5.07	5.11	5.14	5.18	5.21	5.25	5.28
4.75	5.15	5.19	5.22	5.26	5.29	5.33	5.36	5.40	5.43
5.00	5.30	5.34	5.38	5.41	5.45	5.48	5.52	5.55	5.59

Table 20.7 Metabolisable energy requirements for pregnancy (AFRC, 1990)

Weeks	Days	MJ/day
1	7	0.2
2	14	0.2
3	21	0.3
4	28	0.3
5	35	0.3
6	42	0.4
7	49	0.4
8	56	0.5
9	63	0.6
10	70	0.7
11	77	0.8
12	84	0.9
13	91	1.0
14	98	1.2
15	105	1.4
16	112	1.6
17	119	1.8
18	126	2.1
19	133	2.4
20	140	2.8
21	147	3.2
22	154	3.6
23	161	4.2
24	168	4.8
25	175	5.5
26	182	6.3
27	189	7.3
28	196	8.4
29	203	9.6
30	210	11.1
31	217	12.7
32	224	14.6
33	231	16.8
34	238	19.2
35	245	22.1
36	252	25.4
37	259	29.1
38	266	33.5
39	273	38.4
40	280	44.1

Average calf weights for common breeds of cattle

Breed bull	Bull calf	Heifer calf	Average
Angus	27.0	25.1	26.1
Ayrshire	35.0	32.6	33.8
Charolais	44.0	40.9	42.5
Friesian	39.0	36.3	37.6
Guernsey	33.0	30.7	31.8
Hereford	36.0	33.5	34.7
Holstein	45.0	41.9	43.4
Jersey	26.0	24.2	25.1
Limousin	39.0	36.3	37.6
Simmental	44.0	40.9	42.5

The figures in the left hand table relate to a 40 kg calf and should be corrected for other calf weights. The correction is linear. For example to correct for a Hereford cross calf multiply by 34.7/40 or 0.87

The combined weight of twins are generally considered to be 1.75 times the weight of a single calf.

Table 20.8   Metabolisable energy value (MJ ME) of weight change in milking and pregnant dry cows on rations of differing qualities (derived from AFRC, 1990 and AFRC, 1993) (Assumes weight loss during lactation used to produce milk. Assumes weight loss during pregnancy/dry period used to support foetus.)

Milking cows								
q	-1.00	-0.75	-0.50	-0.25	0.25	0.50	0.75	1.00
0.50	-23.3	-17.4	-11.6	-5.8	9.7	19.4	29.1	38.8
0.60	-22.0	-16.5	-11.0	-5.5	9.2	18.3	27.5	36.7
0.70	-20.8	-15.6	-10.4	-5.2	8.7	17.4	26.1	34.7

Dry, pregnant cows								
q	-1.00	-0.75	-0.50	-0.25	0.25	0.50	0.75	1.00
0.40	-24.8	-18.6	-12.4	-6.2	17.3	34.5	51.8	69.0
0.50	-24.8	-18.6	-12.4	-6.2	13.9	27.7	41.6	55.4

Table 20.9 Metabolisable energy requirements for activity

Weight	Moderate	Extensive
400	7.7	12.3
410	7.8	12.6
420	8.0	12.8
430	8.2	13.1
440	8.4	13.3
450	8.5	13.6
460	8.7	13.8
470	8.9	14.1
480	9.0	14.3
490	9.2	14.6
500	9.4	14.8
510	9.5	15.0
520	9.7	15.3
530	9.9	15.5
540	10.1	15.8
550	10.2	16.0
560	10.4	16.2
570	10.6	16.5
580	10.7	16.7
590	10.9	17.0
600	11.1	17.2
610	11.2	17.4
620	11.4	17.7
630	11.6	17.9
640	11.7	18.1
650	11.9	18.4
660	12.1	18.6
670	12.2	18.8
680	12.4	19.1
690	12.6	19.3
700	12.7	19.5
710	12.9	19.8
720	13.1	20.0
730	13.2	20.2
740	13.4	20.5
750	13.6	20.7

Moderate exercise may be considered as walking long distances on level ground such as may occur when cows graze distant pastures or have access to a large number of paddocks. Extensive exercise is walking long distances on hilly ground as when dry cows are turned out onto moorland or uplands.

Table 20.10 Correction for level of production (APL) (AFRC, 1990)

APL	C_L
0.60	0.993
0.70	0.995
0.80	0.996
0.90	0.998
1.00	1.000
1.10	1.002
1.20	1.004
1.30	1.005
1.40	1.007
1.50	1.009
1.60	1.011
1.70	1.013
1.80	1.014
1.90	1.016
2.00	1.018
2.10	1.020
2.20	1.022
2.30	1.023
2.40	1.025
2.50	1.027
2.60	1.029
2.70	1.031
2.80	1.032
2.90	1.034
3.00	1.036
3.10	1.038
3.20	1.040
3.30	1.041
3.40	1.043
3.50	1.045
3.60	1.047
3.70	1.049
3.80	1.050
3.90	1.052
4.00	1.054
4.10	1.056
4.20	1.058
4.30	1.059
4.40	1.061
4.50	1.063
4.60	1.065
4.70	1.067
4.80	1.068
4.90	1.070
5.00	1.072

Table 20.11 Protein (MP) requirements for maintenance (g/day) (AFRC, 1992)

Weight (kg)	MP	Weight (kg)	MP
400	216	580	286
410	220	590	290
420	225	600	293
430	229	610	297
440	232	620	301
450	236	630	304
460	240	640	308
470	244	650	312
480	248	660	315
490	252	670	319
500	256	680	322
510	260	690	326
520	264	700	329
530	267	710	333
540	271	720	336
550	275	730	340
560	279	740	343
570	282	750	347

Table 20.12 Protein (MP) requirements for lactation (g/day) (AFRC, 1992)

Yield (l)	\multicolumn{11}{c}{Milk protein (%/l)}									
	2.8	2.9	3.0	3.1	3.2	3.3	3.4	3.5	3.6	3.7	3.8
2	80	83	85	88	91	94	97	100	103	105	108
4	160	165	171	177	182	188	194	199	205	211	217
6	239	248	256	265	274	282	291	299	308	316	325
8	319	331	342	353	365	376	387	399	410	422	433
10	399	413	427	442	456	470	484	499	513	527	541
12	479	496	513	530	547	564	581	598	615	633	650
14	558	578	598	618	638	658	678	698	718	738	758
16	638	661	684	707	729	752	775	798	821	843	866
18	718	744	769	795	821	846	872	897	923	949	974
20	798	826	855	883	912	940	969	997	1026	1054	1083
22	878	909	940	972	1003	1034	1066	1097	1128	1160	1191
24	957	992	1026	1060	1094	1128	1162	1197	1231	1265	1299
26	1037	1074	1111	1148	1185	1222	1259	1296	1333	1370	1407
28	1117	1157	1197	1237	1276	1316	1356	1396	1436	1476	1516
30	1197	1239	1282	1325	1368	1410	1453	1496	1539	1581	1624
32	1276	1322	1368	1413	1459	1504	1550	1596	1641	1687	1732
34	1356	1405	1453	1502	1550	1598	1647	1695	1744	1792	1841
36	1436	1487	1539	1590	1641	1692	1744	1795	1846	1898	1949
38	1516	1570	1624	1678	1732	1786	1841	1895	1949	2003	2057
40	1596	1653	1710	1766	1823	1880	1937	1994	2051	2108	2165
42	1675	1735	1795	1855	1915	1974	2034	2094	2154	2214	2274
44	1755	1818	1880	1943	2006	2068	2131	2194	2257	2319	2382
46	1835	1900	1966	2031	2097	2163	2228	2294	2359	2425	2490
48	1915	1983	2051	2120	2188	2257	2325	2393	2462	2530	2598
50	1994	2066	2137	2208	2279	2351	2422	2493	2564	2635	2707
52	2074	2148	2222	2296	2371	2445	2519	2593	2667	2741	2815
54	2154	2231	2308	2385	2462	2539	2616	2692	2769	2846	2923
56	2234	2314	2393	2473	2553	2633	2712	2792	2872	2952	3032
58	2314	2396	2479	2561	2644	2727	2809	2892	2975	3057	3140
60	2393	2479	2564	2650	2735	2821	2906	2992	3077	3163	3248

Table 20.13 Protein (MP) requirements for pregnancy (g/day) (AFRC, 1992)

Weeks	Days	MP
1	7	1
2	14	1
3	21	1
4	28	1
5	35	1
6	42	2
7	49	2
8	56	2
9	63	3
10	70	3
11	77	4
12	84	5
13	91	6
14	98	7
15	105	8
16	112	9
17	119	11
18	126	12
19	133	15
20	140	17
21	147	20
22	154	23
23	161	26
24	168	30
25	175	34
26	182	39
27	189	44
28	196	50
29	203	57
30	210	64
31	217	73
32	224	82
33	231	91
34	238	102
35	245	114
36	252	127
37	259	141
38	266	156
39	273	173
40	280	191

Average calf weights for common breeds of cattle

Breed bull	Bull calf	Heifer calf	Average
Angus	27.0	25.1	26.1
Ayrshire	35.0	32.6	33.8
Charolais	44.0	40.9	42.5
Friesian	39.0	36.3	37.6
Guernsey	33.0	30.7	31.8
Hereford	36.0	33.5	34.7
Holstein	45.0	41.9	43.4
Jersey	26.0	24.2	25.1
Limousin	39.0	36.3	37.6
Simmental	44.0	40.9	42.5

The figures in the left hand table relate to a 40 kg calf and should be corrected for other calf weights. The correction is linear. For example to correct for a Hereford cross calf multiply by 34.7/40 or 0.87.

The combined weight of twins are generally considered to be 1.75 times the weight of a single calf.

Table 20.14 Protein (MP) requirements for weight change (g/day) (AFRC, 1992)

Weight change	MP
-1.50	-197
-1.25	-164
-1.00	-131
-0.75	-98
-0.50	-66
-0.25	-33
0.00	0
0.25	61
0.50	122
0.75	183
1.00	245
1.25	306
1.50	367

Table 20.15 Calcium allowances for maintenance (g/day) (AFRC, 1991)

DMI (kg)	Body weight (kg)						
	400	450	500	550	600	650	700
10.0	13.3	13.8	14.4	15.0	15.6	16.2	16.8
10.5	13.8	14.3	14.9	15.5	16.1	16.7	17.2
11.0	14.2	14.8	15.4	16.0	16.6	17.1	17.7
11.5	14.7	15.3	15.9	16.5	17.0	17.6	18.2
12.0	15.2	15.8	16.4	16.9	17.5	18.1	18.7
12.5	15.7	16.3	16.9	17.4	18.0	18.6	19.2
13.0	16.2	16.8	17.3	17.9	18.5	19.1	19.7
13.5	16.7	17.2	17.8	18.4	19.0	19.6	20.1
14.0	17.1	17.7	18.3	18.9	19.5	20.1	20.6
14.5	17.6	18.2	18.8	19.4	20.0	20.5	21.1
15.0	18.1	18.7	19.3	19.9	20.4	21.0	21.6
15.5	18.6	19.2	19.8	20.3	20.9	21.5	22.1
16.0	19.1	19.7	20.3	20.8	21.4	22.0	22.6
16.5	19.6	20.2	20.7	21.3	21.9	22.5	23.1
17.0	20.1	20.6	21.2	21.8	22.4	23.0	23.5
17.5	20.5	21.1	21.7	22.3	22.9	23.4	24.0
18.0	21.0	21.6	22.2	22.8	23.4	23.9	24.5
18.5	21.5	22.1	22.7	23.3	23.8	24.4	25.0
19.0	22.0	22.6	23.2	23.7	24.3	24.9	25.5
19.5	22.5	23.1	23.6	24.2	24.8	25.4	26.0
20.0	23.0	23.6	24.1	24.7	25.3	25.9	26.5
20.5	23.5	24.0	24.6	25.2	25.8	26.4	26.9
21.0	23.9	24.5	25.1	25.7	26.3	26.8	27.4
21.5	24.4	25.0	25.6	26.2	26.8	27.3	27.9
22.0	24.9	25.5	26.1	26.7	27.2	27.8	28.4
22.5	25.4	26.0	26.6	27.1	27.7	28.3	28.9
23.0	25.9	26.5	27.0	27.6	28.2	28.8	29.4
23.5	26.4	26.9	27.5	28.1	28.7	29.3	29.9
24.0	26.9	27.4	28.0	28.6	29.2	29.8	30.3
24.5	27.3	27.9	28.5	29.1	29.7	30.2	30.8
25.0	27.8	28.4	29.0	29.6	30.1	30.7	31.3
25.5	28.3	28.9	29.5	30.1	30.6	31.2	31.8
26.0	28.8	29.4	30.0	30.5	31.1	31.7	32.3
26.5	29.3	29.9	30.4	31.0	31.6	32.2	32.8
27.0	29.8	30.3	30.9	31.5	32.1	32.7	33.3
27.5	30.3	30.8	31.4	32.0	32.6	33.2	33.7

Table 20.16 Magnesium allowances for maintenance (g/day) (ARC, 1965)

Weight (kg)	Mg	Weight (kg)	Mg
400	7.4	560	10.3
420	7.8	580	10.7
440	8.1	600	11.1
460	8.5	620	11.5
480	8.9	640	11.8
500	9.2	660	12.2
520	9.6	680	12.6
540	10.0	700	12.9

Table 20.17 Phosphorus allowances for maintenance (g/day) (AFRC, 1991)

DMI (kg/day)	Phosphorus	
	q ≤ 0.7	q > 0.7
10.0	19.0	9.8
10.5	19.9	10.3
11.0	20.9	10.8
11.5	21.8	11.3
12.0	22.8	11.8
12.5	23.7	12.3
13.0	24.7	12.8
13.5	25.6	13.3
14.0	26.6	13.8
14.5	27.6	14.3
15.0	28.5	14.8
15.5	29.5	15.3
16.0	30.4	15.8
16.5	31.4	16.2
17.0	32.3	16.7
17.5	33.3	17.2
18.0	34.2	17.7
18.5	35.2	18.2
19.0	36.2	18.7
19.5	37.1	19.2
20.0	38.1	19.7
20.5	39.0	20.2
21.0	40.0	20.7
21.5	40.9	21.2
22.0	41.9	21.7
22.5	42.8	22.2
23.0	43.8	22.7
23.5	44.8	23.2
24.0	45.7	23.7
24.5	46.7	24.2
25.0	47.6	24.7
25.5	48.6	25.2
26.0	49.5	25.7
26.5	50.5	26.1
27.0	51.5	26.6
27.5	52.4	27.1

Table 20.18 Calcium, magnesium and phosphorus allowances for lactation (g/day) (AFRC, 1991 and ARC, 1965)

Milk (l/day)	Calcium g/day	Magnesium g/day	Phosphorus	
			q≤0.7 g/day	q>0.7 g/day
2	3.6	1.6	3.2	2.7
4	7.3	3.2	6.4	5.3
6	10.9	4.8	9.6	8.0
8	14.6	6.4	12.8	10.6
10	18.2	8.0	16.0	13.3
12	21.9	9.6	19.2	15.9
14	25.5	11.2	22.4	18.6
16	29.1	12.8	25.6	21.2
18	32.8	14.4	28.8	23.9
20	36.4	16.0	32.0	26.5
22	40.1	17.6	35.2	29.2
24	43.7	19.2	38.4	31.8
26	47.4	20.8	41.6	34.5
28	51.0	22.5	44.8	37.2
30	54.6	24.1	48.0	39.8
32	58.3	25.7	51.2	42.5
34	61.9	27.3	54.4	45.1
36	65.6	28.9	57.6	47.8
38	69.2	30.5	60.9	50.4
40	72.8	32.1	64.1	53.1
42	76.5	33.7	67.3	55.7
44	80.1	35.3	70.5	58.4
46	83.8	36.9	73.7	61.0
48	87.4	38.5	76.9	63.7
50	91.1	40.1	80.1	66.3
52	94.7	41.7	83.3	69.0
54	98.3	43.3	86.5	71.7
56	102.0	44.9	89.7	74.3
58	105.6	46.5	92.9	77.0
60	109.3	48.1	96.1	79.6

Table 20.19 Calcium, magnesium and phosphorus allowances for pregnancy (g/day) (AFRC, 1991 and ARC, 1965)

| Weeks | Days | Ca g/day | Mg g/day | Phosphorus | |
				q≤0.7 g/day	q>0.7 g/day
1	7	0.0	0.0	0.0	0.0
2	14	0.0	0.0	0.0	0.0
3	21	0.0	0.0	0.0	0.0
4	28	0.0	0.0	0.0	0.0
5	35	0.1	0.0	0.0	0.0
6	42	0.1	0.0	0.0	0.0
7	49	0.1	0.0	0.1	0.0
8	56	0.1	0.0	0.1	0.1
9	63	0.1	0.1	0.1	0.1
10	70	0.2	0.1	0.1	0.1
11	77	0.2	0.1	0.1	0.1
12	84	0.3	0.1	0.2	0.1
13	91	0.3	0.1	0.2	0.2
14	98	0.4	0.1	0.3	0.2
15	105	0.5	0.2	0.3	0.3
16	112	0.6	0.2	0.4	0.3
17	119	0.7	0.2	0.5	0.4
18	126	0.8	0.3	0.6	0.5
19	133	0.9	0.3	0.7	0.5
20	140	1.1	0.4	0.8	0.6
21	147	1.3	0.5	0.9	0.8
22	154	1.5	0.5	1.1	0.9
23	161	1.7	0.6	1.2	1.0
24	168	2.0	0.7	1.4	1.2
25	175	2.3	0.8	1.7	1.4
26	182	2.7	0.9	1.9	1.6
27	189	3.1	1.1	2.2	1.8
28	196	3.5	1.2	2.5	2.1
29	203	4.0	1.4	2.9	2.4
30	210	4.5	1.6	3.3	2.7
31	217	5.2	1.8	3.7	3.1
32	224	5.8	2.1	4.2	3.4
33	231	6.6	2.3	4.7	3.9
34	238	7.4	2.6	5.2	4.3
35	245	8.2	2.9	5.8	4.8
36	252	9.2	3.3	6.5	5.4
37	259	10.2	3.7	7.2	6.0
38	266	11.4	4.1	8.0	6.6
39	273	12.6	4.5	8.8	7.3
40	280	13.9	5.0	9.6	8.0

Table 20.20 Calcium, magnesium and phosphorus allowances for weight changes (AFRC, 1991 and ARC, 1965)

| Liveweight change kg/day | Ca g/day | Mg g/day | Phosphorus | |
			q≤0.7 g/day	q>0.7 g/day
-1.50	-22.2	-3.9	-15.4	-12.8
-1.25	-18.5	-3.2	-12.8	-10.6
-1.00	-14.8	-2.6	-10.3	-8.5
-0.75	-11.1	-1.9	-7.7	-6.4
-0.50	-7.4	-1.3	-5.1	-4.3
-0.25	-3.7	-0.6	-2.6	-2.1
0.25	3.7	0.7	2.6	2.1
0.50	7.4	1.4	5.1	4.3
0.75	11.1	2.1	7.7	6.4
1.00	14.8	2.8	10.3	8.5
1.25	18.5	3.5	12.8	10.6
1.50	22.2	4.3	15.4	12.8
1.75	25.9	5.0	18.0	14.9

Table 20.21 **Principal nutrient composition of feeds. All analyses per kg DM except DM which is per cent of fresh weight (AFRC, 1993, MAFF, 1992 and MAFF, 1986)**

Feed name	DM %	GE MJ	ME MJ	FME MJ	CP g	Ca g	Mg g	P g	NDF g	Fat g	Sugar g	Starch g
Hays and other dried forages (INFIC Classes 10 and 11)												
Hay average	87	18.4	8.8	8.2	107	5.2	1.4	2.6	657	17	108	2
Hay DOMD <450	87	18.1	6.1	5.6	90	3.7	1.6	2.0	752	14	38	n/a
Hay DOMD 450-500	85	18.2	6.5	6.1	101	4.9	1.5	2.8	741	12	38	n/a
Hay DOMD 500-550	85	18.4	8.1	7.5	109	5.0	1.5	2.7	699	16	68	2
Hay DOMD 550-600	85	18.6	8.7	8.1	120	5.2	1.4	2.6	692	16	59	2
Hay DOMD 600-650	86	18.5	9.6	9.0	131	6.3	1.6	3.0	650	18	93	1
Hay DOMD 650-700	87	18.4	10.3	9.5	121	5.3	1.4	2.8	595	22	153	2
Hay DOMD > 700	86	18.6	11.5	10.8	140	5.0	1.3	3.1	560	21	167	1
Dry grass all	89	18.4	9.5	8.2	197	9.2	1.7	3.3	536	38	110	5
Dry Gr 500-550	88	16.2	8.1	6.7	206	9.3	2.1	3.1	444	39	72	9
Dry Gr 550-600	90	18.2	8.9	7.6	192	9.4	1.7	3.2	556	36	100	6
Dry Gr 600-650	89	18.4	9.9	8.6	196	7.2	1.7	3.4	532	37	111	2
Dry Gr 650-700	88	18.7	10.5	9.0	209	7.6	1.6	3.6	511	42	136	5
Dry lucerne	90	18.6	8.6	7.5	192	14.0	2.0	3.0	473	32	56	13
Dry lucerne v. poor	90	18.6	7.1	6.0	182	14.0	2.0	3.0	523	32	33	8
Dry lucerne poor	90	18.6	8.2	7.2	188	14.0	2.0	3.0	471	28	52	11
Dry lucerne average	89	18.7	9.1	7.8	196	15.0	2.0	3.0	471	36	64	16
Dry lucerne good	90	18.2	10.1	8.8	212	15.0	2.0	4.0	436	36	90	n/a
Dry lucerne v. good	92	18.3	10.4	9.2	191	10.0	2.0	4.0	408	33	n/a	n/a
Straws (INFIC Class 12)												
Cereal straw	87	18.3	6.4	5.9	40	4.1	0.8	0.9	802	13	14	n/a
Barley straw	87	18.5	6.5	6.0	43	4.5	0.8	0.9	809	14	18	n/a
Spring barley straw	86	18.6	6.8	6.3	44	4.8	0.8	1.0	805	15	13	5
Winter barley straw	88	18.2	6.3	5.8	38	4.0	1.0	0.8	808	13	35	n/a
Wheat straw	87	18.1	6.1	5.6	38	3.8	0.8	0.7	805	13	11	n/a
Spring wheat straw	88	17.9	5.8	5.3	37	4.9	0.8	0.6	818	14	n/a	n/a
Winter wheat straw	87	18.1	6.1	5.6	38	3.7	0.9	0.8	801	13	11	n/a
Winter oat straw	86	18.1	7.0	6.5	37	3.6	0.8	0.9	735	14	19	1
Pea straw	86	17.7	6.7	6.3	63	n/a	n/a	n/a	n/a	11	n/a	n/a
NH$_3$ barley straw	87	18.7	7.5	6.9	68	4.6	0.6	0.8	786	16	17	n/a
NH$_3$ wheat straw	87	18.5	7.4	6.9	69	4.0	0.7	0.8	770	14	13	n/a
NH$_3$ oat straw	87	18.2	7.8	7.1	60	4.1	7.7	0.8	757	19	16	n/a
NaOH straw	77	17.2	8.3	7.9	40	3.3	1.3	0.9	665	12	14	n/a
NaOH barley straw	80	17.3	9.0	8.5	43	3.6	0.8	0.9	671	14	14	n/a
NaOH wheat straw	74	17.1	7.7	7.3	40	3.3	0.8	0.9	672	12	13	n/a

Table 20.21 (cont.)   Principal nutrient composition of feeds

Feed name	DM %	GE MJ	ME MJ	FME MJ	CP g	Ca g	Mg g	P g	NDF g	Fat g	Sugar g	Starch g
Fresh forages (INFIC Class 20)												
Grass average	20	18.7	11.2	10.4	156	5.4	1.6	2.5	576	22	159	3
Grass D 55-60	20	18.1	7.5	6.9	97	4.8	1.2	2.8	664	16	126	3
Grass D 60-65	23	18.4	9.8	9.1	106	4.4	1.4	2.5	629	19	154	3
Grass D 65-70	21	18.6	10.7	10.0	121	4.6	1.4	2.7	610	20	161	3
Grass D 70-75	21	18.6	11.2	10.4	139	4.9	1.4	2.9	576	22	174	3
Grass D 75-80	22	18.9	12.3	11.4	190	5.2	1.5	3.2	531	25	187	3
Grass D>80	21	19.0	12.6	11.7	190	5.3	1.3	2.5	488	24	248	n/a
Italian ryegrass	22	18.5	11.4	10.6	128	4.7	1.3	2.9	534	22	232	n/a
Perennial ryegrass S23	20	18.4	11.5	10.6	102	4.4	1.2	3.4	572	27	197	3
Perennial ryegrass S24	21	18.7	11.1	10.3	127	3.6	1.3	3.1	616	20	160	n/a
Mixed sward	20	18.4	11.7	11.1	162	4.9	1.5	2.5	566	18	207	n/a
Barley whole crop	25	17.7	10.0	9.4	68	n/a	n/a	n/a	n/a	16	n/a	n/a
Cabbage	11	17.6	13.7	13.1	207	8.3	1.5	1.9	244	17	316	4
Forage pea	26	18.8	8.8	7.4	208	12.7	2.0	4.4	517	40	33	1
Kale	13	17.2	11.8	11.5	164	12.5	1.5	3.9	257	22	233	9
Rape	14	18.7	9.5	7.5	200	9.3	2.1	4.2	n/a	57	n/a	n/a
Rye forage	23	18.4	9.5	8.1	126	n/a	n/a	n/a	n/a	39	n/a	n/a
Sugar beet	23	17.6	13.7	13.6	48	1.6	1.0	1.9	n/a	4	n/a	n/a
Sugar beet tops	16	15.4	9.9	8.8	125	8.6	n/a	2.8	n/a	31	n/a	n/a
Silages (INFIC Class 30)												
Grass silage	26	19.0	10.9	8.3	168	6.4	1.7	3.2	582	43	21	10
Silage very poor	32	18.0	8.4	7.2	160	8.4	2.1	2.7	603	31	15	n/a
Silage poor	38	18.6	9.2	7.3	152	6.3	1.3	2.9	595	27	32	5
Silage average	27	19.5	10.4	8.1	151	6.8	1.6	3.1	546	35	17	7
Silage good	27	18.7	10.8	8.4	156	5.8	1.5	3.0	523	37	21	10
Silage very good	21	19.1	11.1	8.2	171	6.0	1.4	2.9	483	51	19	n/a
Lucerne silage	34	19.9	8.0	6.4	194	17.6	1.8	3.0	495	25	12	4
Maize silage	30	18.5	11.5	9.0	88	3.9	2.4	1.8	390	30	5	206
Urea whole-crop wheat	55	18.2	10.4	9.9	230	2.0	1.0	2.5	500	15	20	216

Table 20.21 (cont.)   Principal nutrient composition of feeds

Feed name	DM %	GE MJ	ME MJ	FME MJ	CP g	Ca g	Mg g	P g	NDF g	Fat g	Sugar g	Starch g
Energy feeds (INFIC Class 40)												
Apples	14	16.8	11.9	11.8	38	0.5	0.3	0.9	126	12	726	2
Apple pomace wet	24	19.8	9.1	7.8	69	1.6	0.6	1.4	489	27	161	30
Barley grain	87	18.5	13.3	12.3	129	0.9	1.2	4.0	201	16	37	562
Bread	65	18.4	14.0	13.5	110	0.8	1.3	3.5	180	13	n/a	n/a
Carrots	13	17.4	12.8	12.3	92	5.9	1.8	3.4	200	15	n/a	n/a
Cassava meal	89	16.8	12.6	12.1	28	2.2	1.4	0.9	114	4	47	1
Caustic wheat	77	18.0	12.6	11.9	118	1.3	3.5	5.7	114	20	58	600
Citrus pulp	89	17.5	12.6	10.7	72	14.6	1.7	1.1	228	22	248	2
Dist. grains + solubles	89	18.5	11.5	10.7	220	3.0	1.5	6.0	390	23	n/a	175
Fodder Beet	18	16.0	11.9	11.8	63	2.8	1.6	1.8	136	3	660	1
Grain maize	87	18.9	13.8	12.6	104	0.1	1.3	3.0	117	39	18	700
High-oil maize residues	45	18.5	14.0	7.0	150	3.0	1.5	6.0	190	200	n/a	175
Maize bran	88	19.9	13.4	12.3	148	0.3	1.4	3.0	538	31	n/a	n/a
Maize gluten feed	89	19.0	12.7	11.5	232	2.8	4.3	10.0	390	34	21	151
Moist barley	55	18.4	12.5	12.0	127	0.8	1.3	3.5	230	13	n/a	n/a
Molasses cane	75	16.4	12.7	12.7	41	9.6	4.4	1.2	0	1	850	0
Oatfeed	88	18.0	9.0	7.8	50	0.8	1.0	3.4	750	34	n/a	471
Oat grain	85	19.6	12.1	10.8	105	0.9	3.0	3.4	310	41	n/a	471
Orange peel	17	17.4	12.5	11.2	85	19.0	1.3	1.2	254	38	217	n/a
Potatoes	20	17.2	13.4	13.2	108	0.4	1.0	2.0	73	2	73	565
Pressed pulp umolassed	26	17.0	11.7	12.1	99	10.3	1.9	1.2	523	6	45	4
Rice bran	90	16.7	7.1	6.9	165	0.9	3.8	17.4	451	7	30	236
Rye grain	87	18.5	14.0	13.3	119	0.6	1.4	4.7	357	12	n/a	n/a
SBF dry molassed	86	17.1	12.5	12.4	129	5.9	1.0	0.7	294	4	296	5
SBF dry unmolassed	86	17.1	12.9	11.3	77	7.6	1.8	0.8	372	7	79	3
SBF ensiled molassed	21	17.6	11.5	12.3	111	7.7	1.4	0.8	341	6	22	0
Sorghum grain	89	18.7	13.2	12.1	110	0.3	1.1	2.7	107	30	n/a	730
Turnips whole stubble	8	18.4	11.6	11.1	112	n/a	n/a	n/a	n/a	15	n/a	n/a
Wheat bran	89	18.9	10.8	9.2	178	1.1	6.2	12.6	475	39	n/a	196
Wheat feed	89	19.1	11.9	10.4	181	1.1	5.2	10.5	364	43	84	277
Wheat grain	87	18.2	13.6	12.9	123	0.6	1.1	3.4	166	19	58	660

SBF = sugar beet feed

Table 20.21 (cont.)   Principal nutrient composition of feeds

Feed name	DM %	GE MJ	ME MJ	FME MJ	CP g	Ca g	Mg g	P g	NDF g	Fat g	Sugar g	Starch g
Protein feeds (INFIC Class 50)												
Brewers' grains (ensiled)	28	21.5	11.7	9.0	245	3.3	1.5	4.1	572	77	10	57
Cottonseed cake	94	20.6	11.1	9.2	375	2.1	5.8	8.9	385	64	68	17
Cottonseed meal	92	20.4	11.1	8.8	375	2.1	5.8	8.9	390	66	68	17
Draff	25	21.5	10.2	9.5	211	1.5	1.8	3.8	672	86	5	18
Dreg	34	18.4	12.0	9.2	370	0.2	0.4	2.8	500	80	n/a	n/a
Fishmeal Chilean	92	20.1	14.9	12.3	708	42.8	2.5	242.0	0	87	2	1
Fishmeal herring	93	22.0	16.4	15.2	782	34.4	2.1	23.6	0	95	4	1
Fishmeal white	92	19.7	14.2	11.4	694	56.2	2.3	38.1	0	75	4	n/a
Full fat soya	90	23.8	15.5	8.4	408	2.7	2.4	5.9	122	222	84	15
Groundnut meal	92	20.6	13.7	11.1	495	2.0	3.5	14.3	180	70	95	53
High-oil maize germ	96	28.0	22.0	6.6	130	2.0	1.0	6.0	100	440	n/a	100
Maize dist. grains	90	22.4	14.7	11.7	317	1.4	3.2	8.4	342	110	50	24
Maize germ meal	88	19.7	14.5	12.8	115	0.2	2.1	5.2	223	82	43	532
Maize gluten feed	89	19.0	12.7	11.5	232	2.8	4.3	10.0	390	34	21	151
Malt dist. grains	89	21.2	12.2	9.9	267	1.4	3.0	9.4	420	65	18	16
Milk	13	18.4	14.0	11.7	200	4.1	2.5	6.0	0	66	350	0
Palm kernel meal ext.	86	20.4	11.6	10.4	170	2.4	3.0	6.9	693	83	39	12
Peas	87	18.5	13.5	13.3	261	1.0	1.6	5.8	116	14	25	440
Pot ale syrup	48	20.0	15.4	15.3	374	1.9	6.4	20.1	6	2	23	13
Prairie meal	91	23.7	17.5	12.5	666	0.6	0.5	2.8	84	29	6	155
Rapeseed meal	89	19.5	12.0	11.2	418	7.8	4.5	12.0	279	23	103	40
Soyabean meal exp.	90	20.7	13.5	11.2	504	2.3	3.0	9.7	290	66	n/a	n/a
Soyabean meal ext.	88	19.7	13.4	12.8	507	4.5	2.9	7.6	154	16	107	11
Spring feld beans	87	18.6	13.4	13.1	333	1.1	1.8	5.2	186	13	n/a	365
Sunflower meal	90	19.5	9.6	9.2	335	4.8	5.8	10.8	473	23	66	3
Urea	99	18.4	0.0	0.0	2,875	0.0	0.0	0.0	0	n/a	n/a	n/a
Winter field beans	85	18.4	13.1	12.8	267	1.3	1.9	8.6	167	13	n/a	395
Wheat dist. grains	90	21.5	12.4	8.3	322	1.8	2.8	8.8	335	55	86	45
Whey	43	18.4	14.0	11.7	240	4.1	2.5	6.0	10	66	n/a	n/a
Whole cotton	90	18.4	13.8	6.8	250	1.3	3.5	5.7	390	200	n/a	n/a

Table 20.21 (cont.)   Principal nutrient composition of feeds

Feed name	DM %	GE MJ	ME MJ	FME MJ	CP g	Ca g	Mg g	P g	NDF g	Fat g	Sugar g	Starch g
Compound feeds (typical composition)												
Cake 16% CP	87	18.4	12.0	10.3	184	15.0	5.0	7.0	300	50	80	120
Cake 18% CP	87	18.4	12.5	10.6	207	15.0	5.0	7.0	210	55	80	150
Cake 20% CP	87	18.4	13.5	11.1	230	11.0	6.0	8.0	180	70	150	250
Cake 24% CP	88	18.4	13.0	10.9	270	12.0	2.5	6.0	170	60	130	220
Cake 27% CP	87	19.0	13.0	10.9	310	10.0	6.5	10.0	180	60	80	280
Cake 30% CP	87	19.0	13.8	11.7	340	10.0	10.0	15.0	180	60	80	280
Cake 44% CP	87	19.0	13.0	10.9	440	10.0	6.5	12.0	80	60	80	280
Minerals and miscellaneous feeds												
$CaCO_3$	99	n/a	0.0	0.0	0	300	0	0	n/a	n/a	n/a	n/a
Calcined magnes	99	n/a	0.0	0.0	0	0	450	0	n/a	n/a	n/a	n/a
Dairy minerals	99	n/a	0.0	0.0	0	122	80	60	n/a	n/a	n/a	n/a
Dairy mins hi P	99	n/a	0.0	0.0	0	160	30	120	n/a	n/a	n/a	n/a
Fat prills	99	35.0	35.0	0.0	0	n/a	n/a	n/a	n/a	990	n/a	n/a
Min high P & Mg	99	n/a	0.0	0.0	0	100	100	125	n/a	n/a	n/a	n/a
Minerals (gen)	96	n/a	0.0	0.0	0	122	60	80	n/a	n/a	n/a	n/a
Sodium bicarb	99	n/a	0.0	0.0	0	0	0	0	n/a	n/a	n/a	n/a

Table 20.22 Protein composition of feeds (adapted from AFRC, 1993 and other sources)

Feed name	DM %	CP g/kg DM	ME	FME MJ/kg DM		≤1.0 / 8.8	1.5 / 9.5	2.0 / 10.0	2.5 / 10.5	3.0 / 10.9	3.5 / 11.2	4.0 / 11.5	≥4.5 / 11.8

Header note: Level of Production (APL); Microbial yield (Y); Protein supply (g/kg DM)

Hays and other dried forages (INFIC Classes 10 and 11)

Feed name	DM %	CP g/kg DM	ME	FME		≤1.0 / 8.8	1.5 / 9.5	2.0 / 10.0	2.5 / 10.5	3.0 / 10.9	3.5 / 11.2	4.0 / 11.5	≥4.5 / 11.8
Dried grass	92	199	10.7	9.4	ERDP	143.3	124.0	113.2	106.4	101.7	98.3	95.7	93.8
					DUP	24.0	41.3	51.0	57.2	61.4	64.5	66.7	68.5
Dried lucerne	90	199	8.8	7.8	ERDP	140.0	128.4	121.9	117.8	114.9	112.9	111.4	110.2
					DUP	21.8	32.2	38.1	41.8	44.3	46.2	47.6	48.6
Grass hay	85	81	9.2	8.6	ERDP	53.4	47.5	43.6	40.9	39.0	37.5	36.3	35.4
					DUP	14.9	20.2	23.7	26.1	27.9	29.2	30.2	31.1
Lucerne hay	86	183	8.5	8.1	ERDP	148.1	142.1	137.4	133.6	130.5	128.0	125.9	124.2
					DUP	14.8	20.2	24.4	27.8	30.6	32.8	34.7	36.2
Lucerne meal	90	160	8.8	7.8	ERDP	95.5	82.9	75.5	70.6	67.2	64.7	62.8	61.4
					DUP	39.3	50.6	57.3	61.7	64.8	67.0	68.7	70.0

Straws (INFIC Class 12)

Feed name	DM %	CP g/kg DM	ME	FME		≤1.0 / 8.8	1.5 / 9.5	2.0 / 10.0	2.5 / 10.5	3.0 / 10.9	3.5 / 11.2	4.0 / 11.5	≥4.5 / 11.8
Amm. barley straw	85	70	7.7	7.2	ERDP	50.5	48.8	47.7	46.9	46.3	45.9	45.6	45.3
					DUP	2.6	4.1	5.1	5.8	6.3	6.7	7.0	7.2
Amm. oat straw	85	78	8.0	7.4	ERDP	55.0	54.1	53.4	52.9	52.5	52.2	52.0	51.8
					DUP	4.7	5.5	6.1	6.6	6.9	7.2	7.4	7.6
Amm. wheat straw	85	68	7.3	6.9	ERDP	47.9	47.1	46.6	46.1	45.8	45.5	45.3	45.2
					DUP	0.6	1.3	1.8	2.2	2.5	2.7	2.9	3.1
Barley straw	85	42	6.4	5.9	ERDP	28.2	26.1	24.7	23.7	22.9	22.2	21.7	21.3
					DUP	4.6	6.4	7.7	8.6	9.3	9.9	10.3	10.7
Caustic wheat straw	85	36	8.6	8.3	ERDP	25.9	25.0	24.4	23.9	23.5	23.2	22.9	22.7
					DUP	0.2	1.0	1.6	2.0	2.4	2.7	2.9	3.1
Oat straw	85	34	7.2	6.7	ERDP	14.0	11.8	10.9	10.4	10.1	9.9	9.7	9.6
					DUP	12.8	14.8	15.6	16.0	16.3	16.5	16.6	16.7
Wheat straw	85	39	6.1	5.7	ERDP	26.1	24.3	22.9	22.0	21.2	20.6	20.2	19.8
					DUP	5.0	6.7	7.9	8.7	9.4	9.9	10.3	10.7

Fresh forages (INFIC Class 20)

Feed name	DM %	CP g/kg DM	ME	FME		≤1.0 / 8.8	1.5 / 9.5	2.0 / 10.0	2.5 / 10.5	3.0 / 10.9	3.5 / 11.2	4.0 / 11.5	≥4.5 / 11.8
Carrots	10	105	12.0	11.8	ERDP	86.4	84.0	82.0	80.4	79.1	77.9	77.0	76.2
					DUP	8.1	10.3	12.0	13.5	14.7	15.7	16.5	17.2
Fodder beet	18	63	11.9	11.8	ERDP	51.8	50.4	49.2	48.2	47.4	46.8	46.2	45.7
					DUP	3.3	4.6	5.7	6.5	7.2	7.8	8.3	8.8
Grass 55-60D	20	97	7.5	6.9	ERDP	56.9	50.2	45.8	42.8	40.5	38.8	37.5	36.5
					DUP	29.4	35.4	39.3	42.1	44.1	45.6	46.8	47.7
Grass 60-65D	20	120	9.5	8.8	ERDP	85.1	77.0	71.6	67.8	65.0	62.8	61.1	59.8
					DUP	21.4	28.7	33.5	37.0	39.5	41.5	43.0	44.2
Grass 65-70D	20	135	10.7	10.0	ERDP	101.1	92.9	87.2	83.2	80.1	77.8	76.0	74.5
					DUP	15.5	22.9	28.0	31.6	34.4	36.5	38.1	39.5
Grass 70-75D	20	150	11.6	10.7	ERDP	117.8	107.9	101.0	95.9	92.1	89.0	86.6	84.7
					DUP	16.6	25.5	31.7	36.3	39.8	42.5	44.7	46.4
Grass 75-80D	20	190	12.3	11.4	ERDP	156.7	146.8	139.5	133.8	129.3	125.8	122.9	120.5
					DUP	14.8	23.7	30.3	35.4	39.4	42.6	45.2	47.3
Grass >80D	20	190	12.6	11.7	ERDP	159.3	143.8	132.7	124.5	118.2	113.3	109.4	106.2
					DUP	19.9	33.8	43.8	51.1	56.8	61.2	64.8	67.6
Kale	14	160	11.8	11.1	ERDP	129.0	123.5	119.1	115.7	112.9	110.6	108.7	107.1
					DUP	16.8	21.8	25.7	28.8	31.3	33.3	35.0	36.4
Potatoes	20	108	13.4	13.3	ERDP	88.8	86.3	84.3	82.7	81.3	80.2	79.2	78.4
					DUP	8.5	10.7	12.5	14.0	15.2	16.2	17.1	17.8
Turnips	9	112	13.0	12.9	ERDP	91.3	88.0	85.5	83.4	81.7	80.3	79.2	78.2
					DUP	9.7	12.6	14.9	16.7	18.3	19.5	20.6	21.5

Table 20.22 (cont.) Protein composition of feeds (adapted from AFRC, 1993 and other sources)

						Level of Production (APL)							
						≤1.0	1.5	2.0	2.5	3.0	3.5	4.0	≥4.5
Microbial yield (Y)						8.8	9.5	10.0	10.5	10.9	11.2	11.5	11.8
Feed name	DM %	CP g/kg D	ME FME MJ/kg DM			Protein supply (g/kg DM)							
Silages *(INFIC Class 30)*													
Baled grass silage 55D	39	151	8.8	7.2	ERDP	102.9	90.2	83.5	79.5	76.7	74.8	73.4	72.3
					DUP	28.2	39.7	45.7	49.3	51.8	53.5	54.8	55.8
Baled grass silage 65D	36	160	10.6	8.6	ERDP	99.7	96.4	94.2	92.6	91.4	90.5	89.7	89.2
					DUP	34.8	37.7	39.7	41.2	42.2	43.1	43.7	44.2
Baled grass silage 75D	23	180	12.2	8.8	ERDP	136.3	132.5	129.8	127.8	126.3	125.2	124.2	123.5
					DUP	13.5	16.9	19.4	21.1	22.5	23.5	24.4	25.1
Grass silage 65D	25	140	10.3	7.6	ERDP	102.5	99.3	97.1	95.3	94.0	93.0	92.1	91.5
					DUP	10.5	13.4	15.5	17.0	18.2	19.1	19.9	20.5
Grass silage 70D	25	174	11.7	8.6	ERDP	125.6	122.4	120.0	118.2	116.7	115.6	114.7	113.9
					DUP	16.9	19.7	21.9	23.5	24.8	25.8	26.7	27.4
Grass silage UK mean	25	142	11.0	8.1	ERDP	104.0	100.8	98.4	96.7	95.4	94.3	93.5	92.8
					DUP	10.8	13.7	15.8	17.4	18.6	19.5	20.3	20.9
Grass and clover silage	23	174	9.8	7.0	ERDP	130.3	122.3	116.6	112.4	109.3	106.8	104.8	103.3
					DUP	13.8	21.0	26.1	29.9	32.7	35.0	36.7	38.1
Lucerne silage	34	194	8.0	6.4	ERDP	146.0	142.3	139.5	137.4	135.8	134.5	133.4	132.5
					DUP	10.1	13.4	15.9	17.8	19.2	20.4	21.4	22.1
Maize silage	29	98	11.3	9.0	ERDP	68.7	67.5	66.5	65.8	65.2	64.7	64.3	64.0
					DUP	9.1	10.2	11.1	11.7	12.3	12.7	13.0	13.3
Urea whole-crop barley	55	244	10.0	9.3	ERDP	175.8	172.8	170.9	169.6	168.6	167.8	167.2	166.8
					DUP	20.6	23.3	25.0	26.2	27.1	27.8	28.3	28.7
Urea whole-crop wheat	55	244	10.3	9.6	ERDP	175.3	172.1	170.1	168.7	167.8	167.0	166.4	166.0
					DUP	21.1	23.9	25.7	27.0	27.9	28.5	29.0	29.4
Whole-crop barley	39	90	9.1	7.5	ERDP	64.3	60.9	58.6	57.1	56.0	55.2	54.6	54.1
					DUP	7.8	10.9	12.9	14.2	15.2	16.0	16.5	17.0
Whole-crop wheat	41	99	10.0	8.3	ERDP	71.4	67.8	65.5	63.8	62.6	61.7	61.0	60.4
					DUP	8.5	11.7	13.9	15.3	16.4	17.2	17.9	18.4

Table 20.22 (cont.) Protein composition of feeds (adapted from AFRC, 1993 and other sources)

						Level of Production (APL)							
						≤1.0	1.5	2.0	2.5	3.0	3.5	4.0	≥4.5
Microbial yield (Y)						8.8	9.5	10.0	10.5	10.9	11.2	11.5	11.8
Feed name	DM %	CP g/kg DM	ME	FME MJ/kg DM		Protein supply (g/kg DM)							
Energy feeds (*INFIC Class 40*)													
Barley grain	87	129	13.3	12.3	ERDP	111.3	107.5	104.4	101.8	99.8	98.1	96.6	95.5
					DUP	7.8	11.3	14.1	16.4	18.3	19.8	21.1	22.1
Citrus pulp	89	99	12.6	10.7	ERDP	78.4	72.1	68.1	65.4	63.5	62.0	60.8	59.9
					DUP	1.6	7.2	10.8	13.3	15.0	16.4	17.4	18.2
Distillers' grains + solubles	89	220	11.5	10.7	ERDP	171.2	142.2	127.1	117.9	111.8	107.4	104.2	101.7
					DUP	15.5	41.5	55.1	63.4	69.0	72.9	75.8	78.0
Maize grain	86	102	13.8	12.4	ERDP	45.1	36.2	32.5	30.5	29.3	28.4	27.8	27.4
					DUP	44.2	52.2	55.5	57.3	58.4	59.2	59.7	60.1
Oat feed	88	50	9.0	7.8	ERDP	29.6	28.1	27.2	26.6	26.1	25.8	25.5	25.3
					DUP	7.3	8.6	9.4	10.0	10.4	10.7	10.9	11.1
Oat grain	85	105	12.1	10.8	ERDP	83.5	82.6	81.8	81.2	80.7	80.3	80.0	79.7
					DUP	3.5	4.3	5.0	5.5	6.0	6.4	6.7	7.0
Rice bran	90	165	7.1	6.9	ERDP	122.0	107.3	98.3	92.3	88.0	84.8	82.3	80.4
					DUP	26.5	39.7	47.8	53.2	57.1	60.0	62.2	63.9
Soya hulls	86	141	13.2	12.6	ERDP	103.1	87.5	78.3	72.3	68.0	65.0	62.6	60.8
					DUP	18.1	32.2	40.5	45.9	49.7	52.5	54.6	56.2
Sugar beet feed -molassed	86	103	12.5	12.4	ERDP	73.1	64.1	59.4	56.5	54.6	53.2	52.2	51.4
					DUP	12.6	20.7	24.9	27.5	29.2	30.5	31.4	32.1
Sugar beet feed -unmolassed	86	103	12.9	11.3	ERDP	74.2	64.4	58.3	54.2	51.3	49.1	47.5	46.2
					DUP	15.8	24.7	30.2	33.8	36.5	38.4	39.9	41.1
Triticale grain	86	131	13.8	13.3	ERDP	105.5	102.7	100.5	98.9	97.5	96.4	95.5	94.8
					DUP	6.8	9.3	11.2	12.8	14.0	15.0	15.8	16.5
Wheat feed	89	181	11.9	10.4	ERDP	142.2	131.3	123.7	118.2	114.1	110.9	108.3	106.3
					DUP	27.5	37.3	44.1	49.0	52.8	55.7	58.0	59.8
Wheat grain	87	123	13.6	12.9	ERDP	108.2	105.6	103.5	101.7	100.3	99.2	98.2	97.4
					DUP	5.8	8.1	10.0	11.6	12.8	13.9	14.8	15.5
Compound feeds (*typical composition*)													
18% dairy cake -high ME	87	205	13.0	10.3	ERDP	153.0	142.1	134.4	128.2	124.7	121.4	118.6	116.3
					DUP	29.6	39.6	46.6	51.8	55.7	58.8	61.2	63.1
18% dairy cake -moderate ME	87	207	12.2	10.0	ERDP	156.2	144.8	136.8	130.9	126.4	122.9	120.2	117.9
					DUP	27.2	37.5	44.7	50.0	54.0	57.2	59.7	61.7
26% dairy cake	87	300	12.7	9.9	ERDP	225.2	206.7	193.7	184.1	176.8	171.1	166.6	163.0
					DUP	46.5	63.1	74.9	83.5	90.1	95.2	99.2	102.5
Calf weaner	87	206	12.8	11.0	ERDP	155.4	144.1	136.1	130.3	125.8	122.3	119.6	117.4
					DUP	29.3	39.5	46.7	52.0	56.0	59.1	61.6	63.6
Dry cow cake	87	166	12.0	10.3	ERDP	128.1	120.0	114.1	109.8	106.4	103.7	101.6	99.9
					DUP	19.1	26.4	31.7	35.7	38.7	41.1	43.0	44.6
Maize balancer	87	285	12.7	10.2	ERDP	211.0	194.5	183.0	174.7	168.4	163.5	159.7	156.6
					DUP	43.4	58.3	68.6	76.1	81.8	86.2	89.6	92.4

Table 20.22 (cont.) Protein composition of feeds (adapted from AFRC, 1993 and other sources)

						Level of Production (APL)							
						≤1.0	1.5	2.0	2.5	3.0	3.5	4.0	≥4.5
Microbial yield (Y)						8.8	9.5	10.0	10.5	10.9	11.2	11.5	11.8
Feed name	DM %	CP g/kg	ME	FME MJ/kg DM		Protein supply (g/kg DM)							

Protein feeds (INFIC Class 50)

Feed name	DM %	CP g/kg	ME	FME		≤1.0	1.5	2.0	2.5	3.0	3.5	4.0	≥4.5
Beans	86	333	13.1	12.7	ERDP	278.2	263.3	252.4	244.1	237.6	232.5	228.4	225.0
					DUP	21.4	34.7	44.6	52.0	57.8	62.4	66.2	69.2
Brewers' grains (ensiled)	28	245	11.7	9.0	ERDP	147.4	128.7	116.7	108.5	102.6	98.1	94.7	92.0
					DUP	50.4	67.3	78.1	85.5	90.8	94.8	97.9	100.3
Coconut meal	86	215	12.9	9.3	ERDP	132.4	103.9	89.1	80.0	74.0	69.7	66.5	64.1
					DUP	52.1	77.7	91.0	99.2	104.6	108.5	111.3	113.5
Cottonseed meal	92	375	11.1	8.8	ERDP	268.9	238.1	219.2	206.4	197.4	190.6	185.5	181.4
					DUP	55.2	82.9	100.0	111.4	119.6	125.7	130.3	133.9
Dried brewers grains	86	249	12.2	9.9	ERDP	126.5	102.9	89.0	79.9	73.6	68.9	65.3	62.6
					DUP	79.9	101.1	113.6	121.8	127.5	131.7	134.9	137.4
Feather meal	90	889	13.0	11.7	ERDP	324.9	238.0	202.3	182.9	170.9	162.8	157.0	152.6
					DUP	458.7	537.0	569.1	586.5	597.4	604.7	609.9	613.8
Fishmeal	92	694	14.2	11.4	ERDP	388.3	319.9	287.4	268.6	256.5	248.0	241.9	237.2
					DUP	209.6	271.1	300.3	317.2	328.2	335.8	341.3	345.5
Groundnut meal	92	570	13.7	11.1	ERDP	461.2	411.3	377.8	354.1	336.5	323.1	312.5	304.2
					DUP	64.1	109.0	139.1	160.5	176.3	188.4	197.9	205.4
Linseed meal	88	379	11.9	8.9	ERDP	305.6	281.2	264.5	252.5	243.5	236.6	231.2	226.8
					DUP	29.5	51.4	66.5	77.3	85.3	91.6	96.4	100.4
Lupins	86	342	14.2	10.5	ERDP	288.3	265.4	249.1	237.0	227.7	220.5	214.7	210.0
					DUP	29.5	50.1	64.8	75.7	84.0	90.6	95.8	100.0
Maize dist. grains	90	317	14.7	11.7	ERDP	186.1	164.9	152.4	144.2	138.4	134.2	131.0	128.6
					DUP	26.4	45.5	56.8	64.1	69.3	73.1	76.0	78.2
Maize gluten feed	89	232	12.7	11.5	ERDP	162.3	153.8	148.1	144.1	141.1	138.8	137.0	135.6
					DUP	9.6	17.3	22.4	26.0	28.7	30.7	32.4	33.6
Maize gluten meal	90	666	17.5	16.4	ERDP	349.7	269.1	227.0	201.4	184.2	172.0	163.0	156.1
					DUP	239.0	311.6	349.5	372.6	388.0	399.0	407.1	413.3
Palm kernel meal	86	170	11.6	10.4	ERDP	133.6	115.6	104.2	96.4	90.7	86.5	83.2	80.6
					DUP	10.4	26.5	36.8	43.9	48.9	52.8	55.7	58.0
Peas	87	261	13.5	13.3	ERDP	204.1	191.5	183.0	177.0	172.6	169.2	166.5	164.4
					DUP	14.9	26.3	33.9	39.3	43.3	46.3	48.7	50.6
Rapeseed meal	89	418	12.0	11.2	ERDP	320.0	300.5	286.3	275.4	266.9	260.2	254.8	250.4
					DUP	25.4	42.9	55.7	65.5	73.1	79.1	84.0	88.0
Shea nut	86	164	9.2	5.0	ERDP	85.2	71.9	65.6	61.9	59.5	57.9	56.7	55.8
					DUP	30.5	42.5	48.2	51.5	53.6	55.1	56.2	57.0
Soyabean meal	88	507	13.4	12.8	ERDP	399.6	344.4	308.2	282.9	264.4	250.4	239.5	230.9
					DUP	68.1	117.8	150.4	173.1	189.8	202.4	212.2	220.0
Sunflower meal	90	335	9.6	9.2	ERDP	276.6	260.0	247.6	238.2	230.8	224.9	220.2	216.3
					DUP	24.0	39.0	50.1	58.6	65.3	70.6	74.9	78.4
Urea	95	2600	0.0	0.0	ERDP	2574.0	2574.0	2574.0	2574.0	2574.0	2574.0	2574.0	2574.0
					DUP	0.0	0.0	0.0	0.0	0.0	0.0	0.0	0.0
Wheat dist. grains	90	302	12.4	8.3	ERDP	177.3	157.1	145.2	137.4	131.9	127.9	124.8	122.5
					DUP	21.7	39.9	50.6	57.7	62.6	66.2	68.9	71.0

REFERENCES

ADAS Feed Evaluation Unit (1989) Tables of rumen degradability values of ruminant feed stuffs. ADAS FEU, Stratford upon Avon. 21pp.

Agricultural and Food Research Council (1990) Technical committee on responses to nutrients, Report No 5. Nutritive requirements of ruminant animals: Energy. Nutrition Abstracts and Reviews, Series B: *Livestock Feeds and Feeding* **60**: 729

Agricultural and Food Research Council (1991) Technical committee on responses to nutrients. Report No 6. A reappraisal of the calcium and phosphorus requirements of sheep and cattle. *Nutrition Abstracts and Reviews, Series B: Livestock Feeds and Feeding* **61**: 573

Agricultural and Food Research Council (1992) Technical committee on responses to nutrients, Report No 9. Nutritive requirements of ruminant animals: Protein. Nutrition Abstracts and Reviews, Series B: *Livestock Feeds and Feeding* **62**: 787

Agricultural and Food Research Council (1993) Energy and protein requirements of ruminants. An advisory manual prepared by the AFRC Technical committee on responses to nutrients. First edition. Wallingford, UK, CABI

Anon (1984) Dairy herd fertility Ref Book 259. London, HMSO

ARC (1965) The Nutrient Requirements of Farm Livestock: No 1, Ruminants. London, HMSO

ARC (1980) *The nutrient requirements of ruminant livestock.* Farnham Royal, Slough, CAB

Ascarelli, I., Edelman, Z., Rosenberg, M. and Folman, Y. (1985) Effect of dietary carotene on fertility of high-yielding dairy cows. *Animal Production* **40**: 195

Baggot, D.G., Bunch, K.J. and Gill, K.R. (1988) Variations in the inorganic components and physical properties of claw keratin associated with claw disease in the British Friesian cow. *British Veterinary Journal* **144**: 534

Bailey, C.B. (1959) The rate of secretion of mixed saliva in the cow. *Proceedings of the Nutrition Society* **18**:xiii

Batajoo, K.K and Shaver, R.D. (1994) Impact of non-fiber carbohydrate on intake, digestion, and milk production by dairy cows. *Journal of Dairy Science* **77**: 1580

Bazeley, K. and Pinsent, P.J.N. (1984) Preliminary observations on a series of outbreaks of acute laminitis in dairy cattle. *Veterinary Record* **115**: 619

Bee, D. J. (1986) 5th International symposium on disease of the ruminant digit., Dublin, Ireland

Beede, D.K. (1992) The DCAD concept: Transition rations for dry pregnant cows. *Feedstuffs* **64**: 12

Blaxter (1962) *The Energy Metabolism of Ruminants.* Hutchinson. 329 pp.

Bonomi, A., Bosticco, A., Quarantelli, A., Sabioni, A. and Superchi, P. (1988) *Zootecnica Nutrizione Animale* **14**: 21

Bourchier, C.P., Garnsworthy, P.C., Hutchinson, J.M. and Benton, T.A. (1987) The relationship between milk yield, body condition and reproductive performance in high-yielding dairy cows (Abstr). *Animal Production* **44**: 460

Braak, A. v. d. and Klooster, A. v. (1987) Effect of calcium and magnesium intakes and feeding level during the dry period on bone resorption in dairy cows at parturition. *Research in Veterinary Science* **43**: 7

Browne, I., Allen, D., Phipps, R.H. and Sutton, J.D. (1995) *Mixed Forage Diets for Dairy Cows.* UK Milk Development Council. p.5

Butler, W.R. and Smith, R.D. (1989) Interrelationships between energy balance and postpartum reproductive function in dairy cattle. *Journal of Dairy Science* **72**: 767

Carroll, D.J., Barton, B.A., Anderson, G.W. and Smith, R.D. (1988) Influence of protein intake and feeding strategy on reproductive performance of dairy cows. *Journal of Dairy Science* **71**: 3470

Chamberlain, A.T. (1994) The gas production capacity of purified chemicals and feedstuffs when incubated *in vitro* with rumen microbes as a possible indicator of energy availability in the rumen. *Animal Production* **58**: 449

Chamberlain, A.T., Seyoum, K., Chapman, D. and Piotrowsky, C. (1993) The fermentable metabolisable energy in grass silage (Abstr.). *Animal Production* **56**: 455

Chillard, Y., Rouel, J., Ollier, A., Bony, J., Tanan, K. and Sloan, B.K. (1995) Limitations in digestible methionine in the intestine (metDI) for milk protein secretion in dairy cows fed a ration based on grass silage (Abstr.). *Animal Science* **60**: 553

Cortese, V. (1988) Selenium and reproductive performance in dairy cattle. *Agri. Practice* **9**: 5

Dado, R.G., Mertens, D.R. and Shook, G.E. (1993) Metabolizable energy and absorbed protein requirements for milk component production. *Journal of Dairy Science* **76**: 1575

David, G.P. (1989) Epidemiological factors associated with a high incidence of solar ulcer and white line disease in dairy cattle. Proceedings of Society of Veterinary Epidemiology and Preventive Medicine. Conference held at Exeter, UK. Pubs. SVEPM, Edinburgh. p. 149

Dermertzis, P.N. and Mills, C.F. (1973) Oral zinc therapy in the control of infectious pododermatitis in young bulls. *Veterinary Record* **93**: 219

Donkin, S.S., Varga, G.A., Sweeney, R.F. and Muller, L.D. (1989) Rumen-protected methionine and lysine: effects on animal performance, milk protein yield, and physiological measures. *Journal of Dairy Science* **72**: 1484

Edmonson, A.J., Lean, I.J., Weaver, L.D., Farver, T. and Webster, G. (1989) A body condition scoring chart for Holstein Dairy cows. *Journal of Dairy Science* **72**: 68

Ferguson, J.D. (1994) Production and reproduction in dairy cows. The *Bovine Practitioner* **28**: 79

Ferguson, J.D., Blanchard, T., Galligan, D.T., Hoshall, D.C. and Chalupa, W. (1988) Infertility in dairy cattle fed a high percentage of protein degradable in the rumen. *Journal of the American Veterinary Medical Association* **192**: 659

Forbes J.M. (1983) *The Voluntary Food Intake of Farm Animals*. Butterworths, London. 206pp.

Galligan, D. T. (1991) *The role of the veterinarian as a nutritional advisor in dairy practice. Large animal clinical nutrition*. London, Mosby Year Book. 239

Garnsworthy, P.C. and Topps, J.H. (1982) The effect of body condition of dairy cows at calving on their food intake and performance when given complete diets. *Animal Production* **35**: 113

Gordon, F.J. (1984) The effect of level of concentrate supplementation given with grass silage during the winter on the total lactation performance of autumn calving cows. *Journal of Agricultural Science, Cambridge* **102**: 163

Gordon, F.J. (1988) Harvesting systems for the production of grass silage for dairy cows. In: *Nutrition and Lactation in the Dairy Cow*. (ed.: P.C. Garnsworthy) Butterworths. p. 355

Hallberg, G.R. (1989) Nitrate in ground water in the United States. Nitrogen management and ground water protection. (ed.: R.F. Follett)

Hallberg, M.C. (ed.) (1992) *Bovine somatotropin and emerging issues*. Westview Press, Oxford

Haresign, W. (1980) *Body condition, milk yield and reproduction in cattle. Recent advances in animal nutrition*. London, Butterworths. p.107

Herrera-Saldana, R. and Huber, J.T. (1987) Synchronization of protein and starch degradability in lactating dairy cows. *Journal of Dairy Science* **70**: 114

Hodgson, J. (1990) *Grazing Management*. Longman. 200pp.

Howard, H.J., Aalseth, E.P., Adams, G.D., Bush, L.J., McNew, R.W. and Dawson, L.J. (1987) Influence of dietary protein on reproductive performance of dairy cows. *Journal of Dairy Science* **70**: 1563

IDWP (1983) Mineral trace element and vitamin allowances for ruminant livestock. The report of an interdepartmental working party set up to consider the findings contained in the ARC (1980). Technical Review 'The nutrient requirements of ruminant livestock'. ADAS, Horseferry Road, London. 40pp.

Jones, G.P. and Garnsworthy, P.C. (1988) The effects of body condition at calving and dietary protein content on dry-matter intake and performance in lactating dairy cows given diets of low energy content. *Animal Production* **47**: 321

Kara, M.R., Little, C.O. and Mitchell, G.E. (1966) Starch disappearance from different segments of the digestive tract of steers. *Journal of Animal Science* **25**: 652

Leaver, J.D. (1983) Effect of condition score and milk protein content at service on conception rates. Annual Report. Crichton Royal Farm, West of Scotland Agricultural College, Dumfries. p. 36

Leaver, J.D. (1992) Whole-crop forages and alkali-treated straights. In: *Practical Cattle Nutrition*. Proceedings, British Cattle Veterinary Association Summer Meeting 1992. p.45

Livesey, C. T. and Fleming, F. L. (1984) Nutritional influences on laminitis, sole ulcer and bruised sole in Friesian cows. *Veterinary Record* **114**: 510

Lucy, M.C., Staples, C.R., Michel, F.M. and Thatcher, W.W. (1991) Energy balance and size and number of ovarian follicles detected by ultrasonography in early postpartum dairy cows. *Journal of Dairy Science* **74**: 473

Maclean, C.W. (1971) The long term effects of laminitis in dairy cows. *Veterinary Record* **89**: 34

Mansbridge, R.J., Blake, J.S. and Spechter, H.H. (1994) The effect of increasing starch intake and source in supplements fed in a complete diet to dairy cows on total dry-matter intake, milk yield and milk composition, and fatty acid content of milk fat when supplements were fed in complete diets or three times a day (Abstr.). *Animal Science* **60**: 509

Manson, F.J. and Leaver, J.D. (1988) The influence of dietary protein intake and of hoof trimming on lameness in dairy cattle. *Animal Production* **47**: 191

Massey, C.D., Wang, C., Donovan, A. and Beeder, D.K. (1993) Hypocalcaemia at parturition as a risk factor for left displaced abomasum in dairy cows (abstract). *Journal of American Veterinary Association* **203**: 852

Mayer, E., Liebich, H.G., Armitman, R., Hagemeister, H. and Dirksen, G. (1986) Nutritionally induced changes in the ruminal papillae and in their capacity to absorb short-chain fatty acids in high producing dairy cows. XIVth World congress on diseases of cattle, Dublin, Ireland. p. 806

McClure, T.J., Eamens, G.J. and Healey, P.J. (1986) Improved fertility in dairy cows after treatment with selenium pellets. *Australian Veterinary Journal* **63**: 144

McCullough, M.E. (1973) Optimum feeding of dairy animals for meat and milk. Athens, USA, University of Georgia Press

McCullough, M.E. (1986) Feeding Dairy Cows. The how and why of feeding programming. W D Hoard and Sons, Fort Atkinson, Wisconsin, USA. 80pp.

McDonald, P. (1976) Silage. In: *Microbiology in Agriculture, Fisheries and Food*. (eds.: F.A. Skinner and J.G. Carr) Society of Applied Biology Symposium Series 4. Academic Press. p.109

McDonald, P., Edwards, R.A. and Greenhalgh, J.F.D. (1988) *Animal Nutrition*. 4th edition. Longman Scientific, Harlow, UK. 543pp.

McDonald, P., Henderson, A.R. and Heron, S.J.E. (1991) *The Biochemistry of Silage*. Second edition. Chalcombe Publications. 340 pp.

Mertens, D.R. (1973) PhD Thesis. Cornell University, Ithaca, New York, USA

Miettinen, P. (1984) The influence of post-partum energy level on reproductive performance of dairy cows. 10th International Congress on Animal Reproduction and Artificial Insemination, June

Ministry of Agriculture, Fisheries and Food (1979) Lime and Fertilizer Recommendations No 1. Arable crops and grassland. Booklet 2191. p.18

Ministry of Agriculture, Fisheries and Food (1984) Energy Allowances and Feeding Systems for Ruminants. Second edition. MAFF Ref. Booklet 433

Ministry of Agriculture, Fisheries and Food (1986) *Feed Composition: UK Tables of Feed Composition and Nutritive Value for Ruminants*. Chalcombe Publications, Marlow, 69pp.

Ministry of Agriculture, Fisheries and Food (1990) *UK Tables of Nutritive Value and Chemical Composition of Feed Stuffs*. (ed.: D.I. Givens) Rowett Research Services, Aberdeen, 420pp.

Ministry of Agriculture, Fisheries and Food (1992) *Feed Composition. UK Tables of Feed Composition and Nutritive Value for Ruminants*. Second Edition. Chalcombe Publications, Canterbury, 99pp.

Ministry of Agriculture, Fisheries and Food, Department of Agriculture and Fisheries for Scotland, Department of Agriculture for Northern Ireland (1975) *Energy Allowances and Feeding Systems for Ruminants*. Technical Bulletin 33. HMSO, London. 79p p.

Morrow, D.A. (1976) Fat Cow Syndrome. *Journal of Dairy Science* **59**: 1625

Mortellaro, C. (1986) 5th International symposium on diseases of the ruminant digit., Dublin, Ireland

Mortensen, K., Hessleholt, M. and Basse, G. (1986) Pathogenesis of bovine laminitis (diffuse aseptic pododermatitis). Experimental models. 14th World congress on diseases of cattle, Dublin, Ireland. p. 1025

Mulvaney, P.M. (1977) Improving cow fertility. *Better Management, MMB* **29**: 3

Nalsen, T., Bush, L.J., Adams, G.D. and Deetz, L.E. (1987) Amino acid supplementation of high-wheat concentrate mixtures for dairy cows. *Journal of Dairy Science* **70**: 117

Naylor, J. N. and Ralston, S.L. (eds.) (1991) *Large animal clinical nutrition*. London, Mosby Year Book.

Nombekela, S.W. and Murphy, M.R. (1992) Preference ranking of diets by cows in early lactation as affected by additives representing primary tastes and some common feed flavours. *Journal of Dairy Science* **75** Supplement 1 p.294

Offer, N.W. (1993) Background to the new *in vitro* ME silage prediction equation. In: Proceedings, Society of Feed Technologies Ruminants Conference, Coventry, July 1993. p.E1

Offer, N.W., Dewhurst, R.J. and Thomas, C. (1994) The use of electrometric titration to improve the routine prediction of silage intake by lambs and dairy cows. Proceedings, 50th British Society of Animal Production Winter Meeting, March 1994, Paper 1

Offer, N.W., Rooke, J.A., Dewhurst, R.J. and Thomas, C. (1993) Rapid assessment of silage fermentation characteristics by electrometric titration. British Society of Animal Production Winter Meeting, Paper 19

Olson, W.G., Link, K., Otterby, D.E. and Stevens, J.B. (1989) Assessment of sodium deficiency and polyuria/polydipsia in dairy cows. *Bovine Practitioner* p.126

Olson, J.D. (1994) The role of selenium and Vitamin E in mastitis and reproduction of dairy cows. *The Bovine Practitioner* **28**: 47

Ørskov, E.R. (1987) The Feeding of Ruminants. Chalcombe Publications. 90pp.

Ørskov, E.R. (1989) Optimising rumen function: getting the best out of feeds. In: *Ruminant Feed Evaluation and Utilisation*. (eds.: B.A. Stark, J.M. Wilkinson and D.I. Givens) Chalcombe Publications. p. 101

Payne, J.M., Dew, S.M., Manston, R. and Faulks, M. (1970). The use of a metabolic profile test in dairy herds. *Veterinary Record* **87**: 150

Peterse, D.J. (1986) 5th International symposium on diseases of the ruminant digit., Dublin, Ireland

Peterse, D.J., Korver, S., Oldenbrock, J.K. and Talmon, F.P. (1984) Relationship between levels of concentrate feeding and incidence of sole ulcers in dairy cattle. *Veterinary Record* **115**: 629

Phillips, C.J.C. and Chiy, P.C. (1994) Sodium for dairy cows at pasture. *British Grassland Society Newsletter* **48**: 26

Pike, I.H., Miller, E.H. (1994) The role of fishmeal in dairy cow feeding. IFOMA

Plym Forshell, K. (1994) Metabolic profiles in milk. BCVA Proceedings, Held at St Peter Port, Guernsey, UK. Pubs BCVA

Poole, A.H., Aston, K. and Sutton, J.D. (1992) *Milk from grass silage*. UK Milk Marketing Board

Rider, S. (1994) Diet supplement gives profit boost to milk protein. *Farmers Weekly* **121**(19): 44

Roever, G., Claus, J., Kaufmann, W. and Kalm, E. (1982) Milk constituents as indicators of physiological stress and the consequences for fertility in cows. Physiologie und Pathologie der Fortpflanzung. Verhandlungsbericht VII. Veterinar Humanmedizinische Tagung. Giessen **18**: 96

Ruiz, T., Bernal, E. and Staples, C.R. (1992) Effect of dietary NDF concentration on productive responses by lactating dairy cows fed four forage sources. *Journal of Dairy Science* **75**: 209

Russel, A.F.J. (1986) Hill and upland beef cattle production: some nutritional considerations. SVEPM Proc. 1986. p. 77

Ryan, W. (1964) Concentrations of glucose and low molecular weight acids in the rumen of sheep following the addition of large amounts of wheat to the rumen. *American Journal of Veterinary Research*. **25**: 646

Saun, R.J. v., Idleman, S.C. and Sniffen, C.J. (1993) Effect of undegradable protein amount fed pre-partum on post-partum production in first lactation Holstein cows. *Journal of Dairy Science* **76**: 236

Shappell, N.W., Herbein, J.H., Deftos, L.S. and Aiello, R.J. (1987) Effects of dietary calcium and age on parathyroid hormone, calcitonin and serum and milk minerals in the peripaturient dairy cow. *Journal of Nutrition* **117**: 201

Smit, H., Verbeek, B., Peterse, D.J. and Jansen, J. (1986) The effects of herd characteristics on claw disorders and claw measurements in Friesians. *Livestock Production Science* **15**: 1

Soest, P.J. v. (1982) The Nutritional Ecology of the Ruminant. O & B Books, Corvallis, Oregon, USA. 374pp.

Soest, P.J. v. (1994) Nutritional Ecology of the Ruminant. Second edition. Cornell, Cornell University Press. 476pp.

Sutton, J.D. and Morant, S.V. (1989) Nutrition and milk quality in dairy cow nutrition - the veterinary angles. Conference Proceedings (Ed.: A.T. Chamberlain). Reading University, Reading, UK

Thomas, P.C., Robertson, S, Chamberlain, D.G., Livingstone, R.M., Garthwaite, P.H., Dewey, P.J.S, Smart, R. and Whyte, C. (1988) Predicting the metabolisable energy (ME) content of compounded feeds for ruminants. In: Recent Advances in Animal Nutrition. (eds.: W. Haresign and D.J.A. Cole) Butterworths, London. p. 127

Tomlinson, P. and Perry, A. (1993) An analysis of Genus management costed dairy farms 1992-93. Genus management

Treacher, R.J., Reid, I.M. and Roberts, C.J. (1986) Effect of body condition at calving on the health and performance of dairy cows. *Animal Production* **43**: 1

Vadiveloo, J. and Holmes, W. (1979) The prediction of voluntary feed intake of dairy cows. *Journal of Agricultural Science, Cambridge* **93**: 553

Vincent, I.C., Hill, R., Williams, H.L. and Noakes, D.E .(1985) The absence of effect on fertility of high levels of inclusion of British rapeseed meal in the diet of yearling heifers. British Society of Animal Production. Winter Meeting

Wainman, F.W., Smith, J.S. and Blaxter, K.L. (1971) Voluntary intake and energy metabolism of sheep fed chopped dried grass and the same material milled and pelleted. *Proceedings of the Nutrition Society* **30**: 23A

Waite, R., White, S.C.D. and Robertson, A. (1956) Variations in the chemical composition of milk with particular reference to the solids-non-fat. (1. The effects of the stage of lactation, season, year, age of cow.) *Journal of Dairy Research*, June 23, p.65

Wilkinson, J.M. (1990) *Silage UK*. Sixth edition. Chalcombe Publications. 167pp.

Wilkinson J.M. and Stark, B.A. (1992) *Silage in Western Europe. A survey of 17 countries*. Second edition. Chalcombe Publications. 156pp.

Wright, I., Russel, A. and Russel, A.J.F. (1984) Partition of fat, body composition and body score in mature cows. *Animal Production* **38**: 32

Xin, Z., Tucker, W.B. (1989) Effect of reactivity rate and particle size of magnesium oxide on magnesium availability, acid-base balance, mineral metabolism, and milking performance of dairy cows. Journal of Dairy Science 72: 462

Younge, B.A., Murphy, J.J., Rath, M. and Sloan, B.K. (1995) The effect of protected methionine and lysine on milk production and composition on grass based diets (Abstr.). *Animal Science* **60**: 556

Zamet, C.N., Colenbrander, V.F., Callahan, C.J., Chew, B.P., Erb, R.E. and Moeller, N.J. (1979) Variables associated with peripartum traits in dairy cows. I. Effect of dietary forages and disorders on voluntary intake of feed, body weight and milk yield. *Theriogenology* **11**: 229